DATE DUE

*Paris and London
in the Eighteenth Century*

By the same author

The Crowd in the French Revolution (1959)
Wilkes and Liberty (1962)
Revolutionary Europe (1964)
The Crowd in History (1964)
Captain Swing (with E. J. Hobsbawm, 1969)
Hanoverian London, 1714-1808 (1970)

Paris and London in the Eighteenth Century

Studies in Popular Protest

George Rudé

NEW YORK · THE VIKING PRESS

Contents

Acknowledgements

My thanks are due to the following journals for allowing me to reproduce in this volume a number of articles that originally appeared in their columns (numbers denote the order in which they feature in the present volume):

Annales historiques de la Révolution française (no. 5); *Bulletin of the Institute of Historical Research* (no. 6); *Economic History Review* (no. 7); *Flinders Journal of History and Politics* (no. 1); *Government and Opposition* (no. 12); *The Guildhall Miscellany* (nos. 8, 9); *The Historical Journal* (no. 11); *History Today* (no. 4); *Past and Present* (no. 3); and *Transactions of the Royal Historical Society* (no. 10).

G.R.
November 1969

Introduction

The articles reproduced in this volume relate, in one form or another, to popular protests and revolts breaking out in Paris and London during the eighteenth century. They are the outcome of work carried out over a period of nearly twenty years in libraries and archives in the two cities—mainly in the Archives Nationales and the archives of the Prefecture of Police and Bibliothèque Nationale in Paris, and in the Guildhall Library, the British Museum, the Public Record Office and county Record Offices in London. It has been a rewarding and exhilarating experience, though somewhat tempered by the irritations that the researcher suffers from the bureaucracy and archaic methods of cataloguing of the Bibliothèque Nationale in the one city and the ban placed on the use of pens (even biros) in the Public Record Office in the other. However, with such minor reservations, I am deeply grateful to the librarians and archivists in the two capitals who have helped me in my work—and not least to the caretaker of the annexe to the Archives Nationales in Paris who, on a memorable occasion in the summer of 1953, locked Richard Cobb and myself in the building at night so that we had to shin down a drain-pipe into the Rue Vieille du Temple to get out!

There are certain threads linking these two sets of studies together, of which some are no doubt more obvious than others. In the first place, the events they describe took place in the same century in two closely related capital cities. They were at this time (with the possible exception of Tokyo, then called Edo) the two largest cities in the world. They had similar problems of population-growth and of cultural, economic and political development. They both bore the mark of a predominantly aristocratic society;

they both had 'rising' middle classes; and they both had large overcrowded central districts inhabited by wage-earners, craftsmen and petty tradesmen (those whom Frenchmen of the Revolution called *sans-culottes*); but, being at the 'pre-industrial' stage of their development, they neither had factories, 'captains of industry' nor an industrial working class. So they had much in common; yet the differences were equally important. London (after the mid-century at least) had a larger population, a larger port and a wealthier merchant class; her industrial suburbs were more developed, and her wage-earners more independent and class-conscious. Besides, London was largely self-governing where Paris was not; she even enjoyed a measure of political democracy, and the City of London, in particular, was governed by a 'middling' class of merchants, shopkeepers and craftsmen, who had long enjoyed a degree of political authority which their Parisian counterparts would not attain until the years of revolution.* A consequence of this was that, in London, popular disturbance was inclined to be more militant, more sophisticated and 'political', than it was in Paris during the greater part of the century—we shall see examples of this maturity in our pieces on 'Wilkes and Liberty' and the Gordon Riots of 1780. London was, in fact, by far the more turbulent of the two; and it is not so surprising that after the latter of these events a French observer should have written that such excesses would be impossible in a city as well policed as Paris! Of course, the French Revolution would tip the balance the other way; so that as London (after 1780) became relatively quiet, Paris became noticeably more disturbed. If is therefore perfectly sensible that we should have selected our examples of London popular movements from the period 1736–80 and the Parisian from the revolutionary years 1789–95.

Yet, with all these differences, the pattern of popular revolt in the two cities was basically the same. In both

* See 'Society and Conflict in London and Paris . . .' (piece 2 in this book).

cities it conformed, by and large, to the 'pre-industrial' model I have outlined in the first contribution to this volume. But, in the case of large cities, there were always variations from the norm. For one thing, food riots were far less frequent than in country districts and market towns: there were comparatively few in Paris, and in London none before the wartime inflation of 1795. For another, riots tended to have political undertones, largely due to the influence exerted on the 'lower orders' by political groups in the city: in Paris by the aristocratic Parlement; in London by the 'middling'-class elements of the City's Common Council and Common Hall. For the rest, city riots, like those in country districts, were led by a combination of short-term local 'captains' and longer-term 'outside' leaders, and disturbances tended to assume a 'direct-action' form with assaults on property, the 'pulling-down' of houses and the burning in effigy of unpopular politicians or employers. We shall find examples from both cities of these forms in the pieces that follow: notably in those dealing with the Gordon Riots in London and the Réveillon riots of April 1789 in Paris. But, in certain respects, the latter event marks a transition from an older form to a new. With the Revolution, the older style of more primitive, near-spontaneous protest tends to give way to the more organised armed revolt, as in the case of the Bastille, the armed attack on the Tuileries, the expulsion of the Girondin leaders from the National Convention; and, even more spectacularly, in the *sans-culottes*-led revolt of Prairial of the Year III (referred to in pieces 6 and 7 below). Yet the older style lingered on, as in the Paris grocery riots of February 1793 (see piece 6); and, in provincial cities and rural centres, the old 'pre-industrial' forms of disturbance did not die out entirely in either France or England until half-way through the following century.

Another common thread linking these pieces together is the method of investigation on which they are based. It is, of course, a truism that the historian's end-product depends almost as much on the questions he asks as on the records he uses to answer them. I suppose that in my case the most commonly reiterated questions have been *what?* and *who?* and *how?* and *why?*, with the emphasis being more frequently placed on the second and the last. In this I have perhaps followed, though not always consciously, the precept of the late Georges Lefebvre: 'D'abord, il faut constater les faits; ensuite, il faut chercher à les expliquer.' This probably seems common-sensical enough; yet my own particular concern with the question *who?* has, I suspect, been considered by some to amount almost to an obsession. (Piece 5 among those that follow may perhaps appear to the reader to be a case in point.) Yet, though pleading guilty to the charge, I shall offer no apology; for how can one know what revolutions or popular movements are about if one does not take the trouble to find out who played the most active part in them? And this was precisely the question that bothered me when I began to study the French Revolution a few years after the war. I was struck by the vague or prejudiced generalisations of historians, who were quite prepared to write off the captors of the Bastille or the assailants of the Tuileries as a 'mob' or *canaille*, or (if they felt better disposed towards them) as *les ouvriers* or *le peuple*, without any closer investigation. And elsewhere (in my book on *The Crowd in History*) I have argued that, in this respect, the record of sociologists has been no better than that of historians.

So I began by asking (it seems a simple enough question): who actually took the Bastille? and followed this with the questions: who marched to Versailles, stormed the Tuileries, drove out the Girondin leaders, or stood silently by while Robespierre was toppled from power? Whose, in fact, were the 'faces in the crowd'? In the case of the Bastille—at least, in so far as its immediate captors were concerned—the answer proved surprisingly easy. For the names of the captors are neatly set out, with full details of ages, occupations, addresses and military units, in a list drawn up by one of their leaders.* (The list had, in fact,

* See piece 5 below.

been used fifty years before in a footnote and without acknowledgment, by Gustave Bord, a Frenchman, whose aim—somewhat different from mine—was to show that the capture of the Bastille was part of a Masonic conspiracy!) But this list was something of a historical freak (insurgents don't usually leave their names around); and, in other cases, I had to use a sampling method (as previously used by Marcel Rouff and Alexandre Tuetey in the 1890s) by resorting to the police reports of the Châtelet and Paris Sections and to the records of military and hospital authorities, relating to those arrested, killed or wounded in the various Paris *journées*. But such records were 'chancey' to say the least. Sometimes they proved to be reasonably adequate, as, for instance, the police records of the series F^7 in the Archives Nationales, which have been used to good effect by Albert Soboul and Richard Cobb. At other times, as in the case of those relating to the women's march to Versailles and the Massacres of September 1792, they were very meagre indeed; and, to fill in the gaps I had, like others, to resort to the more tendentious and subjective accounts of eyewitnesses, journalists or political leaders.

But this problem became considerably greater when I began to apply a similar method of enquiry to the study of the London rioters of the eighteenth century; for the English administrative records of the time were far less adequate than the French. This is due, no doubt, to a combination of factors. In the first place, the French judicial system, unlike the English, subjected the prisoner to a detailed cross-examination before trial; this might be hard on the prisoner, but it has proved a useful asset to the historian. Secondly, the omnicompetent State, with its profusion of administrative records, developed far earlier in France than in England; and, of course, the French Revolution itself, being a time of social movement and disorder, brought many more persons before the law or within range of the guillotine or the soldier's bullet. In contrast, London was comparatively peaceful after the last wild outburst in 1780; so it is not really surprising that the Gordon Riots, being the most violent episode of the century, should be the best documented, both as to the identity of the rioters and the victims of their assault. So here, at least, with the aid of the Old Bailey sessions papers, I was able to draw on reasonably adequate samples (see paper 10 in this book), similar to those I was able to draw on in the case of the assault on the Tuileries and the grocery riots in Paris. But it is an exception, and it will hardly escape the reader's attention that, in most cases, the identity of those taking part in popular disturbance emerges far more clearly, in these pieces, from those relating to Paris than from those relating to London.*

But, in order to get into the skulls of the participants—that is, to attempt to write what Lefebvre called 'history from below'—it was not sufficient merely to establish their identity; something also had to be done to unravel the motives and impulsions that urged them to take part in these and similar events. This was, in itself, nothing new. Generations of liberal-minded historians, and not only those of labour and popular movements, had explored the question *why?* in more or less rational terms: in terms of bread-and-butter issues such as wages, prices or enclosures, or of 'forward-looking' demands for political change or social improvement; while others, sharing Burke's antipathy to the 'mob', had ascribed its activities to bribery or conspiracy. Yet this is to oversimplify the picture. For modern social psychology, and those historians and social scientists who have learned some of its more relevant lessons, have now begun to explore the underlying or

* This is, however, not the case when one comes to the protesters and victims of the 'middling' sort. London is liberally provided with Rate Books and Land Tax (or Riot Tax) registers, which help to establish the identities and assess the values of the properties of men like those who voted for Wilkes against the Court candidates in the Middlesex elections of 1768–9 (see piece 9 below). In Paris, however, it happened that the taxation records were destroyed by fire during the Paris Commune of 1871, i.e. before historians began to ask the sort of questions that we are concerned with here.

hidden motives that are equally potent in impelling men to riot or rebel, often in a 'backward-looking', illiberal or irrational manner. And these could play a most effective part not only in primitive outbursts, food riots or Vendée-style peasant movements, but in radical-political and revolutionary outbreaks as well. Here again, Georges Lefebvre was an innovator and formulated new ideas on 'collective mentality' in a brief study of 'revolutionary crowds' and in his longer study on the rural panics of 1789 (*La grande Peur de 1789*, published in 1932). In this latter work he portrayed the potency of rumour as a historical force in French country districts during the summer of 1789. The Bastille had fallen and soldiers, disbanded after the event, were straggling homewards along roads already choked with unemployed villagers made jobless by the economic crisis. Out of this confusion grew the peasants' fear of an 'aristocratic plot', to further which roaming bands of 'brigands' were marching on the villages to destroy their crops and demolish their properties. The fear served, in turn, as a stimulus to peasant assaults on the *châteaux* and the destruction of the landlords' manorial rolls. It was a similar pattern of rumour, carried from market to market and village to village, that I found to have propagated the corn and bread riots around Paris in May 1775 (referred to in piece 3 in this book); so here again I owed a debt to Lefebvre. The same potent force of rumour can be seen at work in the Gordon Riots, when it was whispered that George III had broken his Coronation Oath by granting favours to the Roman Catholics; and it was even believed by some that he had become a Catholic himself! Other aspects of this irrational element in popular disturbance are briefly discussed in the first of the pieces that follow. They are more fully treated in Eric Hobsbawm's *Primitive Rebels* (1959), which shows how millenarial and other archaic notions have, even in European communities, spilled over into modern times. But such investigations are still in their infancy and await a closer collaboration between historians and social psychologists.

In conclusion, I should like to acknowledge with gratitude the help and friendship that have been so generously extended to me in both cities in the course of preparing my work. In the first place, like so many others working in the field, I owe a particular debt to Georges Lefebvre, the grand old master of French Revolutionary history and the progenitor of the study of history 'from below'. I am also indebted to the late Alfred Cobban, who saw me over the first hurdles by supervising my doctoral thesis on the Parisian wage-earners in the events of 1789–91: this served as a launching pad for much of the work that is reproduced in this volume. I have also valued, over many years, the friendship and collaboration of Albert Soboul and Richard Cobb, who, since Lefebvre's death, have probably done more to stimulate the study of the French Revolution in France, Britain and America than any other scholars. To Dr. Albert Hollaender, Deputy Librarian at the Guildhall Library, I owe just about everything I have learned about London judicial, fiscal and vestry records. In addition, I should like to thank Richard Ollard, of Collins and Fontana, for serving as my editor for a second time. And, most of all, I am indebted to my wife, who has had to live with the two-score articles and half-dozen books that have, intermittently over the past eighteen years, come from my pen.

Part One   Paris and London

The 'Pre-Industrial' Crowd

What I am mainly concerned with here is the changing complexion or 'face' of popular movements from one type of society to another. And by 'face' I don't mean only the physical appearance of crowds, or even their modes of behaviour. In addition to these I am also concerned with the issues involved, the forms of action in which they engage, their leaders and motives, and their social composition. My contention is, rather, that the 'crowd' or popular movement has to be studied as a historical phenomenon, and not as a stereotype that is equally suited to any form of society. Thus popular movements occurring in ancient times tended to be different in kind from those of the Middle Ages; and these in turn tended to have distinctive characteristics that separate them from those that have arisen in 'pre-industrial' or industrial society.

By 'pre-industrial' I mean broadly the period—it may extend over a hundred years or it may be more or it may be less—during which a society is adapting itself to the changes brought about by rapid industrialisation and at the end of which that society has (as in Britain in the nineteenth century) become radically transformed, so that we may speak of a new society—an 'industrial' society—as having come into being. This 'pre-industrial', or transitional, period naturally arises (if it arises at all) in different countries and different continents at different times. In England and France, with which I am most directly concerned, we may date it roughly from the early eighteenth century to about the 1840s (or, possibly, in France a little

From *Flinders Journal of History and Politics*, vol. I (1969).

later). In Central Europe, Australia and North America, it followed shortly after; in Eastern and Southern Europe not till 1900; in parts of Africa and Asia and in Latin America during the present century; and there are still countries in Asia, Africa and the Pacific (not to mention the 'aboriginal' areas of Australia) where the process has not yet begun.

So I am arguing that in each of these societies—whether ancient, medieval, 'pre-industrial' or industrial—popular movements have had their own distinctive and particular characteristics; and in each case, it is the historian's job to sort these out and not be content with readymade all-embracing answers. Which are these distinguishing features in the case of movements arising in 'pre-industrial' societies as, for example, those of France and England in the eighteenth and early nineteenth century?

Broadly speaking, it is convenient to classify them under the following six heads:

First, the types of disturbance. In the earlier phases food riots predominate, and these occur more frequently in villages and market towns than in cities; while industrial disputes, though fairly frequent, play only a secondary role. This is understandable enough at a time when there were no national or durable trade unions, when bread accounted for something like half, or more, of the working-man's budget, and when even the wage-earner was more concerned with the price of bread than with the amount of money in his pay-packet. But with growing industrialisation and working-class organisation, the roles became reversed: the strike tends to take over and the food riot tends to recede into the background. Similarly, political issues, always tending to obtrude in *urban* riots, play a relatively insignificant role in the earlier phase; but they come in greater evidence (as in England and France) from the latter part of the eighteenth century. This was largely due to early Radicalism in England and to the French Revolution of 1789, and to the advent, in both countries, of a working-class movement and socialist ideas half a century later.

Secondly, the forms of action. Predominantly, these are of the 'direct-action' type: in cities, 'pulling-down' of houses and burning the villain-of-the-hour in effigy; in country districts, arson (and particularly, in Britain, in the 1830s and 1840s), machine-breaking, and the imposition of price control by riot—what the French call *taxation populaire*. In brief, violence applied to property, but not (and I shall comment on this later) to life and limb. In addition, in the course of revolution, there are armed rebellions (assuming a progressively more organised and sophisticated form, as in Paris after 1789). At the same time, more 'modern' or 'industrial' forms of action are by no means absent; such as petitions to Parliament, marches, and modern-type industrial disputes of a more-or-less peaceful character. But the prevailing form of protest is the violent assault on property.

Thirdly, 'spontaneity' and lack of organisation; and therefore, a common feature is the *transformation* of a disturbance from a relatively small beginning (say, a meeting of housewives outside a baker's shop) into a wholesale rebellion and attack on property. This 'spontaneity' applies even to a highly developed movement like the popular outbreaks of the French Revolution; but notably more to its opening than to its later stages. And, generally speaking, as trade unions and political parties develop, this element of 'spontaneity' (which, of course, was never complete) begins to recede.

Fourthly, leadership: a point that is closely associated with the last. The typical leader of the 'pre-industrial' popular movement, certainly in its more sophisticated manifestations (in urban riots, revolutions and rebellions) comes from 'without' rather than from 'within' the crowd. Where the typical rioter or rebel is a craftsman, a labourer or a peasant, he may be a small nobleman, a lawyer, a journalist or a government official. Strictly speaking, there may be three types of leader: the leader-in-chief, in whose name the crowd riots or rebels; the intermediate leader—a sort of N.C.O.—who passes on the slogans or tells the rioters whose house has to 'come down'; and the most articulate or militant among the rioters themselves, whose leadership is purely local and purely temporary. Of these three, the last alone emerges from the 'crowd' itself. He may be an anonymous figure who rides on a white horse, brandishes a sword or blows a bugle; he may bear a pseudonym like the countless Rebeccas, Ned Ludds and Captain Swings of the early nineteenth century, or like Tom the Barber who led the anti-Irish rioters in London in the 1730s; or he may be known by his proper name like the local leaders of London's Gordon Riots and several of the real or alleged leaders of the early disturbances of the French Revolution in Paris. But, whether anonymous or not, his authority is purely temporary and, after the riot which thrust him forward, he sinks back again into the obscurity of the crowd. Two further points may be worth making here. One is that the leader-in-chief in whose name the crowd riots or rebels may be an involuntary leader, whose leadership has been quite literally thrust upon him. Louis XVI of France, for instance (like other French Kings before him), claimed no more personal responsibility for the activities of the peasants who burned down *châteaux* in his name than Luther did for the rebellious German peasants of 1525. The other point is that, with the rise of a working-class movement in both England and France in the 1830s, the temporary and anonymous (or near-anonymous) local leader tends to give way to a more permanent and articulate successor. So, by the 1830s, we find men emerging as leaders from the crowd itself, who are no longer occasional, sporadic and anonymous, but continuous and openly proclaimed. Such a man was George Loveless, the leader of the Dorchester labourers of 1834, who was transported to Australia as a labour militant and political Radical and returned to his homeland, with similar opinions, three years later.

Fifthly, the composition of the 'pre-industrial' crowd. This is the feature of popular disturbance that has perhaps been more neglected than any other—and probably even more by sociologists than by historians. The main point I want to make here is that the typical protesting crowd of this transitional 'pre-industrial' period is not confined, or largely confined, to a single class. This has not always been the case. I suppose that the typical medieval crowd was composed of craftsmen in cities and peasants in country districts; and, in industrial society, industrial workers have—until recent times, at least—perhaps played a predominant part in urban riots. In 'pre-industrial' society, however, the composition is noticeably—and no doubt significantly—*mixed*. By this I don't mean that all classes of the community are represented in more or less equal proportions. Members of the upper and 'middling' classes have never been particularly noted for their participation in riots or street demonstrations: a notable exception here, of course, are the younger people, in particular the students—though even they played an altogether insignificant role in the disturbances of the eighteenth century—and, in Britain, even in the nineteenth. It is 'mixed', therefore, only in relation to the 'lower set of people' (as they were called in the eighteenth century): that is, the cottagers, small freeholders, rural craftsmen, weavers, farm labourers and miners of the countryside; and, in the towns, the small shopkeepers and stall-holders, the master craftsmen and wage-earners (whether skilled or unskilled); those, in short, who, during the French Revolution, acquired the name of *sans-culottes*. The very term *sans-culottes*—meaning originally those who wore trousers and not breeches—denotes not a single class but an amalgam of classes: both small employers and work-people who had a common interest in a cheap and plentiful supply of bread.

Sixthly, the Motives or ideology of disturbance, or what some sociologists have termed the 'generalised ideas' underlying all forms of collective behaviour. This is the most difficult and most elusive question of all, as it raises all sorts of problems that the historian may not be particularly well qualified to handle; all the more so as his visual sources of enquiry all too rarely provide him with any satisfactory answers. It was all very well for the historians of the nineteenth century—before the days of mass observation or social psychology—to say that men rioted or rebelled simply because they were hungry or because this or that political leader or party had given them a new vision of the world or a taste for political reform. But the historian of today is expected to probe more deeply and cannot get away with such easy generalisations. And having read Tocqueville and Marx (and possibly Freud and Durckheim), he can hardly fail to realise that human motivation is extremely complex. This complexity applies, of course, as much to ancient and medieval as to 'pre-industrial' and industrial society. But it does not mean that the same motives for certain types of collective behaviour are equally predominant at all times and in all places—even though so respectable a figure as Gustave Le Bon, the 'father' of crowd psychology (he was writing about sixty years ago), appears to have thought so. It is fairly evident, for example, that 'political' motivation (whether of the Right or Left) played a more important role in popular disturbance at some stages than at others. It played a considerable part, as we shall see, in the latter part of this 'pre-industrial' period in France and England, though it is certainly not a distinctive feature of the period as a whole.

What *is* the distinctive feature of the 'pre-industrial' crowd is, I believe, its attachment to the *traditional* ways (or believed traditional ways) of the old village community or urban craft and its violent reaction to the sort of changes promoted, in the name of 'progress', by governments, capitalists, corn-merchants, speculative landlords or city authorities. So we find the constant and continuous presentation of demands for the 'restoration' of 'lost' rights, such as the 'just wage' and the 'just price', and even (later in the period) the right to vote. This is, of course, only a part (though a very important part) of the whole picture. I will return to the wider question later.

So far, then, I have argued that the distinctive hall-marks of the 'pre-industrial' crowd (at least, in its Western European manifestations) are: (1) the prevalence of the rural food riot; (2) the resort to 'direct action' and violence to property; (3) its 'spontaneity'; (4) its leadership from 'without' the crowd; (5) its mixed composition, with the emphasis on small shopkeepers and craftsmen in the towns and weavers, miners and labourers in the village; and (6) its concern for the restoration of 'lost' rights. I am arguing, too, that these features are 'distinctive' in the sense that, by and large, they distinguish the 'pre-industrial' popular movement from those that occur in both earlier and later periods. But I am certainly not insisting that all movements of the 'pre-industrial' age conform to this pattern or 'model'; nor am I blinding myself to the obvious fact that many popular disturbances of later times share common features with them. If such exceptions were frequent enough, they would of course invalidate the whole case I am putting forward. I don't think they were; but I'll return to this point a little later.

Before doing so, I should like to discuss certain of these 'common features' a little more fully, once more drawing my illustrations mainly from the history of England and France.

To return first to the types of disturbance and the behaviour of crowds. I have already said that food riots were the most common type of popular disturbance and I have tried to explain why this should have been so. But it would be a mistake to assume that the whole period, in both France and England, was punctuated by an almost unbroken succession of food riots. This, for obvious reasons, was not the case. Food riots generally occurred, as one might suspect, in the wake of bad harvests and shortage which sent prices rocketing upwards, and they may be said to have been the direct outcome of a fear of famine and not famine itself. (The great famine year of 1709 in France, for example, was not conspicuous for popular disturbance.) In their most characteristic form such riots were attended by popular price-fixing (or *taxation populaire*), which took the form of a violent invasion of markets, granaries, flour-mills and bakers' shops in the course of which the crowd, or its 'local' leaders, insisted that the baker, miller or farmer should reduce the price of his wheat or bread or flour to a 'just' or traditional level. Such movements made their appearance in England soon after Parliament passed the first Corn Law in 1660 and, in France, in the early part of the eighteenth century. In both countries the lean years were more frequent after 1760 than in the half-century before; and the 'peak' years for this type of rioting were, in France, 1768, 1775, 1789 and the 1790s, and, in England, 1766, 1795 and 1800. In both, the French Revolution served as a watershed, tending to inject a political content into such disturbances where it did not exist (or hardly existed) before. So we must look for their most classic, simon-pure, non-political expression, to the great English corn riots of 1766 and the French of 1775. The latter took the form of a vast rural rebellion in which the small consumers invaded the markets, flour-mills and bakers' shops in half a dozen provinces and in Paris itself, imposing a reduced price on corn, flour and bread, which, owing to the potency of rumour and of the 'bush-telegraph' of the market far more than to any organised conspiracy, was remarkably similar within the whole area over which the riots progressively spread. Such movements gained a new lease of life from the French Revolution; and they survived, through a couple of further revolutions, until the early 1850s. In England, they barely survived the Napoleonic Wars. There the last great outbreak of popular price-fixing by riot took place in East Anglia in 1816; after that, they persisted only in remote parts of the country (in Cornwall as late as 1830); and gave way to machine-breaking, arson and, later, to rural trade unionism.

In England (rather more than in France), the other most common type of rural riot was the attack on enclosures and toll-gates which spanned a roughly similar period; though, in West Wales (as remote from the centre of things as Cornwall), the last great manifestation of this kind, the so-called Rebecca Riots, took place as late as the early 1840s, at a time when the People's Charter was already winning wide support in the industrial districts of England, Scotland and South Wales.

Industrial disputes, during this 'pre-industrial' period, were also attended, in their most typical form, by attacks on machinery or the destruction of the mill-owner's or coal-owner's house or personal possessions. This has generally been called 'Luddism'; but as Dr. Hobsbawm and others have pointed out, 'Luddism' had two sides to it: its purpose was not always to arrest the growth of machinery (though this was certainly the prevailing intention in the Luddite riots in Yorkshire and Lancashire in 1812); it was also a traditional method of bringing pressure on the employer to raise wages or improve the conditions of work: this was generally the idea in the machine-breaking activities of the miners and weavers in the years preceding the Industrial Revolution and was also the case with the frame-work knitters of the Midlands 'hosiery' counties in the Luddite outbreak of 1811 and 1812. And in 1816, in 1822, and, above all, in 1830, the same method of settling what was primarily a wages dispute was adopted by the country labourers of East Anglia and the South of England. In 1830, the labourers fired stacks, extorted money, engaged in wages riots and—most characteristically—destroyed threshing machines in a score of counties. And so convinced were they of the justice of their cause that they exacted payment from the farmers for obliging them by breaking their machines. In Berkshire, the usual rate for breaking a threshing machine of a reasonable size was £2; and the treasurer of the

Kintbury 'gang' of rioters, a bricklayer named Francis Norris, was found with £100 and a couple of receipts in his pocket when arrested by the troops.

So a common factor in most of these disturbances— whether food riots or industrial disputes, whether they were rural or urban—was violence to property. And this goes as much for riots taking place before, during and after the French Revolution, and even for a short while, at least, after the birth of a working-class movement and the emergence of socialist ideas in the 1830s. Why this violence? In the case of individuals, it might perhaps be claimed that violent behaviour then, as now, is a release from tension or a way of canalising innate aggressive instincts. But, whatever the merit of such explanations in regard to individuals, we are dealing here with collective behaviour and we cannot assume that the urges stimulating the crowd are identical with the urges prompting the individuals that compose it or that crowd behaviour is simply individual behaviour writ large. The old-fashioned historian was inclined to identify the two and attribute the violence of the crowd to the natural violence of the rather unsavoury persons who composed it. Similarly, an old-fashioned crowd psychologist like Gustave Le Bon, who quite obviously was appalled by all such collective manifestations and had acquired his knowledge of the French Revolution from Taine, believed that the crowds that took the Bastille and stormed the Tuileries were displaying a 'collective mentality' that reduced all those taking part to a common level of bestiality.

The historian, however, cannot afford to neglect the political and social aspects of the case. The eighteenth century crowd, in particular, could hardly fail to be corrupted by the example set them by their social betters. It was an age of brutal floggings, torture of prisoners and public executions: in London, the desiccated heads of the Jacobite rebels executed after the 'Forty-Five' still grinned down from Temple Bar in the early 1770s; and in Paris men were broken on the wheel before the City Hall to the accompaniment of the consoling incantations of officiating clergy. Babeuf, the later promoter of a so-called 'conspiracy of the Equals', deplored the lynching by the crowd of a handful of victims after the fall of the Bastille, but ascribed their savagery to the lessons learned from their social superiors. Besides, was there a practical and effective alternative to violence (I am no longer talking of its grosser forms, like lynching) at a time when those composing these crowds were not allowed to organise in trade unions and were, almost without exception, excluded from the vote? In theory, there were, of course, alternatives such as carrying petitions to Parliament or engaging in peaceful processions. This was sometimes done in capital cities; but this was not much good in villages or in the suburbs of the new industrial towns where most of the disturbances took place. So the obvious and the most effective form of action, in times of hardship or dispute, was to take the law into your hands (as in the case of food riots) or to strike at the employer where it hurt most: at his house, his mill, his mine or his machinery. And it is perhaps no coincidence that the great debate on the relative virtues of 'physical force' and 'moral force' should have taken place at the time of Chartism, when many workers saw for the first time the possibility of finding a viable alternative to violence in the winning of the vote.

But it is important to note that violence was overwhelmingly applied to property and not to persons. This was so, with certain important exceptions, even in the most violent phases of the French Revolution. In the year 1789, for example, the crowd that stormed the Bastille massacred the governor, a municipal officer and half a dozen Swiss Guards; and, in the months that followed, four persons (including a baker) were lynched in Paris, two Household Guards were shot dead at Versailles and three or four persons were reported killed in the peasant attacks on the *châteaux* in the summer. In all, a total of a little short of twenty victims of the crowd in the opening year of revolution. This contrasts sharply with the greater savagery of the crowd's opponents. In the Réveillon riots of April 1789, 'several hundred' (the exact number is not known) were killed by troops and three were hanged after the event. At the siege of the Bastille, 150 assailants were killed or wounded. Five were hanged as a result of the disturbances in the capital that followed; and, two years later, in the great demonstration in the Champ de Mars in Paris, the crowd took two victims in return for fifty. In the case of all the English (and Welsh and Scottish) urban and rural riots of the 1830s to 1840s, the toll of death was even more one-sided. From my (no doubt) incomplete and imperfect record of the twenty-odd major riots and disturbances taking place in Britain between the Edinburgh Porteous Riots of 1736 and the great Chartist demonstration of April 1848 in London, I have totted up the following score: the crowds killed a dozen at most; while, on the other side, the courts hanged 118 and 630 were shot dead by the troops. We are told that Japanese students today, armed with sticks and helmets, inflict a heavier toll of casualties on the police than is inflicted on them by their opponents; but this was evidently far from being the case in similar engagements in the eighteenth and early nineteenth centuries in France and England. In brief, all talk of the famous 'blood-lust' of the crowd is largely based on legend and a few selected episodes in the French Revolutionary Terror; but it is a legend that dies hard.

What also dies hard is the legend of the crowd as riff-raff or *canaille*, or as a 'mob', 'foreigners', lay-abouts, or simply (to quote Dr. Dorothy George on the Gordon Riots) of 'the inhabitants of the dangerous districts who were always ready for pillage'. That historians should have helped to perpetuate this legend is perhaps hardly surprising. On the one hand, they have often had to cater for their own prejudices which reject the 'mob' (or *mobile vulgus*) as a squalid and dangerous intruder on the historical scene. On the other, they have had the more respectable justification of deriving their picture from that presented of the crowd by the great majority of contemporary observers, to whom the 'lower orders', particularly when engaged in acts of violent protest, readily appeared as gangs of criminals, drunkards or marauding 'strangers'. Doubtless for sound historical reasons, this picture tended to become less lurid and less one-sided by the early nineteenth century; but even in 1830, the 'Swing' labourers who fired stacks or broke threshing machines in the South of England were still being described in reports to the Home Office (often by clerical magistrates) as 'smugglers and deer-stealers', 'strangers dressed as labourers' (sometimes reported to be riding about in 'green gigs'), as 'the lowest description of persons' or 'men of indifferent character'. Usually these epithets fell wide of the mark, as these rioters, in particular, turn out, from the voluminous records that have survived in their case, to have been mainly respectable labourers and rural craftsmen of almost unimpeachable character: this, at least, is the general picture that emerges from the records relating to the 480 who were transported to Australia. And, similarly, the Parisians who stormed the Bastille and the Tuileries, though described by the historian Taine as cut-throats, vagrants, bandits and foreigners, are now fairly widely accepted as having been typical craftsmen, small employers and workmen of the Paris *faubourgs*; and generally of fixed abode and settled occupation.

A rather more refined variant of the 'crowd-as-mob' thesis is that put forward by M. Louis Chevalier in his book on the 'industrious and dangerous classes' of Paris in the 1830s and 1840s. From a wealth of sources, both literary and demographic, M. Chevalier paints a horrifying picture of the growth of Paris in the early nineteenth century, in terms of a growth of slums and overcrowding; and, with them, of crime, suicide, violence and prostitution. The main agents of this transformation are the 'nomads' or 'uprooted' who flock into the capital from the provinces and proceed, almost literally, to wage war on the old settled population. The 'industrious' and 'dangerous' classes turn out to be much the same; and the author infers

—though he never specifically states—that these 'dangerous' and overcrowded districts were the nurseries not only of poverty and crime but also of riot and rebellion. If this was so, one would expect to find a fair sprinkling of criminals and down-and-outs among the rioters and rebels of the period—and more particularly in the revolutions of 1830 and 1848. Yet such studies as have been made on the subject by Pinkney, Tilly, Gossez and others do not bear this out; and the Parisian crowd of the 1830s and 1840s appears, when every allowance has been made for the changes brought about in certain occupations, to be remarkably similarly constituted to that of 1789 and 1793.

This is, of course, a bald generalisation; and it is not being suggested either that the crowd remained largely identical whatever the nature of the disturbance, or that it remained unchanged from one decade to another. In Paris, for example, political and para-military engagements like the assault on the Bastille and the Tuileries involved a far higher proportion of craftsmen than food riots, in which both women and unskilled workers were more conspicuously represented. And the French Revolution was an important turning point, after which nothing was ever quite the same as before, not only because it gave a new political dimension to riot (and this applies to riots of the Right as well as to those of the Left), but also because it drew a wider range of social forces into political, or semi-political, activity. Not that political issues were entirely absent from rioting in the period up to the 1780s. The urban riot in big cities like London and Paris always tended to have political undertones; and in London, even before the early eighteenth-century riots of Anne's reign, the Common Council of the City had begun to serve as the political educator of the crowd in much the same way as the Paris Parlement, which did not scruple to clothe its appeal to uphold ancient privilege in popular terms, served to educate the French. In Paris, the big change came with the Revolution, when the crowd took a sharp and decisive turn to the Left and the popular movement even gained a considerable degree of independence, not only in breaking loose from its former aristocratic allies but even to a large extent from its new-found *bourgeois* allies as well. In London, this happened in two stages: in the 1760s, the crowd attached itself to the City Radicals and the person of John Wilkes; after the revolution in France it began to throw up leaders and organisations of its own. And this whole process was vastly speeded up in both countries by the emergence of working-class movements and socialist ideas in the 1830s.

So we come back to the most complex question of all: that of ideology and motivation. The question: why did people riot or rebel? is a simple one, but, as I have said before, it has no simple answer. The best I can hope to do here is to indicate certain motives and attempt to classify them. But how? as short-term and long-term motives? As 'economic' and 'political'? as overt or submerged? as 'forward-looking' or 'backward-looking'? as 'progressive' or 'reactionary'? This is largely a matter of choice as one type of classification cannot claim to be intrinsically more suitable than any other. For myself, I prefer to distinguish broadly between motives that are 'indigenous' (that is, directly experienced) and those that are 'derived', or borrowed or adapted from another quarter. As I see it, 'indigenous' motives are of two kinds: there are those that are concerned with the immediate problems relating to the rioters' daily bread, such as wages and prices, enclosures, turnpikes, land; and I assume that in food riots, turnpike riots and wages movements such overt motives play a predominant, though by no means an exclusive, role. But there are also, both in this type of riot and in others, certain underlying ideas and traditional, or 'generalised', beliefs that, for lying partly submerged, are none the less important. Such is the 'levelling' instinct or the belief in a rough sort of social justice, which prompts the poor to settle accounts with the rich by smashing their windows or burning their property or destroying their fences; we find examples of this both in English rural riots of the 1830s and 1840s and in the London riots of the 1760s and 1780s. There was also the strong belief among both 'middling' classes and poor in England in the 'Englishman's birthright' and his right to certain basic freedoms (as in Good King Alfred's day!), which distinguished him from poor benighted foreigners, like Frenchmen or Spaniards who had to put up with Popery and Wooden Shoes; and it seems that the fear that these freedoms were being threatened served on occasion as a powerful stimulus to riot. Again, in countries of absolute monarchy like France or Russia, the King or Tsar was frequently seen in the guise of Protector of his People; and this belief was no doubt strong among the French peasants who rioted in the King's name for bread in 1664 and 1775 and against feudal dues in August 1789. Again, as I have mentioned earlier, there was a strong attachment among both English and French labourers and small consumers to the traditional principles of a 'fair price' and a 'fair wage' untouched by the new-fangled notions of supply and demand. And this may do a great deal to explain the peculiar tenacity with which crowds broke machines and imposed price-controls by riot.

On the other hand, political motives and beliefs came, as we have seen, to be of increasing importance after the French Revolution; and these were, in the first place at least, *derived* from outside sources; from the Common Council or Parlement, from Radical journalists and politicians, or from liberal aristocrats or revolutionary *bourgeois*. Such was the notion and slogan of 'liberty' absorbed by the London crowds in the 1760s; and such were the ideas of the Rights of Man and Popular Sovereignty which Rousseau passed on to the Parisian *sans-culottes* via the Parlement and the revolutionary journalists and orators of 1789. And, later, socialist ideas were similarly derived from Babeuf, Owen and Marx.

But though originally derived from outside, such ideas were given a particular twist in the course of their assimilation by the small masters, craftsmen and wage-earners, who adapted them, as it were, to their own social and political needs. This is particularly striking in the case of the *sans-culottes* in Paris, who gave new meanings to the ideas of 'equality', 'Liberty' and 'sovereignty' which were quite unacceptable to their Jacobin teachers.

And to formulate more clearly what I only hinted before: it was a feature of this 'pre-industrial' period that the predominant traditional and 'indigenous' beliefs, which played so important a part in the ideology of the eighteenth century crowd, were gradually rivalled or eclipsed by the new political ideas emanating from the French Revolution and the working-class movements of the 1830s and 1840.

Thus, in spite of my somewhat tentative 'model', the face of the crowd, far from being firmly fixed, was constantly changed as society moved from its 'pre-industrial' to its industrial phase; and there was certainly no sharp cutting-off point between the two. So we have recognisable points of transition that mark the passing-over from the earlier to the later type of society. Examples of this are found in the revolution of 1848 in France and Chartism in England. We see signs of the old 'pre-industrial' forms in the February stage of the 1848 revolution: in the initial alliance of classes between bourgeoisie and *sans-culottes* (reminiscent of 1789), in food riots, industrial 'Luddism', not to mention the frequent repetition of the slogans, organisations and ideas of the older revolution. On the other hand, there is a reaching forward to the newer industrial society (particularly in the June insurrection) in the armed clash between capital and labour, in the working-men's clubs and socialist ideas, and in the emergence of new types of worker, such as railwaymen and engineers. Chartism, too, has a similar dual complexion. On the one hand, the six points of the People's Charter look back to a similar programme drawn up in Westminster in 1780; and Feargus O'Connor's Land Plan as a cure for industrial ills and the old-style 'house-breaking' riots in Staffordshire in 1842 are stamped with the traditions of a 'pre-industrial' society. On the other hand, the Chartist political organisation, the industrial aims of the miners and textile workers, and the activities of the Manchester 'turn-outs' in the 'Plug-Plot' riots of 1842 were new and 'forward-looking'.

Again, it may occur to the reader that there have been plenty of cases of 'pre-industrial'-type riots in our modern industrial society. In 1914, for example, German bakers' shops were attacked in London in much the same way as the Gordon rioters attacked the property of Roman Catholics and their reputed sympathisers in 1780. In Kalgoorlie, in Western Australia, striking miners in the 1930s wrecked pit-head machinery as their forbears in the Durham coalfields had done a hundred years before. The Japanese rice riots of 1918 were accompanied by the same sort of direct action and popular price control as the food riots in France and England in the eighteenth and early nineteenth centuries. Dr. Hobsbawm gives us plenty of illustrations of archaic and strictly non-'industrial' forms of popular protest in his book on twentieth century 'Primitive Rebels'. The Mexican Cristeros of 1936 hailed Christ the King and damned the radical *bourgeois* in a manner highly reminiscent of the Vendée peasants of 1793 and of the 'King and Church' movements in Spain, Italy and the Tyrol at the time of the Revolutionary and Napoleonic Wars. And what of the Negro rebellion that has been erupting in the northern cities of the United States since 1964? Hasn't this, in certain of its aspects at least, a distinct flavour of the 'pre-industrial' riot? I think the answer is yes. But why this should be so, and why Japanese rice-rioters should have behaved as they did at a time when Japan was already considered to have moved into its 'industrial' stage, I prefer to leave to my readers to work out for themselves.

Society and Conflict in London and Paris in the Eighteenth Century

The main purpose of this paper is to compare the social structure and government of London and Paris, and the social and political tensions arising within them, during the latter part of the eighteenth century. But it may be useful first to consider when and how the population grew in both cities, while the reader may be left to judge for himself how far such factors are relevant to the main discussion that follows.

Population

Throughout the century, these were the two largest cities in Europe, and of the two Paris may have been the larger when the century began. But, by the 1750s, London had overtaken Paris and, from now on, she grew more quickly and now (as indeed before), Londoners formed a far higher proportion of the population of England and Wales than Parisians did of the population of France.

To look at the problem more closely. The population of Paris, having reached the 500,000 mark before 1700, rose comparatively little, or even stagnated or declined, in the course of the next hundred years. Calculations before the census of 1801 are notoriously defective and erratic and it is quite impossible to assert with any confidence what, at any point, the size of the Parisian population actually was; so much depended on the methods used to determine it. Thus the official calculation of 1789 (based on the believed number of 'hearths' within Paris and its adjoining suburbs) was 524,000, a figure that showed only a slight increase on

Paper read at University of Melbourne on 9 July 1969.

similar estimates made in 1700 and 1760. Yet, as Jacques Necker, a former (and future) Finance Minister, pointed out, such estimates omitted the thousands of foundling children and the great 'floating' population of the hotels and furnished lodgings; and these, he believed, if taken account of, would have added a further 100,000 or 120,000 to the official figures—a total that was certainly further inflated in the summer of that year, when many thousands of villagers from the surrounding countryside, driven by economic necessity, sought refuge within the walls of the capital. So there may have been as many as 700,000 people (both permanent and temporary) within the city in the opening months of the French Revolution, but even if this were so, that population most certainly declined during the next ten years, and the first official census—Napoleon's census of 1801—put it no higher than 546,000. Meanwhile, the population of France had ranged between about 24 million and 27 million so that Parisians formed throughout the century a more or less constant proportion of 1 in 40 or 50 of all the people of France.[1]

The population of London, on the other hand, grew markedly and rapidly in the course of these years. Far smaller than that of Paris during the seventeenth century, it progressed (according to Mr. Wrigley's calculations) from 200,000 in 1600 to 575,000 in 1750 and to 900,000 in 1801. Meanwhile, during the century, the population of England and Wales rose from $5\frac{1}{2}$ million to 9 million. Thus at almost any time during these hundred years, as many as one Englishman in ten was living in the capital.[2]

1. M. Reinhard, 'Paris pendant la Révolution', *Les Cours de Sorbonne*, 2 vols. (Paris, n.d.), I, 25–34; G. Rudé, 'La population ouvrière parisienne de 1789 à 1791', *Ann. hist. Rév. franc.*, no. 1 (1967), pp. 15–21; F. Furet, C. Mazauric, L. Bergeron, 'Les sans-culottes et la Révolution française', *Annales (Economie, Société, Civilisation)* (Nov.–Dec. 1963), pp. 1124–5.

2. E. A. Wrigley, 'A Simple Model of London's Importance in Changing English Society and Economy 1650–1750', *Past and Present*, no. 37 (1967), pp. 44–5; M. D. George, *London Life in the Eighteenth Century* (1951), pp. 24, 329–30.

In both cities, the rise or fall or the 'movement' of population could be attributed to any one (or more) of four demographic factors. One was the excess of annual births over deaths, or vice versa. Another was the influx of new arrivals offset by the number of those going out. A third was the movement of population within the city itself; and a fourth the progressive absorption by the city of parts of the adjoining countryside. In Paris, the number of annual births and deaths both tended to increase; but, taking the century as a whole, there was a slight excess of births over deaths. Meanwhile, there was a steady influx of new arrivals and, in the eighteenth century (as in the early nineteenth), it was commonly noted that six out of every ten Parisians were born outside France or in the provinces; and as the population increased so little, it is evident that the number of those leaving the city (including several thousands of seasonal workers) must have been almost as great. As for those who migrated *within* the city, there was a dual movement: on the one hand, there were the nobility and the rich who moved westwards from the centre or north-centre of the new fashionable districts of the west (the Palais Royal, the Faubourg St. Honoré and the Champs Elysées); on the other, there was the working population which, in ever-increasing numbers, came and settled in the old overcrowded quarters of the centre, near the markets, off the Place de Grèves, or along the Seine. And, finally, the city of Paris as a whole burst through its old boundaries and swallowed up a large part of the outer suburbs, a fact that was clearly recognised by the Farmers-General when they built their new customs wall, or *barrières*, around Paris in 1785.[3]

London followed a similar development, if we consider the century as a whole. But, in the first half-century, there was a regular excess of deaths over births; in the next

3. Reinhard, *op. cit.*, I, 35–9; L. Chevalier, *Classes laborieuses et classes dangereuses à Paris pendant la première moitié du XIXe siècle* (Paris, 1958), pp. 263–4; G. Rudé, *The Crowd in the French Revolution* (Oxford, 1959, pp. 10–15); P. Lovedan, *Histoire de Paris* (1960), pp. 65–6.

forty years births frequently eclipsed deaths; but it was
not until the 1790s that births were regularly in excess of
mortality. Throughout the century, the growth of population was largely accounted for by the continuous influx
of migrants from the countryside and here again, as in
Paris, it was noted (around the 1770s) that two Londoners
out of three (the proportion is much the same as for
Paris) were born abroad or in the provinces. Mr Wrigley
adds, further, that, about the mid-century at least, one
Englishman in every six had at some time lived in the
capital. Moreover, he estimates that, at this time, there was
a *net* intake, after every allowance had been made for those
returning to the provinces, of about 8,000 persons a year.
And, as in Paris, there was a continuous movement of the
urban population—above all of the City's merchants and
shopkeepers—towards the new parishes to the north and
the west, such as Kensington, Chelsea, Hammersmith
and Marylebone. Largely as a result of this internal
migration, the population of the City actually declined
while that of the five new 'parishes outside the Bills'
increased from 9,000 in 1700 to 123,000 in 1801. London,
too, like Paris, overflowed into the neighbouring countryside, and the census of 1801 took stock of the situation by
including a score of new villages—in Surrey and Middlesex—within the metropolitan boundaries.[4]

In short, in the course of the century there was a broadly
similar demographic development in the case of the two
cities. They both experienced a continuous influx of new
arrivals from outside; in both, there was a movement of
the more prosperous classes from the old quarters of the
centre towards the newer quarters in the west, and in
both a similar invasion of the adjoining country by the
town.

Yet, in other respects, the differences were perhaps even
more striking. In the first place, the King's Court at

4. George, *op. cit.*, pp. 329, 401; Reinhard, *loc. cit.*; Wrigley, *op. cit.*,
pp. 46–9; Sir Walter Besant, *London in the Eighteenth Century* (1902), p.
76.

St. James's lay well within the boundaries of London, whereas the French Court was (until October 1789) at Versailles, a dozen miles beyond the outer walls of Paris. Thus Versailles served as a magnet, as a considerable diversion from the political, social and artistic life of France's capital city. But, apart from this, Paris was, as a metropolis, far more uniform and compact than London. It had one single administration with jurisdiction all over the capital; and there was a wall, the so-called 'wall of the Farmers-General', which ringed it all around over a stretch of fifteen miles, enclosing the *faubourgs* as well as the old city and sharply dividing the capital from the country outside. London, on the other hand, even before Defoe wrote in the 1720s, sprawled over a circuit of thirty-six miles, with neither wall nor *barrières* to fence it in. Moreover, far from being uniform, it was composed of a number of ill-assimilated parts, each separately governed: the old City of London, the centre of its trade; Westminster, the centre of Court, Parliament and Government; the old commercial Borough of Southwark and its dependencies across the river; and the urban or near-urban parishes of Surrey and Middlesex. We should note, too, that London was more effectively divided by the Thames than Paris was by the Seine; and, even in the eighteenth century, the 'Left Bank' formed a far more integral part of Paris than the South Bank parishes did of London. And yet, by way of compensation, the city of London as a whole was more intimately linked with its rural hinterland than Paris. For not only was there no physical barrier separating London from the villages around but there was also no *economic* barrier as formed by the Paris wall, along which the Farmers-General had set up customs posts to levy duties on the cattle, timber, wine and food brought in to the capital by the villagers from outside. Moreover, parts of Essex to the east, Surrey to the south, and Middlesex to the west were already being converted into 'dormitory' areas for the London merchant class; and even early in the century it was not unknown for a London merchant to commute daily between his City or Westminster office and his country home in Middlesex.[5]

There were also certain differences in the *functions* of the two capital cities. Both, admittedly, were centres of government, politics, law, manufacture, entertainment, intellectual life and the fine arts: if we consider the century as a whole, perhaps here there was little to choose between them. Paris, too, like London, was a centre of trade and finance, in the latter respect at least the greatest in France. But in neither of these fields did it reach the international eminence of London. The Bank of England was founded in 1694, the Bank of France not until 1800. Paris was admittedly a large port: M. Marcel Reinhard tells us that, at the time of the Directory, 9,700 boats loaded and unloaded at its quays and carried 500,000 tons of merchandise in their holds.[6] But Paris was not a great international port like Marseilles, Nantes or Bordeaux. Still less was it like London, which not only far eclipsed all other British ports but was fast becoming the largest port in the world. More than half of all the ships coming to English ports unloaded their wares in London; and in one single year, in 1794–5, more than 14,500 ships (one quarter of them from overseas) brought with them cargoes totalling 1,800,000 tons, or nearly four times the tonnage handled by Paris.[7] And Ralph Davis, in his history of the English merchant navy, estimates that something like one-quarter of London's total working population in 1700 was employed in one or other of the numerous trades and occupations associated with the port of London.[8]

Society

Let us now consider the society, or the social structure, of the two cities. It is not an easy task, as the observers of the

5. M. Robbins, *Middlesex* (1953), pp. 190–1.

6. Reinhard, *op. cit.*, II, 44.

7. Sir Joseph D. Broodbank, *A History of the Port of London*, 2 vols. (1921), I, 74–81.

8. R. Davis, *The Rise of the English Shipping Industry* (1962), p. 390.

day differed widely among themselves as to what should constitute a social category, and social classes were seen by all of them in terms quite different from our own. And we have the further problem of choosing a form of classification which is as appropriate for Paris as it is for London. This is one reason—and it is an important one—why it is not practical, in a study of this kind, to adopt the social classification of either Mercier (of 1782) or Massance (of 1788), both of which are discussed by M. Reinhard in his Sorbonne lectures.[9] I have preferred to fall back on Daniel Defoe's classification of 1709. Although it is considerably earlier than the others and has certain other defects, it is concerned with 'classes' rather than 'orders' and therefore provides a better basis for a comparative study.

Defoe divides the population of England into seven main groups, of which six will be seen to be applicable to an urban society. They are as follows:

The *great*, who live profusely.
The *rich*, who live very plentifully.
The *middle sort*, who live well.
The working trades, who labour hard but feel no want.
The *country people*, farmers, etc., who fare indifferently.
The *poor*, that fare hard.
The *miserable*, that really pinch and suffer want.[10]

It is a little crude and there is no provision made for either the lower nobility or gentry or the considerable class of professional people—artists, doctors, lawyers and the like—who formed an important element in both cities. But in the absence of better, it will serve our purpose reasonably well.

To begin at the top of the social pyramid with Defoe's 'great', or the nobility. In both cities, a wealthy nobility lived within easy reach of the Court; in both, a wealthy upper clergy ranked with the nobility; and, in both, a

9. Reinhard, *op. cit.*, I, 41.
10. George, *op. cit.*, p. 363.

lesser provincial nobility (in England they were termed the 'gentry') paid occasional social visits to the capital—though, in England, many sat in Parliament as Members of the House of Commons. But the differences were more striking than the similarities. For one thing, in France *les grands* (if we limit the term to the top nobility) were excluded from playing any direct part in politics. For another, they generally lived in far more splendid style in Paris than their opposite numbers did in London. There were notable exceptions, such as the Earl of Chesterfield, the Dukes of Bedford and Richmond, Lord Holland (the father of Charles James Fox) in the 1760s and 1770s and the Prince Regent after the turn of the century. But even their style of living was eclipsed by that set by the French Princes of the Blood: by the Duke of Orleans at the Palais Royal or Monsieur (the future Louis XVIII) at the Luxembourg, and even by several of the bigger aristocratic *hôtels* of the Marais or the Faubourgs St. Germain and St. Honoré. In contrast, the London nobility led comparatively simple lives in their comparatively simple terrace houses; and foreign visitors to the English capital were astounded by their lack of ostentation, which contrasted so oddly with that displayed by their own privileged classes. St. James's Palace, in particular, aroused amusement, if not derision, and provoked von Bielfeld's famous quip: 'Les Rois de la Grande Bretagne sont logés au Palais de St. James comme des invalides, et les invalides de l'Armée et de la Marine comme des Rois à Chelsea et à Greenwich!'[11]

But the most important difference of all was the existence in Paris of the privileged legal caste known as the *noblesse de robe*; they may have numbered some 1,500–2,000 persons and had no equivalent in London. They were the people who sat in the Parlements, or 'sovereign' courts, and held (by purchase or inheritance) the main administrative, financial and judicial offices in the capital or at Versailles,

11. M. D. George, 'London and the Life of the Town', in *Johnson's England*, ed. A. S. Turberville, 2 vols. (1965), I, 170.

and who alone among the nobility claimed the right to play a direct part in political affairs. It was they, as we shall see, who formed the main opposition to the Royal Government in the years preceding the revolution of 1789.

We come to those whom Defoe termed 'the rich'. These were the financial and commercial *bourgeoisie*, who played a significant (if not the predominant) role in the economic life of both Paris and London. In Paris, there were the *gens de finance*, like the brothers Pâris in Louis XV's time; there were the large bankers and *négociants*, and the tax-farmers or Farmers-General, who, even if they were, as *roturiers*, the social inferiors of 'the great', often eclipsed them by the 'nobility' of their style of life. Among them were many of the greatest holders of the city's real estate: in Jaurès' words, they had become by 1789 'la force souveraine de propriété, de production et de consommation'.[12]

In London, there were the bankers, the large holders of government stock, and the directors and governors of the main insurance offices and of the great chartered trading companies like the Hudson Bay, the East India and the South Sea Companies, men who, in politics, were more vitally interested in national than in purely London affairs. At the end of the century, the City of London probably contained about one-half of the 2,000 'eminent merchants and bankers' who, according to Patrick Colquhoun, lived in Britain at this time; he attributed to them an average income of £2,600 a year.[13] Some were, of course, far wealthier than this: William Beckford, a West India merchant and the elder Pitt's principal lieutenant in the City, had an annual income of £36,000; and Samson Gideon, the Jewish financier, left a fortune of £500,000. Some of them, like the aristocracy, lived in St. George's or St. James's at 'the polite end of the town'; Gideon,

12. J. Jaurès, *L'histoire socialiste de la Révolution française*, 8 vols. (Paris, 1922–4), I, 149–50.
13. M. D. George, *England in Transition* (1953), pp. 152–3.

for example, ended his days in Arlington Street, off Piccadilly. Others, however, preferred to live out their lives in the City or (like Beckford) in a once, but no longer, fashionable district like Soho Square.[14]

Defoe's 'middle sort' is a far larger and more comprehensive group and, in the case of both cities, might more suitably be divided into three. For there are important distinctions to be drawn between the 'middling' or comfortable merchant class, which, in its upper ranges, merged with the class of 'the rich'; the more prosperous master craftsmen, wholesale dealers, manufacturers and substantial shopkeepers; and those whom we term the 'professional' classes, the doctors, artists, poets and lawyers, to whom Defoe and other contemporary observers paid little or no attention. Such groups were both numerous and important in the lives of the two cities; but there were significant differences between them in their numbers and in the role they played. In London these 'middling' merchants and shopkeepers were wealthier and more numerous and enjoyed a higher social status than those in Paris. They may have had fewer grievances: they were certainly not subject to the vexations of the *droits d'entrée* exacted on the approaches to the city. Moreover, they enjoyed the protection (far transcending that of the Paris petty gilds) of the Corporation of the City of London and, in Westminster, had other minor 'citadels' on and off the Strand. In Westminster, their shops were particularly brightly lit and well installed; Archenholtz, on a visit in 1789, wrote: 'The magnificence of the shops is the most striking thing in London; they sometimes extend without interruption for an English mile. The shop front has large glass windows and a glass door . . . The largest shops of this kind [he is talking of silversmiths' and jewellers' shops in particular] in Paris, in the Rue St. Honoré, are mean compared to those in London.'[15]

14. G. Rudé, *Wilkes and Liberty* (Oxford, 1962), pp. 2–5; H. Phillips, *Mid-Georgian London* (1964), pp. 288, 302.
15. M. D. George, in *Johnson's England*, I, 175.

But if the merchants and shopkeepers of London were both socially and politically more significant than those in Paris, in the case of the lawyers—the attorneys, the *avocats* and the *procureurs* and their clerks—it was the other way round. As the commercial classes in London had their stronghold in the City, so the *hommes de loi* ('ces gens de la basoche') had theirs in the Palais de Justice. London, admittedly, had its Inns of Court and (by 1791) over 2,000 counsel and attorneys—and there were wealthy and influential men among them; but, collectively, they never enjoyed the prestige or commanded the authority of the legal profession in Paris. Closely associated with the privileged *parlementaires*, whose aspirations they shared and whose direction they accepted, they played a political role that was quite disproportionate to their actual numbers within the community.

Yet, if we consider these 'rich' and 'middling' classes as a whole, there was one further respect in which the impact of the Londoners was far more potent than that of the Parisians. This was in the field of culture, the arts and intellectual discussion. In both cities (as in both countries), culture and the arts bore the stamp of a predominantly aristocratic society. But in London, far more than in Paris, this aristocratic monopoly had for long been undermined, corroded and challenged by new 'values' emanating from the commercial middle classes. Voltaire had noted it in his visit to London in the 1720s and had discussed it at length, and with evident approval, in his *Lettres philosophiques*.[16] The London coffee-houses had become centres of political and intellectual discussion, frequented by 'middling'-class citizens, from as far back as the 1660s; there were 450 of them in Queen Anne's time and a further hundred by 1739, of which the great majority lay in the City or within easy reach of the Strand. In Paris, there were perhaps as many in the course of the eighteenth century (there were 380 in 1723, according to Daniel Mornet, and

16. Voltaire, *Lettres philosophiques* (Paris, 1728); English edition: *Letters Concerning the English Nation* (London, 1759).

600–700 in 1782, according to Mercier); but, the same authors tell us, politics were hardly discussed in them until the 1780s.[17] This same middle-class outlook, which Voltaire admired so much among the English, found other means of expression: in the novel, for example, which began to flourish in 1740, and, more explicitly, in the Press. The first London daily newspaper, the *Daily Courant*, was launched in 1702; its Paris equivalent, the *Journal de Paris*, first appeared in 1777. Two years later, Paris already had 35 newspapers and journals, but London had 160. Of course, the French Revolution helped, as in so many other respects, to redress the balance; but even by the end of 1789, when Paris had 169 papers and journals of every kind, London had 205.[18]

Government and politics

It is perhaps appropriate at this point, before we leave the propertied classes altogether, to say a word on the government and politics of the two capital cities. Here the contrasts are considerably sharper. Paris, before the Revolution, was still the particular jewel, 'la bonne ville', of the King of France. He governed it despotically and centrally, through his Intendants, lieutenants and officials, either from Versailles itself or from the Châtelet in Paris. The Paris city government was only nominally vested in a small oligarchy of its wealthier citizens—the self-perpetuating *échevins* and *prévôts*—established at the City Hall. And in so far as there existed an alternative authority to that of the absolute monarch, it lay with the 'aristocratic' group of *parlementaires* at the Palais de Justice, and least of all with the citizens at large.

17. Bryant Lilliwhite, *London Coffee Houses* (1963); D. Mornet, *Les origines intellectuelles de la Révolution française (1715–1787)* (Paris, 1933), pp. 277–85.

18. R. S. Crane and F. B. Kaye, *A Census of British Newspapers and Periodicals 1620–1820* (1927), pp. 182–201; Mornet, *op. cit.*, p. 343 *et seq.*

In London, however, municipal government was diverse, autonomous, largely middle-class and even, to a surprising degree, democratic. The City of London had its two governing and elective Courts, the Court of Aldermen and the Court of Common Council, its 26 (or 28) wards and its 100 parishes. The County of Middlesex was governed by its justices, recruited largely from the 'middling' class or gentry; and, after the election of John Wilkes in 1768, at least one of its two representatives in Parliament tended to be a man of radical (rather than of Whig or Tory) leanings. The City of Westminster alone retained, in its local administration, an aristocratic complexion. Although it was nominally governed by a Court of Burgesses, composed of local tradesmen, this body had its functions progressively usurped by the Middlesex justices, supported by the local vestries of its nine parishes, most of which, in the latter half of the century, fell into the hands of 'select' groups of notables—aristocrats, gentry and prosperous merchants. But, in parliamentary elections, the opposite was the case, as Westminster had a franchise even more broadly based than that of the City of London. Every householder, or 'pot-walloper', had the vote, and its 10,000 electors included, in addition to a majority of small and 'middling' tradesmen, a sprinkling of watermen, chairmen and even labourers. In London, whose franchise was only slightly more restricted, about 8,000 freemen of the livery companies voted within their Common Hall; and these freemen not only had the duty of returning the City's four Members of Parliament but they also played a leading part in the City's administrative affairs. In 1739, an enquiry revealed that of the 236 members of the Court of Common Council (which shared with the more august Court of Aldermen the direction of the City's affairs), 152 were tradesmen and 'artificers' as compared with a mere 30 merchants, bankers, attorneys, surgeons and distillers. And the influence of these 'middling' groups increased as the century went on; for, with the growing volume and complexity of municipal affairs, the aldermen were compelled to transfer ever more of their business to the Court of Common Council.[19]

After what has been said, it is perhaps hardly surprising that the political confrontation between groups and parties should have assumed quite different forms in London from what it did in Paris. In Paris, the principal conflict was between the magistrates of the *noblesse de robe* (with some support from the professional *bourgeoisie*) and the Royal government, and the main challenger to the 'despotism' of Ministers was the Paris Parlement, which, intermittently since 1720 and almost continuously since the early 1770s, opposed the attempts made by a succession of ministries to impose taxes on the privileged classes. In this engagement, which was essentially one between 'despotism' and 'privilege', the *bourgeoisie* played a comparatively passive role and wavered in its loyalties between King and Parlement. As the *bourgeois* had no representative institutions of their own, their voice could only be heard through that of the writers, journalists and lawyers. Some of these— Voltaire, Turgot and Mirabeau were among them—saw the main danger in the 'privileges' of the aristocracy of the sword or the robe; while others (and they included a great many of the lawyers, who were largely dependent on the Parlements) saw it in the 'despotism' of Ministers. In 1788, during the 'aristocratic revolt', it looked as if the whole nation would unite behind the Parlements against the King; but, in September of that year, the tables were turned when the Parlement of Paris scandalised the Third Estate by rejecting its claim to a double representation and a 'vote by head' at the Estates-General which had been summoned to meet at Versailles. From that moment, the *bourgeoisie*, in Paris as elsewhere, found a voice of its own and condemned the pretensions of the Parlements and aristocracy before going on to challenge the 'despotism' of the King and his Ministers.[20]

19. S. and B. Webb, *English Local Government from the Revolution to the Municipal Corporations Act. The Manor and the Borough* (1908), pp. 569–692.

20. See J. Egret, *La pré-révolution française 1787–1788* (1962), p. 367.

In London, the situation was a very different one. Here the main challenger to government, from early in the century, was not the aristocracy, nor even those whom Defoe termed the 'merchant princes' or 'the rich'. It was, rather, the small and middling *bourgeoisie* of the City of London, who held a more or less firm control of the City's government. And, through them, the City of London was, from about 1730 to the 1780s, almost in continuous opposition to the Court of St. James's and the government at Westminster. The main protagonist in this duel was, as I have said, the small merchant and shopkeeping and artisan class of the Common Hall and Common Council, which often spoke with a different voice from that of the wealthier and more conservative Court of Aldermen. But, in the great crises, the City tended to form a common front against its opponents at Whitehall, Westminster and St. James's. Thus the City united to oppose Sir Robert Walpole over Excise in 1733 and the Pelhams over the Jewish Nationalisation Act of 1753, to champion William Pitt in the 1750s, to defend the cause of John Wilkes and the Middlesex electors in 1769 and the City's printers and journalists in 1771, and to demand the repeal of the Catholic Relief Act, on the eve of the Gordon Riots, in 1780. It is perhaps of interest to note, in passing, here that, in the aftermath of these riots, which thoroughly scared the worthy magistrates and householders of the capital, the City demanded—nine years before the Third Estate in Paris—the right to form a military volunteer association of its own, staffed by its own officers; in short, a *bourgeois* National Guard, both to protect their properties against the riotous 'banditti' and to uphold their traditional 'liberties' against government encroachment. But the riots also marked the separation of the London *bourgeois* from their allies in the streets. Popular Radicalism had lost its appeal for them. Soon after, they broke with Fox and the Whigs and, in the General Election of 1784, they rallied to George III and his Minister, the younger William Pitt. Thus the City and its allies in Westminster and Middlesex, having challenged the King and his Ministers for half a century, entered into an alliance with Pitt's new Tory—and King's—party just at the moment when the Parisian *bourgeoisie* was beginning to establish itself as an independent force in opposition to the Court and the privileged classes.[21]

The 'lower orders' or *menu peuple*

So I come at last to the poorer classes—to Defoe's 'working trades', his 'poor' and his 'miserable'—those whom the French termed the *menu peuple*. Following Defoe, I propose to treat them in three main groups. First, his 'working trades', which comprised (roughly) the small shopkeepers and craftsmen, both masters and journeymen. Francis Place numbered them (in 1818) at about 100,000 in London; and, in Paris, they correspond broadly to those 'cent cinquante mille ouvriers et artisans', who, in May 1789, protested to the Assembly of the Parisian Third Estate against their exclusion from the franchise.[22] Secondly, there were the unskilled workers in more or less regular employment: the porters, watermen, water-carriers, day-labourers and domestic servants—those, roughly, whom Sir John Fielding (writing in 1758) called the 'infinite number of chairmen, porters, labourers and drunken mechanics', and whom his half-brother Henry had previously defined as 'the Mob'.[23] It was these two groups (reinforced, in Paris, by the smaller shopkeepers) who, during the French Revolution, acquired the collective

21. L. S. Sutherland, 'The City of London in Eighteenth-Century Politics', in *Essays Presented to Sir Lewis Namier*, eds. R. Pares and A. J. P. Taylor (1956), pp. 49–74; R. R. Sharpe, *London and the Kingdom*, 3 vols. (1895), vol. III, *passim*.

22. George, *London Life*, p. 361; *Pétition de cent cinquante mille ouvriers et artisans adressée à M. Bailly, dimanche 3 Mai 1789*, Bib. Nat., Lb 39 1667.

23. Sir John Fielding, *An Account of the Origin and Effects of a Police* (1758), p. 44; J. P. de Castro, *The Gordon Riots* (1926), p. 249.

label of *sans-culottes*. But, in both cities, there was also an equally large, but 'submerged', group of poor, destitute, beggars, homeless, vagrants, part-employed, sempstresses and home-workers, criminals, prostitutes and *lumpen*-proletarians (Marx's later term), whom the more respectable workers, like Francis Place in London, and the *sans-culottes* in Paris thoroughly despised and rejected. How many were there? If we judge by the figures for poor relief in Paris in the 1770–90s (the numbers remained remarkably stable) and Colquhoun's figures of the 'criminal' element in London, perhaps 100,000–120,000 in both cities.[24] But, in spite of all that has been written about them by Taine, Louis Chevalier and other writers, they played little or no part in political or protest movements (except, possibly, in food riots). We know remarkably little about them; and rather than speculate further on their social role and identity, it may perhaps be best to leave them out of further consideration.

So we return to Defoe's other categories—the 'working trades' and 'the poor'; to the small workshop masters, craftsmen, journeymen and labourers. Again there were similarities in the two cities. Neither had distinctive working-class districts, such as developed in the nineteenth century. Yet there were the elements of these in the streets around the docks, the markets and the City Hall in Paris; and, in London, in certain parishes on the fringe of Westminster and the City, in St. Katherine by the Tower, East Smithfield and around the Mint in Southwark. In both cities, it was common for small employers and workmen to live on different floors of the same tenement building, the room rising the higher in inverse proportion to the tenant's status or daily wage.[25] In both, a large proportion of the working population lived in rented furnished rooms or lodgings: there were perhaps 50,000 such *non-domiciliés* in Paris in the early years of the Revolu-

24. Rudé, 'La population ouvrière parisienne . . .', p. 17; P. Colquhoun, *Treatise on the Police of the Metropolis* (1797), pp. vii–xi.
25. George, *London Life*, p. 104; Reinhard, *op. cit.*, I, 91.

tion and 2,837 lodging-houses were recorded in March–April 1795.[26] Rents were not dissimilar: the occupant of a room in a doss-house or cheap lodging-house might pay 2*d.* in London and 2 *sous* (the equivalent amount) in Paris: and more 'respectable' lodgings might cost 4*d.* or 6*d.* a night (2*s.* to 3*s.* 6*d.* a week) in London where they would cost 3–5 *sous* in Paris. Hours of work were long in both cities: in London, they varied between twelve and fifteen hours a day (and this was as true of the 1780s as it was of the thirties and fifties) according to the trade and the season; and we find Paris bookbinders in 1776 striking for a fourteen-hour day.[27] Wages are harder to compare, as they varied greatly, in both cities, according to season, occupation and skill; but there was a similar differential between skilled and unskilled and between skills that were rare and those that were not. Thus, around 1789, a labourer in London earned between 12*s.* and 14*s.* a week, where he might earn 125–150 *sous* (based on a five-day week) in Paris; and a tailor or carpenter might earn 18–22*s.* a week in London and 250 *sous* in Paris; and a journeyman sculptor or goldsmith 60–80*s.* in London and 500 *sous* in Paris. Moreover, bread, the basic diet in both cities, might, in a normal year in London between 1765 and 1790, cost 1½*d.* or 2*d.* a pound and 2 *sous* in Paris between 1776 and 1787.[28]

Yet, once again, there were important differences, which will be merely briefly recounted here. The wage-earners in London were more advanced as an identifiable and separate social class. In Paris, the typical unit of manufacture was still the small workshop, deriving from the middle ages, in which the master craftsmen worked with a regulated number of apprentices (perhaps one and rarely more

26. Rudé, 'La population ouvrière parisienne . . .', pp. 18–21; Arch. Nat., F⁷ 3688⁴.

27. George, *London Life*, pp. 100–1, 205–6; Rudé, *The Crowd in the French Revolution*, pp. 15, 20, 251.

28. G. D. H. Cole and R. Postgate, *The Common People 1746–1938* (1945), pp. 71–6; George, *London Life*, pp. 166–7; Rudé, *The Crowd in the French Revolution*, pp. 21–22, 25, 251–2.

than three) and a small, but larger, number of journeymen. There were, of course, exceptions, like the textile 'manufactories' in the north of Paris, some employing several hundred men, and the 'free' manufacturing enclaves in the Louvre and in the Faubourg St. Antoine. But these were, indeed, the exception and not the rule. In London, on the other hand, it was the other way about and the gild system, with its close regulation of wages, hours and quality of workmanship, was generally in full decline, where, in Paris, it had only been dented by Turgot's Six Acts of 1776. In Paris, too, the journeyman was more closely associated with his master, often slept under his roof, sometimes married his daughter or widow, and still— although admittedly more rarely than of old—aspired himself to become a master, or, at least, to set up in business of his own.[29]

A further difference was that the 'lower orders' in London were probably less poor than those in Paris, and less haunted by the fear of famine. So much appears from an admittedly rough-and-ready comparison of wages and the price of bread. In Paris, a labourer of the 1780s, with a daily wage of 25–30 *sous* and a daily purchase of 4 lb. of bread, would, in normal times, spend something like 50–60 per cent of his weekly earnings on bread; the London labourer, with a wage of 12–14*s*., would, under similar circumstances, spend 35–40 per cent.* During this same period, a medium or lower-paid journeyman in Paris might spend 30–37 per cent of his income in this way, while in London he might spend 25–33 per cent; and a highly paid craftsman 15 per cent in Paris and as little as 7 per cent in London. And the disparity was considerably greater in times of shortage, as (on such occasions) prices rose less steeply in London than they did in Paris. Thus (to

29. George, *London Life*, p. 158 *et seq.*; Rudé, *The Crowd in the French Revolution*, pp. 18–19.

* The assumption is that, in Paris, a worker worked for only five days a week (there are reputed to have been 111 feast-days in the course of the year), while in London he worked six.

take the last third of the century alone), the 4-lb. loaf in Paris rose, in three of the most critical years, from a norm of 8–9 *sous* to 16 *sous* in 1768, to 14 *sous* in May 1775, and to 14½ *sous* in February 1789; whereas, in London, the quartern loaf rarely rose above 8*d.* or 9*d.*, and the quarter of wheat rose from a current 'norm' of 55–60*s.* in 1767, to 64*s.* in 1774 and 1783, and to 62*s.* in 1789. It was only in the inflationary war-years of 1795 and 1800 that London knew sharp increases in the price of bread comparable to those in Paris in these earlier years.[30]

Moreover, the English craftsmen and wage-earners had inherited a long political and dissenting tradition, reaching back to the 1640s and based on chapel and on 'revolution principles'.[31] This had no equivalent in Paris before the Revolution. In Paris, it is true, there had been the earlier experience of the militant Catholic democracy of the Parisian *menu peuple* of the Religious Wars and the Fronde, which had been a force that both sides had to reckon with; but this was a long time before, and the memory of it had been largely stamped out under the long despotic rule of Louis XIV and his Ministers.

Popular disturbances

In neither city were the wage-earners or craftsmen of the eighteenth century considered a part of the political community. In Westminster, there were, admittedly, a small number of watermen, labourers and journeymen who, as householders, were entitled to the vote. But these were, of course, quite exceptional and, in Paris, there was no equivalent at all. In consequence, at moments of crisis and social and political tension, the *menu peuple* or 'lower orders' sought redress for their grievances through street demonstrations, in strikes or in riots.

30. D. G. Barnes, *A History of the English Corn Laws from 1660 to 1846* (1965), pp. 31–7, 76–7; Walter M. Stern, 'The Bread Crisis in Britain, 1795–96', *Economics*, XXXVI (1964), 168–87.

31. See E. P. Thompson, *The Making of the English Working Class* (1963), pp. 51–68.

In both countries, there were in the course of the century numerous years of bad harvests, followed by food shortage and high prices, which were generally attended by riots. Food riots were more common in France than in England. In England, there were provincial riots in 1727 (sporadically), in the 1730s, in 1740, 1756 and 1757, 1766 (by far the worst year of all), 1772 and 1773, and 1783. In France, Daniel Mornet has recorded them in forty separate years between 1724 and 1789 and, according to his figures, they occurred in twenty-two of the twenty-five years following 1763, the only exceptions being 1769, 1779 and 1780.[32] Compared with these provincial outbreaks, riots in the capital cities were relatively few. Even in Paris, before the crisis of 1789, serious bread-rioting occurred only in 1725, 1740, 1752 and 1775, with minor outbreaks in 1771 and 1778. In London, if we except a few slogans and handbills in 1768, there was no food-rioting at all.

The explanation for this relative immunity of the capitals from bread-rioting is perhaps not hard to find. On the one hand, both cities had exceptionally favourable access to sources of supply and had machinery to hand for regulating prices and ensuring distribution. London drew its supplies of wheat directly from Kent, Middlesex, Essex and Lincoln (Defoe noted in the 1720s that 'this whole Kingdom' was employed 'to supply the city of London with provisions'); and the Assize of Bread fixed the weight, size and price of the loaf according to the price of corn and flour in the nearest markets.[33] Paris had access by road or river to the granaries of Picardy, Brie, Soissonnais, Champagne, Beauce and the Norman Vexin; it had a normal reserved zone for buying grain over a radius of thirty miles and further reserved zones, over a far more extensive area, in cases of emergency; it had a Bureau des Subsistances, attached to the Ministry of Finance, for

32. Mornet, *op. cit.*, pp. 444–8.
33. D. Defoe, *A Tour Through the Whole Island of Great Britain*, 2 vols. (1966), I, 12; S. and B. Webb, 'The Assize of Bread', *Economic Journal*, XIV (1904), 196–218.

making purchases; and the Lieutenant of Police had powers to protect convoys, to keep a watchful eye on bakers and millers, and, at times of crisis, to forbid a rise in prices. (Admittedly, in Turgot's day, such measures failed to operate in the crisis of May 1775.)[34] Secondly, both cities (and especially Paris) had to hand comparatively large, and comparatively effective, police forces for coping with disturbance. London had, by the 1770s, a combined force of some 1,000 peace officers and 3,000 watchmen and patrolmen, supported, in emergency, by several thousand troops. Paris had in all some 7,000 police and soldiers, including a reserve force of 5,000–6,000 Gardes Françaises and Suisses.[35] Though small by later standards, these forces were far larger and more effective than any operating in the provinces. Yet there were occasions when they proved inadequate, or at least unsuited, to withstand the shock of a large-scale outbreak, such as in London in June 1780 and in Paris in the summer of 1789.

But the complete absence of food-rioting in London before the 1790s calls for further explanation. We have already noted that Londoners rarely had occasion to fear a famine: this, in itself, must be a factor of some importance. Another was that London was separated from the surrounding countryside at its most vulnerable point by the protective shield of the near-urban county of Middlesex. This might have two effects: it might absorb the shock of any bread-riots spreading into the capital from the villages to the north or west; and it might prevent any large-scale irruption of hungry villagers seeking food in London's more privileged markets. Paris, on the other hand, was exposed, in times of shortage, to the inrush of hungry consumers from the nearby villages of Issy, Vaugirard, Neuilly, Auteuil and St. Denis, who, when food was scarce in the *banlieue*, forced their way through

34. E. Faure, *La disgrâce de Turgot* (Paris, 1961), pp. 195–225.
35. Besant, *op. cit.*, pp. 494–533; R. C. Cobb, 'The Police, the Repressive Authorities and the Beginning of the Revolutionary Crisis in Paris', *The Welsh History Review*, III, iv (1967), 427–40.

the gates of the capital and invaded its markets. Such was the case in May 1775, when rioting was literally swept into the city by bands of invading peasants.[36]

Writing of France in the eighteenth century, Mornet noted that strikes were noticeably less frequent and less significant than food riots.[37] The observation is true enough of the country as a whole, and it applies equally (up to the 1780s at least) to England. But it is not true of Paris, and, of course, it is even less true of London. I have noted a dozen strikes (though there may well have been more) in Paris between 1720 and 1789 and in London perhaps a score. In both cities, strikes tended to occur at time of falling or stable rather than of rising prices; and they were generally untouched by political issues. In Paris, the most militant workers, before 1770, appear to have been the hatters and, after 1770, print-workers and builders. In London, they were tailors and Spitalfields silk-weavers; these engaged in repeated industrial disputes. The tailors had their own committees from 1719, and both sailors and weavers had committees to conduct their strikes in 1768 and 1769. The Paris workers had their *compagnonages*, or associations of journeymen; but these were as much concerned with welfare as they were with their members' wages and lacked the sustained militancy of the Londoners' committees. And, in general, it is probably true that London industrial disputes, apart from being more frequent and more prolonged, were more militant and violent, and probably more varied and more sophisticated in their means of agitation.[38]

Even more typical of the outbreaks in both cities were riots with political undertones, that is disturbances in which

36. G. Rudé, 'La taxation populaire de mai 1775 à Paris et dans la région parisienne', *Ann. hist. Rév. franç.*, no. 2, 1956, pp. 139–79.

37. Mornet, *op. cit.*, p. 448.

38. For Paris, see Mornet, *op. cit.*, p. 449; M. Rouff, 'Une grève de gagne-deniers en 1786 à Paris', *Revue historique*, CV (1910), 332–47; and F. Funck-Brentano, 'La question ouvrière sous l'Ancien Régime', *Revue retrospective*, XVII (1892), 1–24. For London, see Rudé, *Wilkes and Liberty*, pp. 90–104.

the participants, even if not professing any political allegiance of their own, were touched by the political ideas of others. In Paris, for example, there were the disturbances of July 1720, which arose from John Law's financial speculations. In 1743, and again in 1752, there were riots over the balloting for the militia. Also in 1720, and again in 1750, there were great popular protests against the abduction (or believed abduction) of children by the police. In 1752 there were riots against the Archbishop of Paris for refusing the sacrament to dying Jansenists. From 1753 onwards, there were frequent commotions and disturbances in support of the Parlement of Paris in its duel with the Ministers: minor incidents occurred in 1753, 1757, 1758, 1768, 1771, 1772 and 1786, and major riots broke out, during the *révolte nobiliaire*, in 1787 and 1788. Most of these outbreaks (the last two were the exception) did not greatly alarm the authorities or contemporary opinion. 'Une émeute,' wrote Mercier hopefully in 1783, 'qui dégénérerait en sédition est devenue moralement impossible.'[39] Meanwhile, Londoners rioted against Nonconformists (the Sacheverell Riots) in 1709 and again in 1715 and 1716; against Walpole's Excise in 1733 and against the Gin Bill and the Irish in 1736; and, in 1753, there were 'commotions' (though hardly riots) against the proposal to grant easier naturalisation to alien Jews. Up to now, such disturbances had had 'Tory' rather than 'Whig' undertones. But from the mid-1750s, when the great William Pitt was becoming the hero of the streets, popular rioting became impregnated with the new Radical (or Whig-Radical) ideas emanating from the City of London. There followed the riots of 1763 and of 1768–74 associated with the astonishing career of the Radical John Wilkes; and, in 1780, the anti-Papist riots that bear the name of Lord George Gordon, a Member of Parliament and the son of a Scottish duke. After this, London's popu-

---

39. L. S. Mercier, *Tableau de Paris*, 12 vols. (Amsterdam, 1783), pp. 22–25.

lar Radicalism was silenced for a dozen years and revived only under the impact of the French Revolution and the writings of Paine and the English democrats in the 1790s.

First, let us note the similarities between these political, or near-political, disturbances in Paris and London. In neither case is there any sign of an independent political movement of the 'lower orders' or *menu peuple*, let alone of such a movement among the wage-earners or working class. (The first signs of this will appear, in Paris, among the *sans-culottes* in 1793 and, in London, among the petty craftsmen of Hardy's London Corresponding Society of 1792.) And, in both cities, we note that the political impetus given to these movements came from outside the ranks of the classes most actively engaged. In Paris, it was the Parlement that provided the slogans and political ideas: at first in the riots of 1720 and, more continuously, after 1753. In London, a similar role was played by the City's Common Council and the liveried freemen of the Common Hall; it was they who inspired, even if they did not deliberately provoke, all such movements, whether Tory or Radical-inclined, from 1709 to 1780. In these respects, there are close, even striking, resemblances between the popular movements of the two cities.

The differences, however, are equally remarkable. The most important is that the London popular outbreaks of this kind were more mature and sophisticated than those taking place in Paris before 1789. Above all, there was no sign in Paris at this time of the political awareness expressed by the 'lower orders' in the Wilkite Riots of the 1760s and 1770s. Nor was there any equivalent in Paris of the scope and violence of the Gordon Riots; and we can sympathise with Mercier when he wrote, soon after the event, that such 'terrors and alarms' would be inconceivable in a city as well policed as Paris![40]

Nor is this difference so surprising. The Londoners had had a longer, and more sustained, revolutionary-radical

40. Mercier, *loc. cit.*

tradition. Besides, their political mentors—the 'middling' shopkeepers and craftsmen of the City—were closer to the journeymen and labourers and more appropriate educators of the *menu peuple* than the quasi-aristocrats of the Parlement of Paris; but, in Paris, before 1789 there were no others at hand. And, furthermore, in London, even the *menu peuple* itself had had some direct political experience not only as voters in the parishes of Westminster but also as vociferous supporters of the popular candidates on the hustings of Middlesex and the City of London.

The French Revolution would, of course, serve to redress the balance, though it may be argued that the London wage-earners (if not the 'middling' classes) retained a degree of independence that, even with their revolution, the Parisians did not attain until the 1830s. But this is to look far beyond the scope of the present paper.

Part Two   Paris

The Outbreak of the French Revolution

Although there is a tendency to reopen the debate on the
causes of the French Revolution, most reputable historians
of the event have by now accepted the thesis that the
Revolution was the product of a conflict of social classes
rather than the outcome of a conspiracy hatched by
philosophes, lawyers, disgruntled officials or Freemasons.[1]
Since the publication of Jaurès' *Histoire Socialiste* at the
turn of the century, a serious effort has been made, as well,
by a number of historians to treat the problems, aspirations
and movements of the peasant and urban masses in their
own right instead of as an echo or reflection of the speeches
and actions of the revolutionary leaders in Paris.

Such studies have, of course, done more than merely
throw a fresh light on the general causes and course of the
Revolution; they have made it possible to measure with
greater accuracy the point of revolutionary outbreak and
the part played by the masses of town and countryside in
relation to it. The revolutionary explosion, therefore, no
longer appears as a more or less fortuitous climax to a
series of purely political, though interrelated, crises—the
rejection of Calonne's proposals by the Notables, the convocation of the States General, the dismissal of Necker,
etc.—but as the sharp collision of a complex of social
forces at a moment of acute revolutionary crisis.

Even when this is accepted, however, the picture may still
become lop-sided if one or other of the social forces,

From *Past and Present*, no. 8, 1955, pp. 28–42.

1. The main exponents of this 'conspiracy' thesis are Taine,
Cochin and Gaxotte. More recently, a more modern version of it has
been put forward by J. L. Talmon in his *Origins of Totalitarian
Democracy* (1952).

whose coming together—either in alliance or in opposition —provoked the revolutionary crisis, is not seen in its proper perspective. The most familiar distortion of this kind is that which presents the revolutionary action of the peasant and urban masses as 'waiting upon' that of the *bourgeoisie*, or even of the privileged orders themselves. Mathiez, in particular, has made us familiar with the picture of the origins of the great Revolution as a gradual 'unfolding' of minor revolutions—first the '*révolte nobiliaire*'; then the '*révolution bourgeoise*'; and, finally, the popular revolution. While such a presentation is convenient and has more than a grain of truth in it, it tends to reduce the intervention of the masses to one of secondary importance and fails to show that the popular movement, while intensified and accelerated by the revolutionary crisis, had its origins in the Old Régime and, in fact, preceded by many years the revolutionary activity of the *bourgeoisie*.

On the other hand, writers like Daniel Guérin have gone to the opposite extreme by exaggerating the independence and the degree of coherence and political maturity of the popular movement, and particularly emphasising those aspects of it which appear to look forward to the working class movements of the nineteenth and twentieth centuries.[2] In the view of such historians, of course, it is not the wage-earners or *sans-culottes*,[3] but the *bourgeoisie* itself which ceases to be a revolutionary force.

Yet another tendency has been to present the revolutionary crisis almost exclusively in terms of more or less short-term economic factors, particularly of rising or falling prices. No one will deny the great contribution

2. D. Guérin, *La Lutte de Classes sous la I^e République*, 2 vols. (1946).

3. The term *sans-culottes* is here used, as elsewhere in this article, to denote the mass of small producers and the non-propertied classes of town and countryside. Strictly speaking, it did not come into use until after June 1792; but then it tends also to acquire a wider, political significance.

made to our knowledge of the origins of the Revolution by Ernest Labrousse: before his work appeared,[4] little was known of the movements of prices and wages in eighteenth-century France, particularly in the crucial years preceding the revolutionary outbreak. Labrousse's insistence, however, on the primacy of 'natural' (i.e. uncontrollable economic) over 'anthropomorphic' causes has the effect of reducing the popular movement to the automatic product of purely economic factors.[5]

The present study introduces new material to illustrate the range and diversity of the movement in town and countryside—particularly in the Paris region—in the years leading up to the Revolution; it also attempts to place the revolt of the privileged orders and the Parlements (the '*révolte nobiliaire*') and the revolutionary action of the *bourgeoisie* in the crisis of 1788–9 in their correct historical setting; but, above all, it is concerned to trace the main stages and currents of the popular movement during the last years of the Old Régime up to the point where its 'merger' with that of the *bourgeoisie* touched off the revolutionary explosion.

Let us begin with the year 1775. There had, of course, been numerous other movements provoked by hunger and the high cost of bread in earlier periods of the century—as, for example, in 1725, 1739–40, 1752 and 1768;[6] but that of 1775 is not only the nearest to the point of revolutionary outbreak but the most extensive, the best documented and that which bears the closest resemblance to the popular movements of the Revolution itself. Turgot had been appointed Comptroller-General in August 1774. He started

---

4. C.-E. Labrousse, *Esquisse du Mouvement des Prix et des Revenus en France au XVIII Siècle*, 2 vols. (1933); *La Crise de l'Economie Française a la Fin de l'Ancien Régime et au Début de la Révolution*, vol. 1 (1944).

5. *La Crise de l'Economie Française*, p. 180 et seq.

6. *Journal et Mémoires du Marquis d'Argenson*, 9 vols. (1859), I, 54; II, 153, 159, 184, 213; III, 61–2, 131–73; VII, 81–7, 218–333, 353–9. See also S. Lacroix, *Actes de la Commune de Paris*, 2nd series., 8 vols. (1900–14), VI, 398.

with no particular record of unpopularity as far as the common people were concerned: at any rate, his predecessor and most vocal opponent, the Abbé Terray, was, soon after his appointment, burned in effigy in the Faubourg St. Antoine.[7] Yet, to the delight of his enemies at Court, he was soon to lose any semblance of popular favour by his over-haste in applying Physiocratic doctrine to the grain-trade: an *arrêt* of 13 September restored freedom of trade in grain and flour. This, combined with a bad harvest, led to a shortage and a rapid rise in the price of corn, flour and bread in the following spring and summer. The price of the 4-lb. loaf in Paris (normally 8–9 *sous*, though, in recent years, more often 10–11 *sous*) rose to $11\frac{1}{2}$ *sous* in early March and to $13\frac{1}{2}$ *sous* at the end of April. Grain riots had already broken out in Bordeaux, Dijon, Tours, Metz, Rheims and Montauban—and, in their wake, sprang up that particular series of riots, centred in Paris and its adjoining provinces, known to history as '*la guerre des farines*'. The movement spread from market to market and took the form of a popular price control of wheat, flour and bread—the price of bread being generally fixed at 2 *sous* per pound, that of flour at 20 *sous* a bushel and wheat at 12 *francs* a *setier* (2 quintals). Starting on 27 April at Beaumont-sur-Oise, twenty miles north of Paris, it reached Pontoise on the 29th, St. Germain on 1 May, Versailles on the 2nd and Paris itself on the 3rd. It then spread eastwards and southwards up the valleys of the Seine and Marne, lingered for several days in the markets and villages of Brie, reached Beaumont-sur-Gâtinais (fifty miles south of Paris) on the 9th, and petered out somewhere near Melun on the 10th.

It is instructive to note the main features of this remarkable movement. It was essentially a spontaneous movement —in spite of some historians' claim to the contrary— provoked by hunger and the fear of shortage. It saw the massive invasion of markets and farms by urban poor,

7. Métra, *Correspondance secrète, politique et littéraire . . . depuis la Mort de Louis XV*, 18 vols. (London, 1787–90), I, 87.

farm-labourers, village artisans, and even occasional farmers and well-to-do *bourgeois*. It was directed, in the main, against farmers or prosperous peasants (*laboureurs*), grain-merchants, millers and bakers; and aroused some sympathy among other classes—certain parish priests, for example, either encouraged, or did little to restrain, their parishioners from taking part in the movement, and more than one market official helped it along by himself fixing a 'just' price for grain or flour.

Why, then, did a movement of such magnitude and bearing striking similarities with certain movements of the Revolution yield no tangible result? In the first place, the food crisis itself, though protracted, was overcome by the end of the summer: prices began to fall in October. Secondly, Turgot managed to crush the movement by a combination of propaganda—via the Bishops—and the use of troops, who remained entirely loyal to the Government. More important still, the bulk of the peasantry was not involved: the question of tithes, feudal dues or game laws did not arise. Lastly, and perhaps most important of all, the *bourgeoisie* had not yet begun to challenge the existing order and, in any case, were bound to be hostile to a movement directed against members of their own class and against a Minister, whose accession to office they had hailed with enthusiasm and whose reforms—including that of free trade in grain—they actively supported: in several towns, in fact, the *milice bourgeoise* was mustered in order to crush the riots.[8] The main lesson of 1775 was, in short, that, in the conditions of eighteenth-century France, no isolated movement of wage-earners, artisans and village poor could hope to yield revolutionary results. This truth was to be realised on more than one occasion both before and during the Revolution.

The twelve years that followed (1775–87) were, despite

8. For the movement of 1775, see my study, 'La taxation populaire de mai 1775 à Paris et dans la région parisienne', shortly to appear in *Annales Historiques de la Revolution Française.*

a general sharpening of the longer-term economic crisis,[9] years of comparatively stable food prices and social peace. In Paris, at least, the price of bread remained remarkably steady: from the manuscript Journal of the Parisian bookseller Sébastien Hardy we learn that, whereas, in the period 1767-75, the price of the 4-lb. loaf rarely fell below 11 *sous* (and, for a few days in November 1768, actually reached 16 *sous*), in the later period, the normal price was 8 or 9 *sous*, and it only rose to 10½ or 11 *sous* for very brief spells in 1784.[10]

Popular movements during these years were scattered and sporadic, arising on a number of separate issues. In June 1778, bread riots took place in Toulouse and Grenoble and, in 1785, at Rennes; in all three, rioters were fired on by troops.[11] In 1784 and 1786, there were protest movements in Paris against the *barrières*, or ring of customs posts, recently erected by the Farmers-General to tax livestock, meat, wine, firewood and other commodities entering the capital;[12] and, also in 1786, Hardy noted protests against the cost of meat and firewood.[13] In Paris, too, there appears to have been a resurgence of anti-clerical feeling among the people: Hardy recorded a number of incidents between 1783 and 1789[14] that are reminiscent of the hostility to Jesuits in the 1720's and to the Archbishop of Paris over the *billets de confession* in 1752.[15]

9. See Labrousse, *Esquisse* ... II, 597–608. Already in 1778, there were said to be 120,000 poor and needy in Paris out of a population of about 600,000. (M. C. Bloch, *L'Assistance et l'Etat en France à la Veille de la Révolution* (1908), p. 6).

10. S. Hardy, *Mes Loisirs, ou Journal d'événements tels qu'ils parviennent à ma connoissance* (Bib. Nat. fonds français, nos. 6680–7), vols. 1–7 *passim*.

11. Hardy, *op. cit.*, IV, 9; Métra, *op. cit.*, V., 295.

12. Hardy, VI, 18, 35, 435.

13. *Ibid*, VI, 332, 479.

14. *Ibid.*, V, 322–3, 394–5, 410; VI, 330, VIII, 184.

15. E. J. F. Barbier, *Journal historique et anecdotique du Règne de Louis XV*, 4 vols. (1847), I, 263–4; *Journal et Mémoires du Marquis d'Argenson*, VII, 226–7.

More remarkable perhaps is the number of strikes, involving the journeymen in a number of trades and, in the case of the Lyons silk-workers, assuming almost insurrectionary proportions. Jules Flammermont may be right in attributing these, in part at least, to the special penal measures in restraint of combination introduced in August 1776 and to the anger of the workers at the reversal of the decision to abolish the guilds;[16] but it is worth observing that, in 18th century France, a crop of strikes usually coincides, as here, with a period of comparatively stable prices. In 1776, a general strike broke out among Parisian bookbinders who were demanding a fourteen-hour day.[17] In July 1785, there was a large-scale and successful strike of Paris building-workers against a wage-cut imposed by the employers; in March 1786, the carpenters were on strike again and, this time, Hardy reported *'une espèce de fermentation'* among the journeymen of several trades.[18] In January of the same year, the carriers and porters of the capital struck against the institution of a rival monopoly by Court favourites, and seven to eight hundred of them marched to Versailles to see the King.[19] In Lyons, the strikes of the silk-weavers led to widespread rioting and bloodshed.[20] Yet, with the exception of the movement in Lyons, which had its sequel in the domination by the *maîtres-ouvriers* of the meetings called to draw up the *cahiers de doléances* for the silk industry in 1789, it is doubtful if these labour disputes gave any appreciable impetus to the widespread and varied popular movement that was to arise in the period of revolutionary crisis.

The year 1787 saw the opening of the *'révolte nobiliaire'*

16. J. Flammermont, 'Mémoire sur les grèves et les coalitions ouvrières à la fin de l'Ancien Régime', *Bull. du Com. des Trav. hist. et scient.* (Section des sciences écon. et soc.) (1894), pp. 194–205.

17. Hardy, III, 281.

18. *Ibid.*, VI, 149–50, 315.

19. *Ibid.*, VI, 266–71.

20. Jaurès, *Histoire Socialiste de la Révolution Française*, 8 vols. (Paris, 1922–4), I, 97–116; Hardy, VI, 413–4, 424–5.

which served as a curtain-raiser to the revolutionary crisis of 1788–9. In February, an empty exchequer and mounting deficit forced the Government to convene the Assembly of Notables. Calonne, as Comptroller-General, proposed a number of stop-gap measures to meet the crisis, including a stamp-duty and a tax on landed estates. The privileged orders refused to co-operate. Calonne was dismissed on 8 April and succeeded by Loménie de Brienne, Archbishop of Toulouse. Brienne's proposals being no more acceptable than Calonne's, the Notables in turn were dismissed on 25 May, and the '*révolte nobiliaire*' began. The opening shot was fired, as so often in the past, by the Paris Parlement which, while accepting Brienne's plan to relax controls on the sale and export of grain and protesting against the stamp-duty, refused absolutely to register the decree on the land-tax and demanded that the States General be convened to deal with the matter. When the decrees were, none the less, promulgated in a *lit de justice* in August, the provincial Parlements rallied to the support of Paris, and Brienne was forced to capitulate; the decrees on the land-tax and stamp-duty were withdrawn on 21 September and the Paris Parlement was reinstated a few days later.[21]

The return of the Paris Parlement from exile was the occasion of wild scenes of jubilation in the Place Dauphine, the rue du Harlay and other approaches to the Law Courts. Calonne was burned in effigy, bonfires were lit on the Pont Neuf, fireworks and squibs were let off at the Guards. From Hardy's description and from the arrests made on 28 September (the climax of the disturbances) it is clear that the shock-troops in these riots were formed by the clerks of the Palais—'*une jeunesse effrénée*' Hardy calls them— and the apprentices and journeymen of the luxury trades in the Place Dauphine; the 'populace' of the surrounding

21. For a brief, but adequate, account of the '*révolte nobiliaire*', see G. Lefebvre, *La Révolution Française* (Peuples et Civilisations No. XIII, 1951), pp. 107–12; also A. Goodwin, *The French Revolution* (Hutchinson's Univ. Lib., 1953), pp. 27–42.

quarters joined them but played only a subordinate part.[22] The *bourgeoisie* was as yet uninvolved.

In the months that followed it was the economic crisis, above all, that brought the 'fourth estate' once more into the picture, either on their own account or (as in Paris) as the temporary ally of the dissident privileged orders. Brienne's return to the 'free trade' measures of Turgot had led to a sharp rise in the price of grain; by July 1788, in the North at least, speculators were at work again and widespread complaints were voiced against forestalling and hoarding.[23] At Troyes, the *milice bourgeoise* was already mustered in April to overawe the textile workers;[24] and, in Paris, as we shall see, the high price of bread was to contribute to a popular outbreak in the late summer. Peasant revolt, however, lay dormant until the following spring, when long-simmering discontent with food prices and seignorial exaction was to be touched off into violent outbreak by the political ferment emanating from the local electoral assemblies.

Meanwhile, the political crisis had sharpened. Brienne had fallen back on the expedient of raising a loan, which the Paris Parlement was willing to accept, provided the States General should be summoned. But negotiations broke down again in November; the Duke of Orleans and two *conseillers* were exiled; and, in May 1788, the Parlement issued a declaration, condemning the whole system of arbitrary government, including the *lettres de cachet*. The Government riposted by ringing the Palais with troops, forced the *Parlementaires* to surrender their ringleaders to royal justice and promulgated six edicts, prepared by Lamoignon, the *garde des sceaux*, which restricted the jurisdiction of the Parlements and vested the royal courts and officials with greater powers. A new phase of violence followed: there were mass riots in Grenoble and Rennes in

22. Hardy, VII, 178–255; Arch. Nat. Y 13014.
23. G. Lefebvre, *Les Paysans du Nord pendant la Révolution Française* (1924), pp. 339–41.
24. G. Lefebvre, *La Grande Peur de 1789* (1932), pp. 55–6.

June;[25] in the Dauphiné, nobility and Third Estate joined forces against the Crown in July. In early August, troops were concentrated around the capital for fear of an 'insurrection', not so much of the Palais clerks and apprentices as of the *menu peuple* of the markets and the Faubourgs St. Antoine and St. Marcel.[26]

These fears proved well-founded. The Government was compelled to bow before the storm and promised that the States-General would be called in May 1789; on 24 August, Brienne was replaced by Necker and the Parlement was recalled soon after. The news was greeted with another outburst of celebrations in the Place Dauphine and the approaches to the Palais: bonfires were lit and the occupants of coaches crossing the Pont Neuf were compelled to bow low to the statue of Henri IV and to shout 'A bas Lamoignon!' A new factor, however, was to extend these disturbances far beyond the scope and limits of those of the previous year. On 17 August, the price of the 4-lb. loaf, after long remaining at 9 *sous*, rose to $9\frac{1}{2}$ *sous*, on the 20th to 10 *sous*, on 2 September to $10\frac{1}{2}$ *sous* and on 7 September to 11 *sous*. Under this stimulus, the inhabitants of the Faubourgs joined in the riots on the third day (29 August) and changed their whole character: they spread to the markets and University quarter, continued—with short lulls—until the end of September and took a heavy toll in casualties and arrests; the latter were mainly composed of craftsmen and wage-earners of widely-scattered districts.[27] The Parisian *sans-culottes* had entered the arena as a decisive force, but not yet as the ally of the *bourgeoisie*; the real revolutionary crisis was yet to come.

This developed in the winter of 1788–9 and was to bring

25. For Rennes, see B. de Moleville, *Histoire de la Révolution de France*, 14 vols. (1801–3) II, 100–20.

26. Hardy, VIII, 35.

27. For a detailed account of the above, see Hardy, *op. cit.*, VIII, 58–109; for the arrests, see Bib. Nat. MSS Collection Joly de Fleury, doss. 1113; and Arch. Nat. Y 9491, 9989, 11206, 11517, 18756, 18795.

about a radical realignment of classes. The harvest was generally bad, and, in the Paris region, crops had been flattened by a freak hailstorm in July.[28] There followed a winter of phenomenal severity which threw thousands out of work and brought further thousands of villagers flocking to the capital;[29] in December, Hardy wrote of 80,000 unemployed.[30] The price of the 4-lb. loaf in the Paris markets rose to 12 *sous* on 8 November, to 13 *sous* on the 28th, to 14 *sous* on 11 December and, finally, to 14½ *sous* on 1 February; it was to remain at this level until after the fall of the Bastille.[31] In April, in the grain-starved markets of the Paris region, the price of wheat rose to the fantastic sum of 40–44 *francs* the *setier*.[32] Meanwhile, the crisis in industry—itself the offshoot of the agrarian crisis,[33] though doubtless aggravated by the results of the Commercial Treaty with England in 1786[34]—had thrown thousands out of work in every textile centre: according to the reports of the industrial inspectors for September 1788 to January 1789, there were 46,000 unemployed in Amiens, 10,000 in Rouen, 8,000 in Falaise, 30,000 in Carcassonne, 25,000 in Lyons; while at Troyes and Sedan half the looms were idle.[35]

It was against this economic background that the *bourgeoisie* made its entry on the revolutionary stage. The cause of conflict had its roots deep in the Old Régime:

28. Arch. Nat. H 1453.

29. See A. Tuetey, *L'Assistance Publique à Paris pendant la Révolution*, 4 vols. (1895–7), I, cxlii.

30. Hardy, VIII, 168.

31. *Ibid.*, VIII, 154–5, 408, 426.

32. Arch. Nat. H 1453.

33. Labrousse, *La Crise de L'Economie Française*, pp. xxxviii-xl.

34. The older view—that the Vergennes Treaty was a primary cause of the depression—is argued by Charles Schmidt in 'La crise industrielle de 1788 en France', *Revue Historique*, LCVII (1908), 78–94; this is contested by L. Cahen, 'Une nouvelle interprétation du traité franco-anglais de 1786–7', *Rev. Hist.*, CLXXXV (1939), 257–85; and by Labrousse (*loc. cit.*).

35. Schmidt, *loc. cit.*

while colonial trade, land values and luxury spending had enormously increased in the course of the century, capital investment and expansion of manufacture were everywhere impeded by the restrictions imposed by privileged corporations, feudal landowners and Government on the elementary capitalist freedoms—the freedom to hire labour, the freedom to produce and the freedom to buy and sell. Yet, while the ensuing conflict owed its eventual sharpness and finality to these deeper social antagonisms, the clash between the *bourgeoisie* and the privileged orders arose, in the first instance, over representation and voting in the States General. Already in September, the Paris Parlement had shattered its reputation as the spokesman for 'popular liberties' by demanding that the States General be constituted as in 1614—i.e. that each order should have equal representation and vote separately. An even more forthright insistence on the maintenance of privilege was voiced in the Manifesto of the Princes of the Blood in December. Necker, however, persuaded the Council to allow the Third Estate double representation; but the question of voting 'par tête' (as demanded by the *bourgeoisie*) or 'par ordre' (as insisted by the nobility and clergy) remained open and led to bloody clashes between nobles and commoners at Rennes. By January, the new alignment of forces was becoming clear and Mallet du Pan noted that it was no longer a question of a constitutional conflict between the King and the *privilégiés* but a 'war between the Third Estate and the two other orders'.[36] In February, the conflict was raised to a higher pitch by the publication of the Abbé Sieyès' pamphlet *Qu'est-ce que le Tiers Etat?*, in which the *bourgeoisie*, for the first time, laid claim to control the destinies of the nation irrespective of the wishes or privileges of the other orders.

It is not surprising that, with these developments, the winter of 1788–9 should see the beginnings of a popular movement of an altogether vaster scope and intensity than

36. Quoted by Lefebvre, *La Révolution Française*, p. 113.

those of the preceding years. This movement had other, even more significant, features: it became a continuous movement that did not cease until after the point of revolutionary outbreak; it grew from a movement concerned, in the first place, with purely economic ends into one with more or less clearly defined political aims; it developed a common bond of interest between the wage-earners, craftsmen, wine-growers[37] and small tradesmen of town and countryside against monopolists, hoarders and grain-speculators; this movement, in turn, began to 'merge' with that of the small peasant proprietors against feudal game laws, tithes and dues; and, finally (though not always in point of time), the movement of townsmen and villagers 'merged' with the political action of the *bourgeoisie* against feudal privilege and the whole apparatus of government of the Old Régime.

The revolt against shortage and rising prices started in the last days of December 1788 and is recorded in the reports of the Intendants (or their *sub-délégués*) of several provinces. It variously took the form of pillaging of grain-boats and granaries; of enforcing price-control of bread, flour and wheat; of rioting in bakers' shops and markets, and at town halls; of assaulting customs officials, dealers and farmers; and the widespread destruction of property. In December and January, such reports come in from Brittany and Touraine; in March and April, from Burgundy, the Ile de France, Langeudoc, Nivernais, Orléanais, Picardy, Poitou, Provence and Touraine; in May and June, from the Limousin and Lyonnais; in July, from Champagne and Normandy.[38] Hardy records bread riots at Rheims in March and at Nancy and Toulouse in April.[39]

In the Faubourgs and markets of Paris, the high cost of

37. For the importance of the wine-growers as a factor in the revolutionary crisis, see Labrousse, *op. cit.*, pp. 207–630.
38. Arch. Nat. H 1453.
39. Hardy, VIII, 262, 278.

meat and bread provoked a mounting wave of anger[40] which broke out into destructive violence in the Réveillon Riots in the Faubourg St. Antoine at the end of April.[41] Ten 'smugglers' were arrested at the *barrières* in early May; this movement reached its climax on 12–14 July, when forty of the fifty-odd customs posts ringing the capital were burned down.[42]

In the country north of Paris, the fight against famine developed into a movement against the game laws and the hunting rights of the nobility. On the estates of the Prince de Conti at Cergy, Pontoise, l'Ile Adam and Beaumont, peasants and land-workers, having reaped no harvest owing to the ravages of hail, set out to trap and destroy the rabbits that infested their fields. The movement spread in the spring to Conflans Ste. Honorine and adjoining villages, and led to clashes with the *maréchaussée*.[43] At Oisy, in the Artois, the peasants of a dozen villages banded together to exterminate the Count of Oisy's game and refused in future to pay him the traditional *soyeté*, or *terrage*.[44] More violent clashes occurred near Corbeil and at Chatou; south and west of the capital, whole parishes, suspected of large-scale poaching on royal and aristocratic preserves, were disarmed in June.[45] In Lorraine and the

40. For this *'fermentation'* in Paris and the posting of troops at bakers' shops and in markets to contain it, see Hardy, VIII, 158–184, 310, 344 *et seq.*

41. Although the immediate cause of the riots were remarks attributed to two manufacturers concerning wages, it is evident that the real issue was that of the shortage and high cost of bread. (See my article, 'The Motives of popular Insurrection in Paris during the French Revolution', *The Bull. of the Inst. of Hist. Research*, XXVI (1953), 53–74.)

42. Arch. Nat. Y 18795, pp. 446–7; Z^{ia} 886.

43. Arch. Nat. H 1453.

44. Lefebvre, *Les Paysans du Nord*, p. 356.

45. Arch. Nat. O^1 1036. Villages in the neighbourhood of the Royal forests of Fountainebleau, St. Germain, etc. had been protesting against damage done to their crops by rabbits, deer, etc., almost continuously for the past fifteen years. There is, however, no sign of armed revolt in these districts until April 1789 (*ibid.*).

Hainaut, landless peasants and small *laboureurs* joined forces in opposition to enclosure edicts and land clearance schemes.[46] Meanwhile, peasant revolt against royal taxes and seignorial exactions had broken out in Provence in March, at Gap in April, and in the Cambrésis and Picardy in May.[47] This movement led, in turn, into that far vaster movement of July and August which, spreading over regions as widely scattered as Alsace, Normandy, the Hainaut, Mãconnais and Franche-Comté, left in its trail the widespread destruction of *châteaux* and manorial rolls.[48] Yet peasant hostility to enclosure and encroachment on rights of pasture led also to attacks on capitalist farmers; and, in more than one case again, the *milice bourgeoise* joined forces with the *maréchaussée* to repress peasant disorder.[49]

Yet, in spite of such contradictions, as the crisis deepened, *bourgeois* and *sans-culottes* were drawn into closer partnership in opposition to the privileged orders and the feudal régime. The urban and peasant masses were never to be fully won for the *bourgeois* conception of 'freedom'—this was to remain a cause of division throughout the Revolution—but it was in their common interest to remove the fetters on production and the high cost of food occasioned by internal customs duties and fiscal charges; to clip the wings of (if not to dispossess entirely) the tithe-owner and the extractor of feudal *rente* and *champart*; to reduce taxes and the ruinous costs of government; to compel the privileged orders to make a fair contribution to the national exchequer; to curb the monopolists and Farmers-General; to destroy such relics of ancient tyrannies as the

---

46. M. Bloch, 'La lutte pour l'individualisme agraire dans la France du xviiie siècle', *Annales d'Histoire économique et sociale*, II (1930), 532–43. I am indebted to Mr. Alun Davies for this reference, as for several other valuable suggestions concerning the peasant movement of the period.

47. Lefebvre, *La Révolution Française*, p. 130.

48. Lefebvre, *La Grande Peur*, pp. 146 *et seq.*

49. Lefebvre, *La Révolution Française*, p. 138.

Bastille, the *lettre de cachet* and the vexatious inquisitions of the Parlements. It is precisely such demands that we find voiced most frequently in the *cahiers de doléances* which began to be drawn up in the early months of 1789—usually drafted, it is true, by the professional *bourgeoisie*, but often endorsed by meetings of peasants, small tradesmen and workshop masters, and even, though more rarely (as at Rheims, Marseilles, Troyes and Lyons) by guilds of journeymen or *maîtres-ouvriers*.[50]

And the States General roused such ardent hopes—'la grande espérance', Georges Lefebvre has called it[51]—because it was widely believed that, cleared of the obstruction and domination of the privileged orders, it could realise a radical programme of this kind. From these hopes stem the enthusiastic adoption of the slogan, '*Vive le Tiers Etat!*' (which is certainly thought to include the 'Fourth Estate' as well),[52] and the passionate belief, once the Court Party began to threaten to dash these hopes to the ground, in the existence of an 'aristocratic plot'. It was in direct response to this stimulus that the Parisian journeymen, labourers, workshop masters and shopkeepers—already roused to action by the ruinous cost of bread, meat and wine—rallied to the call of the revolutionary leadership installed at the Palais Royal and—less certainly—to that set up by the Electors of the Paris Third Estate at the Hôtel de Ville; it was also this conviction that the Court Party was preparing to disperse the States General and to

50. For the latter, in particular, see G. Laurent, *Cahiers de Doléances pour les Etats Généraux de 1789*, 6 vols. (Rheims, 1906–30), IV, 94–5; G. Fournier, *Cahiers de Doléances de la Sénéchaussée de Marseille* (Marseille, 1908), pp. 70, 228–34; J.-J. Vernier, *Cahiers de Doléances du Bailliage de Troyes et de Bar-sur-Seine pour les Etats Généraux de 1789*, 3 vols. (1909), I, 179–80; C.-L. Chassin, *Le Génie de la Révolution*, 2 vols. (1863), I, 428–33.

51. *Op. cit.*, pp. 130–1.

52. The earliest popular use that I have found in police records of the term '*tiers état*' in this militant sense is on 21 April 1789 (Arch. Nat. Y 18762). The slogan '*Vive le Tiers Etat!*' was heard in the Réveillon Riots a week later (Arch. Nat. KK 641, fo. 17).

subdue Paris with the aid of foreign troops, far more than the gold of the Duke of Orleans, that won over the main body of the Paris garrison, the Gardes Françaises—so recently engaged in shooting down the Réveillon rioters—to the side of the Revolution. When Necker, the popular Finance Minister, was dismissed by the King on 12 July, the people of the Faubourgs and the markets joined with the *bourgeois* revolutionaries and the disaffected troops in carrying through the Paris insurrection—the first great armed uprising of the Revolution. The gunsmiths, arsenals and religious houses were raided for arms, the hated *barrières* were destroyed, a *milice bourgeoise* (including journeymen, but excluding 'vagrants' and unemployed workers) was organised, a revolutionary government was installed at the Hôtel de Ville, and, finally, the Bastille was taken by storm. The popular movement had fully 'merged' with that of the revolutionary *bourgeoisie*; the example was quickly followed in other parts of France.

Labrousse tells us that the Bastille fell on the very day when the price of grain throughout France reached its cyclical peak.[53] This is no doubt significant, but it would be a mistake to attempt to explain the revolutionary crisis wholly in such terms. To do so would be to discount entirely the revolutionary action of the *bourgeoisie* and the permeation of the Parisian *menu peuple* with the political ideas and slogans of the Third Estate. It is evident that the basic motive prompting popular action was the high cost of food and the fear of famine. This continued to be so and is the most constant element in the repeated upsurge of the popular movement during the years of the Revolution—in August–November 1789, in the years 1792–3 and, above all, in 1795.[54] Yet there was a similar fear of

53. Quoted by Lefebvre, 'Le mouvement des prix et les origines de la Révolution française', *Ann. Hist. Rév. Franç.*, XIV (1937), 324.

54. For an elaboration of this point, see my aforementioned article in *The Bulletin of the I.H.R.*; also 'Prices, Wages and popular Movements in Paris during the French Revolution', *Econ. Hist. Rev.*, vol. VI, no. 3 (April 1954), pp. 246–67.

famine in 1768; and, in 1775, as we have seen, the fears thus aroused led to a massive movement of popular protest; yet in neither case did a revolutionary outbreak result. This was because the economic and political crisis as a whole—and not one single aspect of it, however important—had not fully matured and because the conflict of social classes which it occasioned was as yet only one-sided and partial; above all, it was because one of these classes, the *bourgeoisie*, although dissatisfied with the inequalities, the corruption, the extravagance and the restrictions of the Old Régime, had not yet begun seriously to challenge the absolute monarchy or the privileged orders, or the social system on which they depended. It was only when the *bourgeoisie* entered the revolutionary struggle, as it did in the winter of 1788–9, that the popular masses were able to acquire a political direction and a set of political aims and concepts—such concepts as Third Estate, Nation, '*complot aristocratique*' and the Rights of Man—without which they would have expended their energies on actions limited to economic ends. This is not to underrate the importance of their contribution; without their intervention, the *bourgeois* revolutionaries of July 1789—many of whom were stricken by panic at the crucial moment of insurrection—would have been doomed and the recently constituted National Assembly dispersed by royal troops. Yet, for all their vacillations and fears—fears of the Court Party and of the masses themselves—in the social conditions of the day, the insurrection could not have been successfully carried out without the direction and political guidance of the deputies, journalists, pamphleteers and Electors of the Third Estate.

It was, in fact, to be one of the great lessons of the French Revolution that the popular movement, however militant and widespread, could only succeed and survive as an effective revolutionary force as long as it was allied to an important section of the *bourgeoisie*; conversely, that the *bourgeoisie* could only carry out its historical task of destroying feudal property relations as long as they, or a substantial part of them, maintained their links with the broad masses of town and countryside. Nothing is to be gained by omitting one side or other of this picture, as some historians have done. In July 1789, as we have seen, at the moment of revolutionary crisis, the immediate interests of the masses coincided with those of the main body of the *bourgeoisie* and even of a minority of the privileged class itself. In the following autumn, as so often in the course of the Revolution, the preoccupation of the Parisian *menu peuple* with the problems of high prices and shortage threatened to disrupt the alliance by directing their main fury against the monopolists and the newly constituted city authorities; and it was only by the harnessing of this movement to the political tasks set by the Constitutional Monarchists that the Royal Family was brought to Paris and the National Assembly was once more saved. Similar situations arose— though with changing forms of alliance, as the *bourgeois*-democratic revolution advanced—in the years 1791–4; but, in the summer of 1794, when the Revolutionary Government was compelled by its own contradictions to sacrifice the interests of the *sans-culottes*, the alliance was broken and Robespierre fell an easy victim to the intrigues of his enemies. In the spring and early summer of 1795, attempts were made to reconstitute it at the time of the massive popular insurrections of *Germinal* and *Prairial*; but, at the crucial moment, the radical wing of the *bourgeoisie* deserted, either from weakness or from fear of the masses, and the popular movement was finally crushed. It was only to rise again—and under very different conditions— in 1830.

The Fall of the Bastille
14 July 1789

The storming of the Bastille, though commemorated on France's National Day, is still the object of bitter controversy. The legendary valour of the 'men of 14 July' has become part of the Republican tradition and most Frenchmen might be inclined to accept Michelet's verdict that the Bastille was taken as 'an act of faith' and that its capture symbolised the overthrow of age-old tyrannies. Yet some Frenchmen—and there have been prominent historians among them—have denounced the 'legend' of the Bastille as a propagandist stunt and have claimed that its captors were prompted by the basest motives. It has been argued that the Bastille, far from being a symbol of despotism, was a credit to the humanity of its administrators; that it was gradually being abandoned as a State prison (at the time of its capture no more than seven prisoners were released from its cells); and that the common people of Paris could, in any case, have had little interest in its fall, as it had long ceased to be a place of detention for men of humble station.

While there is more than a grain of truth in this argument, much of it is really beside the point in so far as it invites us to see the storming of the Bastille as a single, isolated event, divorced from the circumstances in which it took place and from the passions which the onset of the Revolution had already aroused. To present a faithful picture, it would therefore seem necessary to place this episode in its proper setting; and, in so doing, not merely to relate it to the political events of July 1789, but to attempt to see it from the viewpoint of the many thousands of Parisians who played a part in the drama of which it was the climax.

From *History Today*, IV, no. 7 (July 1954), 448–58.

In one sense at least it is indisputable that the Bastille had become an anachronism. Built by Charles V in the fourteenth century as a fortress to defend the eastern approaches of the capital, it still stood, four hundred years later, as a grim reminder of a turbulent past. The awe inspired by its eight towers and eighty-foot walls was enhanced by the jealousy with which the Government guarded its secrets and the pledge of silence imposed on its prisoners as a condition of their release. Meanwhile, the face of the city was being rapidly transformed. While the Temple and Châtelet prisons vied with the Bastille as survivals from a feudal past, and the medieval splendours of Notre Dame and the Sainte Chapelle still dominated the approaches to the Cité, the work of reconstruction, begun under Louis XV and actively supported by the nobility and wealthy *bourgeoisie*, went on apace. The houses on the old bridges were being pulled down; work on the Pont Louis XVI—the present Pont de la Concorde—had been begun, and the Pont Neuf, though only completed in 1600, was, by the time of the Revolution, second only to the Pont Notre Dame in point of age. Medieval cemeteries were being cleared from the centre and pavements were beginning to appear, in imitation of London. In 1788 Sébastien Mercier was able to write that, in the last thirty years, 10,000 houses had been constructed and that one-third of Paris had been rebuilt. In the fashionable Marais, the aristocratic quarter of the Right Bank, the new town houses of the Rohans and the Soubises eclipsed the former splendours of the Hôtels de Bourgogne and de Sens. Further west, at the entrance to the elegant Faubourg St. Honoré, the Duke of Orleans, wealthiest and most popular of the Princes of the Blood and a near claimant to the throne, built the magnificent arcades and gardens of the Palais Royal, shortly to become a centre of lavish entertainment and a meeting place of journalists, pamphleteers and political gossips. On the Boulevards, the Théâtre Italien was erected in the gardens of the Duc de Choiseul; on the Left Bank, the Théâtre Français (the later Odéon) was built in 1789 on the site of the Hôtel de Condé, recently purchased for 3 million *livres*. Regiments of building workers had been enrolled from outlying provinces and the speed of construction was often phenomenal: the Opéra was built in seventy-five days and the Château de Bagatelle in six weeks!

It was not only the walls of the Bastille that stood out in sharp contrast against this feverish progress of modernisation; so did the old tenements, workshops and lodging houses in which the bulk of the Parisian population still lived and worked. It would be wrong, however, to define them—as some historians have done—in terms of a distinctive working class: while already accounting for nearly half the population of Paris, the wage-earners and their families did not as yet form a clearly defined social group, identifiable by their dress, method of living or social outlook. There was as yet no factory system or industrial 'belt', though enterprising textile manufacturers had set up establishments that, on occasion, employed up to 400 or 500, or even 800, workpeople under one roof. Apart from the multifarious petty trades plied in the markets, on the riverside, in the Place de Grève or on the Pont Neuf, the prevailing mode of production was still that of the traditional workshop in which the journeyman, though his prospects of promotion were becoming ever more remote, still shared the work and gossip, and often the board and lodging, of his master. This mixed, yet closely related, population of craftsmen, petty traders, shopkeepers, journeymen and labourers—the later *sans-culottes* of the Revolution—must, in 1789, have already accounted for five out of every six inhabitants of a city of over 600,000 souls. They lived closely packed in the older quarters of the capital—in the central market area adjoining the Louvre (the most densely populated of all), on the island of the Cité and in the *faubourgs* of the north, south and east. Among these, though not the poorest, the traditional centre of popular agitation and disturbance, even before the Revolution, was the Faubourg St. Antoine, where a closely knit community of craftsmen, petty workshop masters and their journeymen lived within easy range of the walls and guns of the Bastille.

Although writers like Sébastien Mercier considered that the common people of Paris were incapable of committing the excesses witnessed in London during the Gordon Riots, there had been precedents for the great social disorders of the year 1789. Paris had, it is true, an international reputation for being well 'policed'; yet diarists and the reports of the Châtelet have recorded the periodic outbursts of popular anger, usually aroused by a shortage or the high price of bread, which alarmed the respectable *bourgeois* and fashionable society of the times: the outbreaks at the time of the Law scandal in 1720; the food riots during Fleury's Ministry in 1740; the violent outcry against the kidnapping of children in 1750; the burning of the Abbé Terray in effigy in the Faubourg St. Antoine after the death of Louis XV; and, above all, the bread riots of May 1775, when every baker's shop and stall in the *faubourgs* and city centre was sacked by angry crowds. More recently, in the autumn of 1787 and 1788, when the Paris Parlement was still able to pose as the popular champion of ancient liberties, the journeymen and labourers of the city centre and southern *faubourgs* had joined with the clerks of the Palais de Justice in violent demonstrations on the Pont Neuf and in the Place Dauphine to demand the withdrawal of unpopular Ministers.

In the winter of 1788–9, as so often in the past, famine and high prices gave the initial stimulus to the popular movement. Throughout the eighteenth century the shortage and high cost of bread—which, even in normal times, accounted for half the household budget—had been endemic. Prices had far outstripped the level of wages. It has been calculated that, between the two periods 1726–41 and 1771–89, wages all over France had risen by only 22 per cent, while prices had risen by 65 per cent. This tendency became more marked in the last three years of the Old Régime. In Paris, the normal price of a 4-lb. loaf was 8 or 9 *sous* (8*d.* or 9*d.*). Between August and September

1788, it rose from 9 to 11 *sous*; and Hardy, the bookseller-diarist, who lived within a stone's throw of the great popular market of the Place Maubert, wrote: 'In the markets and among the people all the talk is of future revolutions.' Worse was to come: on 28 November the price of bread rose to 13 *sous*, and a bitterly cold winter, that was to throw thousands out of work, began. Early in December the price rosè to 14 *sous* and Hardy reported that there were 80,000 unemployed. As the cold weather ended in the last days of January, the price of bread reached its peak at 14½ *sous*; it was to remain at this level until the week after the storming of the Bastille. We can get some idea of what this meant in terms of hardship and suffering to the ordinary Parisian when it is realised that, at prevailing rates of wages, a builder's labourer, in order to maintain his normal diet, would, between February and July 1789, have had to spend four-fifths of his earnings on bread.

Yet hunger was not the only stimulus to popular unrest. A new hope had been born—French historians have called it 'la grande espérance'—with the Government's promise to summon the States General to meet in Versailles in May. At last something would be done to relieve the sufferings of the poor! The words 'Third Estate' and 'nation' were beginning to gain currency among the people; and, in the riots which shook the Faubourg St. Antoine at the end of April, demonstrators who raided foodshops and burned down the properties of the manufacturers Henriot and Réveillon shouted, 'Vive le Tiers Etat!' But, as the conflict sharpened between the Third Estate and the Privileged Orders, it appeared that the hopes centred on Versailles would be dashed to the ground by aristocratic intrigue. From mid-summer, foreign troops were being concentrated on the outskirts of Paris: already on 3 June, Hardy had noted the arrival of German and Hungarian regiments, brought in on the pretext of preventing a renewed outburst of rioting in the Faubourg St. Antoine. The intentions of the Court Party, grouped around Marie-

Antoinette and the King's younger brother, the Comte d'Artois, were becoming clear: on the night of 22 June the King was persuaded to dismiss Necker, his popular Finance Minister, and to overawe the National Assembly by a display of military force. The plot miscarried: thousands invaded the courtyard of the Palace to demand that Necker be retained in office; soldiers under the command of the Prince de Conti would not obey the command to fire; and the deputies, rallied by Mirabeau in an historic speech, refused to disperse. The King was compelled to yield.

Up to now, the insurrectionary temper developing in Paris, fed on economic hardship and rumours of 'aristocratic plots', had been without effective leadership. With the latest news from Versailles, however, the professional and commercial classes, who had hitherto been prepared to wait passively on events and had viewed the simmerings in the *faubourgs* and markets without sympathy, began to give a direction to affairs without which the July revolution could not have taken place. From this date, the pamphleteers and journalists in the entourage of the Duke of Orleans (who had himself gone over to the Third Estate at Versailles) began to establish a permanent headquarters at the Palais Royal; here thousands congregated nightly and acquired the slogans and directives—and, possibly, too, the funds—of what Hardy called 'the extreme revolutionary party'. Also at this time, the 407 Electors of the Paris Third Estate, whose original task it had been to appoint the Parisian deputies to the Third Estate at Versailles, began to meet regularly at the Hôtel de Ville in the heart of the capital. These two bodies were to play distinctive, yet complementary, parts in the events of July. In the early days, however, it was the Palais Royal alone that gave a positive direction to the popular movement. Whereas the Hôtel de Ville contented itself with drafting paper schemes for the institution of a *milice bourgeoise*, or citizens' militia, the Palais Royal took effective measures, by public agitation and liberal expenditure, to win over the

Gardes Françaises, the main body of troops stationed in Paris, from their loyalty to the Court. On 30 June, crowds directed from the Palais Royal forcibly released from the Abbaye prison eleven Guardsmen who had been jailed for refusing to fire on the people at Versailles on the night of 22–23 June; while on 10 July, eighty artillerymen, who had broken out of their barracks in the Hôtel des Invalides, were publicly fêted in the Palais Royal and the Champs Elysées.

Reacting to these developments, the Court Party attempted a new show-down: on 11 July Necker was sent into exile and replaced by the Baron de Breteuil. This proved to be the spark that touched off the insurrection in Paris. The news reached the capital at noon on the 12th. During the afternoon, Parisians flocked in their thousands to the Palais Royal, where orators—the young journalist Camille Desmoulins among them—gave the call to arms. Groups of marchers quickly formed; the busts of Necker and the Duke of Orleans were paraded on the Boulevards; theatres were compelled to close as a sign of public mourning; in the Place Louis XV demonstrators clashed with cavalry commanded by the Prince de Lambesc, who had been ordered to clear the Tuileries gardens. Besenval, commander of the Paris garrison, withdrew to the Champ de Mars; the capital was in the hands of the people. Barricades were manned and the tocsin was sounded. Bands of insurgents joined those who had already two days earlier—on their own initiative or on that of the Palais Royal—begun to burn down the hated *barrières*, or internal customs posts, that ringed the city. While the Palais Royal probably had a direct hand in this operation—it was reported that two posts belonging to the Duke of Orleans were deliberately spared by the incendiaries—the common people of Paris had their own account to settle with an institution which levied a toll on all wines, meat, vegetables and firewood that entered the capital. During the night, too, armed civilians, Gardes Françaises and local poor broke into the monastery of St. Lazare on the northern fringe of the city, searched it for arms, released prisoners and removed fifty-two cartloads of corn and flour to the central grain market.

But the main feature of the night of 12–13 July was the search for arms; religious houses were visited and gunsmiths, armourers and harness-makers were raided all over the capital. A number of statements drawn up in support of their claims for compensation have come down to us. Thus, Marcel Arlot, master gunsmith of the Rue Grenéta in the parish of St. Leu, reported that his shop was broken into at 2 a.m. by a crowd headed by a journeyman armourer of the Rue Jean Robert; muskets, pistols, sabres and swords to the value of 24,000 *livres* (£2,000) were removed. A harness-maker of the Pont St. Michel reported the theft of belts and shoulder-straps to the value of 390 *livres*; while a sword-cutler of the parish of St. Séverin, on the Left Bank, complained that his shop had been invaded several times on 12 and 13 July and that a very considerable quantity of sabres, swords and unmounted blades had been forcibly removed by numerous persons who had refused to pay for them 'on the pretext that they would serve for the defence of the capital'; he had suffered a loss of 6,684 *livres* (nearly £600). The total losses eventually submitted to the National Assembly by the Parisian gunsmiths amounted to more than 115,000 *livres* (over £9,000).

Of considerable interest, too, is the eye-witness account of the events of that night given by Jean Nicolas Pepin, a tallow chandler's labourer, who, as a subpoenaed witness in the St. Lazare affair, later told the story of how he was caught up in the milling throngs of civilians and French Guards that, all night long, surged through the streets, shouting slogans, ringing the tocsin and searching for arms. From his account it is doubly clear that, at this time, the guiding centre of the revolutionary movement lay in the Palais Royal to which, rather than to the Hôtel de Ville, the angry, bewildered masses looked for leadership and guidance.

On the morning of the 13th, however, the Electors made a firm bid to gain control of the situation. They formed a Permanent Committee to act as a provisional government of the city and determined to put a stop to the indiscriminate arming of the whole population. They had been alarmed by the burning of the *barrières* and the sacking of the monastery of St. Lazare. To them the bands of unemployed and homeless, who had played some part in these operations, were as great a menace as the Privileged Orders conspiring at Versailles. Accordingly, a regular citizens' militia was hastily mobilised for the dual purpose of defending the capital from the military threat without and the danger of 'anarchy' within. Each of the 60 Electoral Districts was to contribute 200 (later 800) men. While each District drew up its own conditions of enrolment, in most cases property and residential qualifications were imposed that virtually debarred a large part of the wage-earning population; certainly all unemployed and vagrants were excluded. All 'irregulars' were to be immediately disarmed. According to Dr. Rigby, an English observer, this process had already begun during the afternoon of the 13th; yet it is doubtful if it went far as long as the insurrection lasted. Crowds besieged the Hôtel de Ville, demanding arms and powder. Jacques de Flesselles, *prévôt des marchands* and acting head of the provisional city government, being anxious to limit the distribution of arms, made vague promises and sent parties off on fruitless expeditions to the Arsenal and the Carthusian monastery; this 'treachery' was to cost him his life on the morrow. During the night, the insistence of half-armed crowds surging round the Hôtel de Ville compelled an Elector, the Abbé Lefebvre, to distribute eighty barrels of gun-powder that had been placed in his safe-keeping.

On the next morning, 14 July, the quest for arms and ammunition continued: a spectacular raid was made on the Hôtel des Invalides across the river. According to Salmour, the Saxon ambassador, who witnessed the affair, 7,000–8,000 citizens took part. The Governor, the Marquis de

Sombreuil, was abandoned by his troops and forced to open his gates. He later reported the removal of more than 30,000 muskets, of which 12,000 at least were 'in dangerous hands'. Meanwhile, the cry had gone up, 'To the Bastille!'

Royalist historians have scoffed at the picture of thousands of Parisians hurling themselves at the Bastille in order to release seven prisoners. Such criticism falls wide of its mark. The immediate aim was to find the powder which was known to have been sent there from the Arsenal. Other motives no doubt played a part. It was believed that the fortress was heavily manned; its guns, which that morning were trained on the Rue St. Antoine, could play havoc among the crowded tenements. In the night it had been rumoured that 30,000 Royalist troops had marched into the Faubourg St. Antoine and had begun to slaughter its citizens. Besides, though it had ceased to harbour more than a trickle of State prisoners, the Bastille was widely hated as a symbol of 'ministerial despotism': the *cahiers de doléances* of the Paris Districts bear witness to this fact. Yet there was no intention of taking it by storm (such a notion seemed preposterous, anyway), least of all on the part of the Permanent Committee of Electors who directed operations, with fumbling uncertainty, from the Hôtel de Ville. They made their intentions clear from the start: to negotiate with de Launay, the Governor, for the surrender of the gunpowder in his keeping and for the withdrawal of the guns from his battlements. That this plan failed, and that the Bastille fell only after the threat of a frontal assault, was due to circumstances outside their control.

Numerous eyewitness accounts of the siege of the Bastille, or accounts purporting to be such, have come down to us. Fact and fiction are often richly blended in them. Among the most trustworthy, perhaps, are those left by the Electors themselves, both in the form of the official minutes of their Assembly and in that of individual memoirs. From these it appears that the first deputation sent to parley with de Launay arrived at the Bastille at 10 o'clock. Having received a friendly welcome and an invitation to dine, they did not emerge for some time. The dense crowds waiting outside, fearing a trap, now raised a shout for the surrender or capture of the fortress. To allay suspicions, a second delegation, sent by the neighbouring District of La Culture, urged the Governor to surrender. Its leader, Thuriot de la Rozière, brought back word to the Permanent Committee that the Governor, while refusing to surrender, had withdrawn his cannon and had promised not to fire unless attacked. Up to this point, the crowds surging in from the Rue St. Antoine had penetrated only into the outer of the two courtyards leading to the main drawbridge and gate of the Bastille. This outer courtyard was, as usual, unguarded; it was separated from the inner Cour du Gouvernement by a wall and a drawbridge which de Launay had, unaccountably, left raised but undefended. Half an hour after Thuriot's departure, two men climbed the wall from a neighbouring building and lowered the drawbridge. Believing a frontal attack to be imminent, de Launay gave the order to fire. In the affray that followed, the besiegers lost ninety-eight dead and seventy-three wounded; only one of the defenders was struck. Two further deputations, sent to the Bastille in the course of this affray, were fired on and failed to gain admittance.

The worthy Electors were now at their wits' end. Their policy of peaceful negotiations had proved a complete failure. Had it not been for the angry insistence of the bands of armed citizens who swarmed in the rooms of the Hôtel de Ville, in the Place de Grève outside and along all the approaches to the Bastille, calling for vengeance for blood spilt and suspected treachery, they would certainly have abandoned their efforts. Meanwhile, two detachments of Gardes Françaises, drawn up outside the Hôtel de Ville, responded to the summons of Hulin, a former non-commissioned officer, who marched them off to the Bastille with five cannon removed from the Invalides that morning. Joined at the fortress by a few hundred armed civilians, they fought their way under fire to the inner courtyard and trained their cannon on the main gate. This proved to be decisive. The Governor offered to surrender provided that the garrison were spared; but the angry crowds would not hear of conditions and the siege continued. At this point, de Launay seems to have lost his head and threatened to blow up the fortress. He was, however, dissuaded by his garrison and, in desperation, gave orders for the main drawbridge to be lowered. So the Bastille fell.

It is perhaps surprising that the angry and triumphant crowds, pouring through the open gates of the Bastille, did not exact a more complete and indiscriminate vengeance. They had lived through days of nervous tension, continuously subject to the fear of sudden attack and disaster; they had been betrayed, they believed, by some of their leaders; over 150 of their fellows had been killed and wounded. Of 110 members of the defending garrison, six were slaughtered; de Launay, though promised a safe-conduct to the Hôtel de Ville, was struck down on the way and his head severed with a butcher's knife. De Flesselles, who had aroused popular fury by his reluctance to distribute arms, met a similar fate as he followed his accusers from the Hôtel de Ville.

Meanwhile, the seven prisoners of the Bastille had been released from their cells. Among them, there were four persons charged with forging bills of exchange, locked up without trial since January 1787; and two lunatics, of whom one had been confined for the past forty years as a would-be regicide and the other had lost his reason before his transfer to the Bastille from Vincennes prison five years earlier. The seventh, the Comte de Solages, was a young rake who, in accordance with the custom of the times, had been committed by *lettre de cachet* at his father's request 'pour cause de dissipation et de mauvaise conduite'. In fact, while the arbitrary manner of their confinement—without formal charge or trial—was no great credit to the prevailing system of justice, as victims of tyranny the prisoners made a decidedly poor showing. And so, after the initial toasts and celebrations which the occasion demanded, little serious effort was made to dress them up in a heroic guise. The two lunatics, at least, enjoyed neither fame nor freedom for long: after a short interval, they were despatched to the Charenton asylum.

Among the many 'legends' of the Bastille, there have been few as persistent as that which represents its captors as vagabonds, criminals, or a mercenary rabble hired in the wine-shops of the St. Antoine quarter. Yet not only is there is no evidence to support this view, but the available evidence directly refutes it. From lists of the accredited captors of the Bastille, the so-called *vainqueurs de la Bastille*, drawn up by the National Assembly, we know the occupations and addresses of the great majority of those— some 700–800 in number—who played a direct part in its surrender. Most of them, far from being vagrants or down-and-outs, were settled residents of the Faubourg St. Antoine and the adjoining parishes of St. Gervais and St. Paul; most, again, were members of the citizens' militia, from which such elements were rigorously excluded. Among them appear the names of some who were to distinguish themselves in the course of the Revolution— Jean Rossignol, goldsmith of the Faubourg St. Antoine and, later, general of the Republic; Antoine Joseph Santerre, wealthy brewer and commander-in-chief of the citizens' battalions that overthrew the monarchy in August 1792; Stanislas Maillard, who played a big part in the surrender of the Bastille and, a few months later, led the market women on their historic march to Versailles. But most of them were men of no particular distinction, drawn from the typical crafts and occupations of the Faubourg and adjacent Districts: joiners and cabinet-makers, locksmiths and cobblers—these alone accounting for more than a quarter of the civilian captors —shopkeepers, gauzemakers, sculptors, riverside workers and labourers. Among them small masters and independent craftsmen, rather than journeymen or wage-earners, predominate, thus faithfully reflecting the social structure of the Faubourg.

Yet, in a wider sense, we may agree with Michelet that

the capture of the Bastille was not the affair of a few hundred citizens of the St. Antoine quarter alone, but of the people of Paris as a whole. It has been said that, on that day, between 180,000 and 300,000 Parisians were under arms; and, taking an even broader view, we should not ignore the part played by the great mass of Parisian petty craftsmen, tradesmen and wage-earners—in the Faubourg St. Antoine and elsewhere—whose revolutionary temper had been moulded over many months by the rise in living costs and, as the crisis deepened, by the growing conviction that the great hopes raised by the calling of the States General were being thwarted by an 'aristocratic plot'.

Of little importance in itself, the capture of the Bastille had far-reaching consequences, and the news of it echoed round the world. The National Assembly was saved and received Royal recognition. The Court Party began to disintegrate and the Comte d'Artois went into voluntary exile. In the capital, power passed firmly into the hands of the Committee of Electors, who set up a City Council with Bailly as mayor. On 17 July, the King himself made the journey to Paris, was received at the Hôtel de Ville by the victors and, in token of acquiescence in the turn of events, donned the red, white and blue cockade of the Revolution. As it turned out, the Revolution was far from completed, but a decisive step had been taken. To many —and not in France alone—it seemed the dawn of Liberty. In distant St. Petersburg, we are told, at the news of the fall of the Bastille, strangers embraced in the street and wept for joy.

The Social Composition of the Parisian Insurgents of 1789–91

One of the aspects of the French Revolution that has been neglected by historians is the social composition of the revolutionary crowd. Georges Lefebvre, it is true, published an important study on the psychology of revolutionary crowds,[1] but few attempts have been made to determine with any degree of precision the nature of the crowds that carried through the Paris revolution of July 1789, that brought back the King from Versailles in October, and overthrew the monarchy in August 1792. Ignoring more precise definitions, historians have been content, when describing these rioters and insurgents, to use such vague generalisations as 'the people' or 'the mob' (or variations on these themes), according to their prejudices and according as to whether they followed the tradition established by Michelet or by Taine.[2]

Although it is not possible to give a detailed description of all those taking part in these revolutionary crowds, there are documents in the Archives Nationales and elsewhere that make it possible to present a fairly exact analysis of the various social elements engaged in the Parisian insurrections of the period. The most valuable sources for research of this kind are the reports of the police commissioners of the Paris Châtelet[3] and of the Parisian

Translated from *Annales historiques de la Révolution française*, no. 127 (July–August 1952), pp. 256–88.

1. G. Lefebvre, 'Foules révolutionnaires', in *Ann. hist. Rév. franç,,* XI (1934), 1–26.

2. H. Taine, *Les origines de la France contemporaine: La Révolution* (Paris, 1876), I, 18, 41, 53, 54, 81, 130, 135.

3. A[rchives] N[ationales], series Y: Archives du Châtelet de Paris; sub-series Z: Juridictions spéciales et ordinaires.

Sections of 1790–5,[4] whose classification by Alexandre Tuetey over half a century ago opened up a rich store-house of records for the social historian.[5] It is evident that these reports refer only to a minority of those engaged in riots and demonstrations—the arrested, the imprisoned, the killed and the wounded; yet the samples provided are often large enough to enable us to draw some general and reasonably valid conclusions.

It was Marcel Rouff who first demonstrated the value of this method of research in a short study that he made of the reports of the police commissioners on begging and vagrancy in the streets of Paris in January–February 1789.[6] By making an analysis of the addresses and occupations of prisoners, and of the periods during which they had been unemployed, M. Rouff was able to show that the great majority were not professional beggars or vagrants, but victims of recent unemployment in a certain number of Paris trades who had been thrown out of work by the economic crisis that broke out on the eve of the Revolution. Here I shall attempt to use a similar method to present a picture of the social composition of the Parisian rioters and insurgents of 1789–91.

The Réveillon affair of 28 and 29 April 1789, although it took place a few days before the assembly of the Estates General at Versailles, is now generally recognised as the first great popular outbreak of the Revolution. It was the direct outcome of the 'inconsiderate' remarks made by two manufacturers of the Faubourg St. Antoine who, in their local electoral assemblies, had deplored the high costs of production and had expressed the desire to see wages return to their old level of 15 *sous* a day.[7] During the disturbances

4. A[rchives de la] P[réfecture de] P[olice], series Aa: Sections de Paris. Procès-verbaux des Commissaires de police.

5. A. Tuetey, *Répertoirs général des sources manuscrites de l'histoire de Paris pendant la Révolution française*, 11 vols. (Paris, 1890–1914).

6. M. Rouff, 'Le personnel des premières émeutes de 1789 à Paris', *La Révolution française*, LVII (1909), 213–31.

7. A. N., C 221, no. 160/146, fos. 54, 58.

that followed—mainly in the Faubourg St. Antoine, but with considerable support from neighbouring districts[8]— the houses of the two manufacturers were looted and burned down. According to official reports, twenty-five rioters were killed and twenty-five wounded by the Gardes Françaises, and thirty-five men and women were arrested, of whom three were hanged for sedition and five branded and sent to the galleys.[9]

It is, of course, impossible to determine the full number of those who took part in the riot; but eyewitnesses were agreed that 500–600 *ouvriers* demonstrated in the Faubourg St. Antoine and neighbouring districts during the afternoon of 28 April[10] and that their numbers rose to 3,000 in the course of the evening.[11] It seems that the crowd was far denser still on the evening of the 29th at the approaches to Réveillon's manufactory in the Rue de Montreuil. And, according to eyewitness accounts, most of these people were wage-earners.

Both Hardy, the bookseller, in his diary of events, and de Crosne, the lieutenant-general of police, in the despatches that he sent to Versailles, describe the rioters as '*ouvriers*';[12] the term is also used by the authors of the pamphlet, *Acte patriotique de Trois Electeurs*, who saw the bands of rioters assembled in the Place de Grève on the evening of 28 April.[13] Of course, these indications need hardly be taken as conclusive in view of the lack of precision in the use of the term *ouvriers* in the eighteenth

---

8. A. Hardy, *Mes loisirs, ou Journal d'événements tels qu'ils parviennent à ma connoissance*, 8 vols. (Paris, 1764–89), VIII, 297–9. Bib[liothèque] Nat[ionale], fonds français 6687.

9. A.N., Y 11033, 15019, 15101, 13582, 10491; 10530, fos. 129–30, 132–3; 18795, fos. 444–5, 447–50, 457, 462. C. L. Chassin, *Les cahiers et les élections de Paris en 1789*, 4 vols. (Paris, 1889), III, 72 *et seq.*

10. See de Crosne to Louis XVI, A.N., C 221, 160/146, fo. 53; Hardy, VIII, 297.

11. Hardy, VIII, 298; *Acte patriotique de Trois Electeurs du Tiers Etat*, Bib. Nat., Lb³⁹ 1620.

12. Hardy, VIII, 297, 299; de Crosne, fos. 53, 54, 58.

13. Bib. Nat., Lb³⁹ 1620.

century. Yet they are confirmed by the more precise evidence of the persons interviewed by the police after the disturbances were over; their testimony, in fact, shows that direct appeals were made to wage-earners both at home and at their place of work. Thus, Gilles, a marble-worker, told Commissioner Desmarets that he and his companions left their work at three o'clock in the afternoon on the day that Réveillon's manufactory was destroyed; and J. B. Hallier, a master farrier, declared before Commissioner Guyot that his workers stopped work at two o'clock on the same day; while the 500 workers of the Royal Glass Manufactory in the Rue de Reuilly, ignoring de Crosne's instructions that they should be kept at work, were persuaded or compelled by the bands of rioters to join them. Marchand, a port-worker, declared that no work was done on the docks that afternoon; a fellow port-worker, Téteigne, stated that he had been forced to join the rioters and that he went with them to a place where several dockers and other workers were assembled. In the Temple district the rioters went to fetch out the journeymen from their homes.[14]

There is further evidence to support the view that the predominant element in the Réveillon Riots was formed by wage-earners rather than by independent craftsmen, small employers or other sections of the *menu peuple*: this emerges from a study of the occupations of the persons killed, wounded or arrested by the troops. Of sixteen corpses identified and examined at the Montrouge cemetery, the Hôtel Dieu hospital and the Force prison, and whose occupations are known, thirteen were wage-earners.[15] Among twenty wounded cross-examined by the police at the Hôtel Dieu, the Charity Hospital and the Force, there were fifteen wage-earners.[16] It may perhaps be admitted that the thirty-five men and women that were arrested, many of them in the cellars of Réveillon's house, probably

14. A.N., Y 15101, 13582, 12218, 13454, 11033; de Crosne, fo. 51.
15. A.N., Y 10519, 15101; Chassin, III, 72 *et seq.*
16. A.N., Y 11033, 13582, 15101; Chassin, *loc. cit.*

took a more direct part in the affair than the chance victims of the soldiers' bullets. And of these as many as thirty appear to have been wage-earners: the remainder were a sculptor, a writer, a wine-merchant, a master upholsterer and a Knight of the Holy Roman Empire.[17] In all, fifty-eight rioters, out of seventy-one whose occupations have been established, were wage-earners. This is a far larger proportion than any we shall find in similar documents relating to later riots and disturbances occurring in this period. Yet it is perhaps not so surprising in view of the special circumstances attending the Réveillon affair and the particular appeal to action addressed to the wage-earners of the Faubourg St. Antoine and its adjoining districts; such an appeal has no parallel in the history of the Revolution.

The Paris revolution of July 1789, whose climax was the capture of the Bastille and the transfer of municipal authority to the Assembly of Electors, took the form of an armed popular insurrection which lasted from 10 to 14 July. Its principal stages were marked by the support given to the popular cause by the armed forces, the burning of the *barrières* (customs posts), the sacking of the St. Lazare monastery, the arming of the civil population, and the siege and capture of the Bastille. With the aid of the police reports of the Châtelet and other documents, we may determine with fair precision the social composition of the crowds taking part in a number of these events. For example we find in the *dossier* relating to the burning of forty of the fifty-four customs posts surrounding Paris a most important document: the depositions of eighty-one witnesses who were heard between 29 March and 29 April 1790.[18] This document provides us with a detailed eye-witness account of what took place at thirty-one *barrières* spread over a wide area of the suburbs surrounding the city. It gives us a picture of the rioters, their leaders and

17. A.N., Y 10530, fos. 129–30, 132–3; 18795, fos. 444–5, 447–50, 457, 462; 13454, 13981.
18. A.N., Z^{Ia}886.

their aims such as we could not obtain from any other source.

Thus we learn that the leaders included a few people whose behaviour and manner of dress marked them out as aristocrats or *bourgeois*. The adventurer Musquinet de St. Félix was seen at the Fontainebleau and Hôpital *barrières*, both of which gave entry to the Faubourg St. Marcel. Among the incendiaries of the *barrières* St. Georges and Trois Frères were two persons described as being 'fairly well dressed'. The leader of the rioters at Longchamps 'appeared to be a person of quality'; at Passy, their leader 'wore a white frock-coat, with a round hat, and was fairly well dressed besides'. Among eighty rioters against whom warrants were issued by the Public Prosecutor on 10 May, one is described as wearing 'a blue habit and carrying a stick with a gold top', a second was wearing a fine watch chain and a third was 'riding on a white horse'.[19]

But these were the exception. Those most frequently mentioned in eyewitness accounts were men and women of the people, shopkeepers, craftsmen and wage-earners. It is perhaps not surprising that wine-merchants and smugglers figured conspicuously among those most actively engaged. Bataille, a smuggler and wine-merchant's assistant, was the leader of the rioters at the *barrières* Blanche, Clichy and Monceaux. The leader at the Temple and Marais customs posts was a professional smuggler called Coeur de Bois.[20] Of the eighty rioters against whom warrants were issued, fifteen are described as smugglers; they include three women: the *femme* La Forest and two sisters, Henriette and Edmée Buratin.[21] Smugglers and wine-merchants were closely connected. Four wine-merchants—Bissard, Maréchaux, Billard and Chevet—directed the riots at La Croix and Haute Borne, where they levied the customs duties themselves. The same eighty included nine wine-merchants and five others working for wine-merchants or lodging in their homes. Of eleven

19. A.N., Z^{Ia}886.   20. *Ibid.*   21. *Ibid.*

other suspects named in warrants, two were wine-merchants and there were four other wine-merchants among twelve persons arrested in June 1790. Yet there is nothing surprising in these figures in view of the particular nature of the disturbances.

There is perhaps no more striking illustration of the hostility of small tradespeople to the *barrières* system than the attitude to these events of the National Guard. This body, which had recently been formed to maintain public order and uphold the law, showed itself less than enthusiastic to protect the properties of the Farmers-General and, on occasion, sided openly with the rioters. Admittedly, it played its part in extinguishing the fire at the Versailles customs post on 16 July, the protective force of the Royal German Regiment having been withdrawn two days earlier; but the fire had already been burning for forty-eight hours before the Guard appeared. At Vaugirard, the Guards seem to have been particularly well disposed towards the rioters. The sub-brigadier in charge of the post relates how he and the controller were threatened by a dozen Guards, conducted under armed escort to the headquarters of the local electoral committee, and advised to keep away from the post for a while. Another witness reports that, a few days later, when he was trying to get a butcher to pay the duty on a consignment of meat, the latter called the National Guard 'who let him through without paying'. So, it is hardly surprising that the Public Prosecutor, in issuing his warrants on 10 May of the following year, should have prefaced them by commenting on the Guard's lack of enthusiasm in such terms as these: 'In those early days, the National Guard was far from displaying that zeal for maintaining order and repressing disturbance that it displays today.'

Wage-earners also appear to have played a part in this destruction, though they rarely took the initiative. At the *barrière* St. Martin, lying at the northern end of the great north–south road dividing Paris, officials challenged a group of men and women who were trying to smuggle through some bottles of brandy. 'A moment later,' a witness reports, 'there arrived on the scene a large number of workers from the neighbouring Public Workshops (*ateliers de charité*) to whom the first-comers cried: "Stand by us, Third Estate!" ' The customs officers were overwhelmed and the liquor went through. A similar incident involving unemployed engaged on public works was reported from the St. Louis *barrière* on 18 July. There must have been other attacks on customs guards by unemployed workers in co-operation with smugglers, as on 19 July the newly installed Paris Municipality made a special request for armed assistance to protect the *barrières* against such assaults.[22] At Montmartre barrel-workers were said to have been among the incendiaries; and Vionnet, the sub-brigadier at the post, recognised among them a number who worked for a certain Geoffroy, barrel-maker of the Rue Coquenard. At the Barrière de l'Hôpital, three men refused entry on 13 July threatened to bring to their aid the workers from a neighbouring goods' yard, 'and then they would get through whether the guards opposed them or not'. At Le Roulle it was said that the assailants included building workers who had worked at the building at the time of its erection. At Fontainebleau two labourers were seen sharing out the money picked up in the controller's office. At Le Roulle, again, a navvy and a daily labourer were reported as having threatened the officers in charge. A water-carrier's mate and a journeyman wheelwright were recognised at St. Georges, a textile worker at La Rapée and a porter at Le Roulle.

There seem to have been no more than seventeen wage-earners among the eighty persons scheduled for arrest, though there may have been more among the 'smugglers' or those whose names do not appear. The seventeen include three wine-merchants' assistants, three labourers, two dockers, a porter, two water-carriers, a grocer's assistant, a mattress-worker, a gardener, a coachman, a plaster-beater

22. A.N., C 134, doss. 8, fo. 29; doss. 7, fo. 8.

and a journeyman wheelwright. Among the eleven against whom writs of summons were issued there are three wage-earners—a grocer's assistant, a porter and a navvy. There are three further wage-earners among the twelve arrested: a mattress-worker, a coachman and a sempstress. In addition, four young workers were arrested by the National Guard on 14 July and sent to the Châtelet prison for breaking the windows of the customs post at St. Denis.[23]

These documents make it evident that the men and women who burned down the *barrières* were mainly drawn from the *menu peuple* living in the *faubourgs* on the outskirts of the capital. It is true that among the leaders of the operation were well-dressed *bourgeois* and occasional aristocrats, but the mass of the rioters were local shop-keepers, wine-merchants and their clerks, employers and wage-earners, employed and unemployed, united in a common hatred of the local customs system. Although smugglers played a part in these events, there is little evidence to support the view that criminals, vagrants or organised bands of urchins played any significant rôle.

The sacking of the St. Lazare monastery, which took place in the early hours of 13 July, was also the work of local people, of small tradesmen, craftsmen and workers living about the intersection of the Faubourgs St. Denis and St. Lazare, to the north of Paris. This clearly emerges from the depositions of the thirty-eight witnesses (five of them subpoenaed), who appeared before Laurent de Courville, police lieutenant of St. Lazare and St. Laurent, between 20 and 30 July 1790.[24]

From their evidence we learn that there were two distinct phases in the St. Lazare operation. The first comprised the entry into the building, the transportation of grain and flour to the Corn Market, the destruction of registers and the liberation of prisoners; the second, the ransacking

23. A.N., Y 10649, fo. 18; 15683 (15 July 1790).
24. A.N., Z² 4691.

of rooms and furniture, and the pillage of wine, food, silver and every sort of object of real or imaginary value. The first phase appears to have been subject to a central plan of operations and was carried through by armed citizens supported by soldiers of the Gardes Françaises and directed by *bourgeois* leaders; while the second was quite unorganised and was the work of local people, men and women, small shopkeepers and craftsmen, employed and unemployed workers, impelled by hunger and hatred of the *accapareur*.

Wage-earners and local poor were numerous among these raiders. Two witnesses reported that they had seen several poor who were in receipt of regular relief at St. Lazare. A market-women, who had entered the building soon after 5 a.m., said that she recognised a number of market porters and several workers from the Public Workshops. Of twenty-three men and women against whom writs of arrest were issued and whose occupations appear in the reports, sixteen may be presumed to have been wage-earners—two quarrymen, three housewives, a groom, two labourers, a carter, a water-carrier, a ribbon-weaver, a button-maker, a mason, a joiner, a shoemaker and a wheel-wright (the last four all journeymen). The remainder were tradespeople and included a master shoemaker and his wife, a market-woman, a shopkeeper and the wife of a cork-seller. They all lived locally; six of them were women. It is evident, moreover, that the rioters enjoyed the support or sympathy of the local population: only three of these twenty-three witnesses made any personal accusations; and of thirty-one persons against whom writs were issued only fourteen appeared for cross-examination. Not a single sentence followed.

We can determine with far greater precision the identities of those who took a direct part in the capture of the Bastille. It is true that contemporary accounts are notoriously imprecise and have given rise to the tradition which presents its captors as being the 'people' or the 'workers' of the Faubourg St. Antoine. Thus Bailly noted in his

Memoirs that they 'dared not oppose the people who, eight days before, had taken the Bastille'.[25] On 14 July Hardy wrote in his *Journal* that 'the workers of the St. Antoine quarter had decided on the formal siege of the fortress';[26] and Marat later claimed that the siege had been the work of 'ten thousand poor workmen of the Faubourg St. Antoine'.[27]

If one takes account of the current meaning of the term 'ouvrier' and of the undoubted support that the actual assailants enjoyed not only in the Faubourg but among the Parisian population as a whole, these statements appear accurate enough. But if, on the other hand, one is more concerned with the few hundred persons who were directly involved in the capture of the fortress, one can arrive at a greater degree of precision by referring to a number of documents concerning those officially recognised as 'Vainqueurs de la Bastille'. The first complete and official list of the *Vainqueurs* was published by order of the Constituent Assembly on 17 June 1790. It contained the names of 871 assailants, sixteen widows, nine children and two orphans.[28] A second official list, drawn up a little later, bears 954 names in alphabetical order, giving occupations in some cases, details of the maimed and wounded, and including the same sixteen widows, nine children and two orphans.[29] The third list forms part of the Osselin dossier in the Archives Nationales; it bears only 662 names.[30] These are the names of those who were waiting for the muskets, bayonets, swords, bandoliers and other weapons offered to the *Vainqueurs* by the Assembly and whose distribution was in the hands of Osselin, the administrator

25. *Mémoires de Bailly*, 2 vols. (Paris, 1821), II, 108.
26. Hardy, VIII, 398.
27. *L'Ami du peuple*, no. 149 (30 June 1790), pp. 1–2.
28. *Tableau des citoyens Vainqueurs de la Bastille*; Musée des Archives Nationales, no. 1166.
29. *Tableau des Vainqueurs de la Bastille, ibid*; reproduced in F. Bournon, *La Bastille* (Paris, 1893), appendix V, pp. 219–23. See also J. Durieux, *Les Vainqueurs de la Bastille* (Paris, 1911).
30. *Noms des Vainqueurs de la Bastille*, A.N., T 514 (i).

of the Parisian National Guard. The list bears no date, but the correspondence attached to it dates from the summer and early autumn of 1790, a time when the *Vainqueurs* were beginning to be equipped; and this proves that it had no claim to be a complete list (the reason, however, is not quite clear). Thus, on 13 July 1790, Maillard, the *Vainqueurs'* secretary, whose own name does not appear on the list, signed for 870 articles of equipment; and in a note to Osselin, dated 23 August of that year, he acknowledged the receipt of '870 bandoliers, and as many shoulder belts, but this number is not sufficient to meet our needs, for there have been further names added to the records, as we shall demonstrate anon'.[31]

However, even if this last list is incomplete, it is the only one that can help us determine the social composition of the assailants. The first official list is difficult to follow, badly spelt, with a repetition of names and a lack of Christian names and other details that pose serious problems of identification. The second has the advantage of being in alphabetical order and of including first names or initials, but occupations appear in only about fifty cases, and here, too, there are many repetitions.[32] It is, in fact, only in Maillard's list that we find almost complete details of addresses and occupations set against the names of 600 civilian captors. So, of the three, this list alone gives us a clear idea of the social status and occupation of each of the *Vainqueurs* without having to resort to fanciful speculation.

Jaurès wrote: 'On the list of combatants there is no sign of the stockholders and capitalists on whose behalf the Revolution, in part at least, was fought.'[33] It appears, indeed, that very few men of means and affluence were among the captors of the Bastille. Three manufacturers are listed, four *négociants*, the brewer Santerre, three naval

31. A.N., T 514 (i).
32. Bournon, pp. 219–23; Durieux, p. 13.
33. J. Jaurès, *L'Histoire socialiste. La Révolution française*, 4 vols. (Paris, 1922–4), I, 303.

officers, perhaps a handful of wealthy among the thirty-five *marchands* of every kind, and four described as *bourgeois*. The rest, apart from sixty-three soldiers and fourteen cavalrymen of the Maréchausée de la Garde Nationale (whose civilian professions are not stated) are almost to a man small tradesmen, artisans and wage-earners. Among these, however, the great majority are small businessmen, shopkeepers, master artisans, employers or independent craftsmen, rather than wage-earners.[34]

A detailed analysis of trades and occupations shows that the majority were small workshop masters and their journeymen. There were 49 joiners, 48 cabinet-makers, 41 locksmiths, 28 shoemakers, 20 sculptors and modellers, 11 metal-chasers, 10 turners, 10 hairdressers and wig-makers, 7 potters, 9 monumental masons, 9 nailsmiths, 9 dealers in fancy ware, 8 printers, 7 braziers, 7 tailors, 9 founders, 5 jewellers, 5 goldsmiths, 5 stove-makers and 3 upholsterers. This already accounts for more than half of the 585 civilians appearing on this list. If we add to these the tinsmiths, farriers, watchmakers, dyers, wheel-wrights, stonecutters, sawyers, saddlers, bakers, butchers, pastrycooks and other craftsmen, we shall find that about 380 of the civilians belonged to crafts associated with the small workshop.

It is not always easy to tell which are wage-earners and which are independent craftsmen or small employers. The word *garçon* or *compagnon* does not always prefix the occupation in the case of wage-earners, and a so-called *compagnon* (or journeyman) may be working on his own account, or may even be a small employer. Equally, the absence of the prefix *maître* does not necessarily denote a wage-earner. The following estimate of wage-earners from small crafts must, therefore, be treated with some caution: 8 joiners, 8 to 10 cabinet-makers, 7 to 9 locksmiths, 5 cobblers, one sculptor, one monumental mason, 1 nailsmith, 1 worker

34. Durieux (p. 5) sees most as 'ouvriers'; a view shared by G. Bord in 'La conspiration maçonnique de 1789', in *Le Correspondant*, vol. 10 (25 May 1906), pp. 544, 567, 757.

in fancy ware, 4 print and paper workers, 1 brazier, 1 tailor, 2 founders, 1 goldsmith, 3 stove-makers, 1 upholsterer, 2 tinsmiths, 1 farrier, 3 butcher's boys, 1 furrier, 4 stocking-weavers, 1 cooper: in all, perhaps sixty whom we may with reasonable certainty term wage-earners of about 380 craftsmen and artisans.

Of those employed in manufacture, distributive trades, building, the professions and general trades, there are to be found 11 wine-merchants, 3 café-proprietors, 2 innkeepers, 21 storekeepers of various kinds, 9 hatters, 3 manufacturers, 4 businessmen, 6 gardeners, 3 carpenters and 7 stonemasons. The wage-earners in this category are more numerous than in the small crafts. There are no fewer than 22 gauze-workers, 17 porters, 5 shipyard-workers, 8 riverside workers and bargemen, 2 labourers, 2 navvies, 6 coachmen and carters, 2 cooks, 2 clerks, one ex-postman, 3 gardeners, 1 brewer's boy, 1 shop assistant, 1 silk worker, 1 glass worker from the Royal Glass Manufactory, 1 laundress, 5 journeymen stone-masons, 4 stone-cutters, 4 hatters and 3 ribbon weavers. In all, some eighty-five to ninety wage-earners out of about 200 persons not directly associated with the small workshops.

It is of interest to note that about 400 of the 635 captors of the Bastille whose origins are known were of provincial extraction.[35] Yet the majority were settled inhabitants of the Faubourg St. Antoine. Of the 602 civilians on Maillard's list whose addresses are known, 425 lived in the Faubourg, the greater part of them in the streets immediately adjoining the Bastille; of these 102 were wage-earners. Of those not living in the Faubourg, sixty came from the neighbouring districts of St. Paul and St. Gervais, and over thirty from the central markets. Under fifty came from the Left Bank of the river, with perhaps a dozen from the Faubourg St. Marcel. Very few lived more than a mile and a half from the Bastille: among them was a locksmith

35. See Durieux, pp. 261 *et seq.*

of the Faubourg St. Honoré and a tinsmith of the Gros Caillou district, near the Champ de Mars.

Maillard's list, of course, relates only to the survivors. According to Loustalot (whom Jaurès quotes), there were a hundred dead and, of these, 'over thirty left their wives and children in such a state of distress that they required immediate assistance'.[36] Other evidence, too, suggests that there were several wage-earners and poor among the dead. Hardy reports a burial service for Charles Dousson, a journeyman edge-toolmaker of the Rue de la Huchette, in St. Séverin church on 18 July.[37] According to police records, five corpses of persons killed at the Bastille were brought to the Châtelet for identification. Three of them were the subject of a report by commissioner Duchauffour. One was a journeyman shoemaker of the Faubourg St. Antoine; a second a street lighter whose rough clothing suggests that he may have been a worker ('heavy shoes attached with string; a shirt of rough cloth'); and a third who remained unidentified.[38]

What part was played in the siege by the unemployed? The records do not generally distinguish between employed and unemployed, though Maillard's list tells us that there were four participants from the *ateliers de charité*: two navvies, a foreman and a *chef d'atelier*. Moreover, other evidence suggests that many of the *Vainqueurs*, whether wage-earners or independent craftsmen, were without work. We know that substantial monetary contributions were made after the fall of the Bastille by Paris deputies and others to relieve the distress of the Faubourg St. Antoine, after appeals by M. Damoye, president of the St. Marguerite District, and by M. Bessin, *procureur* at the Châtelet.[39] There was also the evidence of the 900 unemployed stone-cutters who, in a petition which Camille Desmoulins presented to the Constituent Assembly in

36. Jaurès, I, 303.
37. Hardy, VIII, 388.
38. A.N., Y10598, 12698 (14 July 1789).
39. A.N., C 134, doss. 6. fos. 14–15.

July 1791, claimed to have been engaged on the demolition of the Bastille after many of them had taken part in its capture.[40] Such evidence suggests that there may have been many unemployed among the wage-earners, independent craftsmen and small masters who formed the great majority of the *Vainqueurs de la Bastille*.

So we may conclude that the capture of the Bastille was largely the work of the inhabitants of the Faubourg St. Antoine and its neighbouring districts. Four in five of the civilian captors lived within little more than half a mile of the fortress. Of the remainder, over two in three lived in the adjoining parishes of St. Paul and St. Gervais. Secondly, if we leave aside the important contribution made by the sixty-odd Gardes Françaises, the capture was mainly the affair of independent craftsmen, small masters and their journeymen; these formed about two-thirds of the civilians taking part. Nor should we be too astonished that, among these, wage-earners appear to have accounted for no more than one in four. It must be remembered that the Faubourg was essentially an area of small workshops and that the wage-earners and their families represented a comparatively small proportion of its inhabitants.[41] Besides, several of the Paris Districts (including that of Petit St. Antoine) had, in forming their contingents of the National Guard, adopted measures to limit the distribution of arms to employers and men of property.[42]

As for the march to Versailles on 5 October 1789, there are no lists of participants to guide us and the police reports on those arrested or killed at Versailles are a mere handful and, consequently, quite insufficient to enable us to draw any valid conclusions.[43]

40. S. Lacroix, *Actes de la Commune de Paris pendant la Révolution française*, 2nd series, 8 vols. (Paris, 1900–14), V, 260.

41. F. Braesch, 'Un essai de statistique de la population ouvrière de Paris vers 1791', in *Rév. franc.*, LXVIII (July–Dec. 1912), 289–329.

42. For Petit St. Antoine, see A.N., C 134, doss. 1, fo. 3.

43. Archives de Seine-et-Oise, series B, Prévôté de l'Hôtel du Roi, Greffe 1789.

At first sight, one might be tempted to believe that a suitable compensation would be found in the findings of the Châtelet enquiry into the events of 6 October, which were published in March 1790 after the examination of 388 witnesses.[44] It is certain that Taine, among others, was largely inspired by this document when he painted his unflattering picture of the men and women who escorted the King and Queen back to Paris.[45] Yet the document should be treated with the greatest caution. The proceedings appear to have been set afoot to attribute the October events solely to the intrigues of Mirabeau and the Duke of Orleans. By this means, it was hoped, no doubt, to exonerate the Royal Family and the dominant party in the National Assembly, which benefited most directly from the insurrection. Besides the police selected their witnesses with the greatest care; and the Cordeliers District justly complained, in a written protest which served as an example for other Districts to follow, that 'on the list of witnesses . . . one finds few other than aristocratic names'.[46] Most of these witnesses are, in fact, persons whose evidence can hardly inspire confidence: officers of the Flanders Regiment, courtiers or servants of the Royal household or of the aristocracy, much of whose evidence, besides, is second-hand. It would, therefore, be unwise to use this material without reservation in order to draw an impartial picture of the insurgents or of the motives that brought them to Versailles. However, in spite of its faults, the document should not be dismissed entirely: it contains a large number of eyewitness accounts, which are of considerable value in helping to trace the events and the social groups taking part, and which accord, moreover, fairly closely with the reports on these events made by other contemporary observers.

44. *Procédure criminelle, instruite au Châtelet de Paris, sur la dénonciation des faits arrivés à Versailles dans la journée du 6 Octobre 1789*, 2 vols. (Paris, 1790).
45. Taine, I, 130–6.
46. Brit. Mus., Croker collection, R 655 (6).

On one point, at least, all witnesses are agreed: that the bands of women who took the lead in marching to Versailles on 5 October were composed not only of market-women but also of well-dressed *bourgeoises* and of women of different social classes. Thus, a Châtelet witness saw at the Palais Royal on the evening of the 4th a group of people listening to a woman of about thirty-five, 'whose manner of dress was that of a woman above the common station'.[47] Among those [declared another witness] who, on the morning of the 5th, forced the bell-ringer of St. Margaret's church in the Faubourg St. Antoine to summon the citizens to revolt by sounding the tocsin, was a woman 'who appeared not to be of the common people'. Hardy describes the assault that took place on the City Hall that morning as 'an insurrection of the women of the *Halles* and of the various markets'. Another witness of the invasion of the City Hall recorded that there were among the assailants a large number of fashionably dressed women, and he describes 'a first platoon of women, most of them young, clad in white, wearing hats and powdered'; and he added that 'he observed very few that could be classed among the lowest order of people'.

Hardy, too, in describing the women's departure for Versailles on the afternoon of the 5th, reports that 'several thousands of women, having recruited all the women they met with on the way, even women wearing hats (whom they forced to follow them), had removed the cannon from the courtyard of the Châtelet'.

In their accounts of what took place at Versailles, eye-witnesses also confirmed the presence of women of a variety of social classes. The *curé* of St. Gervais reported seeing 'women, of whom some were well dressed'; and Hardy relates the scene in the hall of the Assembly: 'This strange spectacle was all the stranger for the apparel of several of the women who, in elegant clothes, had hunting knives or short sabres hanging over their skirts'; while the

47. *Procédure criminelle . . .*, witness no. 62; see also witnesses nos. 119, 126.

Marquis de Paroy wrote to his wife that, in the deputation of six women received by Louis XVI, 'I observed two that appeared to be well dressed and not to be of the common people, although they affected to speak their language.' On the other hand, the demagogue Fournier l'Américain boasted of having affected the speech of the fish-wives in order to win the support of the market-women for the proposed return with the King and Queen to Paris; and the *Révolutions de Paris*, in its report of the events of 5 and 6 October, insisted that it was 'the women of the people, particularly the stall-holders of the *Halles* and the working women of the Faubourg St. Antoine, that had undertaken to save the country'.[48]

But it was not only on the October 'days' themselves that women played so outstanding a part. Their action in October had already been anticipated in the popular movement that sprang up in August and September in protest against the scarcity and high price of bread. . . . Hardy relates in his *Journal*, in the course of these months, the particular contribution made to this movement by the market-women and working-class housewives.[49] On 16 September, he noted that women had stopped five cart-loads of grain at Chaillot and had brought them to the Paris City Hall; and in relating the incident of the women who besieged the Hôtel de Ville on the 18th of that month and compelled Mayor Bailly and the Municipal Council to receive them, he wrote the significant phrase: 'These women said aloud that the men knew nothing of this business and that they would now lend a hand.'[50] Such incidents help to explain the initiative taken by women on 5 October and the predominance of the women of the markets and the central districts among those leading the march to Versailles.

48. For the above, see *Procédure criminelle* . . ., witnesses nos. 35, 91, 92; Hardy, VIII, 501–2, 506; *Revue de la Révolution*, I (1883), docs. 1–7; Fournier's *Mémoires secrets* . . ., A.N., F⁷ 6504; *Révs. de Paris*, no. XIII (3–10 Oct. 1789), p. 9.

49. Hardy, VIII, 478, 479, 480, 489–90, 499–505.

50. Hardy, VIII, 479.

It is more difficult to determine the social composition of the men who followed after. A few, as we know, joined the women marchers, but the great majority were formed by the 20,000–40,000 National Guards who paraded on the Place de Grève and, towards five in the morning, compelled Lafayette to lead them to Versailles.[51] We may be certain that most of these were small shopkeepers, workshop masters and independent craftsmen, who constituted the bulk of the Parisian National Guard from which the wage-earners, though not formally excluded, tended more and more to stay apart.[52] Yet there were workers among them. The handful of reports drawn up by the Versailles police record a single death among those who invaded the *château* on the morning of 6 October: that of Lhéritier, a journeyman cabinet-maker and volunteer guardsman of the Faubourg St. Antoine; and they also inform us that one of the two wage-earners picked up by the police for pillaging the Hôtel des Gardes du Corps at Versailles was a journeyman goldsmith and guardsman of the St. Gervais District.[53]

The Châtelet witnesses also give some indication of the presence of wage-earners among many thousands who gathered at the *château* of Versailles. Elizabeth Girard, for example, speaks of 'large numbers of journeymen locksmiths'; and another witness records that butcher's boys ran after the Royal coaches which, it was rumoured, were due to take the King to Rambouillet, and prevented them from leaving.[54]

Of course, these scraps of evidence do not in themselves allow us to drawn any general conclusions. But a brief glance at the popular movements preceding the October events will suggest that the working population, the journeymen, the unemployed and their families contributed a major share to the ranks of the men and women who

51. *Procédure criminelle* . . ., witness no. 81 (Stanislas Maillard).

52. See, e.g., the composition of those recruited in August 1789 to the battalion of the District of Ste. Opportune (Brit. Mus., F 830 (6)).

53. Arch. Seine-et-Oise, series B, Prévôté de l'Hôtel du Roi, Greffe 1789.

54. *Procédure criminelle* . . ., witnesses nos. 29, 90.

marched to Versailles on 5 October. [A brief account of the wages and unemployed movements of the preceding months is omitted from the translation of the original article.]

We may perhaps, therefore, conclude that these movements, which affected such large numbers of the Paris population, played their part in preparing popular opinion for the October 'days' and even in swelling the ranks of those who marched to Versailles. While there is no direct evidence to support this view in regard to one of the most mysterious outbreaks of the Revolution, such documents as there are to hand have clearly shown us that the participants in both the October and the preceding events were drawn largely from the same sections of the population: from the *menu peuple* of Paris.[55]

After the calm of 1790, popular insurrectionary movements developed again in the early months of 1791. Opinion had been alarmed by the departure from France of the King's aunts on 24 February and by the proposal to convert the *château* of Vincennes into a temporary prison. This last measure had provoked several thousand people from the Faubourg St. Antoine and its neighbouring districts to march to Vincennes, and a part of the dungeon had been destroyed. But it was only some weeks later that a continuous movement sprang up; it was directed by the Cordeliers Club and its affiliated societies and supported by a number of Republican and democratic journalists, and it culminated in the popular demonstration and 'massacre' of the Champ de Mars on 17 July.

Unfortunately, as for the October insurrection, very little direct evidence exists to help to determine the social composition of the demonstrators who assembled on the Champ de Mars to sign the petition drawn up by the Cordeliers Club.[56] According to the account given by the

55. See A. Mathiez, 'Etude critique sur les journées des 5 et 6 Octobre 1789', in *Revue historique*, LXVII (1898), 241–81; LXVIII (1899), 258–94; LXIX (1899), 41–66.

56. Braesch, 'Les pétitions du Champs de Mars', in *Rev. hist.*, CXLIII (1923), 17–18.

Révolutions de Paris a few days later, there were 50,000 people present at the end of the afternoon, and of these 15,000 were grouped around the *autel de la patrie* when the troops opened fire.[57] Buchez and Roux tell us that the petition bore, by this time, more than 6,000 signatures; and the organisers of the demonstration claimed that these included the names of more than 2,000 municipal officers and electors. Yet Buchez and Roux, who saw the petition before its destruction by fire in 1871, maintained that 'the mass of the signatures were those of people who could hardly read' and, to prove the illiteracy of the signatories, they instanced the large number of crosses appearing on the sheets.[58] Similarly, a daily newspaper, *Le Babillard*, wrote: 'Citizens must have shuddered on seeing close at hand these poor wretches whom scoundrels had assembled on the Champ de Mars. Among all these people, not one, I believe, can read.'[59]

Even if we allow for a degree of exaggeration in the highly slanted account given by *Le Babillard* and for the uncertainty of illiteracy as a guide to social analysis, we may perhaps accept the suggestion put forward by Buchez and Roux: that, broadly, the signatories belonged to the poorer classes of the community. Such a supposition, moreover, is confirmed by the few documents surviving in the Paris archives, which directly relate to the participants in the event. For example, the report drawn up by Filleul, a municipal officer, on those killed at the Champ de Mars and examined by him at the Military Hospital of the Gros Caillou shows that, of nine identified corpses, three were of workshop journeymen, one of a woman 'in a patched skirt of many colours', and the rest those of a master saddler, the son of a wine-merchant and of two relatively well-dressed *bourgeois*.[60] The reports of the police

57. *Révolutions de Paris*, no. CVI (16–22 July 1791), p. 53 *et seq.*
58. Buchez et Roux, *Histoire parlementaire de la Révolution française* 40 vols. (Paris, 1833–8), XI, 113; *Révs. de Paris. loc. cit.*
59. *Le Babillard*, no. XXXVI (19 July 1791), p. 4.
60. A.N., W 294, no. 235.

commissioners of the Paris Sections mention one solitary corpse, that of a shoemaker of the Section des Invalides which was brought to the police headquarters of the Palais Royal on 17 July.[61] Among those arrested in the Sections after the 'massacre', the only ones who admitted that they had been present at the Champ de Mars or whose presence was confirmed by the police were a journeyman joiner, a café-proprietor's assistant, a gardener, a cook, a tailor and an unemployed shoe-black.[62] Of these, the tailor related that the National Guard had fired 'on the workers as though they were game', and the shoe-black described the resistance that was offered to the armed force 'by all the wig-makers and others'. And Buirette-Verrières, a member of the Cordeliers Club, replied to accusations that he had incited the *ouvriers* to assemble on the Champ de Mars, 'that he could hardly have incited any workers to come to the Champ de Mars, as those whom he is supposed to have incited were on their way to it already'.[63] Unfortunately, the prison register of the Hôtel de la Force only gives the occupation of one Abbé among the twelve persons brought there from the Champ de Mars and interrogated by the police commissioner of the Roi-de-Sicile Section.[64]

But we do have the indirect, though far more voluminous, evidence of the police commissioners' reports and the prison register of the Force, relating to some 260 persons arrested in the Sections between April and November 1791 for having opposed or resisted the municipal authorities. Most of these documents, and certainly the most detailed, are to be found in the archives of the Paris Prefecture of Police;[65] the commissioners' reports, in particular, are a

61. A.P.P., Aa 85, fo. 768.

62. A.P.P., Ab (registre), pp. 33, 38; Aa 148, fo. 30; 215, fo. 463; 182, fo. 312. A.N., T. 214 (3).

63. A.N., F⁷ 4623, fo. 104.

64. A.P.P., Ab 324, p. 60.

65. A.P.P., Aa 56, 72, 74, 76, 84, 85, 134, 137, 148, 153, 155, 157, 166, 172, 173, 182, 198, 205, 216, 219, 220, 224, 239; Ab 324 (Force), pp. 7–60.

most valuable source for the study of the social movement of this period. They tell us something not only about the many men and women whom we may suppose to have taken part in the demonstration itself, but also about the far greater number who were influenced by the continuous agitation carried on, during the preceding months, by the democrats and the Cordeliers Club.[66]

Most of these arrests undoubtedly relate to the widespread popular movement which culminated in the demonstration on the Champ de Mars. Very few of them resulted from counter-revolutionary activity: in almost every case, the men and women concerned were accused of having criticised or abused the Paris administration, the National Guard, or its commander, Lafayette, in terms that indicate the considerable influence exerted at this time by the democrats, Republicans and popular societies on the workers and other social elements among the Parisian *sans-culottes*. Thus, among the fifty-two persons arrested between 14 April and 15 July 1791 whose occupation and status we know, thirty-four were wage-earners, some of them unemployed; the rest were mainly small employers and independent craftsmen. Again, of 186 persons arrested between 16 July and 15 November (most of them for having criticised the Guard and the municipality for the violence they had used against the signatories of the Champ de Mars), 102 were wage-earners, including fifteen unemployed and ten news-vendors who had lost their jobs in other trades. As before, the rest were largely small employers and craftsmen, with a sprinkling of small proprietors.[67] The evidence, although it is indirect, appears to confirm the impression gained by consulting the documents directly relating to the Champ de Mars affair: that the signatories and demonstrators of 17 July were

66. Yet they have been neglected by historians of the period: see Mathiez, *Le club des Cordeliers pendant la crise de Varennes et le massacre du Champ de Mars*, Paris, 1910; and A. Mellié, *Les sections de Paris pendant la Révolution française* (Paris, 1898).

67. See A.P.P., Aa, various boxes.

composed of that same *menu peuple* of shopkeepers, craftsmen and wage-earners that made up the bulk of the population of the Faubourgs and the overcrowded districts in
the centre of the city.

The image is, in fact, almost identical with that created
by the participants in all the other major revolutionary
movements of the time. In the Réveillon affair, the capture
of the Bastille, the march to Versailles, the Champ de Mars
demonstration and the popular movements leading up to
it, we have found a similar predominance of the typical
menu peuple of revolutionary Paris: workshop masters,
shopkeepers, independent craftsmen, journeymen and
workers in manufactories and *ateliers de charité*, both men
and women, the latter being more in evidence when the
question of bread was to the fore. Yet it was only in the
Réveillon affair that we found a great preponderance of
wage-earners involved; for here, as we saw, the issues were
such that the workshop journeymen and other workers
felt themselves to be particularly affected as a social group.

We shall not attempt here a general analysis of the
motives which impelled the different groups of rioters to
play an active part in the 'days' of revolutionary crisis;
but it would perhaps be of some interest to consider
briefly Taine's hypothesis that a great part of them were
made up of hired bands who had been recruited for money.
It is important to note, besides, that underlying the general
thesis put forward by Taine and his disciples is the assumption that bribery and corruption were decisive factors in
stimulating revolutionary activity and participation in
revolutionary events. It has been claimed, for example,
that the market-women who marched to Versailles on
5 October had been 'recruited for several days past for
money'.[68] The craftsmen and workers who besieged the
Bastille had been bribed to do so: 'They were hired in the
workshops at a *louis* per head . . .' Criminal elements had
also been taken care of: 'in the hovels of the great city they

68. Taine, I, 129.

recruited that feckless class whose intemperance had led them to crime'.[69] The 'evidence' of the Royalist Montjoie concerning the prisoners and the wounded in the Réveillon affair is taken at its face value; they had (he wrote) been bought for twelve francs apiece.[70] And little inhibition is shown in quoting Mortimer-Ternaux's dictum that 'in most popular movements, money plays a more important role than passion or commitment'.[71] Indeed, there is no lack of contemporary opinion to support the view. Montjoie, editor of the *Ami du Roi*, claimed he had direct evidence that money had been distributed to the Réveillon rioters: 'I have questioned several of these wretches [he wrote], whether in hospital or in prison, and I have no doubt that all of them were paid and that the rate was twelve *livres*.'[72] And Besenval, commander-in-chief of the armed force summoned to crush the revolt, declared, on the strength of the unanimous verdict of the police spies of the Châtelet, that 'people were seen to excite to disorder and even to distribute money'.[73] A popular pamphlet of the day speaks of the rioters in the following terms:

You know well, Gentlemen of the States-General, that these people had been paid, some six francs, some twelve, to do mischief and, after, to stir up a regular revolt.[74]

Similar accusations were made against the rioters at the St. Lazare monastery and the *barrières* in July 1789; and, in September, Hardy noted in his *Journal* that each one of the rioters arrested at Versailles for attempting to hang

69. A. de Gallier, 'Les émeutiers de 1789', *Revue des questions historiques*, XXXIV (1883), 122.

70. J. Collot, 'L'Affaire Réveillon', *Rev. des quest. hist.*, CXXI (1935), 247.

71. M. Mortimer-Ternaux, *Histoire de la Terreur*, 8 vols. (Paris, 1862–81), VIII, 455.

72. Montjoie, *Mémoires*; cit. Chassin, III, 58.

73. Berville et Barrière, *Mémoires du Baron Besenval*, 2 vols. (Paris, 1921), II, 346.

74. *Cahiers des plaintes et doléances des dames de la halle*, p. 23, B.M., R. 40 (5).

a baker in his shop had 33 *livres* in his pocket.[75] But, at this time, it was above all during the episode of 5 and 6 October that allegations abound concerning the alleged distribution of money among the people in order to provoke disturbance. During the Châtelet enquiry, several witnesses affirmed that the soldiers of the Flanders Regiment, the women of the markets and others had been hired at a good price; and it is generally inferred that it was the faction around the Duke of Orleans that had paid them.[76] It is hardly surprising that Taine and his followers drew heavily on this source to support their thesis.

During the period of social tension leading up to the 'massacre' of the Champ de Mars, the opponents of the administration were liberally branded as paid agents of the enemies of the régime. *Le Babillard* describes the workers in the National Workshops as 'the hired agents of agitators'; and Bailly, mayor of Paris, had earlier attributed to similar influences a riot that broke out in the Faubourg St. Antoine in May 1790, when three thieves had been lynched by the crowd: 'The municipal authorities are informed that money has been distributed in order to promote a dangerous fermentation.'[77]

It was indeed normal for the authorities of the time to take the venality of the masses for granted and to seek the remedy for popular disturbance in the prosecution of alleged conspirators and their hirelings rather than in rooting out the causes of popular grievance. Thus, in the Réveillon affair, the police commissioners of the Châtelet, when interrogating those arrested or wounded, asked them if they had any knowledge of the payment of bribes to promote disorder. When Jean Nicolas Pepin, a tallow-porter, was questioned about the looting of St. Lazare and the general events of 12–14 July at the Palais Royal and elsewhere, he was asked 'if he had received money from

75. Hardy, VIII, 488.
76. *Procédure criminelle* . . ., witnesses nos. 20, 29, 45, 71, 87, 89, 91, 144, 161, 164, 373, 387.
77. *Le Babillard*, no. XXIV (26 July 1791); *Ancien Moniteur*, IV, 465.

these persons'. Michel Adrien, a labourer, later hanged for provoking a 'sedition' in the Faubourg St. Antoine, is asked 'if before or after the 12th July he has not received money from different persons to instigate disturbances in Paris'. François Billon, charged with threatening to hang a baker at the Ecole Militaire, is asked if he has been 'incited to do this by ill-intentioned persons who had tried to suborn him by paying him money'. During the weeks preceding the Champ de Mars affray, the question is insistently put in the cross-examination of those arrested in the Paris Sections. Here is one sample. Gaspard Ballet, a shoemaker, when arrested for making insulting remarks about Lafayette, explained that he had acquired his opinions from reading the democratic press. The report of his cross-examination continues as follows:

It was suggested to him that his condition did not make it possible for him to acquire the great number of papers that appear; so perhaps someone paid for them on his behalf? He was asked to say who this might be.

He replied that he read them at the shop of one Collier, shoemaker, at St. Jean de Latran.

Questioned and called upon to tell us if he had not received money from certain individuals to provoke a public and cruel hatred against a general who, night and day, was sacrificing his all for public peace and order.

He replied no, that this was his own way of thinking, and that his opinions had been formed by his reading.[78]

It might be argued that such substantial contemporary evidence fully justifies the attitude of the authorities and the opinion of that group of historians which sees in mass bribery a mainspring of popular action. But, in fact, the sources from which we have quoted are one-sided and often tendentious. Montjoie's and Besenval's reports of bribery in the case of the Réveillon riots are not substantiated by the police reports of the Châtelet. The editor of *L'Ami du Roi* appears to have been romancing. The

78. A.N., Y 11033; Z² 4691; Y 18768-9; DXXIX *bis* 36, no. 376, fo. 37. A.P.P., Aa 206, fos. 366-7.

police had every motive for making public the discovery of any suspicious objects or sums of money found on the dead, wounded or prisoners. There is no report of any search of the wounded, but the prisoners and dead were, as always, subjected to a thorough examination. The results are almost entirely negative. Of the prisoners only one appears to have been found with any substantial sum of money—the paper-worker Sirier, who admitted having received 4 *livres* from two individuals whom he had met at the Palais Royal—but this was several days after the riots! The eighteen bodies brought to the Montrouge cemetery for identification were examined by commissioner Odent: of these, ten had nothing in their pockets, two a tobacco pouch, one a small key, another a trade instrument, a fifth a silver object (which may have been stolen), and a child had a compass, knife and pencil. Of money not a trace. Here, at least, the case for bribery is not proved.[79]

For the Paris revolution of 1789 the evidence supporting mass bribery is very slight and need not be taken too seriously. Even Gustave Bord, who ascribes the capture of the Bastille to a masonic conspiracy, does not suggest that the *ouvriers du quartier* were bribed to participate.[80] And de Gallier's charge of mass corruption in the workshops is based on no supporting evidence. More specific, it is true, are the charges we have quoted from the riots at St. Lazare and the *barrières*, but the testimony of one witness out of thirty-three in the former and of four out of eighty-one in the latter hardly affords conclusive proof of widespread bribery.

Highly significant of contemporary middle-class opinion on this matter is Hardy's assertion that the Versailles bread rioters of September 1789 were each found with 33 *livres* in their pockets after arrest. The charge is based on rumour. In the detailed police reports of the case in the Versailles departmental archives there is no mention of money being

79. A.N., Y 14119, 15019.
80. G. Bord, *op. cit.*, pp. 521–44, 751–67.

found on any one of the fifteen prisoners.[81] At least Hardy, unlike Montjoie, did not claim to have first-hand knowledge of the facts he reported.

There is perhaps more substance in the numerous charges of bribery made in the Châtelet enquiry into the events of October 1789. Maybe the Orleanist faction did distribute sums of money among the Gardes Françaises, tradespeople and working men and women who thronged the gardens of the Palais Royal: it is known that large sums were spent on fireworks and entertainment; and Gaxotte may be justified in writing that 'the Duke of Orleans once more opened his coffers and money flowed freely'.[82] But the testimony of the *Procédure au Châtelet* should be treated with the greatest reserve. The charges are in many cases based on hearsay and the majority are witnesses whose evidence cannot be considered objective—officers of the Flanders Regiment, Court officials, and domestic servants of the Royal Family or nobility. The only police reports issued immediately after the event are silent on this score.[83] Equally silent are the numerous documents relating to those arrested in the months preceding or following the Champ de Mars affair. On balance, in fact, the evidence on which Taine and the historians of the *Revue des questions historiques* have based their case appears to be extremely slight. It seems likely enough that large sums of money were spent on propaganda by groups interested in the prosecution of the Révolution, and some of this may have found its way into the pockets of the wage-earners and small tradesmen. The documents tell us little. At any rate, the corruption of working men does not appear to have been a major factor in the stimulation of revolutionary activity or mass participation in these events.

If now, in the light of all the evidence we have examined

81. Arch. Seine-et-Oise, series B, Prévôté de l'Hôtel du Roi, Procédures 1789, fos. 7–21.

82. P. Gaxotte, *La Révolution française* (Paris, 1946), p. 146.

83. Arch. Seine-et-Oise, series B, Prévôté de l'Hôtel du Roi, Greffe 1789. These relate to two arrests and one death only.

above, we turn to the picture that Taine has painted of the revolutionary crowd, we shall find an equal absence of solid fact. Whereas he does not deny among the participants the presence of wage-earners and poor, he would have us believe that the main body of the insurgents and demonstrators in these events were vagrants, criminals and other social riff-raff.[84] While we admit that such elements may have mingled with the crowds whose social composition we have tried to establish, a study of the documents does not confirm the importance that has been attached to them by Taine and his disciples.

Marcel Rouff has shown that there was only a small number of professional beggars, vagrants and *gens sans aveu* among the hundreds of unemployed arrested for begging in the last months of the Ancien Régime.[85] Among the fifty-five arrested, wounded and killed in the Réveillon Riots for whom details are available there were three without fixed abode: a cobbler, a carter and a navvy. Of the eighty scheduled for arrest after the burning of the *barrières* and the four arrested for breaking the windows of the office at the St. Denis customs post, all were of fixed abode and occupation. Of the sixty-one persons arrested in connection with the looting of St. Lazare, nine were unemployed workers without fixed abode who probably had no connection with the affair, having presumably been picked up as part of the general round-up of vagrants, down-and-outs and lodging-house inmates at the time of the July revolution. Every one of the 662 *Vainqueurs de la Bastille* was of fixed abode and settled occupation. There is a lack of evidence on this score in connection with the march to Versailles, but contemporary accounts, which stress the role of market-women and journeymen, made no mention of vagrants or professional beggars or of Taine's '*gens sans aveu*, street-prowlers, bandits and thieves'. In the weeks preceding the Champ de Mars demonstration, one beggar was arrested for abusing the King and Queen,

84. See note 2 above.
85. Rouff, *op. cit.*, pp. 213–31.

and another for justifying their flight from Paris; but every one of the 136 workers arrested before and after the demonstration gave a settled address. Doubtless such elements mingled with the rioters and we know that they caused concern to the Paris Electors during the July revolution, but they seem to have played little direct part in the insurrectionary movements.[86]

Yet unemployed workers—whether from the small crafts or of other occupations—played a big part in these movements, thereby reflecting the deep social and economic crisis which ushered in the Revolution and persisted in several trades during the whole of this period. Seven of the thirty-five arrested Réveillon rioters were unemployed.[87] Though precise evidence is not available, we have already suggested that a considerable proportion of the Bastille's captors were out of work. At St. Lazare and the *barrières*, we have noted the frequent reference made to unemployed—not surprising in view of the location of most Public Workshops on the outskirts of the city. Again, we saw that, in the months preceding and following the Champ de Mars affair, several unemployed persons were arrested for criticising the municipal authorities in their Sections. It may, in fact, be concluded that a remarkable feature of the early insurrectionary movements of the Revolution in Paris was the widespread participation of unemployed workers of every occupation; yet they rarely appear in the guise of beggars or vagabonds.

Taine's further contention that criminals and 'bandits' played a large part in the revolutionary *journées* collapses no less readily under close examination. The eight commissioners of the Châtelet who cross-examined the prisoners in the Réveillon affair found only three who had served previous prison sentences, and of these only one had a serious criminal record: this was the port-worker Téteigne who had been branded with an iron. Only one of those arrested for looting St. Lazare had been in prison: the

86. Various records in A.N., series Y, and A.P.P., series Aa and Ab.
87. A.N., Y 18795, fos. 444–62.

butcher's boy Quatreveaux, who had spent seventeen days at the Hôtel de la Force on a previous conviction. Not one of twenty-three persons arrested at St. Denis in August 1789 for the murder of a municipal officer had a criminal record. Of fifteen Montmartre navvies accused of causing a disturbance at Monceaux on 1 August 1789, one had previously served nine years in the galleys. Only three of the fifteen arrested for the food riot at Versailles on 13 September 1789 had served previous sentences— one for stealing four pieces of wood and two for breaches of army discipline.[88] Of 158 persons arrested in the Paris Sections for political offences before and after the Champ de Mars affair, only three had been in prison before, and all for short terms, which ranged between three days and two to three weeks.[89] There is, unfortunately, no evidence available in the case of the Bastille besiegers, the Versailles marchers or the incendiaries of the customs posts. But the evidence of the other *journées* is overwhelming and should prove conclusive. So, once more, Taine's allegations appear to be ill-founded. At most, the elements whom he claims to have been typical of the rioters and insurgents played an altogether marginal role, and their presence in no way invalidates our conclusions concerning the social composition of revolutionary crowds.

These crowds were, as we have seen, largely composed of shopkeepers, workshop masters, independent craftsmen, wage-earners, employed and unemployed. These are the social elements whom Hardy, the bookseller-diarist, frequently terms the 'menu peuple', and whom Mathiez termed 'the still unformed, but emerging, class of the *sans-culottes*'.[90] Does this mean that these people formed a tightly knit social class whose constituent elements can scarcely be told apart? This is certainly not the conclusion that emerges from our study and from the documents we have consulted.

88. Arch. Seine-et-Oise, series B, Prév. de l'Hôtel du Roi. Procédures 1789, fos. 7–21.
89. A.P.P., Aa 137, fos. 177–8; 173, fos. 24, 25–6.
90. Mathiez, *Le club des Cordeliers*, p. 30.

It is true that there is a lack of precise definition as between craftsmen and wage-earners (we noted as much in discussing the captors of the Bastille), and this makes it difficult to draw up an exact statistical analysis of the rioters; yet the indications that we have are numerous enough and precise enough to enable us to draw a broad line of distinction between the wage-earners and the other social groups among the *menu peuple*. In the Réveillon affair, for instance, we saw that wage-earners—journeymen, shop-assistants and labourers—made up the bulk of those wounded, killed and arrested, as of the insurgents in general; a fact that strongly suggests that, in this incident at least, the workers as a group felt a particular concern. In the movement launched by the Cordeliers Club and the democrats and ending in the 'massacre' of the Champ de Mars, it is also possible to trace a fairly accurate picture of the involvement of the wage-earners and their families. Although they played no distinctive role, the wage-earners formed a high proportion of the many hundreds of persons arrested in the different Paris Sections.

Yet we must guard against any tendency to exaggerate the significance of these social distinctions or to follow Daniel Guérin in seeing the expression of a 'proletarian' class consciousness where this had not yet had time to develop. In the social conditions of the day it is not surprising that distinctive workers' movements were still fairly rare and that, in the social struggle, the worker still found himself most often the ally of the small shopkeeper and master craftsman, who had a common interest with him in opposing the claims of the large merchant, the contractor and the monopolist, whether noble or *bourgeois*. It is this which justifies the use of terms such as 'sans-culottes' and 'menu peuple', terms which lack the precision of the social terminology of our day but which reflect aptly enough the social conditions of those times. They also help to explain the composition of the rioters and insurgents who have been the subject of this study.

The Motives of Popular Insurrection in Paris during the French Revolution

Never, perhaps, has the investigator into the nature and motives of revolutionary crowds found ready to hand such rich and varied material as that provided by Paris during the French Revolution. Apart from the year 1790, which was a period of remarkable social calm, Paris was for six years almost continuously subject to social movements and revolutionary upheavals—from April 1789, when the journeymen and labourers of the Faubourg St. Antoine and adjoining districts destroyed the properties of the manufacturers Henriot and Réveillon, until the final, desperate revolts of the Parisian *sans-culottes* against the Thermidorian Convention in Germinal and Prairial of the Year 3 (April–May 1795).[1] Here it is not proposed to attempt a general investigation into the behaviour of the participants in these events. For the study of the process of transformation of groups of individuals into revolutionary crowds and

From *Bulletin of the Institute of Historical Research*, XXVI (1953), 53–74.

1. The most important of these revolutionary *journées* were:
In *1789*: Réveillon Riots (28–29 April), Paris revolution and capture of the Bastille (12–14 July), march to Versailles (5–6 October);
in *1791*: march to Vincennes (28 February), Champs de Mars demonstration and petition (17 July);
in *1792*: first pillage of grocers' shops (January–February), invasion of Tuileries (20 June), fall of monarchy (10 August), September Massacres (2–4 September);
in *1793*: second pillage of groceries (25–26 February), expulsion of Girondin deputies (31 May–2 June), 'Hébertist' insurrection (4–5 September);
in *1794*: overthrow of Robespierre (9 Thermidor = 27 July);
in *1795*: riots of 12 Germinal (1 April) and 1–4 Prairial (20–23 May).

The march to Vincennes (28 February 1791) and the September Massacres are not dealt with in this study.

of the particular behaviour and reaction to external stimuli of such crowds—what is generally termed the psychology of revolutionary crowds—the reader is referred to the work of Professor Georges Lefebvre.[2] In this article I shall be concerned with another aspect of the problem; I shall attempt to see if there is any common pattern linking together the various insurrectionary movements or any underlying unity of purpose motivating their participants.

In their characterisation of the revolutionary crowd historians have tended to fall into two main groups—those who have accepted the revolutionary tradition with Michelet[3] and those who have rejected it with Taine[4]; but whether they refer to the mass of the participants in the great revolutionary *journées* admiringly as 'le peuple', or, slightingly, as 'la canaille', they have been inclined (in Professor Lefebvre's phrase) to treat the Revolution 'from above'[5] and have only considered the revolutionary crowd from the elevation of the committee room or the rostrum of the National Assembly or Jacobin Club. This has been true even of a great social historian like Albert Mathiez.[6] In so far as any attempt has been made at a detailed study of revolutionary crowds, there has been a tendency to explain them in terms of mass bribery and aristocratic or foreign conspiracy, or else as a kind of collective personification of the revolutionary ideal. However, I believe that it is possible to throw more light on the particular motives which prompted Parisian shopkeepers, workshop masters and journeymen to participate so frequently and whole-

2. See his 'Foules Révolutionnaires' in *Annals Historiques de la Révolution Française*, XI (1934), 1–26.

3. J.Michelet, *La Révolution Française*, édition définitive (Paris, 1893).

4. H. Taine, *Les Origines de la France Contemporaine. La Révolution*, 3 vols. (Paris, 1876).

5. G. Lefebvre, *La Révolution Française. La Révolution de 1789* (Les Cours de Sorbonne, Paris, 1946), p. 2.

6. See, e.g., his great work on the social movement of the Parisian *sans-culottes* of 1792–4, *La Vie chère et le Mouvement social sous la Terreur* (Paris, 1927), which is based almost entirely on reports of speeches in the National Convention, the Paris Commune and the Jacobin Club.

heartedly in revolutionary actions, and on the connection between their aims and those of the revolutionary leaders with whom historians of the Revolution have been largely preoccupied. The basis for such a study was laid by Jean Jaurès in his *Histoire Socialiste de la Révolution Française,* first published in 1901–4. More recently it has received a valuable stimulus from the work of Lefebvre and from Labrousse's research into the movements of prices and wages on the eve of the Revolution.[7] The present study draws largely on the police reports (particularly the *procès-verbaux* relating to the cross-examination of prisoners by the *commissaires de police*) of the Paris Châtelet,[8] the Paris Sections of 1790–5[9] and the Comité de Sûreté Générale.[10]

It must be recognised, to begin with, of course, that each of the Parisian *journées* and of the social movements that generally led up to them had its own distinctive features, its own political content and objective, its own leaders and organisation. Thus, the Réveillon Riots in the Faubourg St. Antoine in April 1789, although involving many thousands of people and leading to a considerable loss of life and property, do not, unlike most of the other disturbances, appear to have been organised by anyone in particular or to have furthered the interests of any particular faction; further, they were the only major social disturbance in Paris during this period in which wage-earners appear to have predominated and in which, though confusedly, a worker–employer conflict can be seen. Again,

7. C.-E. Labrousse, *Esquisse du Mouvement des Prix et des Revenus en France au XVIIIe Siècle,* 2 vols. (Paris, 1933); *La Crise de l'Economie Française à la Fin de l'Ancien Régime et au Début de la Révolution,* vol. I (Paris, 1944).
8. Archives des Commissaires au Châtelet. Archives Nationales, series Y.
9. Archives de la Préfecture de Police. Sections de Paris: Procès-Verbaux des Commissaires de Police. Series Aa.
10. The most important of these from the point of view of the present study are contained in the Archives Nationales, series F[7] (Police Générale). I cannot claim, however, to have thoroughly investigated this extremely rich and voluminous source.

there is a marked contrast between the apparent spontaneity of the march to Versailles to fetch the royal family to Paris in October 1789 and such military operations as the assault of the Bastille, the overthrow of the monarchy in August 1792 or the expulsion of the Girondin deputies from the Convention in June 1793; or again, between the predominantly *political* actions, such as the capture of the Bastille or the Champ de Mars demonstration of July 1791, and the more obviously *social* or *economic* movements, such as the various bread riots preceding the march to Versailles or the mass irruption into grocers' shops all over Paris in January–February 1792 and February 1793. If there is a common thread running through these varied insurrectionary and social movements, it is to be found, not in the objectives or organisational plans of their promoters or of the political factions whose interests they often served, but in the social composition and particular aims of the rioters and demonstrators themselves.

A study of the social composition of the participants in these movements, based mainly on the reports of the police commissioners of the Châtelet and of the Sections,[11] reveals, in fact, a fairly constant and uniform pattern. So much is, indeed, conceded by historians like Taine; but they would have us believe that revolutionary crowds were formed, in the main, of criminals, vagrants and down-and-outs. While these no doubt played a certain part in these events, it appears to have been only a minor one. In nearly every insurrection and social movement of the period, as will be seen, the main body of participants seems to have been drawn from the typical *menu peuple*[12] of Paris: wage-earners, craftsmen, small shopkeepers, workshop masters, clerks and

11. See pp. 96–7, n. 3 and 4, above.
12. This term, borrowed from the contemporary manuscript journal of the Parisian bookseller Hardy 'Mes Loisirs, ou Journal d'événements tels qu'ils parviennent à ma connoissance', (Bibliothèque Nationale, fonds français 6680–7), cannot lay claim to any sociological exactitude. It has, however, been found convenient to use it in describing collectively wage-earners, small property owners and urban poor.

others. Within this broad social grouping the proportion of the whole formed by the various constituent elements differs considerably, it is true, from one insurrection to another. Thus, in the Réveillon Riots, where the issues involved were of particular interest to wage-earners, we find, as has already been said, a predominance of journeymen and labourers. We find, also, a higher proportion of wage-earners among those arrested in connection with the Champ de Mars petition of July 1791 than among the assailants of the Bastille, the captors of the Tuileries in August 1792 or (though here the evidence is slighter) among the armed militia which expelled the Girondin deputies—doubtless because the promoters of the Champ de Mars petition had over a long period made a particular appeal to the politically under-privileged and because the latter three operations involved, in the main, citizens organised in the National Guard, from which wage-earners had long been excluded either by law or by economic necessity. Again, it is not surprising that we should find a higher proportion of women participating in those movements in which the 'bread-and-butter' question presented itself most clearly—as in the march to Versailles, the popular invasions of the grocers' shops or the food riots of Germinal–Prairial of the Year 3—than in the more strictly military or political actions. If we leave aside the single case of the Réveillon Riots, these variations have no particular significance, however, for the present discussion, in which I hope to show that the various social groups composing the *menu peuple* of Paris were closely allied in the social conflicts of the period and were prompted to participate in these movements by identical motives. What is important to note is that the political leaders directing, or making political capital out of, these operations—the Paris electors of May–July 1789, the revolutionary journalists, the members of the Commune, of the National Assembly, the Cordelier or the Jacobin Clubs—were, with few exceptions, drawn from social groups whose interests were often at variance with those of the Parisian *menu peuple*—namely the *bourgeoisie*, the professions or the liberal aristocracy. Thus, it is possible to assume a certain discrepancy between the aims of the political leaders and the mass of the participants in the revolutionary movements under review.[13]

Considerable mystery still surrounds the actual preparation and organisation of many of these movements. The absence of exact supporting evidence (either owing to the natural caution of men uncertain of the outcome of their plans or the subsequent deliberate removal of incriminating documents) often makes it difficult to determine how this or that insurrection was planned, who approved it and by what means the mass of its participants were drawn into action. Both Mathiez and Lefebvre have, for example, pointed to this difficulty in the case of the Parisians' march to Versailles in October 1789.[14] Yet this problem need not detain us. Even if we are bound, in most cases, to remain ignorant of the exact mechanism of revolt and, therefore, of the identity of many of those who served as intermediaries between the political leaders and the mass, Cato's old maxim *Cui bono?* usually serves as a useful pointer to the political leaders themselves even where the precise documentary evidence is lacking. The objectives are usually not difficult to determine, either from the declarations of political leaders or the consequences that flowed from the revolutionary actions which they provoked or guided. Thus, the capture of the Bastille—the climax to the Parisian insurrection of July 1789—ensured the transfer of power in the capital from the city government appointed by the absolute monarchy to the assembly of electors, representing the trading, manufacturing and professional middle class and the liberal aristocracy. The October insurrection and the march

13. For the period 1789–91, the above conclusions are drawn from my article on page 96. They remain substantially the same for the later period (the relevant documents are frequently quoted in the course of the present study).

14. See A. Mathiez, 'Etude critque sur les journées des 5 et 6 octobre 1789', *Revue Historique*, LXVII (1898), 241–81; LXVIII (1899), 258–94; LXIX (1899), 41–66; also Lefebvre, *op. cit.*, p. 135.

to Versailles had the effect of consolidating these gains. By placing the king under the watchful eye of the majority in the National Assembly, the Paris city government and Districts, and by destroying the influence of the conservative 'English party' within the Assembly, the ascendancy of the constitutional monarchists was, for the time being, assured. The Champ de Mars petition of July 1791 and the accompanying agitation marked the first, premature challenge of the democrats and republicans, centred in the Cordelier and Jacobin Clubs, to the constitutional monarchy and its supporters—a challenge that was successfully implemented by the armed capture of the Tuileries in August 1792. The Parisian revolution 31 May–2 June 1793, in turn, overthrew the Girondin wing of the republican *bourgeoisie* and transferred power to the Mountain, headed by Robespierre and supported by the Paris Commune and *sans-culottes*. Similarly the *coup d'état* of 9 Thermidor (27 July 1794) overthrew Robespierre, destroyed the Jacobin Club and the Committee of Public Safety and transferred power back to the main body of the republican bourgeoisie. The Parisian insurrections of Germinal and Prairial of the Year 3 (April–May 1795), in turn, marked the final, desperate attempt of the Jacobins, backed by the Parisian *sans-culottes*, to restore their supremacy.

These, then, were, in broadest outline, the political aims of the leaders in provoking or initiating the major insurrectionary movements which concern us in this study. How far can the mass of the participants in these actions be said to have shared these aims and the political ideas with which they were associated? To what extent must their active participation be explained in other terms?

To Taine, Mortimer-Ternaux[15] and many other historians this question presents few difficulties. The revolutionary crowd is a conscienceless rabble, quite incapable of political thought, driven to rebel by the prospect of easy

15. M. Mortimer-Ternaux, *Histoire de la Terreur*, 8 vols. (Paris, 1862–81).

loot or by monetary inducements.[16] Though this view is often upheld by the testimony of hostile contemporary observers,[17] the theory that bribery was a main stimulus to revolutionary activity cannot be sustained against the directly contrary evidence of the police reports of the Châtelet and of the Sections: these show that corruption played, at most, a minor part in drawing the masses into participation in these events.[18] Nor is it possible to maintain that those who took part in the rioting were in general politically neutral or indifferent to the aims and objectives of their promoters. There is ample evidence to suggest that, far from being passive instruments, revolutionary crowds were impregnated with the slogans and ideas of the political groups contending for power as the Revolution advanced. For example, during the Réveillon Riots, which took place on the eve of the convocation of the States General, the demonstrators (though widely believed to have been incited by royalist agents) shouted revolutionary slogans: 'Vive le Roi! Vive Necker! Vive le Tiers Etat!'[19] The same political rallying cry of 'Tiers Etat' was voiced by demonstrators taking part in the burning of the customs posts (the hated *barrières*) and the sacking of the St. Lazare monastery during the Parisian insurrection of 12–14 July of the same year.[20] In the following weeks, as the rift developed in the National Assembly between the constitutional monarchists and the court party over the royal veto, the Parisian *menu peuple* openly championed the liberal wing of the *bour-*

16. Thus, Mortimer-Ternaux writes: 'Dans la plupart des mouvements populaires l'argent joue un plus grand rôle que la passion' (*op. cit.*, VIII, 455).

17. This charge is, for example, made against the Réveillon rioters by Besenval, commander-in-chief of the armed forces mustered to quell them (*Mémoires du Baron Besenval*, II (Paris, 1921), 346) and by Montjoie, editor of the Royalist journal, *L'Ami du Roi* (*Mémoires*, I, 91–3).

18. For a detailed examination of the evidence on which this conclusion is based, see pp. 120–5 above.

19. Arch. Nat. KK 641, fo. 17.

20. Arch. Nat. Z¹ᵃ 886; Z² 4691.

geoisie,[21] and we find the unemployed workers of the Ecole Militaire expressing their readiness to march to Versailles in order to crush reaction almost a fortnight before the march actually took place.[22] After the comparative calm of the year 1790, the social and political ideas of the democrats and republicans, whose main centre of operations was the Cordelier Club, began to circulate among the most active elements of the Parisian *menu peuple*. The results of this in-doctrination were clearly apparent in the Champ de Mars demonstration, called by the Cordelier Club with a purely political object—to sign a petition questioning the king's right to continue in office after his return from his flight to Varennes. More than 6,000 people had signed this petition before the armed militia began firing into the crowd of demonstrators; according to Buchez and Roux, who ex-amined the petition sheets before their destruction by fire during the civil war of 1871, 'la masse des signatures est de gens qui savaient à peine lire'.[23] Many, it is true, may have signed without a clear understanding of the contents of the petition, but the cook, Constance Evrard, at least, stated to the police under cross-examination that she believed its purposes were 'à faire organiser autrement le pouvoir ex-écutif';[24] and of more than 120 persons sent to the Force prison in connection with the Champ de Mars demonstra-tion the great majority had been arrested for expressing political opposition to the National Assembly, the city administration or the armed militia.[25]

21. See Mathiez, *op. cit.*; Malouet, *Mémoires*, I, 367.

22. This is reported by Bailly, mayor of Paris, in a letter to the king's minister, La Tour du Pin (Arch. Nat. C 13, no. 262, fo. 3). One of these workers was arrested on 6 October at Versailles, charged with pillaging the Hôtel des Gardes du Corps. During his cross-examina-tion by the Versailles police, he claimed to have marched 'pour défen-dre les gens de Versailles' (Arch. Seine et Oise. Série B. Prévôté de l'Hôtel du Roi, Greffe 1789).

23. *Histoire Parlementaire de la Révolution Française*, 49 vols. (Paris, 1833–8), XI, 114.

24. Arch. Préf. Pol. Aa 148, fo. 30.

25. Arch. Préf. Pol. Aa (19 cartons); Ab 324 (Registre de la Force), pp. 7–60 (both for period 14–30 July 1791).

It is not possible to produce the same documentary evidence in the case of the armed overthrow of the monarchy in August 1792 and the expulsion of the Girondin deputies in May–June 1793; yet this is hardly surprising as these were insurrections of an entirely different order, dependent for their execution, not on unarmed (or largely unarmed) revolutionary crowds, but on the deployment of a centrally organised armed force—the Parisian National Guard, supplemented in the former case by armed units from Marseilles, Brest and other cities. Yet these actions, too, marked the culmination of many weeks of political preparation in which the Parisian *menu peuple* (now to be distinguished by the title of *sans-culottes*) were thoroughly involved. Thus, the capture of the Tuileries was preceded by the mass invasion of the palace on 20 June, in which may thousands of citizens of the Faubourgs St. Antoine and St. Marcel, both armed and unarmed, presented a petition to the king and shouted patriotic slogans.[26] And already in March 1793 the reports of police agents reveal that the need for a new insurrection, this time directed against the Girondin faction, was openly discussed in the clubs and markets; in April and May this demand had become more insistent and was being supported by countless deputations and petitions to the Convention and the Jacobin Club.[27] Finally, in the riots of Prairial of the Year 3, the crowds that burst into the Convention demanded support for the political programme of the Jacobins and the release of the Jacobin prisoners; in their caps many wore, side by side with the word 'bread', the political slogan, 'The Constitution of 1793'.[28]

There is, therefore, little doubt that these revolutionary crowds enthusiastically supported and assimilated the objects, ideas and slogans of the political groups in the National Assembly, Cordelier and Jacobin Clubs whose leadership they acknowledged and in whose interest they demon-

26. Arch. Nat. F⁷ 4774⁷⁰ (Pétion), pièces 472–600.
27. See police agents' reports for these months in Arch. Nat. F⁷ 3688 (2); AFⁱᵛ 1470.
28. *L'Ancien Moniteur*, XXIV, 497–507; Arch. Nat. W 546–8.

strated, petitioned or took up arms. These were the objects, ideas and slogans of the liberal, democratic and republican *bourgeoisie* (according to the stage reached by the Revolution as it moved leftwards), which the most active elements among the Parisian *menu peuple*, from whom the great bulk of these insurgents and demonstrators were drawn, adopted as their own, because they appeared to correspond to their own interests in the fight to destroy the old régime and to safeguard the Republic. Yet they cannot be regarded as the particular demands of wage-earners, small shopkeepers and workshop masters as such. Therefore, while acknowledging, against the opinion of Taine and his followers, the part played by the political ideas of the leaders in stimulating mass revolutionary activity, we can accept this only as a partial explanation. It does little to explain such 'non-political' movements as the Réveillon Riots, the social unrest that led up to the march to Versailles or the overthrow of the Girondins, the invasion of the grocers' shops in 1792 and 1793, or even the essential character of the riots of Germinal and Prairial—and yet these movements were an intrinsic part of the Revolution and involved people drawn from the same social groups as those who stormed the Bastille, overthrew the monarchy and signed the Champ de Mars petition. Above all, it does not explain the almost continuous undertone of social unrest among the Parisian *menu peuple*, which characterised the whole period under review, and without which it would have been impossible for the contending political groups to mobilise the popular battalions on the great political *journées* themselves. To arrive at a more satisfactory explanation we shall have to find some more constant factor than the changing political slogans of the leaders, look more closely at the social demands of the participants themselves and test the validity of Professor Lefebvre's contention: 'L'intervention de la foule suppose des motifs particuliers'.[29]

Such an enquiry will reveal that the most constant motive

29. Lefebvre, *op. cit.*, pp. 141–2.

of popular insurrection during the Revolution, as in the eighteenth century as a whole, was the compelling need of the *menu peuple* for the provision of cheap and plentiful bread and other essentials, and the necessary administrative measures to ensure it. It is interesting to observe that this *motif particulier* of the Parisian *sans-culottes*, being at variance with the ideas of free trade held by all bourgeois groups, was apt to put a strain on their alliance with even the most advanced of the political leaders. Both Robespierre and Marat, for example, castigated the grocery rioters of February 1793 as being the dupes of Pitt and the counter-revolution.[30] The authorities and the revolutionary leaders themselves on occasion commented on this particular motive of the Parisian *menu peuple* and appreciated its significance for the Revolution. Thus, Barnave, one of the leaders of the constitutional monarchists, wrote significantly in describing the events of the 5–6 October at Versailles to his Dauphinois constituents:

Pendant que nous délibérions, l'impatience des Parisiens s'était portée à l'excès; la bourgeoisie et le peuple, les uns animés uniquement contre la dernière conduite du gouvernement et de l'aristocratie, et *les autres y mêlant l'intérêt du pain qui commençait à être rare*, se sont assemblés dans tous les districts.[31]

The theme of the shortage or high price of bread as a major cause of social disturbance in eighteenth-century France[32] has been given a new emphasis by Professor Labrousse's studies in price fluctuations and budgets in the years preceding the outbreak of the French Revolution.[33] Labrousse has shown the catastrophic effects on the poorer sections of the urban population in particular of the chronic shortage and high price of wheat during these years, reaching a

30. See Mathiez, *La Vie chère et le Mouvement social sous la Terreur*, pp. 153–7.

31. Arch. Nat. W 12, nos. 200–1 (*my italics*).

32. See, e.g., D. Mornet, *Les Origines intellectuelles de la Révolution Française* (Paris, 1933), pp. 444–5.

33. See p. 132, n. 7.

climax in the period 1785–9.[34] We can appreciate the better
the Parisian wage-earners' hostility to the old régime and
their willingness to join with the revolutionary *bourgeoisie* in
destroying it, when we learn, for example, that the proportion of his income that a Paris builder's labourer would
have to spend on bread in order to maintain his normal
consumption rose from about 50 per cent in August
1788 to the fantastic figure of 83 per cent in February
1789.[35]

It is, therefore, not surprising that the price and supply of
bread should emerge so clearly from contemporary documents as a constant source of popular disquiet during the
insurrectionary movements of the early years of the Revolution. There seems little doubt that the Réveillon Riots in the
Faubourg St. Antoine were the direct outcome of remarks
attributed to the manufacturers Réveillon and Henriot
concerning the desirability of lower wages,[36] and that the
bulk of the rioters were wage-earners, who felt particularly
concerned as a social group by the nature of these remarks.[37]
Yet this was not properly speaking a wages movement;
Réveillon had a good reputation as an employer and his
own workpeople were not involved. The primary cause of
the disturbance was, without much doubt, the prevailing
scarcity and high cost of bread. This is attested by the
author of the contemporary pamphlet, *Lettre au Roi*, who
wrote: 'C'est à la cherté du pain qu'on doit attribuer nos
derniers malheurs'.[38] The bookseller Hardy, too, noted in
his *Journal* on the second night of the disturbances that
the rioters, on dispersing, had announced 'que le lendemain
ils feraient grand tapage pour obtenir la diminution du

34. *La Crise de l'Economie Française*, pp. xlii–l.
35. My own calculation, based on figures given by Labrousse
(*Esquisse du Mouvement des Prix*, II, 597–608).
36. Arch. Nat. C 221, no. 160/146, fo. 58.
37. For the predominance of wage-earners among the Réveillon
rioters, see pp. 98–100 above.
38. Bib. Nat. Lb³⁹ 7157.

pain'.[39] Again, it was reported to the police that, during the riots, women had been seen standing at a street corner receiving bread looted from a baker's shop;[40] and De Crosne, lieutenant general of police, in reporting the course of the riots to the king, further stressed the rioters' concern at the high cost of bread: 'Quoique la sédition paraisse toujours dirigée contre le sr Réveillon, on demande vivement la diminution du prix du pain'.[41] The bread motive appears almost continuously as the main stimulus in the protracted popular movement which sprang up at the end of May, rose to a climax in the days of 12–14 July, again on 5–6 October, and did not visibly subside until the early days of November, when the first stage of the political revolution, which placed power firmly in the hands of the constitutional monarchists, was already long completed.

In the weeks preceding the July revolution, which culminated in the seizure of the Bastille, Hardy vividly illustrates in his *Journal* the popular mood and the authorities' constant fear of an outbreak on a larger and more violent scale than that which had occurred in the Faubourg St. Antoine at the end of April. On nine occasions during May, June and the early days of July he records the posting of special guards in the markets to quell bread riots.[42] On 13 June he noted that the police had forbidden a rise in the price of the 4-lb. loaf from 14½ to 15 *sols*, as requested by the bakers, for fear of social disturbance.[43] A few days before the political revolution itself, a crowd publicly burned the pamphlet, *Espérance du Peuple*, which suggested two prices for bread—3 *sols* and 5 *sols* per lb. 'Le but avait été mal saisi par la classe inférieure du peuple,' wrote Hardy.[44] During the July revolution the same theme constantly recurs. A

39. Hardy, *Journal*, VIII, 299.
40. Arch. Nat. Y 11033.
41. Arch. Nat. C 221, no. 160/146, fo. 48.
42. Hardy, *Journal*, VIII, 310, 312, 320, 332, 341, 344, 348, 351, 378.
43. *Ibid.*, p. 348.
44. *Ibid.*, p. 384.

major purpose of the organised attack on the St. Lazare
monastery in the early hours of 13 July was to remove grain
stored in its barns to the central markets, and among the
local raiders, who looted its rooms, the cry of 'allons chercher du pain' was heard;[45] while to the wage-earners,
shopkeepers and traders who burned down the customs
posts under orders from the political leaders at the Palais
Royal the issue was quite a simple one—to ensure cheaper
food and drink: as a locksmith seen smashing the furniture
in the office of the Chaillot *barrière* put it, 'nous allons boire
le vin à trois sols'.[46]

The popular insurrection of 5–6 October, which achieved
its political purpose of bringing the royal family to Paris,
was even more clearly connected with the provision of
bread for the hungry Parisian masses. Popular fury, which
had so well served the revolutionary *bourgeoisie* during the
July revolution, temporarily subsided after the murder of
Foulon and Berthier on 22 July, when the price of the 4-lb.
loaf was reduced from $14\frac{1}{2}$ to $13\frac{1}{2}$ *sols*.[47] But this calm was
short-lived. The bread crisis appeared in a new form. It was
no longer a problem of price—the price of the 4-lb. loaf
was further reduced to 12 *sols* on 8 August—but of supply.
Following the good harvest of 1789, the expected abundance
in the bakers' shops did not materialise[48] and the acute
shortage of bread which lasted until early November kept
the popular movement in a state of continuous animation.
So it is not surprising that the extremely rich, varied and
complex social movement that led up to the march of the
market-women, St. Antoine housewives, journeymen and
armed militia to Versailles on 5 October was continually
punctuated by popular acts of violence against bakers and
other alleged hoarders, by protest meetings in markets and
streets and by mass deputations of angry women to the

45. Arch. Nat. Z² 4691.
46. Arch. Nat. Z¹ª 886.
47. See Hardy, *Journal*, VIII, 401.
48. See J. M. Thompson, *The French Revolution* (Oxford, 1947), p.
93.

Hôtel de Ville.[49] There is little doubt that to a great mass of the marchers on 5 October the purpose of fetching the king to Paris was to ensure an adequate supply of bread. The adventurer, Fournier l'Américain, who played a leading part in this affair, when sent by Lafayette to the district of St. Eustache to fetch arms for the National Guard, appealed to the women to follow him in order 'to fetch bread' for their children.[50] Most historians have repeated the marchers' slogan, 'cherchons le boulanger, la boulangère et le petit mitron' as clearly revealing the immediate role that the *menu peuple* of Paris expected the royal family to fulfil; and Mathiez has pointed out that Maillard, in his address to the National Assembly at Versailles as spokesman of the market-women, freely borrowed from the contemporary pamphlet, *Quand aurons-nous du Pain?* in order to state their case for the necessary measures to ensure more bread for the people.[51]

The Champ de Mars demonstration, on the other hand, although widely supported by the *menu peuple* in a majority of the Paris Sections,[52] was, in many respects, the most purely 'political' of the great Parisian *journées*. By early November 1789 the protracted social movement of the first months of the Revolution had been brought to an end as the result of the energetic measures taken by the National Assembly to supply Paris with cheap and plentiful bread and to curb public disorder. The particular problems arising from the collapse of the *assignat* and wartime inflation were

49. For these events see, above all, Hardy's *Journal* for August–October 1789, especially VIII, pp. 417, 426, 429, 443–8, 458, 460, 478–80, 499–505.

50. 'Mémoires secrets de L. Fournier, Américain. . .' Arch. Nat. F⁷ 6504.

51. See Mathiez, 'Etude critique sur les journées des 5 et 6 octobre 1789', *Revue Historique*, LXIX (1899), 42–3.

52. An analysis of the police reports on those arrested in connection with this event shows that the 125 persons sent to the Force prison between 14 and 30 July (see 138, n. 25) resided in no fewer than forty of the forty-eight Parisian Sections (Arch. Préf. Pol., series Aa and Ab 324).

yet to come; so it happened that the Champ de Mars demonstration of July 1791 was the only one of the great Parisian *journées* which was not associated in any way with a popular demand for the control of bread or of any other commodity of prime necessity. The demonstration was, it is true, preceded by a considerable wages movement, involving many thousands of journeymen in a variety of trades, and by months of agitation among the unemployed, threatened with starvation by the closure of the Public Workshops. Yet these movements, though taken under the protective wing of the Cordelier Club and its affiliated bodies,[53] cannot be directly connected with the Champ de Mars demonstration itself, and the demands of these workers are not reflected in the cross-examination of the numerous wage-earners, shopkeepers and workshop masters arrested during this period in the various Paris Sections.[54] In this respect, the Champ de Mars affair appears to fall outside the general pattern of the insurrectionary movements which we are here examining. The particular demands of the common people are, in this case, rarely expressed in economic terms.[55] Their demands assume, rather, a political form—as witness the numerous insults hurled at the National Guard and the complaints against the National Assembly and city government by those arrested in the Sections in connection with the demonstration.[56] In this respect, the Champ de Mars affair and the

53. See A. Mathiez, *Le Club des Cordeliers pendant la Crise de Varennes et le Massacre du Champs de Mars* (Paris, 1910), pp. 21–31.

54. Arch. Préf. Pol., series Aa, nos. 56, 72, 76, 84, 85, 134, 137, 148, 153, 155, 157, 166, 167, 172, 173, 182, 198, 205, 206, 215, 219, 220, 224, 239.

55. There was, however, the lady who, when accused of insulting Lafayette and the National Guard, retorted that her accuser would not be so willing to assume their defence 'si le comparant avait autant de mal que les autres à gagner le pain qu'il mange' (Arch. Préf. Pol. Aa 153, fo. 7); or the kitchen-maid who, when asked to explain her hostility to the National Guard, said she found difficulty in buying bread owing to the bakers' lack of small change (Arch. Préf. Pol. Aa 85, fo. 117).

56. See p. 138, n. 25.

popular movement of the spring and summer of 1791 mark an important stage in the development of the Parisian *sans-culottes* as a force in the Revolution. With the split in the revolutionary *bourgeoisie* and the determined attempts of the democrats and the republicans of the Cordelier Club and the Fraternal Societies to win a firm basis of support among the people, they are beginning to play a more independent part: not only are they voicing the particular programme of the more radical section of the *bourgeoisie*, but they are beginning, however hesitatingly, to express their own social grievances in a political form.

With the spring of 1792 the Revolution entered upon a new stage which was to give a new intensity and a new direction to the whole social movement. The fall in the value of the *assignat* had already begun to react on the price of articles of daily consumption in the autumn of 1791, but it was above all the war upon which revolutionary France embarked in April 1792 that ushered in a long period of catastrophic inflation,[57] during which the attention of the *sans-culottes* was almost continuously riveted to the problems of prices, food shortage and the compelling need to force measures of control in the price and supply of the necessities of life on unwilling authorities. From the point of view of the social historian, the whole period is dominated by this preoccupation. It was only by degrees, however, that the Parisian *sans-culottes*, under the guidance of the Hébertists and, above all, of Jacques Roux and the *Enragés*,[58] found a programme of social demands which corresponded to their particular needs and which they were eventually to force for a brief period on the Jacobin Convention in the shape of the *Maximum Général*. In the first place their anger was directed against the grocers, as it had been previously against the bakers and millers, and found expression in the

57. See R. G. Hawtrey, 'The Collapse of the French Assignats', *The Economic Journal*, XXVIII (September 1918), 300–14; S. E. Harris, *The Assignats* (Cambridge, Mass., 1930).

58. See Mathiez, *La Vie chère et le Mouvement social sous la Terreur*, pp. 113 ff.

direct attempts of revolutionary crowds to compel pro-
vision-merchants (particularly the more substantial among
them) to sell their wares at the prices obtaining before the
Revolution. In this connection, the two movements of
January–February 1792 and of February 1793 are of particular interest. The first of these seems to have been mainly
concentrated in the north–central Sections (Beaubourg and
Gravilliers) and the Faubourgs St. Antoine and St. Marcel,
in which crowds of men and women (laundresses were to the
fore in the Section des Gobelins) forced grocers to distribute sugar at the pre-revolutionary price of 20–25 *sols* a lb.[59]
The archives of the Préfecture of Police contain the records
of fourteen persons arrested for playing a direct part in
these disturbances on 22–24 January and of five others for
'tumult, riot and sedition' in the Faubourg St. Marcel on
14–15 February.[60] That the prisoners, who were sent to the
Conciergerie, enjoyed considerable popular support is
evident from a petition in their favour submitted to the
Assembly by 150 residents of the Gobelins Section.[61]
The immediate cause of the disturbances ('la subite aug-
mentation du sucre', as the rioters in a grocer's shop in the
Faubourg St. Antoine told the police commissioner of the
Montreuil Section)[62] seems to have been temporarily removed, or its urgency obscured, by even more pressing
considerations, as the movement petered out and does not
appear to be reflected in any way in the political *journées* of
20 June and 10 August 1792, which overthrew the monarchy. Here, at least, we cannot trace any continuity in the
social movement; yet such a gap is rare.

The riots of 25 and 26 February 1793 were more widespread, of wider scope and of far greater political importance. Documents in the police archives show us that the
rioters on this occasion extended their operations to a large

59. Arch. Nat. D III 256⁴; Arch. Préf. Pol. Aa 173, fo. 39. See also
Mathiez, *op. cit.*, pp. 36–41.
60. Arch. Préf. Pol. Aa 9 (Arrestations), fos. 103–37, 200–4.
61. Arch. Nat. D III 256⁴.
62. Arch. Préf. Pol. Aa 173, fo. 39.

majority (if not to all) of the Parisian Sections.[63] Large crowds compelled grocers to sell not only sugar, but soap, tallow, coffee, soda and other wares at prices determined by the rioters themselves. This time we have the records of some fifty persons arrested, thirty-five of whom were sent to prison and a handful sentenced to long terms of forced labour.[64] Again, despite the disproportionate losses suffered by some grocers and the sinister accusations made against the rioters and their leaders in the Paris Commune and the Jacobin Club,[65] there was no question of a general pillage of foodshops or of creating a state of disorder favourable to the enemies of the Revolution: the documents (particularly the police reports on interviews with grocers and the cross-examination of prisoners) show that the sole purpose of the demonstration was to attempt to force the grocers to sell certain vital commodities at pre-revolutionary prices. On this occasion, however, the movement did not come to a stop after the mobilisation of the National Guard, the arrest of a number of rioters and the adoption of various administrative palliatives. In a general sense, it continued unabated past the enactment of the *Maximum Général* in September 1793, through Robespierre's Revolutionary Government and its fall in Thermidor, to the last outbreak of the *sans-culottes* in Prairial of the Year 3, and beyond. More immediately, it merged with the wider movement, guided by the Jacobin Club, which led to the revolution of

63. I have found reports of such riots in thirty-two of the forty-eight Sections—twenty-one of them in the reports of the police commissioners and the police registers of the Sections (Arch. Préf. Pol., series Aa); 9 others in the various prison registers (Arch. Préf. Pol., series Ab, nos. 132, 319, 325); a further two in the reports sent in to the *Bureau de Surveillance de la Police* (Arch. Nat. AF^{iv} 1470). This is not a complete record, as there are considerable gaps in the commissioners' reports, a great many of which were destroyed by fire in 1871—in the case of eighteen Sections there are no surviving reports for the month of February 1793.

64. Arch. Nat. AA 47, doss. 1387, fo. 54; Arch. Préf. Pol. Aa 11 (Arrestations), fos. 548–52; see, also, police commissioners' reports in a dozen Sections (Arch. Préf. Pol., series Aa).

65. See Mathiez, *op. cit.*, pp. 153–7.

May–June 1793 and the overthrow of the Girondins, by this time identified, in the eyes of the more active elements in the Sections at least, with the hated *accapareurs*. It is not possible to attempt here to analyse the daily reports of the police and the National Guard in April and May of that year,[66] but they establish clearly enough that the next popular insurrection was already anticipated by the authorities in early March, and that, in their opinion, the main motive force behind it was popular concern at the continuous rise in food prices. [It cannot be denied, of course, that, during the May–June revolution itself, a further motive may have played a considerable part in helping to maintain thousands of *sans-culottes* under arms—the promise of the Central Revolutionary Committee to compensate those losing work as the result of their active participation with a payment of 40 *sols* for each day spent under arms.[67] But this was only a last-minute measure and can hardly be regarded as a major motive.]

The expulsion of the Girondins, though transferring power to the Mountain, did nothing immediately to allay public unrest. The reports sent to the *Bureau de Surveillance de la Police* in June are couched in almost identical terms with those in April or May.[68] The shortage of bread in bakers' shops had again begun to arouse concern at the end of March, and by the end of August bread queues and bread riots had become once more a familiar feature of Parisian life.[69] This was the immediate background to the *journées* of 4 and 5 September 1793, directed by the 'Hébertist' Commune under Chaumette. It was under their stimulus that the Convention decided at last to decree the *Maximum Général* and to set on foot the long-delayed *Armée Révolutionnaire* which, as an instrument of the Terror, was intended to ensure the provision of adequate supplies of grain and meat

66. Arch. Nat. F⁷ 3688 (2); AF^Iv 1470; F^Ie III, Seine, 27.
67. Arch. Nat. BB³ 80, doss. 16.
68. Arch. Nat. AF^Iv 1470.
69. Arch. Nat. F⁷ 3688 (2).

to Paris from the surrounding countryside.[70] Under such consistent popular pressure the Convention and the Committee of Public Safety managed, by a policy of controls, to halt inflation and to arrest for several months the fall in the value of the *assignat*.[71] Yet the demands of a revolutionary war and the hostility of the farmers, who tended to hoard their produce in anticipation of better times or failed to produce at all for fear of requisition, kept food in short supply. Throughout this period the reports of the agents of the Ministry of the Interior and others[72] reveal the constant strain that these hardships were imposing on the alliance between the Committee of Public Safety and the Parisian *sans-culottes*. There is little doubt that this dissatisfaction, together with the particular grievance of the wage-earners at the authorities' determined efforts to maintain the *Maximum* on wages as well as that on prices,[73] contributed to the failure of the *sans-culottes* to mobilise in support of Robespierre on 9–10 Thermidor of the Year 2.

The Parisian wage-earners, artisans and shopkeepers certainly lived to regret the fall of Robespierre. The Thermidorians lost little time in destroying the controls created by their predecessors, inflation ran riot[74] and the prices of essential goods soared. The *sans-culottes* took some time to react: they raised no protest at the abolition of their own creation, the *Maximum Général*, in December—partly through indifference and partly because Thermidor had left them confused and leaderless.[75] A police report of 30

70. Arch. Nat. F⁷ 3688 (3); AF^iv 1470; *L'Ancien Moniteur*, XVII. 73–4; E. Soreau, 'Les ouvriers aux journées des 4 et 5 septembre 1793', *Ann. Hist. Rév. Franç.*, XIV (1937), 436–47.

71. See S. E. Harris, *op. cit.*

72. See P. Caron, *Paris pendant la Terreur*, 4 vols. (Paris, 1910–14, 1943, 1949), *passim*; A. Schmidt, *Tableaux de la Révolution Française*, 3 vols. (Leipzig, 1868–71), *passim*; Arch. Préf. Pol. Aa 70, 94, 139, 198, 201, 240.

73. On this question see, particularly, Mathiez, *La Vie chère*, pp. 581–606.

74. See R. G. Hawtrey, *op. cit.*

75. See G. Lefebvre, *Les Thermidoriens* (Paris, 1946), pp. 35–40.

November 1794, however, illustrates the prevailing mood of the people and their growing hostility towards the Thermidorians:

Les plaintes et les murmures se font toujours entendre. La lenteur des distributions du pain, le manque de farine, la cherté sur les places publiques et les marchés de ce pain, le bois, le vin, le charbon, les légumes, les pommes de terre, dont le prix augmente tous les jours d'une manière effrayante, jettent le peuple dans un état de douleur et d'affaissement aisé à concevoir.

Rappelé à lui par le sentiment de ses douleurs et de sa misère profonde, il ne fait entendre que des malédictions contre le gouvernement, mais loin de soupirer après le retour de la Royauté, il prête volontiers l'oreille aux espérances qu'on peut lui donner de la cessation de ce temps de misère et de vraie calamité.[76]

The reports of the local police commissioners and of the Comité de Sûreté Générale on those arrested for expressing opposition to the Convention and its leaders during the coming months show that various elements contributed to the widespread social movement that began around the turn of the year and broke out in violent disorders on 12 Germinal and 1–4 Prairial of the Year 3 (1 April and 20–23 May 1795). The rising cost of living, the closing of the Parisian *ateliers d'armes*, the persecution of Jacobins, the extravagance of rich speculators and war-profiteers, the arrogance of the middle class youth (or *muscadins*)—all aroused the bitter class hostility of the *sans-culottes*[77] and played their part in these explosions; but, above all, it was the extreme shortage of bread—at times reduced to a daily ration of 3 or 4 ounces[78]—that gave this movement coherence and continuity. Thus, on 28 January 1795, the police were told by a pay-clerk of the Indivisibilité Section that

76. Arch. Nat. F⁷ 3688 (4).
77. Most of these factors appear in the cross-examination of J. L. Degré, journeyman joiner and arms worker, before the *Comité de Sûreté Générale on* 9–11 February 1795 (Arch. Nat. F⁷ 4665, doss. 5).
78. See Arch. Préf. Pol. Aa 78, fos. 5–6; Aa 241, fo. 99; Arch. Nat. F⁷ 4734, doss. 1; Arch. Nat. W 547 (Pennan).

the arms workers were only waiting for the price of bread to rise to 20 *sols* per lb. in order to attack the Convention and exterminate the members of the reconstituted *comités révolutionnaires*.[79] On 11 February a discharged arms-worker, arrested for having caused a disturbance outside the Convention, admitted that he had criticised the Convention for not reducing the price of bread.[80] On 18 March a waiter was accused of saying, 'that it was terrible to see Frenchmen reduced to a ration of 1 lb. of bread a day and to eating pota-toes, which were only fit for pigs'.[81] On 21 March there was a fight between workers and *muscadins* near the Porte St. Denis,[82] and on the following day two gentlemen charged three arms-workers with insulting them in the Palais Royal.[83] On 25 March a jeweller of the Rue St. Martin was accused of threatening the Convention and of saying that 'it was not easy to live on a half-lb. of bread'.[84] Two days later (7 Germinal) a more serious movement had developed; on that day women demonstrated for more bread both inside and outside the Convention[85] and there were bread riots in the Gravilliers and Temple Sections, involving wage-earners and housewives.[86] On the following morning eight persons were arrested in the Rue du Temple for attempting to form a procession to the Convention.[87] The movement was already assuming an insurrectionary character: on 31 March a deputation of the Quinze-Vingts Section reminded the Convention that, on occasion, insurrection was a sacred duty;[88] while citizens of the Droits de l'Homme

79. Arch. Nat. F⁷ 3688 (4).
80. Arch. Nat. F⁷ 4665, doss. 5.
81. Arch. Nat. F⁷ 4667, doss. 4.
82. Arch. Préf. Pol. Aa 50, fo. 138.
83. Arch. Nat. F⁷ 4654, doss. 2.
84. Arch. Préf. Pol. Aa 50, fo. 161.
85. Arch. Nat. F⁷ 4693, doss. 1; *L'Ancien Moniteur*, XXIV, 79.
86. Arch. Préf. Pol. Aa 241, fo. 91; Aa 50, fos. 160–5; Arch. Nat. F⁷ 4678, doss. 1.
87. Arch. Préf. Pol. Aa 241, fos. 92–3.
88. *L'Ancien Moniteur*, XXIV, 106.

Section, having received no flour, forced the president of their General Assembly to convene a mass meeting to discuss the food situation and to send a petition to the Convention. Attempts by the police to prevent the meeting from being held were greeted with a unanimous cry of: 'Du pain! Nous voulons du pain!'[89] The following day the Convention was besieged by large crowds of men and women, demanding that adequate measures be taken to ensure an adequate supply of bread to the capital,[90] while disturbances took place in various parts of the city.[91] This was the *journée* of 12 Germinal (1 April).

On 2 April the National Convention decreed that the bread ration, where insufficient, should be supplemented with rice and biscuit, and that priority should be given in their distribution to 'les ouvriers, artisans et indigents'.[92] But this measure did nothing to solve the problem of supplies or to check the popular movement. The same day meetings were being held outside bakers' shops in the Droits de L'Homme Section.[93] On 8 April a porcelain-painter was arrested at the Porte St. Denis for attacking the Convention before a large crowd and complaining of the insufficiency and poor quality of bread.[94] Ten days later a domestic servant was arrested in the Pont Neuf Section, charged with saying, 'Il y a huit mois que nous avions du pain; aujourd'hui nous n'en avons plus, nous sommes dans l'esclavage';[95] while one of two tradesmen arrested in the Arsenal Section on the next day for seditious talk explained his conduct by saying 'qu'il croyait que c'était pour cause de pain'.[96] After a relative lull, on 20 May (1st Prairial) there was a new revolutionary outbreak, this time on a far bigger

89. Arch. Préf. Pol. Aa 136, fo. 193.

90. *L'Ancien Moniteur*, XXIV, 109–14.

91. Arch. Préf. Pol. Aa 80, fo. 178; Aa 241, fos. 99–102; Aa 251, fos. 125–9.

92. *Procès-Verbaux de la Convention Nationale*, LVII, 148.

93. Arch. Préf. Pol. Aa 136, fo. 194.

94. Arch. Préf. Pol. Aa 80, fos. 179–81.

95. Arch. Préf. Pol. Aa 216, fos. 394–7.

96. Arch. Préf. Pol. Aa 71, fos. 28–33.

scale. Armed crowds, among whom the battalions of the Faubourg St. Antoine were much in evidence, invaded the Convention and forced the reluctant majority to adopt a number of decrees, inspired by the Jacobin minority. The deputy Ferraud was struck down and decapitated.[97] On the next day the Faubourg St. Antoine was in open revolt—its citizens were under arms and its shops and workshops closed.[98] The insurrection was only crushed on the fourth day after the fullest mobilisation of the loyal battalions of the western districts, the rounding up of Jacobin suspects in every Section (over 100 from 34 of the 48 Sections were tried by a military tribunal, on the charge of direct complicity in the affair) and the military occupation and disarming of the Faubourg St. Antoine.[99] Thus ended the last great *journée* of the Revolution in Paris. 'Pour la première fois depuis 1789,' writes Lefebvre, 'le gouvernement avait réprimé de haute lutte l'insurrection populaire et brisé ainsi le ressort de la Révolution.'[100]

This crushing defeat of the Parisian *sans-culottes* in the 'days' of the 1st–4th Prairial is a highly important landmark in the history of the Revolution. Here, however, I am only concerned to show, briefly, its connection with the protracted social movement of the Parisian *menu peuple* which, in its latest phase, had developed against the Thermidorian Convention as a result of the calamitous rise in prices and the shortage of the necessities of life, particularly of bread. This connection is not hard to establish. The most common charge against those arrested for taking part in these events was to have worn in their caps a slogan linking the two main demands of the insurrection: 'Du Pain et la Constitution de 1793.'[101] Among the women marchers to the Convention on the 1st Prairial were armed men of the Faubourg St. Antoine, wearing in their caps the more

97. *L'Ancien Moniteur*, XXIV, 497–507.
98. See, e.g., Arch. Préf. Pol. Aa 136, fos. 205–6.
99. *L'Ancien Moniteur*, *loc. cit.*
100. G. Lefebvre, *op. cit.*, p. 124.
101. Arch. Nat. W 546–8 (Commission Militaire).

specific insignia, 'du pain ou la mort'.[102] In the Finistère and Luxembourg Sections the bread ration that morning had been reduced to 2 ounces per head;[103] in both Sections, as well as in the Jardin des Plantes,[104] the *Comité Civil* had been besieged by angry citizens, demanding that it should head a deputation to the Convention to obtain more bread. A characteristic feature of the disorders was the prevalence of women among the rioters in the streets and in the Convention, a sure indication that the 'bread-and-butter' issue was to the fore. In the Faubourg St. Antoine women passers-by were compelled to join the main bodies of marchers on 1st Prairial in a manner reminiscent of the women's march to Versailles in October 1789.[105] Among the persons tried by the military tribunal were four women found guilty of rioting at bakers' shops in the Tuileries Section and of forcing women to march with them to the Convention.[106] A journeyman joiner of the Faubourg St. Denis claimed that he had been called out from work by a crowd of forty to fifty women;[107] while a merchant of the Arsenal Section, presumably scandalised by the determination of the women to make their voice heard, indignantly observed to by-standers, 'que ce n'était pas aux femmes de faire des lois'.[108]

Another feature of this whole period, which emerges both in the insurrection of Prairial itself and in the course of the continuous social movement which precedes it, is the open hostility of the *sans-culottes* to the possessing classes—to merchants, *muscadins*, or simply to 'les riches' or 'les gens bien mis'. An arms worker arrested outside the Convention on 9 February admitted referring to a deputation of respectable citizens from the western Sections as 'blood-suckers, scoundrels and merchants'.[109] On 22 March

---

102. Arch. Nat. AF^{II} 50, plaq. 385, pièce 10.
103. Arch. Nat. W 547 (Rouillère, Pennan).
104. Arch. Nat. W 546 (Paradis).
105. Arch. Nat. AF^{II} 50, plaq. 385, pièce 10.
106. Arch. Nat. W 546 (Legrand, etc.).
107. Arch. Nat. W 546 (Bondy).
108. Arch. Nat. W 548 (Thévenin).
109. Arch. Nat. F^7 4665, doss. 5.

a paper-worker was pounced upon and handed over to the militia for shouting on the Pont Neuf: 'Tous les riches sont des coquins; il y en a à Paris un million à punir!'[110] Among those arrested by their Sections in the round-up of suspected Jacobins and insurgents after the 'days' of Prairial, were a wig-maker and a watchmaker, accused of shouting in the Rue Honoré: 'Ces sacrés foutus marchands, ces bougres ... ';[111] and a water-carrier 'pour avoir vitupéré contre les gens bien mis';[112] while a journeyman locksmith was so convinced of the class-bias of the Thermidorian Convention that he averred, 'que c'était par haine du peuple qu'on ne donnait pas 2 livres de pain par jour'.[113] Such expressions of bitter hostility recall the atmosphere of subdued violence and antagonism between the *menu peuple* and the propertied classes in the weeks preceding the Champ de Mars affair nearly four years earlier. This time, however, the defeat of the *sans-culottes* was final; they were not to rise again for thirty-five years.

It will be observed that no attempt has been made hitherto to distinguish between the particular aims of the wage-earners in the insurrectionary movements that we have been considering and those of other sections of the *menu peuple*. It has been assumed, in the course of our presentation, that the ordinary people of Paris were bound together by one common aim—to ensure adequate supplies of food at a steady and reasonable price. Generally speaking, this assumption is a valid one. Yet it would be surprising if the wage-earners had not, on occasion at least, shown a tendency to press with greater insistence for their own particular demand for higher wages, and if this had not, in one way or another, influenced their participation in the insurrectionary movements of the period. Strikes and wages movements were, indeed, not uncommon in Paris during the Revolution. In June 1789, on the eve of the

110. Arch. Préf. Pol. Aa 216, fo. 389.
111. Arch. Préf. Pol. Aa 153, fos. 264–7.
112. Arch. Nat. F⁷ 4695, doss. 1.
113. Arch. Nat. F⁷ 4728, doss. 1.

July revolution, there was a big strike of journeymen hatters, whose object appears to have been to attempt to compel all hatters to join one single journeymen's association, known as 'les Bons Enfants'.[114] In August and September of the same year, in the middle of the agitation leading up to the march to Versailles, journeymen bakers, tailors, cobblers and domestic servents all demonstrated and petitioned in support of claims for higher wages, employment or improved working conditions.[115] In the spring and autumn of 1791 there developed a far broader wages movement, involving carpenters, printers, farriers and others; the Constituent Assembly, faced with what they believed to be a *coalition générale* of the trades, enacted the famous *Loi Le Chapelier*, which was to make trade unions illegal for nearly a hundred years.[116] The carpenters were in action once more on the eve of the armed assault on the Tuileries: we read of a strike of building workers in the Faubourg St. Antoine on 3 August 1792.[117] There seems, again, to have been considerable labour unrest in the period of steeply rising prices which led to the revolutionary overthrow of the Girondins on 2 June 1793: on 5 March police agents report a projected meeting of paviors, masons and laundrymen to demand a reduction in price 'des denrées qui leur sont le plus nécessaires';[118] on 9 May the journeymen stonemasons and carpenters were claiming higher wages in view of the rising cost of living;[119] and in April and May the journeymen bakers in various Sections were said to be organising for more pay.[120] During the 'Hébertist' insurrection of 4 September of that year the masons and other building workers are again putting

114. Arch. Nat. Y 13016 (12 June 1789).
115. See Grace M. Jaffé, *Le Mouvement ouvrier à Paris pendant la Révolution Française (1789–1791)*, pp. 65–73; Hardy's *Journal*, VIII, 434–9, 455.
116. Jaffé, *op. cit.*, part II.
117. Arch. Préf. Pol. Aa 219, fo. 30.
118. Arch. Nat. AF^{iv} 1470.
119. *Ibid.*
120. Arch. Préf. Pol. Aa 59, fo. 234; Arch. Nat. AF^{iv} 1470.

forward claims, this time for more bread and higher wages.[121]

It was, however, during the period of relatively stable prices, when inflation had been temporarily halted and the revolutionary government of Robespierre was taking energetic measures to impose the *Maximum Général*, that the authorities were faced with the most determined efforts of the wage-earners to improve their standards by raising wages. The shortage of labour, due to the heavy calls of the war and of the arms industry, created conditions particularly favourable for such demands. The Committee of Public Safety, however, was determined to keep wages under control and not to allow them to rise appreciably above a level 50 per cent higher than the rates prevailing in June 1790 (as provided by the law of the *Maximum*). This determination appears in the rejection of the claims of the tobacco-workers, potters, carpenters, water-carriers, printers and riverside workers.[122] Most protracted and stubborn was the agitation of the workers in the *ateliers d'armes*, who, being employees of the state, found their demands more sternly resisted than those in private employment.[123] There is little doubt, as has been suggested above, that this estrangement from the Jacobin government of a considerable proportion of the wage-earning population of Paris contributed substantially to the ease with which Robespierre was overthrown in Thermidor.[124] This period, however, is exceptional. At no other critical stage of the Revolution did an overriding concern with wages on the part of the wage-earners disrupt their alliance with the small shopkeepers and workshop masters and thus vitally affect the relation of

121. *L'Ancien Moniteur*, XVII, 73–4.

122. See A. Ording, *Le Bureau de Police du Comité de Salut Public* (Oslo, 1930), pp. 76–80; A. Mathiez, *La Vie chère et le Mouvement social sous la Terreur*, chap. 10.

123. Mathiez, *loc. cit.*; C. Richard, *Le Comité de Salut Public et les Fabrications de Guerre sous la Terreur* (Paris, 1922), pp. 685–725.

124. There was, in fact, a mass meeting outside the Hôtel de Ville to protest against the most recent wage-rates at 4 p.m. on 9 Thermidor itself (Arch. Nat. AF 47, plaq. 366; AF 48, plaq. 374).

political forces or the outcome of a social or insurrectionary movement of the Parisian *sans-culottes*. This is even true of the period preceding the Champ de Mars petition, when the journeymen of many trades were clearly more concerned with their own particular demand for higher wages even than with the price or supply of bread. It seems probable that it was the measure of support which the Cordelier Club gave to the striking carpenters and to the unemployed[125] which prevented the wage-earners at this time from being divided from the rest of the *menu peuple*, among whom the democratic *bourgeoisie* were carrying on such determined agitation. In the Réveillon affair, it is true, the rioting journeymen were not joined by the bulk of the *sans-culottes*; but the rioters enjoyed considerable local support[126] and, anyway, as we have seen, this was not, properly speaking, a wages movement. It might, of course, be claimed that a demand for higher wages, arising in a period of social unrest—as in the weeks leading up to the fall of the Bastille, to the march to Versailles, the Champ de Mars demonstration and the overthrow of the Girondins—was bound in itself to contribute to the volume of popular discontent and, therefore, directly or indirectly, to help to swell the numbers of demonstrators or insurgents on the great political *journées*. It may well have been so at the Champ de Mars or in the revolution of May–June 1793, but the point should not be pressed too far. In the social and economic conditions of the time, when a small diminution in the supply or increase in the price of bread could have drastic consequences for wage-earners and small urban property owners alike, when there was as yet no factory working class or national trade union movement, even the wage-earners tended to think in terms of cheaper and more plentiful food rather than of higher wages. It is, therefore, no coincidence that the two most considerable wages

125. See A. Mathiez, *Le Club des Cordeliers*, pp. 30–1.

126. According to the documents, there were very few denunciations, and local pressure forced the authorities to release the bulk of the prisoners after a few weeks' detention (Arch. Nat. BB[16] 702).

movements of the Revolution in Paris should have occurred during periods of relative stabilisation of food prices—in April–June 1791 and January–July 1794—and that the broad wages movement that contributed to Robespierre's fall in Thermidor appears to have collapsed during the months of riotous inflation that followed the repeal of the *Maximum Général*.[127] On balance, it may be claimed that the particular demands of the wage-earners—for higher wages and better working conditions—were comparatively unimportant as a stimulus to revolutionary activity and that the wage-earners were more inclined to be drawn into participation in these events by the need for cheap and plentiful bread, a motive which they shared with the *menu peuple* as a whole.

It remains to ask how far the aim which I set myself at the beginning of this study can be said to have been fulfilled. Does a common pattern emerge, underlying the extremely varied insurrectionary movements under review and helping to explain the almost continuous social ferment of the revolutionary period and the repeated willingness of the Parisian *sans-culottes* to participate in large numbers in these events? The evidence suggests that such a pattern does exist, but that it must be sought rather in the particular concern of the *menu peuple* as a whole with the provision of cheap and plentiful food than in the general political ideas that guided the Revolution or in the varying political aims of the leaders.

This does not signify, of course, that the mass of the participants in the events we have examined were prompted by economic motives alone or that they were hostile or indifferent to the political ideas or calls to action which emanated from the revolutionary leaders. On the contrary, the *sans-culottes* wholeheartedly embraced these ideas and identified themselves more closely with the political aims of

127. It should be noted, however, that the agitation in the Parisian *ateliers d'armes*—in which the issue of wages played an important part—continued almost until their closure early in the new year of 1795 (see Mathiez, *La Réaction Thermidorienne* (Paris, 1929), p. 199).

the radical *bourgeoisie* as the Revolution moved leftwards. Without their active support there could have been no overthrow of the monarchy, no *levée en masse* to repel the invader, no revolutionary war or Committee of Public Safety. Yet these political ideas do not by themselves explain the continuity of the popular movement—more continuous than the revolutionary *journées* themselves and often preparing the way for them; even less do they explain the outbreaks of independent revolutionary activity by the *menu peuple* itself, going beyond or running counter to the interests of their bourgeois allies and, therefore, castigated by them as 'counter-revolutionary'. We have seen such examples of independent activity in the blind fury of the Réveillon rioters and in the more constructive attempts of Parisians to impose a form of popular price control in the grocery riots of 1792 and 1793. Such movements are not isolated episodes, as they have sometimes been regarded, but part and parcel of the general history of the Revolution. Indeed, the general social unrest to which they bear witness constitutes the vital link between the successive political *journées*, organised and inspired by the revolutionary leaders. In a sense it may even be said that this was the raw material of which the Revolution, at least in Paris, was made.

Prices, Wages and Popular Movements in Paris during the French Revolution

The work of Labrousse on the movements of prices and wages in eighteenth-century France[1] has thrown a fresh light on the causes of the French Revolution and on the interests, motives and antipathies of the various social groups that participated in it.[2] His work, however, stopped short at 1789 and neither he nor any of his disciples has as yet extended the method used in the *Esquisse des Prix* and *La Crise de l'Economie Française* to the period of the Revolution itself. The present short study lays no claim to bridge this gap. It has the more modest object of examining, in necessarily general terms, the movements of prices and wages in Paris during the revolutionary years, 1789–95, and of relating these to the popular movements of the period. The choice of Paris for such a study has a certain value because of its pre-eminent role in events; but it has, also, the disadvantage of compelling one to rely on fragmentary evidence, as much of the relevant meterial was destroyed by fire during the civil war of 1871.[3] Nevertheless, the various enquiries concerning prices and wages carried out by the Convention and the Committee of

From *Economic History Review*, VI, no. 3 (1954), 246–67.

1. C.-E. Labrousse, *Esquisse du Mouvement des Prix et des Revenus en France au XVIIIe Siècle* 2 vols. (Paris, 1933); *La Crise de l'Économie française à la Fin de l'ancien Régime et au Début de la Révolution* (Paris, 1943).

2. See G. Lefebvre, 'Le mouvement des prix et les origines de la Révolution française', *Annales Historiques de la Révolution Française*, XIV (1937), 289–329.

3. Thus, for example, in the series F[20] (Statistique) in the Archives Nationales, extensively used by Labrousse, there are no materials for Paris.

Public Safety between 1793 and 1795, summarised by L. Biollay,[4] have provided a certain amount of material for 1790 and 1793. For the rest, it has been necessary to draw on excerpts from a variety of sources in the Parisian archives; on the work of d'Avenel[5] and of Bienaymé, the latter based on the account-sheets of the Collège St. Louis-le-Grand and of the Hôtel-Dieu;[6] and, more extensively, on the reports of police agents for the years 1793–5, published by Caron and Aulard.[7]

For the purpose of this article, it will be convenient to divide the revolutionary period[8] into five parts, each characterised by its own distinctive features, and to trace within each of these periods the movements of prices and wages and of social unrest.

4. The Departments' replies to these enquiries are to be found in the Archives Nationales, series F[12], nos. 1546–7 (*Enquête de juin 1793*), 1544 (*Enquête de l'an 2*), 1546 (*Enquête de l'an 3*). It was on the basis of these returns and of the *maximum des salaires*, published by the Paris Commune on 23 July 1794 (Arch. Nat. AD XI/75), that Biollay compiled his useful work, *Les Prix en 1790* (Paris, 1886), on which I have largely relied for prices and wages in 1790 in the course of the present study.

5. G. d'Avenel, *Histoire Économique de la Propriété, des Salaires, des Denrées et des Prix depuis 1200 jusqu'à 1800*, 8 vols. (Paris, 1898).

6. G. Bienaymé, 'Le coût de la vie à Paris à diverses époques', *Journal de la Société de Statistique de Paris*, XXXVI (1895), 57–68, 355–60; XXXVII (1896), 375–90; XXXVIII (1897), 83–90; XXXIX (1898), 369–82; XL (1899), 366–85; XLII (1901), 293–310; XLIII (1902), 87–103.

7. P. Caron, *Paris pendant la Terreur. Rapports des agents secrets du Ministère de l'Intérieur*, 3 vols. (Paris, 1910, 1914, 1944); A. Aulard, *Paris pendant la Réaction Thermidorienne et sous le Directoire*, 5 vols. (Paris, 1898).

8. The date selected for the closure of the revolutionary period is bound to reflect the particular concern of the historian. As I am here concerned, not with the political events of the Revolution in themselves nor with a purely statistical treatment of prices and wages, but rather with the latter in relation to popular movements, it is perhaps permissible to end this study at the point where the last of these popular movements takes place—i.e. in Prairial of the year 3 (May 1795), when the Parisian *sans-culottes* were finally and decisively defeated.

1. The year 1789

In the first place, we must note the importance that Labrousse ascribes to bread as an article of popular consumption in the eighteenth century. According to his calculations, over the whole period 1726–91, the wage-earner's expenditure on bread averaged 50 per cent of his budget; in the acute years of economic crises, 1788–9, it rose to an average of 58 per cent; in the months of famine and top-level prices of 1789, it soared to the fantastic figure of 88 per cent.[9] From this follows the constant popular concern for the price and supply of bread.[10] We shall see that, later in the Revolution, because of the particular measures taken by the National Assembly and the city authorities,[11] bread was to cease in Paris to loom so large as a matter of constant concern and as an issue of social unrest. But in the year 1789, Paris was, in this respect, no different from the rest of the country and the price of bread dominated all other considerations in the popular mind: it is, in fact, no mere coincidence (as Lefebvre and Labrousse have both pointed out) that the Bastille should have fallen on the very day that the price of grain throughout France reached its cyclical peak.[12] It is, therefore, proposed, in considering the year 1789, to

9. Labrousse, *Esquisse du Mouvement des Prix*, II, 597–608.

10. Labrousse calculates that, for the period 1726–91 as a whole, whereas the average wage-earner spent 50 per cent of his budget on bread, he spent 16 per cent on vegetables, fats and wine; 15 per cent on clothing; 5 per cent on fuel; 1 per cent on lighting (Lefebvre, *op. cit.*, p. 315).

11. These measures were not wholly a product of the Revolution. According to Bailly, 18,000 *livres* per day were being spent in June 1789 in order to prevent the price of bread from rising above the already dangerously high level of 14½ *sous* for the 4-lb. loaf (*Mémoires de Bailly*, (Paris, 1821), II, 96). For further details, see S. E. Harris, *The Assignats* (Harvard Univ. Press, 1930), pp. 133–4. I have drawn extensively from Harris's book in this study.

12. Lefebvre, *op. cit.* p. 324.

examine first of all the fluctuations in the price of bread.[13]

The price of a 4-lb. loaf of bread, which had been 9 *sous*[14] in August 1788, had risen by stages to 14½ *sous* in February 1789. It remained at this phenomenally high level until 22 July, when it was reduced to 13½ *sous*; on 8 August it was further reduced to 12 *sous* and remained at this figure until the end of the year.[15] From August till early November, owing to a dearth of flour, it was in almost constant short supply and, during this period, it was the scarcity and poor quality of bread, rather than its price, that were the constant target of popular discontent.[16] Sharp upward movements in the price of flour and bread had been a frequent feature of eighteenth-century life,[17] but these 'famine' periods had usually been of short duration. What was new about the situation revealed in these figures was its protracted nature. The appalling consequences that they entailed for the bulk of the Parisian population will be the

13. It will be observed that no attempt is made in this study to measure the earnings of any other section of the Parisian *menu peuple* than the wage-earners, who, with their families, accounted perhaps for one-half the total population (cf. F. Braesch, 'Un essai de statistique de la population ouvrière de Paris vers 1791', *La Révolution Française*, LXVII (July–Dec. 1902), 289–321). Labrousse has pointed out that all small income-earners of town and countryside were similarly affected by the economic crisis that ushered in the Revolution (*La Crise de l' Economie Française*, pp. xliv–xlv); and the close identity of interest of the various sections of the Parisian *menu peuple*—wage-earners, independent craftsmen, small shopkeepers and workshop masters— in the face of food prices and the large producer may perhaps be taken for granted.

14. It should be noted that 1 *livre* = 20 *sous* and 1 *sou* = 12 *deniers*.

15. Prices of bread are taken from *Observations d'un citoyen habitant de Paris et membre du Tiers* (Bibliothèque Nationale Le[24] 256) and from Hardy's MS. Journal, *Mes Loisirs, ou Journal d'événements tels qu'ils parviennent à ma connoissance* (Bib. Nat., fonds français, 6680–7), VIII, 408, 426.

16. Hardy, *Journal*, VIII, 420 *et seq*.

17. Cf. Labrousse, *op. cit.*, Introduction; cf. also constant references in the *Journal et Mémoires du Comte d'Argenson* and the *Journal* of E. J. F. Barbier (for the period 1725–59).

better realised when they are seen in relation to the wages of typical groups of wage-earners.

The following table, in which we have assumed a normal daily purchase of a 4-lb. loaf by the average employed male worker for himself and family,[18] illustrates the percentage of actual daily income spent on bread by selected groups of workers at the various prices given above:

TABLE 1 Percentage of income spent on bread by Parisian workers in 1789

Occupation	Daily wage *	'Effective' daily earnings †	Expenditure on bread as percentage of income			
			At 9s.	At 14½s.	At 13½ s.	At 12 s.
Labourer in Réveillon's factory	25 s.‡	15 s.	60	97	90	80
Builder's labourer	30 s.	18 s.	50	80	75	67
Journeyman mason	40 s.	24 s.	37	60	56	50
Journeyman lock-smith, carpenter, etc.	50 s.	30 s.	30	48	45	40
Sculptor, goldsmith	100 s.	60 s.	15	24	22½	20

* Wages given here, unless otherwise stated, are from Biollay, *op. cit.* pp. 14–79. Nearly all these, for lack of other evidence, are for 1790. What material there is for 1789 suggests, however, that the differences between the two years are very slight. A notable exception is the case of the journeymen tailors who, in August 1789, obtained an increase of 10 *sous* per day by concerted action (Hardy, *Journal*, VIII, 438–9).

† In computing 'effective' earnings, allowance has been made for the numerous unpaid Feast Days of the *ancien régime*. Here these are assumed to number 111 per year (G. M. Jaffé, *Le Mouvement Ouvrier à Paris pendant la Révolution Française* (Paris, 1927), pp. 26–7). Further allowance should also be made for sickness.

‡ *Exposé justificatif pour le sieur Réveillon, Entrepreneur de la Manufacture Royale des Pap. peints, F. St. Ant.*, Bib. Nat. Lb³⁹ 1618.

18. A. Tuetey estimates for the same period a daily consumption of 6 lb. for a worker with wife and three children (*L'Assistance Publique à Paris pendant la Révolution*, 4 vols. (Paris, 1895–7), I, cxxvi). In March

It will be seen that, at the high price prevailing in the summer months, even a comparatively highly-paid journeyman, such as a locksmith, was spending little short of half his actual income on bread; only the highly skilled journeymen in luxury trades were able to maintain a reasonable balance for other essentials. These figures cannot, of course, all be taken at their face value: it is not possible to imagine, for example, that, in actual fact, a Réveillon labourer would, for months on end, be able to spend 97 per cent of his income on bread: he would almost certainly have to pay 3 *sous* a day for his lodgings (accounting for 20 per cent of his 'effective' daily earnings),[19] not to mention his necessary minimum expenditure on clothing, drink and other foods. He would, therefore, be forced to go hungry rather than buy his full quota of bread. Further, there were periods, particularly after August, when the shortage of supplies made it impossible to maintain one's normal consumption;[20] at other times, the bread was of poor quality and rejected by many as inedible.[21] But, even with these reservations, it may be claimed that these figures are highly significant and help to explain the desperate plight and angry mood of the Parisian wage-earners and

---

1795, the National Convention prescribed a ration of 1½ lb. of bread for each worker and 1 lb. for all others (*L'Ancien Moniteur* (*Réimpression*), XXIII, 701); but this was at a time when the consumption of bread (though often in short supply) had risen owing to a heavy shortage of other consumer goods, e.g. meat (Harris, *op. cit.* p. 154). If, for the period under review (one of shortage and high bread-prices), we allow an average daily consumption of 1 lb. per head and assume that the average male worker had a wife and two dependent children (cf. Braesch, *loc. cit.*), the lower figure of a 4-lb. loaf per day will appear reasonable.

19. Biollay gives 1–5 *sous* as the price of cheap lodgings in 1790 (*op. cit.*, p. 488). Police records that I have seen usually quote 2–4 *sous* for 1789–91.

20. See Hardy, *Journal*, VIII, 348, 378, 460. On 1 September, Hardy was only able to obtain 'la moitié d'un pain de 4 livres, ayant fort mauvais goût'.

21. *Ibid.* pp. 383, 460.

small craftsmen and shopkeepers (whose earnings were not appreciably higher than those of workers) at the outbreak of revolution.

Neither space nor the materials makes it possible to deal here with all other items of the household budget; nor, indeed, does the overwhelming significance assumed by bread during this period make it necessary; yet a word must be said about wine, which probably ranked second in importance.[22] A litre of ordinary wine appears to have cost about 10 *sous*[23] in 1789; half of this was accounted for by tax.[24] It is evident that, at this price and at the prevailing high cost of bread, few wage-earners could afford to buy even the comparatively modest quantity of 1 litre per day for their households; and it is, therefore, not surprising that there should have been such an outcry against the *barrières*, or internal customs posts, and that Parisians should have participated so eagerly in their destruction by fire on the nights of 11–14 July;[25] and it is certainly significant that among those destroying the post at Chaillot on 13 July was a locksmith who was reported as saying, 'nous allons boire le vin a trois sols'.[26]

It was, however, the high price and the scarcity of bread which acted as the main stimulant to the popular movements of the year 1789. This appears from the expressions of contemporary observers, the depositions of witnesses and the statements made by persons wounded or arrested in

22. According to Lavoisier, the average annual expenditure of the Parisian on wine accounted for 15 per cent of his total budget and for 25 per cent of his expenditure on food alone (Bienaymé, *op. cit.* XXXVI, 62–3).

23. I have found no precise figure for 1789. A price of 10 *sous* appears likely in view of (*a*) Bienaymé's figures for 1771–89, suggesting a wholesale price in 1789 of about 8½ *sous* per litre (*op. cit.*, XXXVI, 383); (*b*) the price of 10 *sous* per *pinte* (=0·93 litres) of wine in June 1790 (*Enquête de juin 1793*, Arch. Nat. F¹² 1547ᶜ, doss. 2).

24. Bienaymé, *op. cit.*, XXXVI, 383.

25. Arch. Nat. Z¹ᵃ 886.

26. *Ibid.* This appears to have been a highly optimistic forecast, as we shall see later.

these events.[27] The high price of bread appears as an important motive in the riots of 27 and 28 April in the Faubourg St. Antoine, when journeymen and labourers destroyed the property of two manufacturers, Réveillon and Henriot;[28] it appears again in the continuous agitation in the Faubourg St. Antoine between May and July;[29] and, though the Paris insurrection of 12–14 July had as its culminating and most spectacular episode the seizure of the Bastille, it included such 'economic' measures as the removal of corn from religious houses and the refusal to pay duty on goods passing through the *barrières*.[30] Above all, the protracted shortage of bread appears as the dominant consideration in the continuous social movements in markets, at City Hall and bakers' shops in August to November and in the march to Versailles, which brought the royal family ('le boulanger, la boulangère et le petit mitron') back to the capital in October.[31] It is also not without significance that the reduction in the price of bread from $14\frac{1}{2}$ to $13\frac{1}{2}$ *sous* on 22 July should have coincided with the lynching of Foulon and Berthier;[32] and that the further reduction to 12 *sous* on 8 August should have immediately followed large demonstrations of housewives outside the City Hall.[33]

There were, in addition, during August and September, independent movements of wage-earners—bakers' assistants, journeymen wig-makers, tailors, domestic servants, shoemakers and apothecaries—for work, wages or improved working conditions; but, with the exception of the

27. The most important sources for these are Hardy's *Journal* and the *procès-verbaux* of the *commissaires au Châtelet* (Arch. Nat., series Y).

28. See Hardy, *Journal*, VIII, 299.

29. *Ibid.* pp. 310, 344 *et seq.*

30. Arch. Nat. Z^{1a} 886; Z^2 4291.

31. For details of these movements, see my article, 'La composition sociale des insurrections parisiennes de 1789 à 1791', *Ann. Hist. de la Rév. Franç.* no. 127 (July–August 1952), pp. 256–88 (reproduced, in English, on pp. 96–129 above).

32. Hardy, *Journal*, VIII, 401.

33. *Ibid.*, p. 426.

tailors, who obtained a wages increase of 10 *sous*,[34] they received short shrift from the employers and authorities.[35] The wage-earners of Paris won some concessions as regards the price and supply of bread (the latter after October), but they won little, or nothing, in terms of their nominal wages.

2. November 1789–September 1791

This period, in sharp contrast with the preceding, was one of stable or falling prices, of stable currency[36] and wages. While unemployment still persisted in the former luxury trades,[37] it was a period of general business prosperity and, in a number of Parisian trades, of a shortage of labour.[38]

The price of the 4-lb. loaf, after long remaining at its new 'normal' level of 12 *sous*, was reduced to 11 *sous* in June 1790; after which controls were removed. In the autumn of that year, the price fell to 9 *sous* and, later, to 8 *sous*, where it appears to have remained for the greater part of 1791.[39] In August 1791, however, owing to a bad harvest

34. See p. 167, note to Table 1.

35. For these movements and the hostile attitude of the authorities towards them, see S. Lacroix, *Actes de la Commune de Paris pendant la Révolution Française*, 1st series, 7 vols. (Paris, 1894–8), I, 123–4, 265, 381, 416, 547. See also Hardy, *Journal*, VIII, 434, 438–9, 455; and Jaffé, *op. cit.* pp. 65–73.

36. For the stability of the newly created paper-money, the *assignat*, during this period, see Harris, *op. cit.* pp. 166–71.

37. In June 1791 there were 31,000 unemployed in the Parisian *ateliers de charité* (C. Bloch and A. Tuetey, *Procès-verbaux et Rapports du Comité de Mendicité de la Constituante, 1789–1791* (Coll. des docs inédits sur l'Hist. écon. de la Rév. Franç., (Paris, 1911), p. 278); and, in October, 64,000 *livres* were distributed in alms to 118,184 poor and destitute Parisians (Bib. Nat. nouvelles acquisitions françaises 2656, fos. 342–3).

38. See the speech of de Liancourt, *rapporteur* of the Comité de Mendicité, to the Assembly in June 1791: 'Le commerce reprend une grande vigueur . . . les maîtres ouvriers, notamment ceux de la capitale, se plaignent de ne pouvoir trouver des compagnons . . ', etc. (Bloch and Tuetey, *op. cit.* p. 730).

39. Prices are from *L'Ancien Moniteur* (*Réimpression*), IX, 439; and from Biollay, pp. 103–4.

and the bakers' shortage of flour, the price of bread again rose sharply and, in September, the 4-lb. loaf was once again selling at 12 *sous* or more.[40] Yet, if we consider the period as a whole, it is clear that the wage-earner's position, even though nominal wages showed no appreciable increase,[41] was substantially improved in comparison with 1789. His position was further improved during 1791 by the reduction—short-lived though it proved to be—in the price of a number of other essential goods, including wine. This came about through the abolition of the *droits d'entrée* with the closure of the *barrières* in May 1791. Consequently, the price of a litre of wine appears to have fallen from 10 to 8 *sous*;[42] firewood, which also accounted for a substantial proportion of the wage-earner's budget,[43] was

40. S. Lacroix, *op. cit.*, 2nd series, VI, 455–63. None of these documents gives the figure to which the price of bread actually rose. I have, therefore, had to assume an upper limit—12 *sous*—which appears reasonable in relation to the rise in the price of flour: from 38 *livres* per sack on 1 July to 54 *livres* on 14 September (Lacroix, *op. cit.*, 2nd series, VI, 459).

41. There were considerable wages movements involving a number of trades in the spring and summer of 1791 (see pp. 174–5), but it is doubtful, in view of their hostile reception by the Municipality and the Assembly, if they had an appreciable effect on the level of wages. The journeymen carpenters were, it is true, able to compel the majority of the masters to agree to pay a minimum wage of 50 *sous* per day (*Révolutions de Paris*, no. CXVI, (May 1791), 7–14), but this figure is identical with that given in the *Enquête de juin 1793* for 1790 (Biollay, p. 17). It is possible, therefore, that the outcome of the carpenters' strike was the more general application of a wage already paid to the 'best' workers rather than a general increase. It should be remembered, of course, that there was as yet no general acceptance of the principle of 'the rate for the job'.

42. This figure is put forward tentatively, being based on the uncertain evidence of a journeyman hatter, arrested on 2 May 1791 for abusing Lafayette (Archives de la Préfecture de Police, series Aa, no. 56 (Arcis), fo. 134).

43. Labrousse allows 5 per cent for fuel in his wage-earner's average budget for 1726–91 (see p. 165, n. 10, above), but this is for the whole of France. Lavoisier's estimate of 10 per cent for the average Parisian (Bienaymé, *op. cit.*, XXXVI, 62–3) would appear to be more appropriate.

reduced from 22½ to 17 *livres* per *voie* (56 cubic feet);[44] the price of butter was reduced by one-quarter and that of sugar by somewhat less.[45] The price of meat, however, owing to a persistent shortage of supplies to the market, retained its high price of 10 *sous* per lb.[46]

The improvement in the living standards of the wage-earners resulting from these changes may be illustrated by comparing the hypothetical budgets of groups of workers in 1789 with those in 1791 (Table 2).

TABLE 2 Hypothetical budgets of Parisian workers in June 1789 and June 1791

Budget of a builder's labourer (wage: 30 s.; 'effective' income: 18 s.)		Budget of a journeyman carpenter, locksmith etc. (wage: 50 s.; 'effective' income: 30 s.)	
June 1789	June 1791	June 1789	June 1791
4 lb. bread 14½ s.	4 lb. bread 8 s.	4 lb. bread 14½ s.	4 lb. bread 8 s.
Rent 3 s.	Rent 3 s.	Rent 3 s.	Rent 3 s.
	½ litre wine 4 s.	½ litre wine 5 s.	1 litre wine 8 s.
	¼ lb. meat 2½ s.	½ lb. meat 5 s.	½ lb. meat 5 s.
Balance for oil, vege-tables, clothing etc. ½ s.	Balance ½ s.	Balance 2½ s.	Balance 6 s.
Total 18 s.	18 s.	30 s.	30 s.

These trends are, not unnaturally, reflected in the popular movements of 1790–1. There was no flicker of any public agitation about bread until mid-August 1791 when, as we have seen, a shortage of flour sent the price of the 4-lb. loaf soaring upwards again. Disturbances followed in

44. Cf. Bienaymé, *op. cit*, XXXVII, 389.

45. Cf. Biollay, pp. 167, 288. Other essentials subject to the *droits d'entrée* up to May 1791, but more lightly taxed, were eggs, cheese and tallow candles (*ibid.*, pp. 172, 176, 296).

46. The Paris Council attributed this to the competition of the *mercandiers*, 300–400 of whom operated in the meat market at this time (Lacroix, *op. cit.*, 2nd series, II, 129–33).

different parts of the city and the mayor, Bailly, was threatened with 'la lanterne' in the corn market and was forced to beat an ignominious retreat;[47] while, on the following day, a button-maker was arrested for saying, 'Il nous faut le pain français à deux sols ou se battre.'[48] In the early months of the year there had been, besides, a continuous agitation among 'smugglers' and unemployed directed against the customs posts; this, of course, came to an end with their closure in May.[49]

The major social disturbances of the period, however, took the form of agitation of the unemployed for work schemes, of wages movements and political demonstrations, rather than of food riots. The unemployed workers were threatened with destitution by a decision of the Constituent Assembly in June 1791 to close down the *ateliers de charité*, and they vigorously protested by street demonstrations and petitions.[50] During the spring and summer of the same year, carpenters, farriers, printers and others (their numbers were said in a petition of the master farriers to total 80,000) struck work, or otherwise demonstrated, for higher wages—a movement that afforded the Assembly the pretext for legislating the Loi Le Chapelier, banning trade associations, in June.[51] The political movement in the summer of 1791 was inspired and guided by the Cordelier Club and reached its climax in the Champ de Mars demonstration of 17 July.[52] It is worth noting that the wages movement, one of the two great movements of its kind in Paris during the Revolution, took place at a

---

47. *Le Journal de la Révolution*, no. 391 (7 September 1791); Lacroix, *op. cit.*, 2nd series, VI, 135-6, 374-90.

48. Arch. Préf. Pol., series Aa 167 (Mail), fo. 73.

49. See Bailly-Lafayette correspondence, Bib. Nat. fonds français 11697, pp. 235, 239, 246-8.

50. Cf. Y. Forado-Cunéo, 'Les ateliers de charité de Paris pendant la Révolution française', *La Révolution Française*, LXXXVI (1933), 317-42; LXXXVII (1934), 29-61, 103-23.

51. See Jaffé, *op. cit.*, pt. II.

52. See A. Mathiez, *Le Club des Cordeliers pendant la Crise de Varennes et le Massacre du Champ de Mars* (Paris, 1910).

time when prices were either stable or tending to fall and when there was a shortage of labour in several trades. It is also significant that the political movement culminating in the Champ de Mars petition was the only one of the social movements of the period 1789–91 that did not raise the question of bread or of any other article of popular consumption as an issue.

3. October 1791–June 1793

With the autumn of 1791 we enter a period of rising prices and depreciating paper money, gradual at first but, as the outbreak of war drew nearer, becoming more precipitous. This inflationary movement is reflected in the heavy depreciation of the *assignat*; from a level of 82 per cent of its nominal value (according to the Treasury figures) in November 1791 it declined to 36 per cent in June 1793.[53] Unlike the two preceding periods, it is one, also, of rising nominal wages and, in some trades, at least, of shorter working hours.

From this time until the end of 1794, bread begins to lose its particular significance as an issue of popular concern. After a variety of expedients to keep its price within limits, the Commune eventually fixed it on 4 March 1793 at 12 *sous* for the 4-lb. loaf;[54] and, despite steady increases in the price of other consumer goods and in wages, this price was maintained by subsidies to bakers. Consequently, Parisians were to suffer less from the full rigours of inflation, both in 1793 and in 1795, than the population of small country towns, where the price of bread continued to rise with the rising cost of flour.[55] Yet there were periods,

53. From January to June 1793 alone it fell from 72 to 36 per cent. See Harris, *op. cit.*, pp. 166–76; also R. G. Hawtrey, 'The Collapse of the French Assignats', *The Economic Journal*, no. 111, vol. XXVII (September 1918), pp. 300–14.

54. Cf. P. Caron, *Paris pendant la Terreur*, I, 9, n. 1.

55. Thus, in the Department of the Allier, the price of the 4 lb. loaf rose from 9 sous in 1789 to 20 sous in June 1793 (Harris, p. 104). In February 1795, when the larger proportion of bread sold in Paris was still subsidised, it was reported that the 4-lb. loaf was selling in the Yonne Department at 60 sous. (Arch. Nat. F⁷ 4665, doss. 5.)

even before the end of 1794, when bread was in short supply: such was the case, for example, during the months March–June 1793, when there was a more or less chronic shortage of bread in Paris, to which the reports of police agents constantly refer.[56]

Meanwhile, starting in the late autumn of 1791, the prices of other consumer goods, particularly of colonial products, were beginning to rise sharply. In February 1792, sugar was sold at 50 *sous* per lb., or at nearly double its price of 1789–90.[57] Other commodities followed suit;[58] and, after a temporary pause in the summer and autumn of 1792,[59] the prices of nearly all essentials other than bread took another sharp upward turn in the early months of 1793.[60] It was against a background of rising prices and bread shortage that the National Convention in the early summer of 1793 succumbed to the pressure of the Paris Sections and took the first step to institute a system of price-controls by enacting the first Maximum law on 4 May.[61] Before elaborating a more comprehensive system, the Committee of Public Safety conducted a nation-wide enquiry as to comparative prices and rates of wages in June 1790 and June 1793. The following table, based largely on the Paris returns to this enquiry, illustrates the movement of

56. Arch. Nat. F⁷ 3688 (2); AF^IV 1470.

57. See Mathiez, *La Vie Chère et le Mouvement Social sous la Terreur* (Paris, 1927), pp. 36–41.

58. E.g. the price of eggs rose from 42 to 54 *livres* per 1,000 during 1792 (d'Avenel, *op. cit.*, IV, 598).

59. Cf. Harris, p. 102.

60. On 25 February, sugar was being sold in Paris at prices varying from 47 to 60 *sous* (1790 price: 26 *sous*); candles at 18½ to 20 *sous* (15 *sous*), coffee at 40 *sous* (34 *sous*). 1793 prices are from Arch. Préf. Pol., series Aa (various cartons); 1790 prices (in brackets) are from Biollay, pp. 288–90, 296, 298.

61. This was limited to controlling the price of bread and of flour; it had, therefore, no special significance for Paris, where the price of bread was already controlled. For its terms and debate, see *Archives Parlementaires*, 1st series, 1789–90, 80 vols. (Paris, 1879–1914), LXIV, 56–7.

TABLE 3 Prices and wages in June 1793, contrasted with
June 1790

Occupation	Wages June 1790 (1)		June 1793 (2)		% increase of (2) over (1)
	l.	*s.*	*l.*	*s.*	
Shoemaker	2	5	3	10	+56
Tailor	2	0	3	10	+75
Hatter	2	5	5	0	+122
Locksmith*	2	10	5	10	+120
Joiner	2	5	4	10	+100
Carpenter	2	10	4	0	+60
Mason	2	0	3	0	+50
Harness-maker	2	10	7	0	+180
Wheelwright	2–4 *l.*		6–8 *l.*		+100–200

Commodity	Prices June 1790 (1)		June 1793 (2)		% increase of (2) over (1)
	l.	*s.*	*l.*	*s.*	
Bread † (4 lb.)	0	11	0	12	+9
Wine (litres)	0	10	0	16	+60
Beef (per lb.)	0	11	0	26	}+77 (approx.)
Veal (per lb.)	0	11½	0	14¼	
Mutton (per lb.)	0	14	0	18	
Butter (per lb.) ‡	0	14	1	6⅔	+90
Eggs (per 100) §	4	4	5	10	+31
Rice (cwt.)	47	10	105	0	+121
Olive oil (cwt.)	100	0	180	0	+80
Sugar (lb.)	1	4	5	0	+300
Coffee (lb.)	1	14	4	0	+135
Tallow candles (lb.)	0	15	2	0	+167
Firewood (per 56 cu.ft.)	21	12	30	0	+39

* N.B. Whereas in June 1790 a locksmith worked from 5.30 a.m.
to 8 p.m., in June 1793 he worked only from 6.30 a.m. to 7 p.m.—a
reduction of 2 hours in his working day.

† See pp. 171–2 and 175–6, above. The price of bread is not given in
the *Enquête*.   ‡ Biollay, p. 167.   § *Ibid.* p. 176.

wages in a number of trades and of prices of a number of consumer goods.[62]

On the basis of the evidence here presented it is possible to give a rough indication of the changes in the standard of living between 1790 and 1793. In Table 4, this is attempted in the form of the hypothetical budgets of a journeyman carpenter and a journeyman locksmith for June 1790 and June 1793.

It will be seen that the carpenter, whose wage has increased rather less than the average shown in Table 3, has yet been able to increase his consumption of wine and to have a more reasonable balance over for the purchase of essentials not specified in these budgets. In the case of the locksmith, whose wage has increased more than the average, the improvement is considerably greater: he has increased his purchase of wine, doubled that of meat and has nearly one-quarter of his income over for the purchase of oil, vegetables and clothing. We cannot, of course draw any conclusions for the wage-earners of Paris as a whole owing to the absence of any wages figures for unskilled workers; but we may perhaps tentatively conclude that, among workshop journeymen at least—and they accounted for the majority of the wage-earning population[63]—the rise in the prices of essential commodities during the period 1790–3 was substantially offset by the rise in nominal wages.[64] Yet we must beware of over-confident conclusions, as we have no means of knowing how far this improvement in the nominal purchasing power of wages was offset by the shortage of consumer goods, including bread.

62. Except where otherwise stated, these figures are from the *Enquête de juin 1793* (Arch. Nat. F[12] 1547[c], doss. 2).

63. Cf. Braesch, *op. cit.*

64. Besides, in some trades at least, there appears by this time to have been a substantial reduction in working hours (see the case of the locksmith in footnote to Table 3, above). Long working hours persisted long after 1789. A journeyman tailor, arrested after the Champs de Mars affair in July 1791, claimed that he worked from 5 a.m. until 9 p.m. (Arch. Préf. Pol. Aa 215 (Henri IV), fo. 455).

The popular movement of the years 1792 and 1793 is of exceptional importance for the history of the Revolution. It was dominated, of course, by the great political movements of June–August 1792, which overthrew the monarchy, and of May–June 1793, which expelled the Girondin

TABLE 4 Hypothetical budgets of Parisian workers in June 1790 and June 1793

Budget of a journeyman carpenter			
In June 1790 (wage: 50 s.; *'effective' income: 30 s.)*		*In June 1793 (wage: 80 s.;* *'effective'* * income: 57 s.)*	
4 lb. bread	11 *s.*	4 lb. bread	12 *s.*
Rent	3 *s.*	Rent †	6 *s.*
1 litre wine	10 *s.*	1½ litres wine	24 *s.*
½ lb. meat	5 *s.*	½ lb. meat	9 *s.*
Balance for vegetables, oil, clothing, etc.	1 *s.*	Balance	6 *s.*
Total	30 *s.*		57 *s.*
Budget of a journeyman locksmith			
In June 1790 (wage: 50 s.; *'effective' income: 30 s.)*		*In June 1793 (wage: 110 s.;* *'effective'* * income: 78 s.)*	
4 lb. bread	11 *s.*	4 lb. bread	12 *s.*
Rent	3 *s.*	Rent †	6 *s.*
1 litre wine	10 *s.*	1½ litres wine	24 *s.*
½ lb. meat	5 *s.*	1 lb. meat	18 *s.*
Balance	1 *s.*	Balance	18 *s.*
	30 *s.*		78 *s.*

* 'Effective' earnings are here based on the assumption of a five-day working week. Many of the old Feast Days had, by this time, been abandoned, but the Revolutionary Calendar, which considerably increased the number of working days per year, had not yet been introduced.

† For lack of exact information on rent, I have assumed here an increase of 100 per cent on charges made in 1790, which is roughly in proportion to the rise of other prices. The pressure of population on living space in Paris was still considerable: it was not until the autumn of 1793 that lodging-house keepers were to complain of a dearth of clients (cf. J. de La Monneraye, *La Crise du Logement à Paris pendant la Révolution* (Paris, 1928), pp. 12–13).

leaders from the Convention and prepared the way for the assumption of power by the Jacobins. In the first of these movements the issue of bread or of other consumer goods was almost entirely absent; but, in the second, discontent with the shortage of bread and the continuing scarcity and high prices of colonial products gave a powerful initial stimulus to popular participation and ensured the success of the Jacobins' political aims. Most significant, however, of the swift reaction of Parisians during the Revolution to any sharp upward movement in the prices of consumer goods were the food riots of February 1792 and 1793, provoked by the sudden increase in the price of sugar and of other colonial products. In the riots of 1793 provisions shops all over Paris were invaded by angry crowds, who forced grocers to sell their wares at 1790 prices.[65] In March and April of that year, simultaneously with the broader movement directed against high prices and shortages, there developed an agitation for higher wages by paviours, masons, carpenters and bakers;[66] but this movement was short-lived and cannot be compared, in scope or importance, with that of April–June 1791.

4. June 1793–July 1794

This is the period of *Maximum Général* (general price control) and of the Revolutionary Government, led by Robespierre; but the Jacobin dictatorship was not firmly entrenched until the autumn of 1793. Meanwhile, the *assignat*, according to the Treasury figures, slumped further from 36 to 22 per cent of its nominal value,[67] the bread shortage persisted and prices continued to rise. Police agents' reports testify to the continued shortage of bread, to the rise in the price of every essential and to the existence

65. For details, see my article, 'Les émeutes des 25, 26 février 1793 à Paris', *Ann. Hist. de la Rév. Franç.* no. 130 (Jan.–March 1953), pp. 33–57.

66. Arch. Nat. AF[IV] 1470.

67. Cf. Hawtrey, *loc. cit.*; Harris, *op. cit.*, p. 176.

of angry queues outside bakers' shops.[68] In September, Béraud and Rollin, agents of the Ministry of the Interior, reported prices from the markets, which are contrasted with those for June[69] in Table 5.

It is not surprising that such a sharp upward movement in prices, threatening to destroy the improvements gained since 1790, should have evoked an angry response from the Parisian *menu peuple*, who gave enthusiastic support to the demands put to the Convention by the Paris Commune

TABLE 5 Prices of consumer goods, June and September 1793

(*Prices are for lb. weight, unless otherwise stated*)

Commodity	June 1793 (*1*)	Sept. 1793 (*2*)	% increase of (*2*) over (*1*)
Wine (litre)	16 s.	20 s.	+25
Meat	19 s.	18–22 s.	+16
Veal	14¼ s.	24–26 s.	+85
Eggs (25)	27½ s.	50 s.	+84
Butter	26⅔ s.	35–36 s.	+33
Oil (grade 1)	52 s.	60–70 s.	+25
Sugar	100 s.	110 s.	+10
Coffee	80 s.	90–100 s.	+19
Soap	23–28 s.*	70 s.	+175
Tallow candles	40 s.	44 s.	+10

* This is the price quoted in February 1793, taken from reports of the grocery riots of 25–26 February (see p. 180, n. 65 above).

on 4 and 5 September for the institution of a rigorous system of price-controls and for severe penalties against speculators and forestallers.[70] This was the immediate

68. Arch. Nat. F⁷ 3688 (3).

69. Caron, *op. cit.*, I, 57–60.

70. Cf. *L'Ancien Moniteur* (*Réimpression*), XVII, 73–4; also E. Soreau, 'Les ouvriers aux journées des 4 et 5 septembre 1793', *Ann. Hist. de la Rév. Franç*, XIV (1937), 436–47. For disturbances at bakers' shops in August–September, see police agents' reports (Arch. Nat. F⁷ 3688 (3)); and, for records of arrests in this connection, see Arch. Préf. Pol. Ab. 327 (registre de la Force).

background to the enactment of the *Law of the Maximum Général* on 29 September 1793.[71] The adoption of this law, the creation of the so-called Armée Révolutionnaire to ensure adequate supplies of bread and meat, and the strengthening of the organs of government—all of which are features of the autumn of 1793—ushered in a new revolutionary era, fraught with significant experiment and one which has divided historians of the period ever since.[72]

The law of 29 September, supplemented by an amending law of 1 November, provided for the increase of prices at the point of production by one-third over June 1790, plus a rate per league for transportation, plus 5 per cent for the wholesaler and 10 per cent for the retailer. The law affected thirty-nine commodities, mostly necessities, but excluded firewood, fish, tobacco, salt, soap, milk, crude sugar and poultry. In the case of wages, it provided for a 50 per cent increase over rates prevailing in June 1790.[73] Whatever the merits or otherwise of these laws as a piece of social legislation, there can be no doubt that they arrested the chaotic inflationary trend of January–September 1793. The stabilisation is reflected in the upward movement of the *assignat*, whose nominal value rose (according to the Treasury figures) from 22 per cent in August to 33 per cent in November and to 48 per cent in December 1793.[74] And, as far as the thirty-nine selected

71. For text and debate, see *L'Ancien Moniteur* (*Réimpression*), XVII, 775–6.

72. For the different opinions of historians, see Harris, pp. 147–8.

73. For the foregoing, see H. E. Bourne, 'Maximum prices in France, 1793–1794', *American Historical Review*, XXIII (October 1917), 107–13; and (by the same author) 'Food control and price-fixing in Revolutionary France', *The Journal of Political Economy*, XXVII (1919), 73–94, 188–209.

74. See Hawtrey, *loc. cit.*; also Harris, pp. 176–85. It is true that the *assignat* was to fall again to 34 per cent by July 1794, but if we compare the all-over trend of the *assignat* between October 1793 and July 1794 (period of Jacobin dictatorship) with that of January–September 1793 and, more particularly, with that of July 1794–December 1795 (see Hawtrey), the degree of stabilisation achieved will appear remarkable.

commodities were concerned, the law was enforced: this much at least, is conceded by the main body of historians.[75] Yet the very stringency of its enforcement compelled many producers and dealers either to withhold supplies or to sell both 'taxed' and untaxed goods at prices above the Maximum. Thus, pork butchers, to evade the law, sold only cooked pork (the price of raw meat alone was controlled); an army of *mercandiers* and *revendeurs* invaded the markets and back streets, selling sugar, butter and poor quality meat above the controlled price;[76] and, in December, agents of the Ministry of Interior reported that butter was being sold in Paris markets at 36–44 *sous* per lb. (controlled price: 22 *sous*) and eggs at 80 *sous* for 25 (compared with 21 *sous* in June 1790, $27\frac{1}{2}$ *sous* in June 1793 and 50 *sous* in September).[77] Further, a shortage of bread recurred in December, though it seems to have been overcome, temporarily at least, by a system of rationing.[78] In April, meat was also rationed on the basis of a distribution every five days of $\frac{1}{2}$ lb. per head.[79] Shortages became more acute in the spring, and police reports for this period reveal a growing irritation on the part of wage-earners, housewives and others over the difficulty of obtaining meat, butter, eggs, candles and other commodities.[80] How far these shortages and sales of essentials at 'black market'

75. Cf. Harris, pp. 147–8, 181.

76. H. E. Bourne, *op. cit.*, pp. 206–7 (based on the reports of police agents Grivel and Siret).

77. Caron, *op. cit.* I, 325, 344; II, 20.

78. *Ibid.* I, 305. The consumption of bread per head of population was increasing. With a population certainly no greater than that of 1789–91 (cf. La Monneraye, *loc. cit.*), Paris was consuming 1,800–1,850 sacks of flour per day in February 1794, compared with 1,500 sacks in 1789 (Harris, p. 154) and 1,400 in 1793 (*L'Ancien Moniteur* (*Réimpr.*), XVII, 190.)

79. Bib. Nat. nouv. acquis. franç. 2669, fos. 75–8.

80. See reports by the *commissaires de police* of the Paris Sections for March–April 1794 (Arch. Préf. Pol., series Aa, no. 70 (Arcis), fos. 418, 439–41; 94 (Butte-des-Moulins), fo. 63; 139 (Fidélité), fo. 140; 198 (Observatoire), fo. 260; 201 (Panthéon), fo. 61; 216 (Pont Neuf), fo. 389; 240 (Temple), fos. 156–7).

prices offset the value to the working population of the controlled prices provided by the Maximum laws, it is, of course, impossible to estimate; their total effect, however, must have been considerable.

Marion has suggested that the Committee of Public Safety made a farce of the whole legislation of the Maximum by deliberately ignoring the provisions relating to wages.[81] While this is an exaggeration, it cannot be denied that, had the authorities clung as closely to the letter of the law in regard to wages as they did in the case of prices, they would have found it difficult to man their arms industries and to keep essential services in operation at a time of labour shortage, created by the needs of war. Even on Government contracts rates prescribed tended to be well above the Maximum. Thus, in March 1794, the following rates of wages were laid down for building workers employed on the construction of the Panthéon (here contrasted with rates of pay in June 1790):[82]

Occupation	Wages in June 1790 (1)	Wages in March 1794 (2)	% increase of (2) over (1)
Stonemason	45 s.	85–100 s.	+105
Mason's labourer	32–36 s.	70–85 s.	+128
General labourer	24–32 s.	60–70 s.	+132

Again, wages prescribed for workers in government arms workshops at the end of May 1794 (here contrasted with daily wages of equivalent grades in June 1790) varied as follows:[83]

81. R. Marion, 'Les lois de Maximum et la taxation des salaires sous la Révolution', *Revue Internationale de Sociologie*, XXV (1917), 485–501.

82. The figures for March 1794 are from Arch. Nat. F¹³ 1138; those for 1790 are from Biollay, p. 19.

83. Wages for May 1794 are from C. Richard, *Le Comité de Salut*

Grade of arms worker	Wages in June 1790 (1)	Wages in May 1794 (2)	% increase of (2) over (1)
Highly skilled	3½–4 *l.* 0 *s.*	16½ *l.* 0 *s.*	+340
Average worker	2 *l.* 0 *s.*	8 *l.* 5 *s.*	+312
Lowest paid worker	1 *l.* 16 *s.*	3 *l.* 0 *s.*	+66*

* This last figure is probably an under-estimate. In an address to arms workers, read to the Convention on 15 June 1794, the Deputy Frécine claimed that not one of them was receiving less than double his pay in 1790 (Marion, *op. cit.* p. 491).

Workers in private employment, too, received wages in excess of the Maximum. Thus, an arms worker, suing his private employer for non-payment of wages in March 1794, claimed that 'he had always received 6 *livres*, and more, per day';[84] a journeyman carpenter was said to be receiving 6 *livres* a day in May;[85] in January–February, bakers, previously receiving 8 *livres* per week (and board and lodging), were refusing to work for 15;[86] while brush-makers were paid 90–120 *livres* per month in July,

---

Public et les Fabrications de Guerre sous la Terreur (Paris, 1922), p. 719. Wages for 1790 are those for foundry workers (skilled, semi-skilled and labourers), taken from Biollay, p. 42.

84. Arch. Préf. Pol Aa 49 (Amis de la Patrie), fo. 410. The equivalent rate for his occupation (*forgeron armurier*) in 1790 was 1 *livre* 16 *sous* for an ordinary journeyman, or 3 *livres* 10 *sous* for a highly skilled worker (Biollay, p. 42).

85. Arch. Nat. F⁷ 4662, doss. 1. In March, masons and carpenters had threatened to stop work unless they were paid 6 *livres* per day for skilled work and 3 *livres* 5 *sous* for unskilled work (J. M. Thompson, *The French Revolution* (Oxford, 1947), 483).

86. Marion, *op. cit.*, p. 487. In May, it was reported, from another Section, that bakers were refusing to work for less than 5 *livres* per day, plus food (Arch. Nat. BB³ 76). These examples certainly do not suggest that the shortage of bread was accompanied, as it was in 1789, by unemployment among bakers (see Hardy, *Journal*, VIII, 434).

compared with an average wage of about 42 *livres* in June 1790.[87]

Though the evidence is patchy, it may perhaps be assumed then that, during this period, nominal wages doubled at the very least. Let us then once more examine the hypothetical budget of a journeyman carpenter and contrast it with that of 1793. In Table 6 it is assumed that he is receiving a daily wage of 6 *livres*[88] and that his 'effective' daily earnings are 5 *livres*.[89]

If the improvement in living standards that this budget suggests[90] can be assumed to be of a more general application, why did the mass of the wage-earners and *sans-culottes* desert Robespierre and allow his enemies to overthrow him so easily on the night of 9–10 Thermidor? Mathiez has pointed to the dissatisfaction of the workers with the Committee and the Commune over wages;[91]

87. Arch. Préf. Pol. Aa 163 (Lombards), fo. 297. I have selected here what appear to be typical examples and avoided extreme cases, as, for example, the case of two arms workers, reported in May 1794 to be earning respectively 223 and 185 livres for a few days' work per *décade* (10-day period) (Richard, *op. cit.*, p. 721); or the claim of the Popincourt Section that many workers earning 5 *livres* in March were earning 20 *livres* in June (Arch. Nat. F⁷ 4437); or, again, the oft-quoted complaint of police agents Grivel and Siret that daily labourers were demanding ten times their pay of a year before (Marion, *op. cit.*, p. 487).

88. See p. 185, above.

89. I have here assumed a higher ratio than previously of 'effective' earnings to nominal daily wages owing to the adoption, in the autumn of 1793, of the Revolutionary Calendar, which reduced official holidays to one per 10-day period (*décade*). While this principle was rigorously enforced in the arms workshops from November 1793 onwards (cf. Richard, *op. cit.*, p. 699), it cannot, however, be assumed to have operated in industry generally, particularly as it roused stern opposition among the workers. The ratio here adopted is, frankly, a compromise.

90. It will be seen that, having increased his consumption of bread and wine over that of 1793, the carpenter has a far more generous margin for the purchase of eggs (uncontrolled), oils, clothing, etc. On the other hand, he may be forced, by the shortage of certain essentials, to buy at inflated prices on the 'black market'. On balance, however, it would appear that his general position has substantially improved.

91. See Mathiez, *op. cit.*, ch. 10, 'Le Maximum des Salaires'.

and it is true that, after the removal of the Hébertists in March 1794, the Robespierrist majority aroused the hostility of the wage-earners by their insistence on main-

TABLE 6 Hypothetical budgets of a journeyman carpenter in 1793 and 1794

In June 1793 (wage: 80 s.; 'effective' income 57 s.)		*In June 1794 (wage: 120 s.; 'effective' income: 100 s.)*	
4 lb. bread	12 s.	6 lb. bread	18 s.*
Rent	6 s.	Rent	6 s.
1½ litres wine	24 s.	2 litres wine	30 s.
½ lb. meat	9 s.	2/5 lb. meat	6 s.*
Balance for vegetables, oil, clothing, etc.	6 s.	Balance for vegetables, oil, clothing, etc.	40 s.
Total	57 s.	Total	100 s.

* The higher figure for bread that appears in this budget owes its presence to two considerations: (1) the higher total consumption of bread at this time than in 1789–93 (see p. 183 n. 78, above); (2) the enforced reduction in the amount of meat consumed owing to the introduction of a ration of ½ lb. per head every five days (see p. 183, above). As this worker's full quota of meat only amounts to ⅖ lb. per day (½ lb × ⅕ × 4), it is assumed that he would compensate himself by a larger purchase of bread.

taining some semblance of the 'maximum des salaires' at a time that was particularly favourable to the pressing of claims for higher wages. Hence, the main social movements of the spring and summer of 1794 were wages movements rather than movements in shops and markets over food supplies; and, during this time, the Committee sternly rejected the claims of arms workers, potters, carpenters, tobacco workers, water-carriers, printers and riverside workers and even sent the leaders of the potters and tobacco workers before the Revolutionary Tribunal.[92] In addition, the wage-earners not unnaturally were outraged by the

92. See G. Rudé and A. Soboul, 'Le maximum des salaires parisiens et le 9 thermidor,' *Ann. Hist. Rév. Franç.* no 134 (Jan.–March 1954).

publication on 23 July of the Commune's 'maximum des salaires', which strictly accorded with the provisions of the law of 29 September in respect of wages;[93] so much so that it provoked demonstrations of protest at the City Hall on 9 Thermidor itself;[94] and it was readily believed (and hoped) that the removal of Robespierre would allow wages to resume their upward course unchecked.[95]

5. July 1794–May 1795

Having disposed of Robespierre and his principal associates, the Thermidorians lost little time in dismantling their system of government, in purging the Revolutionary Committees of their Jacobin personnel and in drastically relaxing economic controls.[96] In October 1794, the Maximum legislation was so amended as to allow prices to rise to a level two-thirds above that of June 1790; and, on 23 December, the Maximum laws were virtually abolished: the price of rationed bread was still maintained at 12 *sous* for the 4-lb. loaf (though bread was now allowed, in addition, to be sold freely on the 'open' market); the basic meat ration of ½ lb. every five days was also retained, at its new market price of 21 *sous* per lb.; otherwise, prices were now free to find their 'natural' level.[97] The inflationary movement thus set in motion is reflected in the steady fall of the *assignat* from 36 per cent in July to 28 per cent in October, 24 per cent in November, 20 per

93. *Ibid.*
94. Arch. Nat. AF 47, plaq. 366.
95. It was later reported by a brush-maker of the Section des Lombards that his workpeople had greeted the news of the fall of Robespierre and his principal associates with the observation, 'That puts paid to the Maximum', and promptly put in for a 33% increase to their wages! (See R. Cobb, 'Une "coalition" des garçons brossiers de la Section des Lombards', *Ann. Hist. de la Rév. Franç.* no. 130 (Jan.–March 1953), pp. 67–70.)
96. For the best short account of this process, see G. Lefebvre, *Les Thermidoriens* (Paris, 1946).
97. Cf. Harris, pp. 145–6.

cent in December, 17 per cent in February and to 7½ per cent in May 1795.[98]

The consequences of the new policy were to prove disastrous for the common people of Paris.[99] Already in November, a police agent reported:

Complaints and murmurs are continually heard. The long delays in obtaining rationed bread, the shortage of flour, the high prices, in markets and squares, of bread, firewood, wine, coal, vegetables and potatoes, the price of which is increasing daily in the most alarming manner, are plunging the people into a state of wretchedness and despair that is easy to imagine.[100]

We see, then, developing, side by side with the 'closed' market, still subject to restriction, an 'open' market not only in unrationed goods—eggs, firewood, butter, oil and vegetables—but in meat and bread as well. With the repeal of the Maximum laws and the constantly increasing shortages of every article entering into the wage-earner's budget,[101] not only did the Parisian *menu peuple* have to purchase all commodities other than bread and meat at the higher, 'famine' prices now prevailing, but the inability of the Government to honour its undertaking to provide sufficient quantities of bread and meat at the controlled price[102] forced them to spend an ever higher proportion

98. See Hawtrey, *loc. cit.*; Harris, p. 186.

99. Yet Harris is right to point out that continued Government subsidies in respect of bread and meat probably saved Parisians from the utter depths of calamity suffered by the mass of the population in regions where controls had been taken off altogether. (*Op. cit.*, p. 99.)

100. Arch. Nat. F⁷ 3688 (4) (my own translation).

101. For repeated popular complaints due to high prices and shortages, see Aulard, *La Réaction Thermidorienne*, I, 406–92, 500–17, 560–7, 652–63.

102. On 16 March 1795, the Convention decreed that persons 'living by the toil of their hands' should receive a daily ration of 1½ lb. of bread and all others a ration of 1 lb. per head (*L'Ancien Moniteur* (*Réimpression*), XXIII, 700). On 27 March, workers in the Temple Section were demanding that this pledge be honoured (Aulard, *op. cit.*, I, 608). Indeed, it is apparent from the daily reports of the police that it was rarely, if ever, honoured. For the chronic shortage of meat during 1795, see Harris, p. 107.

of their income on bread and meat in the 'open' market.[103]
Thus, for the first time since the autumn of 1791, the price
of bread reappeared as a social problem. Its importance
may be judged from the rise in the price of a pound of
bread on the 'open' market from 25 *sous* on 28 March
(already eight times its controlled price) to 65 *sous* on 11
April; to 6 *livres* on 21 April; to 9 *livres* on 11 May; while,
a week later—two days before the outbreak of the first
Prairial—it had risen to 16 *livres*.[104] Meanwhile, as the daily
reports of the police reveal, the price of unrationed meat,
of wine, butter, eggs, potatoes (becoming increasingly
an essential part of the Parisian's diet), vegetables and

103. During the year 1795 the proportion spent on bread in the
'open' market appears to have averaged around 40 per cent: at this
time, the Government was contributing daily 1,300 sacks of flour,
earmarked for the rationed loaf, out of a total consumption in Paris
of 2,150 sacks (Harris, pp. 107, 154). It would be surprising, however,
if this proportion were not exceeded, owing possibly to faulty distribution or to 'leakage' into the 'open' market, particularly during the
critical months March–May. (Cf. the almost continuous complaints,
during this period, that this or that body of citizens had only received
¼, ½ or ¾ lb. bread per head, or even no bread at all—see Aulard, vol.
I, *passim*, and numerous documents in Arch. Nat., series F⁷, and
Arch. Préf. Pol., series Aa.)

In this connection, it should be noted that a decree of the Committee of Public Safety of 31 March 1795 debarred lodging-house
keepers, for a short while at least, from obtaining any rationed goods
(i.e. bread and meat) for themselves or their lodgers—a measure which
inevitably compelled a considerable proportion of the wage-earners
(building workers were particularly numerous among the population
of the *chambres garnies*) to obtain all supplies on the 'open' market. A
police report of 2 April considers this decree to be largely responsible
for the participation of wage-earners in the insurrection of 12 Germinal (1 April). (See A. Aulard, *op. cit.*, I, 627.)

104. Cf. Aulard, I, 610, 654, 675, 715, 729. Thus, already by the end
of April, the price of a single pound of bread on the 'open' market
would account for three-quarters of the 'effective' daily earnings of a
labourer at a time when he would be lucky if he could count on a
daily ration of 2 lb. of bread for himself and family at the controlled
price. (For the 'effective' earnings of a labourer, see p. 193 below; for
almost daily complaints throughout April that the ration of bread had,
in effect, been reduced to ½ or a ¼ lb. per head (or, even, to nothing at
all), see Aulard, I, 627–94.)

firewood rose sharply in January and February and, again, in March and April.[105]

In Table 7 the prices of a number of important consumer

TABLE 7 Prices in April 1795 contrasted with June 1790

(*All prices are for lb. weight unless otherwise stated*)

Commodities	June 1790 (*1*)	April 1795 (*2*)	% increase of (*2*) over (*1*)
Bread (unrationed)	2¾ *s.*	65–120 *s.*	+3,260
Wine (per litre)	10 *s.*	59 *s.*	+490
Meat (unrationed)	10 *s.*	150 *s.*	+1,400
Butter	14 *s.*	160–180 *s.*	+1,415
Eggs (per 25)	21 *s.*	140–160 *s.*	+615
Potatoes (per bushel)	14 *s.*	200–320 *s.*	+1,750
Firewood (per 56 cu. ft.)	21 *l.* 12 *s.*	170 *l.*	+685*

 * Figures in this column are approximate.

goods in April 1795 are contrasted with their prices in June 1790.[106]

Unfortunately, information regarding the movement of wages during this period is extremely scanty. Though the Thermidorians were quick to exploit the difficulties that their predecessors encountered in trying to curb the upward movement in wages in the summer of 1794 and criticised the 'maximum des salaires' of the former Paris Commune as being 'insufficient' and 'arbitrary',[107] they made no appreciable amendments to the Paris scales,[108] gave a cold reception to further applications for higher

105. Cf. Aulard, I, 360–520 (January–February), 520–694 (March–April).

106. Prices for June 1790—with the exception of the price of bread —are from the *Enquête de juin 1793*; those for April 1795—again with the exception of the price of bread (see p. 188 above)—are from Aulard, I, 627–94.

107. Arch. Nat. AF II 80.

108. Cf. Biollay, p. 3.

pay[109] and, by their deliberate fostering of inflation and of the freely competitive 'open' market, considerably undermined the gains that had been won by the wage-earners. Though nominal wages appear, by April–May, to have advanced substantially over July 1794, the purchasing power of the workers must have fallen back to, or considerably below, that of 1790. This would appear from the only two examples of wages for these months that I have seen—the first that of two labourers who, though paid 10–12 *livres* per day in April, claimed to be worse off than previously on a wage of 30 *sous*;[110] the second that of a mathematical instrument maker who, in May, was receiving a daily wage of 15–20 *livres*.[111] While this is clearly too slender a basis on which to construct an index of wages of more than very limited validity, we may perhaps obtain some general indication of the rise or fall in the purchasing power of wages since 1790 by relating the increased nominal earnings of these two sets of workers to the rise in prices of selected consumer goods over the same period. The results are summarised in Table 8.

While the over-all decline in real wages indicated by these figures may appear to be relatively slight, it must be remembered that the year 1790 was a year of low wages and low 'effective' earnings and that, had a comparison been made with June 1793 or June 1794, the drop in real earnings would have appeared much greater. The position in April–May, therefore, suggests a sharp reversion to the lean period of the early Revolution—a position, inciden-

109. See, for example, the new Committee of Public Safety's threat to imprison port-workers asking for wages in excess of the revised 'maximum' of 15 August 1794 (Arch. Nat. AF II 80); and the cold reception given by the Convention to the petitions of the arms workers for higher wages on 31 October, 17 and 25 November 1794 (*Procès-Verbaux de la Convention Nationale*, XLVII, 132; XLIX, 244; I, 115).

110. Aulard, I, 658.

111. Arch. Nat. F⁷ 4669, doss. 5. The case is that of Dénot who, as an unemployed cook, had, on 14 July 1789, won notoriety by chopping off the head of de Launay, governor of the Bastille, with a butcher's knife (Arch. Nat. Y 12833).

tally, that was to become worse in the course of the year.[112]

TABLE 8 Earnings index and prices index, April 1795

Base period June 1790 = 100

Occupation	Earnings*	Prices†
Labourer	905	900
Instrument maker	739	900

* This column represents 'effective' daily earnings in April 1795 as a percentage of 'effective' daily earnings in June 1790. I have here assumed a proportion of 'effective' earnings to wages of 3-4, which is lower than that previously assumed for 1794 (see Table 6, above). This is due to indications of unemployment given in the reports of police agents and suggested by the closing of the *ateliers d'armes* in February.

† The price index here used is taken from Harris (pp. 107-8). In drawing up this index, a weight of 3 was given to bread and a weight of 1 to each of the following: eggs, potatoes, soap, fuel, butter, meat (beef, veal and pork are combined as one). Further, in the case of rationed goods, it was assumed that one-third of the bread and one-half of the meat were purchased in the 'open' market.

It is evident that, if the proportion of bread purchased during April in the 'open' market proved, as I have suggested, to be considerably higher than the figure of one-third assumed by Harris, the index figure of 900 for this month would have to be appreciably raised. However, for lack of more precise evidence, I have preferred to accept Harris's estimate.

Space will only permit a brief glance at the social movements of this period; but they serve to underline these conclusions. The Parisian *sans-culottes* had been left confused and leaderless by the *coup d'état* of Thermidor, which they had done so little to avert. Even the movement of

112. In November 1795, bread was sold on the 'open' market at 24 *livres* per lb., in December at 45-50 *livres*, and in May 1796 at 80 *livres* per lb.; while the market price for meat rose from 75 *livres* per lb. in January 1796 to 97 *livres* in March (E. Levasseur, *Histoire des Classes Ouvrières en France de 1789 à 1870* 2nd edition, 2 vols. (Paris, 1903), I, 236-44).

wages, apart from a number of petitions of the arms workers, petered out as the intentions of the new Committee became clear. But after the New Year a social movement developed in response to the Convention's inflationary policy and was to gain powerful momentum before it exploded in the desperate outbreaks of Germinal and Prairial. The rising cost of living, the closing of the *ateliers d'armes* in February, the persecution of Jacobins, the extravagance of the new rich, the arrogance of the middle-class youth (or *muscadins*) were all to play their part in stimulating this movement; but, above all, it was the high price and shortage of bread—at times reduced to a ration of 3 or 4 ounces—that gave it continuity and coherence. Both insurrections adopted as their slogan, 'Bread and the Constitution of 1793'; yet the driving motive was that of hunger.[113] But the spur of hunger was not sufficient to achieve results: for lack of leadership and political purpose the movement was crushed, and the *sans-culottes* were not to rise again as a social force for 35 years.[114]

We may now attempt a brief summary. After the 'famine' year of 1789, when bread was almost continuously in short supply and (when obtainable) swallowed up a disproportionate amount of the incomes of the wage-earners and *menu peuple*, we saw a slight fall in prices and rise in real wages during the period 1790 to September 1791. Already in the autumn of that year the rise in the price of bread threatened to recreate the conditions of 1789; and we have seen that this was followed by a sharp rise in the prices of all commodities, particularly of colonial products, in

113. This is abundantly clear both from the opinions of police agents, published by Aulard, and from the statements of the numerous persons arrested between January and May. (See Arch. Préf. Pol. series Aa, nos. 50, 71, 78, 80, 136, 153, 216, 241, 251; Arch. Nat. W 546–8 (Commission Militaire of 1–4 Prairial); and, above all, the papers of the Comité de Sûreté Générale, the most important of which are in the Archives Nationales, series F⁷.)

114. For a more detailed treatment of these movements, see pp. 151–7 above.

the early months of 1792, consequent upon the hoarding, speculation and shortages arising from the approach of war. This movement was partly arrested in the summer and autumn of 1792, but reappeared more sharply in the early months of 1793. A review of wages and prices in June 1793 suggested, however, that, partly owing to the subsidised provision of cheap bread, wages caught up with commodity prices as a whole. Yet this equilibrium was again disturbed by the continued rise in prices and the chronic scarcity of bread during the summer and autumn. We then saw that the energetic measures of control and requisition carried out by the Committee of Public Safety arrested the inflationary movement, ensured a comparative adequacy of supplies, stabilised the prices of essentials at a level not far exceeding that of 1790, and, though keeping the wages movement in check, allowed real wages to rise substantially. After the fall of Robespierre, we saw that this policy was abandoned by his successors and that there was a steep upward movement in the prices of all commodities—including, in effect, of bread—and the consequent reversion of the Parisian *menu peuple* to the famine conditions of 1789.

A general conclusion that here emerges is that an essential condition for the relative prosperity of the Parisian wage-earners, artisans and small shopkeepers lay, during this whole period, in the provision of cheap and plentiful bread: where that condition was lacking—as it was in 1789, in early 1790, for a period in 1791–2, in the summer and autumn of 1793 and, most strikingly, in the spring and summer of 1795—the *menu peuple* suffered great hardship. From this arises the further conclusion that, during the revolutionary period as a whole, despite the social upheaval and war-time shortage and inflation, the material conditions of the common people of Paris tended to improve. Though there were periodic setbacks in 1791–3, there was a relatively continuous and substantial improvement above the famine conditions of 1789 until their reappearance in 1795.

Our study has indicated, too, how responsive the popular movement was, at every stage, to any shortage or upward fluctuation in the price of essential consumer goods, particularly of bread. Although the special concern of the common people for the supply of cheap and adequate food often merged with, and lent strength to, the political aims of the revolutionary leaders (as in July and October 1789 and in the spring and summer of 1793), and although some popular movements—such as the agitation leading up to the Champ de Mars demonstration in the summer of 1791 or the overthrow of the monarchy in June–August 1792—were essentially political in character, the most typical and continuous of the popular movements were closely concerned with the issues of prices and supplies. So it was in the summer and autumn months of 1789, in the grocery riots of February 1792 and 1793, in the so-called 'Hébertist' insurrection of September 1793 and, most emphatically of all, in the final, desperate risings of April and May 1795. It is not suggested, however, that these movements owed their impetus solely to short-term economic factors. The motives inspiring them are, of course, far more diverse and must ultimately be traced to the complex of economic, social and political relations which the Revolution in part created and in part inherited from the Old Régime. A detailed study of French popular movements in the century preceding the Revolution has yet to be made; but it would be surprising if it were to reveal a pattern closely identical with that of similar movements arising during the revolutionary years themselves. Though sharp upward fluctuations in food prices were not uncommon under the Old Régime and provoked repeated protest and public disturbance,[115] yet the riots thus occasioned could not but be of a different order from those of 1789–95, because the particular social and political relations—not to mention the peculiar

115. See D. Mornet, *Les Origines Intellectuelles de la Révolution Franaise* (Paris, 1933), pp. 444–5.

insurrectionary temper—of the Revolution were lacking.[116]

At various stages of the Revolution there were, as we have seen, strikes and other movements for higher wages: in August–September 1789, in April–June 1791, in the early summer of 1793, in the spring and summer of 1794. Yet in relation to the popular movement as a whole, these were of secondary importance, and they were rarely provoked by sharp upward movements in the prices of food. It is, in fact, significant that the most substantial of them—the movements of April–June 1791 and of January–July 1794—took place at times of a shortage of labour and of falling or stable prices; and that the latter movement collapsed when the Thermidorians relaxed controls and reverted to a policy of high prices and inflation.

These conclusions by no means exhaust the deductions that may be drawn from an examination of the movements of prices and wages and their impact on social movements during the Revolution. Quite apart from its contribution to economic or social history, it may perhaps be claimed that the more detailed study of such factors, and its extension to revolutionary France as a whole, would help to elucidate a number of problems that beset the political historian of the Revolution and whose solution might be brought nearer by the lines of investigation here suggested. These wider possibilities can, of course, be no more than hinted at within the brief and limited compass of the present study.

---

116. The same strictures apply to the revolutionary period itself after the defeat of the insurrections of Germinal and Prairial. How else are we to explain the collapse of the popular movement after this date notwithstanding the continued, and even accelerated, rise in the prices of all essentials in the latter half of 1795 (see p. 193, n. 112, above)?

For a discussion of the relative importance of political and economic factors in stimulating popular participation in insurrectionary movements during the Revolution, see the foregoing article.

Part Three   London

'Mother Gin' and the London Riots of 1736

The year 1736 was a severe testing year for the administration of Sir Robert Walpole. The fractious alliance of the 'Patriots' threatened to disrupt the formidable combination of interests long manipulated and held together by Sir Robert with the aid of the Duke of Newcastle. As ever, the Jacobite menace lurked in the background and was a constant preoccupation of government. In the early months of the year, the West country had been inflamed by turnpike riots, said to have been encouraged by 'gentlemen of fortune', and, owing to strong local feelings of sympathy, rioters arrested in Hereford had been transferred to Worcester for trial.[1] There were further riots at Bristol;[2] and, in the summer and autumn, during the King's absence in Hanover, Parliament's measures against smuggling had touched off the far more dangerous outbreak in Edinburgh, culminating in the murder of Captain Porteous and a renewal of anti-English agitation in Scotland.[3] Even in the Duke of Newcastle's stronghold of Sussex, the government 'interest' was being undermined, if we are to trust the testimony of Archdeacon Thomas Ball of Chichester who, in sending the Duke in early December a list of livings in the gift of the deanery and chapter, referred to a 'new and unnatural' confederacy being hatched by Tories and a group of 'considerable grumbling Whiggs'.[4] And—perhaps most sinister of all—Westminster Hall, on the very threshold of government,

From *The Guildhall Miscellany*, I, no. 10 (Sept. 1959), 53–62.

1. P.R.O., State Papers Domestic, 36/38, fos. 3, 17, 47.
2. S.P. Dom., 36/39, fo. 41.
3. *Gentleman's Magazine* (1736), pp. 230, 422, 486, 514–22, 549–50.
4. S.P. Dom., 36/39, fo. 111.

was rocked by an 'insolent' explosion of gunpowder, the presumed work of 'a sett of low Jacobites', who had concocted 'a preparation which they call a *phosphorus*, that takes fire from the air'.[5]

Not the least alarming of the social disorders of this year were the East London Riots of July and the disturbances that threatened to follow in Holborn, Westminster and Southwark in September. While these outbreaks sprang from different causes, the Government was naturally inclined, in the prevailing state of unrest, to treat them in a common context. Hitherto, historians have either neglected them altogether or considered them in piecemeal fashion;[6] and it is only the recent deposition of the Cholmondeley (Houghton) MSS.—forming part of the private papers of Sir Robert Walpole—with the Cambridge University Library that has made it possible both to relate these episodes in greater detail, to give a picture of the Government's attitude towards them, and to attempt to present them in their correct historical setting. To prepare the present study, I have drawn largely on Group P/70 of these papers (consisting of two small files of some forty letters and scribbled notes),[7] supplemented by materials

5. Sir Robert Walpole to Horace Walpole, 29 July–9 August 1736 (reproduced in Archdeacon William Coxe, *Memoirs of the Life and Administration of Sir Robert Walpole*, 3 vols. (London, 1798), III. 348).

6. See, e.g., M.D. George, *London Life in the XVIII Century* (London, 1925), pp. 117–18; H. J. Bradley, *The History of Shoreditch Church* (London, 1914), pp. 27–30; H. Llewellyn Smith, *The History of East London from the earliest Times to the End of the Eighteenth Century* (London, 1939), p. 163. [These accounts deal only with the preliminary disturbances in Shoreditch and Spitalfields arising from the Anglo-Irish dispute over wages.]

7. I am extremely grateful to the Most Hon. the Marquess of Cholmondeley, G.C.V.O., for giving me permission to use these papers. I am, further, indebted to Mr. G. Allen Chinnery, M.A., for drawing attention to their existence and for his brief analysis of their contents in the *Bulletin of the Society of Local Archivists*, no. 11, April 1953, pp. 27–8; also to Dr. J. H. Plumb, F.S.A., for kindly identifying Sir Robert Walpole's handwriting for me in the case of two of these documents.

from the State Papers Domestic and Entry Books in the Public Record Office,[8] the Sessions papers in the Middlesex County Record Office,[9] the printed *Proceedings* of the Old Bailey,[10] the Walpole correspondence in Archdeacon Coxe's *Memoirs*, the contemporary press, and occasional documents in the British Museum, and in the archives of the Holborn, Mile End, Shoreditch, Westminster and Guildhall Libraries.

In so far as the London disturbances of July and September 1736 had a common origin—how far this was so we shall see later—it lay, ostensibly at least, in the measures adopted by Parliament in that year to restrict the consumption of gin and other 'spirituous liquors'. It was the age when gin-shops proudly advertised: 'drunk for a penny, dead drunk for twopence, and straw for nothing'; the sale of spirits had increased from 3,500,000 gallons in 1727 to nearly 5,500,000 gallons in 1735;[11] and, by the latter year, over 7,000 shops, both licensed and unlicensed, were selling gin and brandy in the Metropolitan area of Middlesex alone.[12] The Act of 1736 arose from a petition presented to Parliament on 20 February by the Middlesex justices, who called for action to restrict the excessive sales of spirits,

by which means Journeymen, Apprentices, and Servants, are drawn in to taste, and, by degrees, to like, approve, and immoderately drink thereof.[13]

8. S.P. Dom., 36/39, fos. 91, 93, 116; S.P. Dom. Entry Books. 44/130, pp. 109–14.

9. Middlesex R.O., Sessions Rolls (Middlesex), no. 2662 (8 September 1736); Gaol Delivery Books, vol. 315 (1736), p. 19. I have been unable to find any documents relating to the riots in the Sessions papers for Surrey and the City of London.

10. *The whole Proceedings on the King's Commission of the Peace, Oyer and Terminer, and Gaol Delivery for the City of London and . . . for the County of Middlesex* (1736), pp. 199–204 [hereafter cited as *Proceedings*].

11. Article in *East London Observer*, 22 May 1915. See also B. Williams *The Whig Supremacy* (Oxford, 1945), pp. 128–9.

12. M. D. George, *op. cit.,* pp. 32–3.

13. *Commons Journals*, XXII, 582–3.

Parliament acted promptly and resolved, a month later,

> That . . . for all Spirituous Liquors which any Retailer thereof shall, from and after the 24th Day of June 1736, be possessed of, there be granted to his Majesty a Duty of Twenty Shillings per Gallon; and
>
> That . . . from and after the 24th Day of June 1736, the Sum of Fifty Pounds yearly shall be paid to his Majesty for a Licence to be taken yearly by every Person keeping a public Brandy-shop, a public Victualling-house, Coffee-house, or Alehouse, or being an Innholder, who shall vend, barter, or utter, any such spirituous liquors.

A Committee, whose members included Sir Robert Walpole, George Bubb Dodington and the Master of the Rolls (Sir Joseph Jekyll), was ordered to prepare a Bill, which quickly passed through its various stages unopposed, and received the Royal Assent on 5 May.[14]

While the operation of the Gin Act was, in fact, postponed until Michaelmas,[15] its adoption in the early summer may, therefore, have contributed to the unrest that broke out in violent rioting in Shoreditch, Spitalfields and Whitechapel in July. Yet the ostensible and immediate cause was quite different. The new church of St. Leonard's, Shoreditch, designed by the City architect, George Dance the Elder,[16] was about to be erected in the place of the old. In the course of demolishing the old church, William Goswell, a vestryman of St. Leonard's parish,[17] who was in charge of the operations, dismissed 'a great number' of his English workmen and engaged Irish labour from Shoreditch and Spitalfields in their place at one-half or

---

14. *Commons Journals*, XXII, 585–7, 638, 658, 677, 690, 703–4.

15. Coxe, *Memoirs*, III, 348.

16. George Dance (b. 1695) also built the Mansion House (completed 1753), St. Luke's, Old Street (1732–3) and St. Botolph, Aldgate (1741–4) (*London County Council Survey of London* (London, 1922), VIII (*Parish of St. Leonard, Shoreditch*), 99–100).

17. Shoreditch Lib., St. Leonard, Shoreditch, Vestry Minute Book, 1727–1771, pp. 93, 115, 124.

two-thirds of their wages.[18] This fact, added to the further grievance of the employment of large numbers of Irish by local master weavers,[19] led immediately to an outbreak of violent rioting against the Irish in these two parishes, which later spread to Whitechapel. In a letter of 29 July to his brother Horace, Sir Robert Walpole gave the following account of the first three days' rioting based on reports received from government agents:[20]

On Monday night last (*i.e.* July G.R.), there was an appearance of numbers being assembled in a very disorderly manner at Shoreditch, near Spitalfields. Their cry and complaint was of being underworked, and starved by the Irish: *Down with the Irish, &c.* But that night the numbers were not very great, and they dispersed themselves without doing any mischief . . . On Tuesday evening they assembled again in bodies, and were about 7 O'clock thought to be 2,000 in number.[21] They now grew more riotous; they attacked a public house, kept by an Irishman,

18. According to Walpole, the Irishmen received 'above one-third less a day'; whereas the anonymous author of 'An account of the parish of St. Leonard, Shoreditch, Middlesex' (Shoreditch Lib. Mid-19th cent. MS. acquired in 1913) follows Malcolm's *Anecdotes* in citing '5 or 6 shillings a week, when the British demanded twelve shillings' (p. 34). According to H. J. Bradley (*op. cit.*, p. 127), the engagement of Irish labour followed a strike by the English workmen for higher wages. This appears to be confirmed by Lord Hardwicke, newly appointed Lord Chancellor, when, in the course of the Lords debate on 10 February 1737, he claimed that the riots 'proceeded from . . . the unlawful and unjust Combination of Journeymen and Labourers to keep up or inhance their wages' (*Gentleman's Magazine* (July 1737), p. 378).

19. C. (H.) MSS., P/70, file 2/14; Coxe, *Memoirs*, III, 350; *Gentleman's Magazine* (1736), p. 422. A contemporary broadsheet, violently hostile to the Irish, may be confusing these two elements when it says that 'Irish weavers' were employed as labourers to demolish the church (British Museum, 515. 1. 2 (236): *Spittlefields and Shorditch in an Uproar OR the Devil to pay with the English and Irish*).

20. These informants—Joseph Bell, Col. John Martin (in Shoreditch and Spitalfields) and John Ibbut (in Whitechapel)—sent in reports every few hours. The reports, though probably incomplete, form a substantial part of the two files of paper in P/70 of the C. (H.) MSS.

21. This information corresponds almost word for word with that sent in by Joseph Bell the same evening (C. (H.) MSS., P/70, file 1 (the papers in this file are not numbered).).

where the Irish resorted and victualled, broke down all the doors and windows and quite gutted the house.[22] Another house of the same sort underwent the same fate. By this time (those places being within the jurisdiction of the City), the Mayor and Deputy Lieutenant of the Tower Hamlets were assembled in order to disperse them. The proclamation was read; but the mob, wholly regardless of the proclamation, increased every minute, and were thought to be about 4,000 strong. The Magistrate upon this gave orders for raising the Militia; and in the Meantime the Deputy Lieutenant wrote to the Commanding Officer at the Tower to send to their assistance such a number of the Guards they could spare.[23] upon which an officer with about fifty men was sent by Major White. Upon the appearance of the Guards the mob retired, shifted from one street and alley to another, and gave no resistance, and by break of day were all dispersed. All Wednesday things seemed very quiet till evening, when the mob rose again to as great a number; but the Militia of the Tower Hamlets being then raised, marched against them; but the mob in same manner retired before them wherever they came, and gave not the least resistance . . . and so dispersed themselves before the morning.

In a 'P.S.' he adds a brief note on the events of Thursday:

It was between ten and eleven before any number at all appeared in bodies; but they did not amount to 300; they fled before the Militia from place to place without any resistance, or doing any mischief but defacing one weaver's house, who, they said, had employed Irish journeymen.[24]

A more detailed account of what took place in Shoreditch on the Thursday night was later written by one J.

22. This may have been 'Goulding's, an Irish Cook's in Shoreditch', said to have offered to give his Irish patrons ten guineas 'for a pint of English Man's blood' (*Spittlefields and Shorditch in an Uproar*). The same account gives the names of seven English and ten Irish reputed to have been 'dangerously wounded' and a boy, Thomas Larkin, said to have been killed, in the battles that ensued.

23. The letter, dated 27 July 1736 and despatched from 'The Angel and Crown taverne in Spittlefields', is in the State Papers Dom., 36/39, fo. 91.

24. Coxe, *Memoirs*, III, 348-9. The first part of this letter, as also the broadsheet, *Spittlefields and Shorditch in an Uproar*, is reproduced in H. J. Bradley, *The History of Shoreditch Church*, pp. 27-30.

Furnell of Shoreditch and sent on to Walpole by George Smith of Red Lion Court, Fleet Street.[25] The writer pays particular tribute to the part played by John Collet, a master carpenter and publican of the King John's Head, King John's Court, of Holywell Lane. As a Militia lieutenant in Major Jones's Company in one of the Tower Hamlets Regiments, Collet was ordered, on the night of the 29th, by the Lieutenancy stationed at *The Three Tuns* tavern in Spitalfields to proceed with eighteen men, a sergeant and a drum to quell the disturbances in Brick Lane[26] and adjoining streets. He caught up with the rioters, now 700 or 800 strong, who had 'nearly pulled down a house in Bryant Street', in Holywell Lane, Shoreditch. Having drawn up his men in King John's Court, adjoining the Lane, he ordered them aloud to load with ball (although only powder was intended) and parleyed with the rioters as follows:

He desired to know the cause of their complaint; to which one who seem'd to be the Captⁿ of the Mobb made answer in the name of the Rest that Mr. Goswell, the builder of Shoreditch Church, had paid off his English Labourers and Imployed Irish because they worked cheaper and several of the Master Weavers Imployed none but Irish by wch means the English Manufacturers were starving and that they chose rather to be hang'd than starved, to wch Mr. Collet replyed that if they wanted redress in this or any other matter their proper Method was to get a Petition drawn to Parliament & no doubt all English Manufacturers would find Encouragement there upon proper Application and that he would find them a Gentleman to settle their case properly and assist them in obtaining Releife. That, as for Mr. Goswell, he had already discharged his Irish Labourers and Employed English in their stead and he doubted not but the Weavers would be prevailed upon to do the same. That Mr.

25. The accompanying note to George Smith, though headed 'Shoreditch Septr 4th 1736', is marked (in Walpole's hand) 'Letter from Spittlefields' (C. (H.) MSS., P/70, file 2/5).

26. According to the *Gentleman's Magazine*, an Irish public house was attacked in Brick Lane, where one young man was killed by the defenders' firearms and seven or eight wounded (July 1736, p. 422. See also *London Magazine* (August 1736), p. 457, and see note 22 above).

Chetham (who as they said Employed near 200 Irish and against whom the Mobb was particularly incensed) had promised him that he would discharge his Irish workmen as soon as they had finished the several peices of work they had in hand. After this short Parley the Mobb gave 2 or 3 huzzas and the Ring-leaders thank'd Mr. Collet for his advice and immediately dispers'd and have never gathered in those parts since.[27]

In a note written to his brother Horace on the next morning July (30), Sir Robert Walpole showed some optimism:

I believe there is now an end to this bustle, and so I hope will all attempts end to disturb the peace of his majestie's government.[28]

Yet a letter sent the same day by the Duke of Newcastle to the Lord Mayor of London was less sanguine and expressed the Government's continued concern at the possibility of the riots spreading, particularly into the City:

You may depend upon all the Assistance, that can be given you, (if it should be necessary), His Majesty having nothing more at heart than the preventing throughout the Kingdom, and especially in the City of London, any Disturbances which might interrupt the Trade, or disquiet the Minds of His Majesty's faithful subjects.[29]

These fears were only too well founded. We learn from a report by Joseph Bell that, between seven and eight o'clock that evening, crowds had begun to re-form in Spitalfields.[30] A glance at the map suggests that they then moved down Brick Lane to Whitechapel to join forces with local rioters who, later that evening, attacked Irish dwelling-houses and ale-houses in Goodman's Fields[31] (Rag Fair) and Rosemary Lane.[32]

27. C. (H.) MSS., P/70, file 2/14: 'An account of some particulars of the late Riot in Shoreditch.' The assurance is added: 'Chetham (though Irish himself) has since begun to dismiss his Irish workers, and the builder of the Church has taken on no new ones.' Collet's esteem is therefore said to be very high among these Poor Ignorant People who chiefly composed this Mobb'.

28. Coxe, *Memoirs*, III, 350.

29. S.P. Dom., 36/39, fo. 93.

30. C. (H.) MSS., P/70, file 1.

31. Goodman's Fields became later in the century a fashionable

Walpole's correspondence, surprisingly, is silent about this phase of the riots, which caused far more considerable damage to property than those in Shoreditch and, moreover, constituted a more direct threat to the security of the City of London. The government agent, John Ibbut, gave a rough picture of events and reported that the general cry was 'Down with the Irish!', occasionally interspersed with cries of 'King George for ever and down with the Irish!'—to which he and his friends replied with 'King George and no Popery!'[33] Far more substantial and revealing are the accounts that emerge from the testimony of witnesses (including publicans, justices and soldiers), who were called upon to give evidence against the five prisoners taken who were tried at the Old Bailey in the following October. John Walden, publican of the *Bull and Butcher* in Cable Street, testified that his eighteen lodgers[34] were all in bed when the crowds approached, shouting, 'Down with the Irish!' Having told his lodgers 'to get up and shift for their lives', he bolted his door, while his assailants set to work. Meat was taken from his window, and six shutters and seventy-odd panes of glass were smashed at a total cost of £3 13s. od.[35] A more comprehensive picture is given by Richard Burton, a brewer's cooper:

On Friday night, July 30, between 9 and 10, I was at the end of Red Lion Street, and I saw the Mob coming down Bell Yard,

residential area of Anglo-Jewry (*East London Observer* (5 August, 9 and 16 September 1911)).

32. At the Old Bailey trials following the Whitechapel events it was said that 'the Mob were come out of Spittlefields and were pulling down some houses' (*Proceedings*, (1736), p. 200). This confirms Joseph Bell's view that it was 'the same mob' which he had seen in Spittlefields that 'operated in Rag Fair later the same night'; but it should not be taken too literally: we shall see (pp. 210–11 below) that the prisoners taken in Goodman's Fields were mainly local men.

33. C. (H.) MSS., P/70, file 1.

34. It may well be significant that Walden generally housed sixty or seventy lodgers, mainly country shopkeepers up in town on a short visit (*Proceedings* (1736), p. 203).

35. *Ibid.*, p. 203.

with Sticks and lighted Links. One of them made a sort of speech directing the rest to go to *Church Lane*, to the *Gentleman and Porter*. My Master serving Mr. Allen who keeps the House with Drink, I ran down to inform him that his Sign was mentioned. There was about 50 or 60 of them then, and they had 2 or 3 Links with them. One read from a Paper the Signs of the *Gentleman and Porter*, the *Bull and Butcher*, and the Tavern in *Well Street*. I did not hear them make any Declaration what was to be done, but I went directly to Allen's to inform him they had great Sticks, like Stakes out of Bakers Bavins. While I was standing at *Allen's* Door, the Mob came down; I told them the House had been mine for a Fortnight, and that the Man who kept it before was gone. One of them was called *Captain Tom* the *Barber*, and was in a striped Banjan. I would have taken notice of him, but he turned away and would not let me see his Face. I desired him to use me favourably and told him it was my House. They said they knew I was not *Irish* by my Tongue, and I should not be hurt. I made them set up Candles in the Windows, and pacify'd the Mob seemingly well, but a Woman telling them it was a sham, and that I was only the Brewer's Cooper, the Sticks flew immediately and beat the Candle out of my Hand, as I stood at the Door; but Justice *Phillips* coming down, and the Captain[36] with his Soldiers, they took some of them, and the rest made off immediately, and were gone as suddenly, as if a Hole had been dug in the Bottom of the Street, and they had all dropped into it at once.[37]

Such reports as these, and the Entry Books in the State Papers, also tell us the names of the rioters' victims and the persons arrested in the course of this episode. We learn, for example, that the following were

The several persons whose houses were broke:
Austin Allen, the Gentleman & Porter in Leman Street.
James Farrell, Church Lane.
Mrs. Austin, ditto.
Patrick Lyon at the Windmill, Back Lane.
Graves Akin, Leman Street.[38]

---

36. This was either Captain Hudson or Captain Litler, both of whom came from the Tower with a troop of thirty men (*ibid.*, p. 201).

37. *Ibid.*, pp. 199–200.

38. S.P. Dom., Entry Books, 44/130, p. 114; also (with slight textual

Other victims, who suffered less material damage, included: John Walden of the *Bull and Butcher*, Rag Fair, who had his shutters and windows 'much broke'; and Ann Pool, wife of Nathaniel Pool, the shutters of whose stall at the *Bull and Butcher* were 'broke' and who had '1 Leg of Lamb' and '2 knuckles of Legs of Mutton' stolen by the rioters.[39]

The drain on parish funds, however, was slight: in the Account Book of Holy Trinity, the Minories, which covered the area of the riots, we note the following 'disbursements' for July and August:

July 28. Gave relief to Wm Reaves he being shott in ye head and neck & was in y^e
    Parish house till cured.   1   –
    Gave relief for food to d° while under cure.   1   –
   „   31. Expended on ye Parish Acc^n in waiting upon y^e
    Justices & at Mr. Lampheres to Preserve ye Parish
    from Insults of the Mobb   7   –
August 5. Gave Mrs Portland for nursing ye Boy w^h was
    Shot   3   –[40]

Nine persons were taken into custody as the result of these disturbances;[41] they were:

Robert Page, journeyman weaver, lodging at Mr. Wilson's, Buckle Street, St. Mary, Whitechapel;
William Ormon Rod, blacksmith, lodging at Mr. Goulby's in Church Lane;

---

variations) C. (H.) MSS., P/70, file 1. There is nothing to indicate the scale of the damages either in these records or in the Treasury Minute Books.

Graves Akin (or Akens)'s house in Leman Street (East side) was valued at £9 p.a. (Guildhall Lib., St. Mary Whitechapel, Land Tax duplicates, 1736, MS. 6015/4, p. 50). Mrs. Austin may be the 'Elizabeth Austin' of Rosemary Lane, whose house was valued at a mere £3 p.a. (*ibid.*, p. 28). I have not been able to find the other victims in the Land Tax records.

39. S.P. Dom., Entry Books, 44/130, p. 112.
40. Mile End Lib., Holy Trinity Minories, Minutes and Account Books, 1720 to 1751, p. 251.
41. The *Gentleman's Magazine* wrongly relates these nine to the 'Riots in Spittlefields' (September 1736, p. 550).

Robert Mickey, brewer's servant, lodging at Mr. Adams' in Church Lane;
John Putrode (or *Puttroyd*), lodging at Mr. Payne's in Castle Street;
John Bates, brewer's servant, of Rupert Street, Goodman's Fields (all these five of St. Mary, Whitechapel);[42]
Edward Dudley, servant to Mr. Gower of Masters Gardens;
John Scott, carpenter, of Cole Yard, Drury Lane;
John Blundridge, presumed to be of St. Mary, Whitechapel;
Joshua Hall, a journeyman sawyer or lath-tender, and a soldier in Colonel Le Ferr's Company.[43]

Of these, five—Page, Ormon Rod, Putrode, Mickey and Hall—appeared for trial at the Old Bailey in October and were found guilty. The first three were sentenced to two years' imprisonment and to find surety for their good behaviour for seven years; the others, to one year in Newgate and to find surety for four years' good behaviour.[44]

A note in the *Gentleman's Magazine*, dated Sunday, 1 August, suggests that the East London riots against the Irish had a brief echo in other parts of the capital:

Mobs arose in Southwark, Lambeth and Tyburn-road, and took upon 'em to interrogate People whether they were for the English or Irish? but committed no Violence; several Parties of Horse Grenadiers dispers'd the Mobs which were gathering in Ratcliff-highway, to demolish the Houses of the Irish.[45]

Yet such incidents were short-lived; and, writing to Horace Walpole on 20 August, Sir Robert assured him that

42. Surprisingly for a 'brewer's servant', Bates appears in the Land Tax register as occupying a house valued at £6 p.a. (Guildhall Lib., St. Mary Whitechapel, Land Tax duplicates, 1736, MS. 6015/4, p. 61).
43. S.P. Dom., Entry Books, 44/130, pp. 111–14 (depositions); C. (H.) MSS., P/70, file 1 (depositions); *Proceedings*, 1736, pp. 199–204; Midd. R.O., Sessions Rolls (Middlesex), no. 2662 (8 September 1736): indictments and Calendar of prisoners committed to Newgate, 21 July–8 September 1736; Gaol Delivery Books, vol. 315 (1736), p. 19.
44. *Proceedings*, 1736, p. 212; *London Magazine* (1736), p. 580.
45. *Gentleman's Magazine*, August 1736, p. 484; quoted by T. Allen, *History of the Parish of Lambeth* (London, 1826), p. 159.

'The tumults and disorders here are quite at an end—the industry of the Jacobites was not able to improve this truly Irish incident into a more general confusion.'

But he added more cautiously:

'Various are the reports, and some apprehensions, that new troubles may arise on Michaelmas-day, the commencement of the Gin Act; but I am fully satisfied that hitherto there is no formed design.' [46]

Yet, a fortnight later, Mr. Furnell, Walpole's Shoreditch correspondent, was writing:

It is the Common Talk of the Tippling Ale houses and little Gin Shops that Sr Robert Walpole and the Master of ye Rolls [47] will not outlive Michaelmas long [48]

During the last week in September, the Government received more certain information of plans to create disturbances by distributing free gin to the 'populace' on the night before the Gin Act became operative. The Government was well prepared and it all amounted to very little; yet it is of some interest to note, from Walpole's private papers, that such attempts were made and what form they took. The information was supplied, unwittingly, by the unknown persons whose hostility to the Gin Act led them to write letters, often in the same hand and couched in similar terms, to a number of distillers and retailers of spirits in Westminister and Holborn, urging them to celebrate 'Madam Geneva's lying-in-state' in the manner described; four of these letters were passed on to Walpole [49] and are among the Cholmondeley (Houghton) MSS. One of them, addressed to William Alexander, a

46. Coxe, *Memoirs*, III, 357.

47. Sir Joseph Jekyll M.P., Master of the Rolls (1717–38) and chief promoter of the Gin Act.

48. C. (H.) MSS., P/70, file 2/14.

49. See a letter of Sir Robert to Horace Walpole of 30 September–11 October, in which he outlines these plans and writes: 'Four of these letters have fallen into my hands' (Coxe, *Memoirs*, III, 359).

retailer of King's Street, St. James's,[50] on Friday, 24 September, runs as follows:

'As you are known to be an honest man & true lover of your Country this comes to inform you that the Body of the Distillers, ffarmers &c., aggrieved by the late pernicious & Enslaving Bill on spirituous liquors have agreed to show they are not blind to the Design in hand of bringing on a general Excise (of which this particular Imposition on us is but the Prelude) & at the same time to testifye our cheerful submission to the will of our Rulers. The Manner is this.

The Dealers in distill'd liquors to keep open shop on Tuesday next, being the Eve of the day on which the act is to take Place and give Gratis what quantities of Gin, or other liquors, shall be call'd for by the populace, provided the said liquors are not carried away, but drunk in the Shops; then christen the (illegible) with the Remainder, & conclude with Bonfires to the Honour of the Ministry—no harm is meant, & you'll be surpris'd both at the number & fashion of those you will give joy in this act of publick spirit.

All Retailers whose Circumstances will not permit them to contribute to the festival shall have quantities of liquor sent in before the time. Gin & Anniseed seem to be most used in your shop & you shall be supplyed with both on Monday. Observe the directions here given & you will find your acct in it as will all your fellow sufferers. The red coats are coming towards London, but we have stanch friends among them, & will not be any prejudice to the Russet. Invite as many neighbours as you can conveniently, & be under no apprehension of the Riot Act, but whenever you hear the words S[r] Robert & S[r] Joseph[51] joyne in the Huzza.[52]

50. William Alexamder's house in King Street (South side) had a rentable value of £10 p.a. (Westminster Lib., St. James's Watch Rate (collector's book), 1736, D 431).

51. Sir Joseph Jekyll.

52. C. (H.) MSS., P/70, file 2/7. An accompanying letter, addressed by William Alexander to Sir Robert Walpole, runs: 'Sir, having received a few days before the Ginn Act took place, a strange Sort of a letter without any name signed directed to me, I was persuaded by a friend to whom I show'd it to divulge it to your Hon.' (*Ibid.*, file 2/6.) Further correspondence suggests that the 'friend' was one James Brettel, of 4 Castle Street, who, in the first instance, brought the letter to Walpole without Alexander's authority (*ibid.*, file 2/15).

Another letter of the same date, addressed to a distiller, urges him to be generous in his supply of liquor to his retailers and adds:

If we are English men let us show we have English spirits & not tamely submit to the yoak just ready to be fastened about our necks. But town and country Ring with the names of Sr Robert and Sr Joseph, let them see that wooden shoes are not so easy to be worn as they imagine.[53]

A third letter, addressed to 'Mr. Moor, Distiller at the Corner of Long Ditch, in Westminster',[54] claimed that the Gin Act struck 'at the very roots of Property' and was a 'prelude to general Excise next Session'. Calling on Mr. Moor to give all the liquor asked for '*gratis* in your several shops', it urged him to 'oblige them to repeal that pernicious Act without the immense sum that will be demanded for it.'[55] The same writer also invited William Jellico, 'at the Distillers Arms in Hide Street, near Giles's Pound',[56] to distribute free in his shops 'what gin &c. shall be necessary to elevate the minds of the People', and ended with the repeated refrain:

Let Town and Country echo that night with Sr Robert and Sr Joseph, make bonfires and give loud Huzzas to their honour.[57]

53. C. (H.) MSS., P/70, file 2/11.

54. John Moore, distiller, had two houses in Broken Cross, at the junction of Thieving Lane and Long Ditch, in Westminster, together valued at £20 p.a. (Westminster Lib., St. Margaret's, Poors Rate, 1736, E 347, p. 81). In the Watch Book of St. Margaret's parish we find that, on 1 July 1736, William Stanton, one of the twenty-six watchmen recently appointed to patrol the parish, was detailed 'to stand at Mr. Mores the Distiller (the Corner of ye Gate house) and he to watch Broken Cross, Long Ditch (including Bennetts Street), both sides of the way as far as John Street and both sides of Tuttle Street from the Gate house to the Swann Inn and from thence to his stand' (Westminster Lib., St. Margaret's Watch Book of Minutes, 1736–1766, p. 11).

55. C. (H.) MSS., P/70, file 2/9.

56. This should read 'High Street' (Holborn), where William Jellico occupied a house of a rentable value of £16 p.a. (Holborn Lib., St. Giles, Bloomsbury, Poors Rate, 1736, 1st Part, p. 43).

57. C. (H.) MSS., P/70, file 2/10.

There were further reports, or rumours, of preparations
for mock-funeral celebrations on the South bank of the
river: an anonymous report sent in to Walpole speaks
of 'the Story of the Coffins of the other side of the Water'
and adds:

They have got a story that Mother Gin is to be buried in great
pomp on Thursday night, when they imagine they shall not be
disturbed by the Guards . . . It was reported last night that a
load of Broomsticks had been delivered out in Kent Street for
the use of the Mob, but upon the strictest enquiry he (Mr.
Draper, the General Surveyor of Distilleries) cant find any
truth in the story.[58]

The Government, while prepared to discount many of
these rumours, took effective precautions. Colonel De
Veil, Sir John Fielding's predecessor as magistrate at
Bow Street, was in continuous contact with the Tilt Yard
and the Horse Guards, in case 'any Disturbance should
suddenly happen';[59] on the morning of 28 September, a
double guard was mounted at Kensington and the guard
at St. James's and at the Horse Guards in Whitehall was
reinforced; Guards paraded Covent Garden 'in order to
suppress any Tumult that might happen at the going down
of Spirituous Liquors'; and, that evening,

a Detachment of 60 soldiers went to guard Sir Joseph Jekyll's
House at the Rolls in Chancery Lane, which was said to be
threatened, among others, by the Populace.[60]

Everything passed off peacefully enough. Summing up the
situation on 29 September, the *London Magazine* reported:

Several people at Norwich, Bristol, and other Places, as well as
at London, made themselves very merry on the Death of Madam
Gin, and some of both sexes got soundly drunk at her Funeral,

58. C. (H.) MSS., P/70, file 2/4.
59. See a letter of De Veil's addressed to the Duke of Newcastle on
1 October 1736 (S.P. Dom., 36/39, fo. 116).
60. *London Magazine* (October 1736), p. 579; *Gentleman's Magazine*
(September 1736), p. 551.

for which the Mob made a funeral Procession, but committed no Outrages.[61]

At first, it seemed as if the Gin Act had justified the hopes entertained by its promoters. The *Gentleman's Magazine*, at least, thought fit to comment on 31 October:

The good effects of the Gin-Act have appeared in the Sobriety and regular conduct of the Soldiery and Common People, so that there have not been half the Number of Courts-Martial, or Quarrels brought to the Justices, as before; and some observed, that the Bakers and Sellers of Old Cloths, had a brisker Trade since Michaelmas.[62]

Yet this optimism turned out to be singularly misplaced. Jekyll's Act, far from bringing the small gin-shops to heel, which had been its main purpose, by the very severity of its provisions, led to wholesale evasions of the law. As Sir Robert Walpole himself—a distinctly lukewarm supporter of the Act—had forecast in a letter to Horace;

The lower sort of brandy-shops, whose poverty secures them from the penalties of the law, may continue to sell in defiance of the law, and in hopes that nobody will think worth their while to prosecute them for what they cannot possibly recover.[63]

However, between September 1736 and July 1738 alone, no less than 12,000 informations were laid against dealers of spirits in the Bills of Mortality, leading to 4,896 convictions and 4,000 claims for the £5 allowed to informers out of the penalty of £100.[64] More gin than ever was consumed, rising to over 8 million gallons in 1743.[65] It needed another Gin Act in that year, and the further Act of 1751, accompanied by Fielding's *Inquiry* and Hogarth's pictorial propaganda, to stamp out the grosser evils of unbridled gin-drinking.[66]

61. *London Magazine, loc. cit.*
62. *Gentleman's Magazine* (October 1736), p. 619.
63. Coxe, *Memoirs*, III, 357.
64. M.D. George, *op. cit.*, p. 332.
65. *Ibid.*, p. 35.
66. *Ibid.*, pp. 35–6; B. Williams, *The Whig Supremacy*, p. 129.

Nevertheless, the London riots and threatened disturbances of 1736 were not wholly concerned with gin, and it still remains to look more closely at their origins and the motives that prompted them. Ostensibly, of course, the riots of July were solely the product of the engagement of cheap Irish labour and those of September of Parliament's measures to curtail the sale of spirits; but the Administration, as we have seen, was inclined to link them together and we must consider its justification for so doing.

It is clear both from Walpole's correspondence and from the assortment of documents in the Cholmondeley (Houghton) MSS. brought together under the common title of 'Riotts', that the Government considered that both sets of disturbances had a common origin—not so much in the Gin Act as in Jacobite agitation. In his letter to Horace Walpole on 29 July (three days after the riots began in Shoreditch), having described the gunpowder explosion in Westminster Hall, Sir Robert continues:

At the same time there are great endeavours, using the same sort of instruments, to inflame the people, and to raise great tumults upon Michaelmas-day, when the Gin Act takes place; and as *these lower sorts of Jacobites* appear at this time more busy than they have for a great while, they are very industrious and taking advantage of everything that offers, to raise tumult and disorders among the people.

And, having related the course of the anti-Irish riots in Shoreditch, he concludes:

But altho' the complaint of the Irish was the first motive, *the Jacobites are blending with all other discontents*, endeavouring to stir up the distillers and ginn-retailers and to avail themselves of the spiritt and fury of the people.[67]

While, in his letter to Horace Walpole on 6 August, he considers the outcome of the East London disturbances

a favourable indication that people are not so ready as the Jacobites flatter themselves to join in general riotts,

67. Coxe, *Memoirs*, III, 349–50 (my *italics*).

he is still apprehensive of 'what may happen Michaelmas-day'.[68]

Among the Cholmondeley (Houghton) MSS., a scribbled note in Walpole's hand, dated 24 September 1736, presents the London disturbances even more explicitly as part of a Jacobite plot:

> Within eight or nine months last past there have been consider-able quantities of Arms, exceeding ten thousand at least, landed on the Northern Coast, viz. Bampff, Pertsey, Peterhead, Aberdeen, Montrose, & some small ports in the Western Islands, & have been distributed among y comon People, who are generally now trained in new Arms, All the Farmers & Peasants have two or three apiece.
>
> If upon y commencement of the Ginn Act there are any tumults in London they are to follow that example.[69]

Similar fears were voiced by some of Walpole's informants during the East London Riots in July. While they were generally agreed that the immediate and ostensible cause was the hostility aroused against the Irish by undercutting the wages of English workmen,[70] some were inclined to look for a deeper design or a 'hidden hand'. Robert Paul, for example, a justice of the peace who examined the first batch of prisoners committed to Newgate after the riot in Goodman's Fields, wrote to Walpole on 31 July:

> It is very difficult to judge whence this Riot arose. Some say the Irish offered to work at an under Rate and others say six of the Irish offer'd to fight any six English were the causes, *but I am afraid there must be something else at the Bottom, either Mother Gin or something worse.* Captain Littler of the Guards said he heard the Word high Church among them, but it was uncon-firmed by anybody else ... By the Seditious Ballads and Dis-

---

68. Coxe, *Memoirs*, III, p. 352.

69. C. (H.) MSS., P/70, file 2/1.

70. Yet Joseph Bell, reporting on the second day of the Shoreditch riots, wrote that while some said they were demonstrating against the Irish, 'in other parts of the crowd they told me their meeting was to prevent the putting Down Ginn' (*ibid.*, file 1).

content that appears about the Gin Act it looks to me as if it would be very difficult to carry it thoroughly into Execution, of which the Jacobites will not be wanting to take Advantage and set us in a Flame if they can.[71]

J. Furnell of Shoreditch, in his 'account' of 4 September, introduces a new element: he had learned from John Collet, who had discussed the matter with the patrons of his public house,

that the greater and more ignorant Part of the Mobb were only led away by the popular cry of English and Irish, but that there were many cunning Intriguing Persons of better sort amongst them in disguise, particularly several who are strongly suspected to be popish preists.[72]

While a great deal of this may be written off as common gossip or the product of fear engendered by the prevailing uncertainty, the Government and its agents may perhaps be excused for searching for a common origin to the many and varied discontents that had sprung up almost simultaneously, arising either from the Government's own conduct of affairs or from circumstances beyond its control. That these grievances were manifold and genuine enough is suggested in another passage of the letter just quoted:

It is evident that there are great discontents and murmurings through all this Mobbish part of the Town. The Ginn Act and the Smuggling act Sticks hard in the Stomachs of the meaner sort of People and the Bridge Act greatly Exasperates the Watermen insomuch that they make no scruple of declaring publiquely that they will join in any Mischief that can be set on foot.[73]

71. *Ibid.,* file 1 (my *italics*).
72. *Ibid.,* file 2/14.
73. *Ibid.* Note Carteret's comment on the riots of 1736 during the House of Lords' debate on the subject on 10 February 1737: 'The People seldom or never assemble in any riotous or tumultuous Manner, unless when they are oppressed, or at least imagine they are oppressed' (*Gentleman's Magazine* (July 1737), p. 374). He could, of course, as spokesman for the 'opposition', afford to be more generous than the Government in interpreting the rioters' motives.

While failing to probe more deeply into its own responsibilities for this state of affairs, the Government had, no doubt, some justification for pointing to the 'hidden hand' of Jacobite intrigue. It seems probable enough that Jacobite agents—as well as Pulteney, Carteret and the growing circle of opposition 'Patriots'—were prepared to exploit these social discontents to further their own political ends; but there is no solid evidence to suggest that they actively promoted them. Nor does it seem likely from the evidence available that the fury displayed against the Irish in Shoreditch, Spitalfields and Whitechapel owed its initial impetus in any way to the widespread dissatisfaction already aroused by the passage of the Gin Act. Yet some connection between the two existed: demonstrators in Shoreditch were heard to voice opposition to the 'putting Down Ginn';[74] and we have seen that 'seditious ballads' were, at this time, already circulating against the Gin Act and that, soon after, plans were being discussed in the 'Tippling Ale houses' for assaulting Sir Robert Walpole and the Master of the Rolls. Similarly, no doubt, the agitation against the Gin Act must have been influenced by, and drawn strength from, the long-standing opposition of distillers, farmers and City merchants to the Government over Excise.[75]

This does not, of course, go to the deeper roots of the matter. If we are to trace the common origins and underlying causes of these conflicts and disturbances—whether they concern the Irish, gin, smuggling or turnpikes—we must seek them in the profounder social changes and upheavals of the age. But this would take us far beyond the scope of the present study.

74. See note 70 above.
75. Coxe, *Memoirs*, I, 372–407.

Wilkes and Liberty, 1768-9

The cry 'Wilkes and Liberty' was first heard in May 1763, when John Wilkes was brought from the Tower to face his judges in Westminster Hall.[1] It was raised again when the exile, lately returned from France, appeared on the City hustings in March 1768, and was frequently repeated during the twelve months that followed. Again, after a lull, it was re-echoed during the years 1771-4, which witnessed the great struggles between the City and Government and Commons over press warrants and parliamentary reports and Wilkes's various campaigns in support of his candidature for office in the City of London. These 'Wilkes and Liberty' movements, besides marking some of the main stages in Wilkes's political career, denote those moments in his career when he touched chords among sections of the community not generally stirred by parliamentary or municipal elections. And, of these movements the most intensive and protracted, and perhaps the most significant for the nation's future, was that of 1768-9 which, in its London context, is the subject of the present paper.

Wilkes has, of course, had his fair share of biographers;[2] but they and others have done less than justice to the popular movements that sprang up in the wake of Wilkite agitation. This is particularly true of the complex movement of 1768-9; though Dr. Maccoby, in his recent work on the origins of English Radicalism,[3] has gone some way

From *The Guildhall Miscellany*, I, no. 8 (July 1957), 3-24.

1. H. Bleackley, *Life of John Wilkes* (1917), p. 107.
2. In addition to Bleackley's work, recent biographies of Wilkes are: O. A. Sherrard, *A Life of John Wilkes* (1930) and R. W. Postgate, *That Devil Wilkes* 2nd edition (1956).
3. S. Maccoby, *English Radicalism, 1762-1785* (1955), pp. 84-115.

towards meeting this deficiency by clearly pointing to the interaction of its political and social aspects. Here it is proposed to go more deeply into the matter and, with the aid of new materials, to submit the movement to a closer analysis. The materials used are, in addition to the usual contemporary journals and pamphlets, the correspondence and Entry Books in the State Papers Domestic of the Public Record Office;[4] the judicial and electoral records relating to the events of 1768–9 in the Record Offices of the Corporation of the City of London and the counties of Middlesex and Surrey; the printed Proceedings of the Old Bailey;[5] and a medley of local records, such as Wardmote Inquest and Vestry Minutes,[6] Rate Books, Land Tax registers, Poll Books, Freeholders' Books and miscellaneous descriptive materials found in the Record Office of the London County Council, the Westminster City Archives, the Guildhall Library Muniment Room and other local collections. These materials, though, in some respects, they have proved disappointing, make it possible to present the popular movement under review in greater detail and in clearer perspective than hitherto.

Wilkes returned to England on 6 February 1768. The winter had been intensely severe: the Thames had been frozen over and the Common Council of the City had been obliged to open a subscription for the destitute.[7] There was widespread economic distress: the price of wheat and bread, having fallen in the last months of 1767, had risen sharply again since January, and the wheaten peck-loaf (17 lb 6 oz.), whose price was settled at the Assize of Bread in London, sold, in February, for 2*s.* 9*d.*[8] The Spitalfields weavers and the coal-heavers of Shadwell and Wapping

4. P.R.O., S.P. Dom, 37/6; S.P. Dom, Entry Bks., 44/142.

5. *The whole Proceedings on the King's Commission of the Peace, Oyer and Terminer, and Gaol Delivery for the City of London and . . . for the County of Middlesex*, ed. J. Gurney (1768–70) (hereafter cited as *Proceedings*).

6. These have proved disappointing as a source in this instance.

7. Sherrard, *op. cit.*, p. 170.

8. *Gentleman's Magazine* (hereafter cited as *G.M.*) (1768), p. 50.

had already embarked on a series of protracted disputes over wages and conditions of work,[9] which were causing the Government concern: an instruction to the Middlesex magistrates drafted in the Earl of Shelburne's office and dated 26 January speaks of

'disorderly persons (having) lately assembled in a riotous manner and committed many outrages in and about Spitalfields'; and, while hoping that 'the power of the Civil Magistrates . . . will be sufficient to quell any Disturbances which may arise'; adds that 'orders have been, however, given, in case of absolute necessity, for a proper Number of soldiers to be marched from the Tower for the support and assistance of the Magistrates when required by them'.[10]

Thus, a popular movement of considerable proportions was already under way before Wilkes's return to the political scene: it is important to stress this fact, as the tendency has been to attribute the movements of 1768–9 too exclusively to Wilkite agitation.

Nevertheless, Wilkes's intervention was dramatic enough and had startling consequences. Having challenged the authorities to take official notice of his presence by a letter to the King on 4 March, he took steps to qualify as a candidate for election in the City of London. The Minutes of the Joiners' Guild record that

On the 10th March 1768 at a Private Court of that Guild held at Joiners' Hall, present Mr. Wm. Hopkins, Master, and others, John Wilkes Esq. (of the Royal Exchange) was admitted into the freedom of this Company by redemption.

Co 10/–, fees and duty 17/8d, on enrolment 3/4d . . . and he paid the Renter Warden Mr. John Sage the sum of Twenty pounds for both his said fines, and paid the fees, and was thereupon excused from serving the office of Steward and admitted on the Livery and took the cloathing of the Company on him accordingly.[11]

9. *Annual Register* (hereafter cited as *A.R.*), 1768, pp. 57–9, 68; *Proceedings* (1768), pp. 244 *et seq.* These movements will be discussed more fully below.

10. P.R.O., State Papers 37/6, No. 80/2, fos. 186–7.

11. Quoted by W. P. Treloar, *Wilkes and the City* (1917), p. 63.

Thus equipped, he presented himself for election on 16 March and received the enthusiastic support of the small City masters and craftsmen who gave him a resounding (though unofficial) majority on a first 'show of hands';[12] but, as expected, when it came to the official poll, from which the great majority of his supporters were excluded, Wilkes emerged bottom of the list of six candidates. Top of the poll were the two Court candidates, Thomas Harley, Lord Mayor, and Sir Robert Ladbroke, followed by the two candidates of the 'patriot' party, William Beckford and Barlow Trecothick, later to become occasional Wilkite supporters.[13] Thereupon, Wilkes announced his intention to contest in the County of Middlesex and, when he left the Guildhall, 'the populace . . . to show their zeal, took the horses from his carriage, and drew it themselves'.[14]

On the morning of the 28th, the first day of the Middlesex election, Wilkes rode to Brentford, 'attended by an amazing number of people to the place of election, which was held in the middle of Brentford Butts'.[15] According to one account, nearly 250 coaches, filled with Wilkite supporters and decked with blue favours, set out for the hustings, every passenger having been give a blue cockade and a 'Wilkes and Liberty' card; 40,000 handbills were distributed.[16] Wilkes headed the poll from the start and his election was never in doubt; but the result was not

12. *G.M.* (1768), p. 139.

13. The votes were cast as follows: Harley, 3,729; Ladbroke, 3,678; Beckford, 3,402; Trecothick, 2,957 (elected); Sir Richard Glyn Bart, 2,823; John Paterson, Esq., 1,769; John Wilkes, Esq., 1,247. None of the other five candidates voted for Wilkes, though he received the votes of two Aldermen: W. Bridgen (Farringdon Within) and Sir W. Barker (Bassishaw); also those of Frederick Bull, salter, of Leadenhall Street, and a later Lord Mayor, and of two Common Council men, Samuel Vaughan, merchant, of Mincing Lane, and George Bellas of Doctors' Commons. Wilkes himself did not vote. (*The Poll of the Livery of London* (1768); A. B. Beaven, *The Aldermen of the City of London*, 2 vols. (1908), I, 292.)

14. *G.M.* (1768), p. 140.

15. *A.R.* (1768), p. 85.

16. Bleackley, *op. cit.*, pp. 189–90.

announced until late in the evening, as a recount had been called for to determine which of the other two candidates— George Cooke and Sir William Beauchamp Proctor— should have second place.[17]

The election itself was perfectly orderly, though some attempt was made at Hyde Park Corner to prevent Wilkes's opponents from reaching Brentford. According to Horace Walpole, the Spitalfields weavers had mustered in strength in Piccadilly, giving out blue cockades and papers inscribed, 'No. 45, Wilkes and Liberty';[18] and objection was raised to a flag carried by Proctor's supporters, bearing the painted words, 'No blasphemer', and other unflattering remarks addressed to the popular candidate. Among victims of the affray was a Mr. Cooke, son of the City Marshal, who was pelted and knocked off his horse and had the wheels stripped off his carriage and his harness slashed. In reporting this incident, the *Annual Register* added the curious observation:

There has not been so great a defection of inhabitants from London and Westminster, to ten miles distant, in one day, since the life-guardsman's prophecy of the earthquake, which was to destroy both those cities in 1750.[19]

The riots that followed Wilkes' victory were far more extensive and, for two nights, his supporters remained masters of the streets of London and Westminster, while the magistrates and constables were almost powerless to intervene. Citizens were compelled to light up their windows and every door from Temple Bar to Hyde Park Corner was said to have been chalked with 'No. 45'.[20] The *Annual Register* reported the disturbances as follows:

At night likewise the rabble were very tumultuous; some persons who had voted for Mr. Wilkes having put out lights,

17. The voting was: Wilkes, 1,292; Cooke, 827; Proctor, 807 (*A.R.* (1768), p. 186).

18. *The Letters of Horace Walpole, Fourth Earl of Orford*, ed. P. Cunningham, 9 vols. (1906), V, 91–2. See also Sherrard, *op. cit.*, pp. 175–6; Postgate, *op. cit.* p. 124.

19. *A.R.* (1768), p. 86.

20. Bleackley, *op. cit.*, pp. 192–4.

the mob paraded the whole town from east to west, obliging every body to illuminate and breaking the windows of such as did not do it immediately. The windows of the Mansion-house, in particular, were demolished all to pieces, together with a large chandelier and some pier glasses, to the amount of many hundred pounds. They demolished all the windows of Ld Bute, Lord Egmont, Sir Sampson Gideon, Sir William Mayne, and many other gentlemen and trades men in most of the public streets of both cities, London and Westminster. At one of the above-mentioned gentlemen's houses, the mob were in a great measure irritated to it by the imprudence of a servant, who fired a pistol among them. At Charing Cross, at the Duke of Northumberland's, the mob also broke a few panes; but his Grace had the address to get rid of them by ordering up lights immediately into his windows, and opening the Ship ale-house, which soon drew them to that side.[21]

An eyewitness account of the events of 29 March tells of a 'Mob of about 100 Men and Boys' setting out from Charing Cross about nine o'clock in the evening, and making their way to the top of Haymarket where, at a house 'which some of the Mob called Cooke's house', several windows were broken before the procession continued via Windmill Street, Prince's Street, Hedge Lane, into Leicester Fields; and thence on via Hemming's Row, Chandos Street, Bedford Street—'where they broke the windows at Mr. Betty's, a Haberdasher'—and Covent Garden into Russell Street, 'where one of the Men, to wit, a Livery Servant with the Coat turned inside out, was taken into Custody, but rescued by the rest of the Mob'. Eventually, having worked their way back to Leicester Fields via the Strand and Longacre, they continued their operations in Oxford Street and Piccadilly, broke the Duke of Newcastle's windows off Lincoln Inn Fields, drank two gallons of beer to 'Wilkes and Liberty' at the 'Six Canns at the Corner of Turnstile Holborn', smashed the lamp at Sir John Fielding's door in Bow Street and became lost to view in Southampton Street, Holborn. Among those arrested in the course of this affray was Mathew Christian

21. *A.R.* (1768), p. 86.

of St. Paul's Church Yard, 'a gentleman of character and fortune', late of Antigua, who was alleged to have 'captained' the rioters and spent £6 or £7 on filling them with beer in a number of ale-houses, where he 'bid them drink "Wilkes and Liberty" '.[22]

Meanwhile, during the riots of the preceding night, 'a vast number of people, some thousands' (it was said) had gathered before the Mansion House and, to shouts of 'Wilkes for ever!', had broken nearly every window and lamp in the building.[23] The cost of restoring the damage was to prove considerable: John Monk of Finch Lane, one of the six glaziers commissioned by George Dance, the City Architect, to do the work, later sent in an account for £20 5s.

to 136 Sash sqrs of the Best Crown Glass cont. 270 Ft. . . . at 1s. 6d. per ft.

A summary of the glaziers' accounts approved by the Mansion House Committee on 25 November 1768 reads as follows:

Mr John Gwyn's Bill	£13 — 3 — 6
Mr Joseph Pulley's Bill	£ 3 — 11 — 6
Mr Thomas Lubton's Bill	£29 — 13 — 6
Mr Anthony Woodland's Bill	£64 — 15 — 6
Mrs Mary Harrington's Bill	£42 — 11 — 0
Mr John Monk's Bill	£20 — 5 — 0
Total	£174 — 0 — 0

In addition, a Mr. Patrick submitted an account 'to the supply of Lighting Lamps destroyed in Riots', amounting to £30 4s. 0d.[24]

22. S.P. 37/6, No. 80/13, fos. 225–6: 'The King ag'st Christian. A State of the Evidence ag'st the Def't touching his being concerned in a Riot on the 29th March 1768.' According to Sir John Fielding on 30 March: 'We yesterday discovered that Mr. Robert Chandler, a Tea-broker in the City, headed a Mob in Westminster' (S.P. Dom, Entry Bks., 44/142, p. 107).

23. *Proceedings* (1768), pp. 192–5.

24. Corp. Lond. R.O. Mansion House Committee Papers, 1768. These accounts include the cost of repairing further (though less extensive) damage incurred in the riots of 9–10 May of the same year.

As may be imagined, the magistrates found considerable difficulty in keeping the disturbances under control. Apart from the chronic shortage of constables and watchmen,[25] a number of the peace officers of Westminster had been directed to attend the election at Brentford,[26] and a call for the protection of any one individual left the forces available to protect the community at large sadly depleted. This dilemma is plaintively voiced by Sir John Fielding in a letter to Lord Weymouth's office on 5 April. At ten o'clock on the night of 29 March, he received a communication from a Mr. Steward, asking

how far resistance was justifiable in case the Mob should break his windows for not putting out lights.

Sir John promised a military force, if the need should arise, and ordered two or three peace officers to stand by in readiness; but, at 1 a.m., he had another call from a tailor in the Strand whose windows were being broken, and accordingly one of the available officers was sent with a sergeant and twelve men to quell this riot. Meanwhile, no further call came from Mr. Steward, whose windows had been broken already. Perhaps it is not surprising that the unhappy Fielding should sign himself 'his (Lordship's) distressed and obedient humble servant'![27]

Under these circumstances, it is little wonder that such few arrests were made: only five are mentioned in the various judicial records. In addition to Mathew Christian, gentleman,[28] there were Thomas Brady, charged with

25. According to a 'Report on the nightly Watch and Police of the Metropolis' of 1812, there were, in 1772, 40 beadles, 180 constables and 267 watchmen in the City and Liberty of Westminster and housebreaking had increased alarmingly over recent years (Parliamentary Papers, 1812, vol. 2, appendices 7–8).

26. See a letter of Sir John Fielding to Robert Wood (S.P. Dom, Entry Bks., 44/142, p 103).

27. S.P. 37/6, No. 80/16, fos. 223–4. There is further correspondence on this episode in Entry Bks., 44/142, pp. 44–5.

28. Christian was admitted to bail and ordered to appear at Westminster Quarter Sessions on 24 June (S.P. 37/6, No. 80/13, fo. 226); but I have found no further trace of him in the Sessions records.

'assembling in the streets of this City in a riotous and tumultuous manner' and sentenced at General Quarter Sessions to a fine of 12*d*. and three months in Newgate;[29] Richard Dakin, charged with 'assembling before the Mansion House . . . and there . . . breaking the front windows of the said House';[30] John Philip Pennie, paperhanger of St. Ann, Westminster, fined 12*d*. at General Quarter Sessions for breaking the windows of a Mr. John Walker 'with large pebble stones';[31] Alexander Thompson, 'labourer' of the same parish, fined 12*d*. on a similar charge;[32] and Daniel Saxton, watch-finisher of Jewin Street, acquitted at the Old Bailey of a charge of 'riotously assembling . . . in the streets of the said City and . . . breaking the windows of the Mansion House of the City aforesaid'.[33]

On 30 March, a Common Council, meeting at the Guildhall, heard a report on the riots and the extent of the damage, and resolved

'to prosecute with the utmost Rigour such Persons who have active (sic!) in the said Riots'; to pay a £50 reward 'upon the conviction of each of the above offenders'; and 'to prosecute withe the utmost vigour all Persons who shall hereafter be guilty of any such Riots or Disorders'.

It further resolved

that the above Order be published in all the Publick Papers and posted in the most public places of this City and Liberties thereof;

29. Corp. Lond. R.O., Sessions Files, 11 April 1768.

30. *Ibid.* Though 'not found' on 11 April, a true bill was found against Dakin on 16 May. I have found no subsequent record.

31. Midd. R.O., Sessions Rolls (Westminster), No. 3199, 5 April 1768; Sessions Rolls (Middlesex), No. 3203, 4 July 1768.

32. Midd. R.O. Sessions Rolls (Westminster), No. 3202, 17 June 1768; Sessions Rolls (Middlesex), No. 3203, 4 July 1768.

33. Corp. Lond. R.O., Sessions Files, 11 April 1768; *Proceedings* (1768), pp. 192–5. Brady, Dakin and Saxton also appear in Lond. R.O., Index of Indictments for 1768.

and appointed a committee of Alderman and Common Council men under the presidency of the Lord Mayor 'to carry on such prosecutions as may arise from the above Resolutions'.[34]

Commenting on these measures, the Crown prosecutor in a later case was to add sadly:

'Notwithstanding the above advertisement and his Lordship's care and vigilance to suppress the Riots & Disturbances, they still continued almost every night from the 28th of March to y 12th or 13th May last.'[35]

There is some exaggeration in the statement, as the first weeks of April passed calmly enough, though there persisted an undercurrent of unrest in parts of the metropolis that needed little pretext to come to the surface.[36] Such a pretext was afforded by Wilkes's brief appearance at the Court of King's Bench, where he formally 'surrendered' to his outlawry on 20 April. On leaving the Court at 2 p.m., he was attended by a large crowd, but there was no immediate disturbance.[37] The same evening, however, in Shadwell, a large band of coal-heavers, who had mustered to settle accounts with an unpopular coal 'undertaker', were swept up in the movement celebrating Wilkes's release and adopted the 'Wilkes and Liberty' slogan as their own. So much appears from the subsequent trials at the Old Bailey of John Green, the 'undertaker', and his principal assailants. Thus Thomas Axford, the publican of the *Swan and*

34. Corp. Lond. R.O., *Journals of the Court of Common Council*, Vol. LXIV (1765–69), fos. 247vo.–248vo.

35. Guild. Lib. MS. 3724: 'Wilkes Riots, 1768; the King v. John Williams, to be tried at the Old Bailey on Saturday 25th of Feb[y] 1769'.

36. On 13 April, the Duke of Northumberland, Lord Lieutenant of Middlesex, suggested to Lord Weymouth that the stored arms of three Battalions of the Middlesex militia should be removed to the Tower for safe custody in case of their seizure by rioters. The proposal, though seriously considered, was not acted upon. (S.P. Dom, Entry Bks., 44/142, pp. 51–4.)

37. *G.M.* (1768), p. 196. For the rigorous precautions taken by the Government and the London magistrates to avoid a repetition of the disturbances of 29–30 March, see Entry Bks., 44/142, pp. 55–63.

Lamb, off New Gravel Lane, Shadwell, testified that, at about 8 p.m., a 'Mob' came running along the Ratcliffe Highway, shouting 'Wilkes and Liberty, and coal-heavers for ever!' There were further cries of 'Damn you, light up your candles for Wilkes', and soon every house was lighted up. On enquiring 'what they had done with Mr. Wilkes', he was told, 'he is cleared till the parliament sits, then he is to be tried by the House of Lords'. But all were not unanimous—in one group an argument took place:

They said, who are you, to one another; one said I am for Wilkes; damn you, said others, I am for Bute; after that, they began to swagger with sticks at one another, and then over their heads.

Yet the main body of coal-heavers, at least, appear to have become staunch supporters of Wilkes.[38]

A week later, the demonstrations became more widespread. On 27 April, Wilkes appeared for trial at Westminster Hall. Having been committed to the custody of the Marshal of the King's Bench prison, he left the Court at 6.30 p.m. in the company of his devoted ally, 'Parson' Horne of Brentford. Crowds formed in Palace Yard and along Westminster Bridge. The horses were unharnessed and the carriage drawn along the Strand and Fleet Street to the *Three Tuns* tavern in Spitalfields, where Wilkes appeared at an upper window and was acclaimed by his supporters, before disappearing in disguise and surrendering to his jailers at the King's Bench prison.[39]

The next day [writes a local chronicler], the prison was surrounded by a prodigious number of persons, but no disturbances happened till night, when the Rails which enclosed the footway were pulled up to make a fire, and the Inhabitants of the Borough were obliged by the Mob to illuminate their houses, but a Captain Guard arriving soon after 12 the Mob dispersed.[40]

38. *Proceedings* (1768), pp. 204–14, 247.

39. Bleackley, *op. cit.*, pp. 197–8; *G.M.* (1768, p. 197. See also Entry Bks., 44/142, pp. 144–6.

40. *Historical Notices of the Borough of Southwark* (MS. account compiled by Richard Corner, gentleman (d. 1820), and preserved in Southwark Library), pp. 134–5. See also *G.M.* (1768), p. 197.

Three persons were taken into custody as the result of this incident: Henry Jefferson, a lighterman of St. John, Southwark, charged with 'being tumultuously and unlawfully assembled';[41] John Robinson, labourer of St. Mary Magdalene, Bermondsey; and Edward Tobias, labourer of Christ Church, Surrey, both charged with 'assembling riotously' before the gates of the King's Bench prison on 30 April and with 'breaking, spoiling, demolishing, burning and destroying sundry wooden posts belonging thereto'.[42] Subsequently, at Surrey Quarter Sessions on 4 October, Robinson was acquitted and Tobias fined 13*s*. 4*d*. and committed to prison for twelve months.[43]

Riots broke out again on 9 May, when Robert Hall was committed and charged with 'forcibly and unlawfully demolishing and breaking down the Lobby of the King's Bench Prison', while Jane Murray was committed for

comforting and aiding and abetting divers other persons unknown . . . who . . . did unlawfully demolish and break down the lobby of the said Prison.[44]

The next day was the opening of Parliament, and many who assembled in St. George's Fields that morning appear to have done so in the expectation of seeing John Wilkes taken to Westminster.[45] Crowds gathered from various

41. Surrey R.O., Sessions Rolls, 1768 (Midsummer); Sessions Bundles, 1768 (Midsummer). Jefferson was admitted to bail and, subsequently, disappears from the records.

42. *Ibid.*

43. Surrey R.O., Process Books of Indictments (1767–1786), QS. 3/5/9, p. 25; Quarter Sessions Order Book (1767–71), QS. 2/1/22, pp. 166–7.

44. According to the *Gentleman's Magazine*, this operation was accompanied by the usual shouts of 'Wilkes and Liberty' (*G.M.* (1768), pp. 323–5). Hall was sentenced at the Surrey Summer Assizes, held at Guildford on 3 August, to a fine of 13*s*. 4*d*. and to twelve months' imprisonment; Jane Murray was 'discharged by proclamation' (P.R.O., Assizes 35/208. Surrey Summer Assizes. 8th Geo. 3rd 1768).

45. *A.R.* (1768), p. 129. One witness, however, later testified that he went there to see Mr. Wilkes, 'who, he heard, that day was going to be tried' (Brit. Mus., Add. MSS. 30, 884, fo. 69: 'The King ag't Mc Lane').

parts of the metropolis.[46] A constable of the parish of St. George the Martyr estimated that, between ten and eleven o'clock in the morning, there were '1,000 or more people' present and that this had grown to 15,000 or 20,000 by the early afternoon; [47] while another account, frankly Wilkite in sympathy, speaks of 'upwards of forty thousand persons'.[48] Shortly before midday, some of the demonstrators broke through the ranks of the Foot Guards surrounding the prison[49] and affixed to the wall a paper bearing the lines

> Venal judges & Ministers combine
> Wilkes & English Liberty to confine;
> Yet in true English hearts secure their fame is,
> Nor are such crowded levies at St. James's.
> While thus in Prison Envy dooms their stay,
> Here, O grateful Britons, your daily homage pay.
> Philo Libertatis no. 45.[50]

When, at the instance of the justices, the paper was pulled down, the demonstrators became restive: there were shouts of 'Give us the paper' and 'Wilkes and Liberty for ever!' and stones were thrown at the soldiers.[51] A

46. Among some 25 persons arrested in Southwark as the result of the events of 10–11 May, 2 were from Bermondsey, 3 from the City of London, 3 from Westminster and 6 from other parts of Middlesex (Surrey R.O., Sessions Rolls, 1768 (Midsummer)); among witnesses at Justice Gillam's trial for murder at the Old Bailey in July, one was from Mile End, a second from the parish of St. George the Martyr, Holborn, and a third from St. George's, Hanover Square (*Proceedings* (1768), pp. 274–83).

47. *Proceedings* (1768), pp. 276–7.

48. *English Liberty: being a collection of Interesting Tracts from the Year 1762 to 1769, containing the Private Correspondence, Public Letters, Speeches and Addresses of John Wilkes Esq. . . .*, 2 vols. bound in one (London, 1770), I, 170. The printed volume is accompanied by a manuscript 'supplement' covering the years 1771–80, 'compiled by Isaac Hitchcock, late of Stafford in Staffordshire' (Guild. Lib., MS. 3332).

49. According to Justice Gillam, one of the magistrates present, the soldiers (100 men of the 3rd Regiment of Foot Guards) had been sent for on Sunday, 8 May and stayed there till the 12th (B.M., Add. MSS. 30, 884, fo. 70).

50. *Ibid.*, fo. 72. A slight variant appears in *English Liberty*, I, 170.

51. According to one hostile witness, the crowd also shouted, 'No

Captain Murray and three grenadiers chased one of the stone-throwers, 'a man in a red waistcoat', off the Fields and, in the adjoining Blackman Street, they entered a cow-house annexed to the *Horse Shoe Inn* and shot dead William Allen, the publican's son, mistaking him for their assailant. Several other casualties followed. After the Riot Act had been twice read, the foot-soldiers, by now reinforced by Horse Guards, were ordered to fire and '5 or 6 were killed on the spot & about 15 wounded'.[52] According to one eyewitness, a constable and peruke-maker:

'The horse occasioned a great disturbance, and the whole disturbance, I believe; the people huzzaed and hissed, but no further riot.' The soldiers fired at random: 'a great number of them loaded three times, and seemed to enjoy their fire; I thought it a great cruelty'.[53]

Wilkes, no King!'; 'Damn the King, damn the Government, damn the Justice!'; and even 'This is the most glorious opportunity for a Revolution that ever offered!' (B.M., Add. MSS. 30, 884, fo. 72); but I have found no confirmation of this elsewhere.

52. *A.R.* (1768), p. 108. In *English Liberty* appears the following 'list of some of the persons killed and wounded in this melancholy affair.

'Mr. William Allen, shot to death in his father's cow-house.

'Mr. William Redburn, weaver, shot through the thigh, died in the London hospital.

'William Bridgman, shot through the breast, as he was fitting a hay-cart in the Haymarket, died instantly.

'Mary Jeffs, of St. Saviour's, who was selling oranges, by the Haymarket, died instantly.

'Mr. Boddington, baker, of Coventry, shot through the thigh-bone, died in St. Thomas's hospital.

'Mr. Lawley, a farrier, shot in the groin, died the 12th of May.

'Margaret Walters, Mint, pregnant, died the 12th of May.

'Mary Green, shot through the right-arm bone.

'Mr. Nichols, shot through the flesh of his breast.

'Mrs. Egremont, shot through her garment under her arm.

'Mr. —— in Kent-Street, stabbed with a bayonet in his loin.

'Mr. —— unknown, stabbed with a bayonet' (*English Liberty*, I, 172–3).

53. *Proceedings* (1768), p. 278. Nevertheless, a soldier outside the prison was heard to say: 'We are all ready to fire on our enemies, the French and the Spaniards, but never will on our countrymen' (*English Liberty*, I, 110).

Such was the 'massacre' of St. George's Fields.[54]

The incident was to have far-reaching effects, as we shall see. Meanwhile, a number of the demonstrators wreaked their own form of vengeance on authority: that night and the following morning, the houses of two of the Southwark magistrates, Edward Russell, a distiller of Borough High Street, and Richard Capel of Bermondsey Street,[55] were attacked and 'pulled down'. According to the *Gentleman's Magazine*, 'the activity of the two gentlemen . . . in suppressing the tumults, occasioned the outrage'.[56] A witness of the events in St. George's Fields was even to declare that Justice Capel had claimed to have 'an order from the Ministry to kill twenty-five of the people'.[57] From Capel's own 'information' relating to the attack it appears

That, on Wednesday, the eleventh day of May between eleven and twelve o'clock . . . after a great number of riotous persons had been dispers'd by the soldiers from before his dwelling house in Bermondsey Street, an intelligence was brought to him that a great number of riotous Persons were assembled at and before the House of Edward Russell Esq[r] the foot of London Bridge in the High Street of the Borough, and that his Presence was necessary, and to bring with him what military assistance he could. Accordingly he went to the said House with an Officer and a Body of the Life Guards, and found there a great number of Persons assembled in a riotous manner. He then and there exhorted them to disperse and told them the Danger of their Behaviour. Then one John Percival took him by the collar and said 'Damn you, I'll mark you'; and accordingly he did mark him with large figures *No.* 45 on the cape of his great Coat. He then immediately took him into Custody and deliver'd him to the Care of the Centinels then and there on duty. After

54. For the foregoing, see *Proceedings* (1768), pp. 274–83; B.M., Add. MSS. 30,884, fos. 65–76; *English Liberty*, I, 169–202; *G.M.* (1768), pp. 323–5; *A.R.* (1768), 227–34.

55. Of the two, only Russell appears in the Surrey Freeholders' Book, 1762–1771 (Surrey R.O., QS. 7/5/2).

56. *G.M.*, 1768, p. 243.

57. *Proceedings* (1768), p. 281.

which several well-dressed persons, and in particular one Richard Gilbert, came up to him and demanded to know by what authority he took the said John Percival into Custody. He told them he was a Magistrate and came there to preserve the Peace. He then insisted on seeing his Authority and otherwise insulted him. He (this deponent) then took hold of him (the said Richard) and delivered him into the Custody of the Centinels on Duty. Soon after which the Mob dispers'd and return'd with the Horse Guards into Bermondsey Street.[58]

There were further disturbances in other parts of the capital. In Fore Street, Limehouse, a band of 500 sawyers, having given prior notice of their intentions, 'pulled down' Charles Dingley's new saw-mill on 10 May:[59] it is unlikely that political motives played any part in this, though Charles Dingley was some months later to distinguish himself by opposing Wilkes in Middlesex and to organize a 'loyal' demonstration of City merchants against him.[60] On 9 and 10 May, too, further riots took place at the Mansion House and more windows, lamps and furniture were broken. On the first occasion, a crowd was seen carrying a gibbet along Cornhill, 'on which hung a boot and petty-coat'.[61] 'There were great hissing and hallooing,' stated a

58. Surrey R.O., Sessions Bundles, 1768 (Mid-summer): 'Rich'd Capel Esq. ag't Percival Gilbert Inform[n] dated 16th June 1768'.

59. *Proceedings* (1768), pp. 256–7; *G.M.* (1768), p. 242; *A.R.* (1768), p. 108. Dingley seems by this date to have occupied fairly extensive business premises in Limehouse. In the local Land Tax register for May 1768 we find the following properties in Fore Street (with their annual rents) under his name:

'£10 empty house and a wharf.
'£70 for a yard.
'£18 for Ashton's lands & late Salmons.
'£8 for City lands.
'£5 for Ashton's Land late Moul.
'£5 for ground late bought' (Guild. Lib., St. Ann's Limehouse, Land Tax Assessments, 11 May 1768, MS. 6006/51, p. 3). In 1769, there is an additional entry: '£31 for Land & Premises late Moul' (MS. 6006/52, p. 3).

60. See page 245 below.

61. This was the current Opposition symbol for Lord Bute and the Princess-Dowager.

witness, and cries of 'Wilkes and Liberty'.[62] On the 10th, crowds threw stones and 'damned the Lord Mayor'; and a demonstrator, later convicted at the Old Bailey, was said to have collected stones for breaking the Mansion House windows 'at the Borough or King's Bench'![63] There was also a disturbance outside the House of Lords.[64]

The riots had their aftermath. On 13 May, the House of Commons passed a vote of thanks to Thomas Harley, Lord Mayor of London,

for his vigilance and active conduct, in support of the Laws, and for the preservation of the public Peace, during the late Disturbances.

The Commons also resolved, *nem. con.*,

That an humble Address be presented to His Majesty, that he will be graciously pleased to order Compensation to be made to Mr. Russell, Mr. Capell, and other Magistrates, for those losses which they have suffered, by exerting themselves to suppress the late seditions and dangerous Riots in this Capital, and the neighbourhood thereof; and to assure His Majesty that this House will make good the expenses thereof to His Majesty.[65]

Accordingly, a Treasury Minute of 16 August reads as follows:

Read the account of the damages done by the rioters in Southwark to the House & Warehouse of Edward Russell Esqre on the 10th of May last amounting to £491—5—6.

Read the account of the damages done . . . to the dwelling-house of Richard Capell Esqre on the 10th of May last amounting to £69—4—7.

Read an Address of the House of Commons to his Majesty of the 13th of May last, on the subject.

Prepare Warrants for paying to Mr Russell and Mr Capell the

62. *Proceedings* (1768), pp. 285–7.
63. *Ibid.*, pp. 287–8.
64. In the Calendar of Prisoners committed to Tothill Fields Bridewell, we find one John Biggs committed on 10 May for 'riotously and tumultuously assembling with divers others and disturbing the Peace of the Rt. Hon. House of Lords' (Midd. R.O. Sessions Rolls (Westminster), No. 3202, 17 June 1768).
65. Commons Journals, XXXII, 11.

amount of the damages they have respectively suffered according to the above accounts.[66]

There was, too, a fair toll of arrests and convictions. John Smith, 'labourer' of Limehouse, was sentenced at Hicks Hall in January 1769 to seven years' imprisonment in Newgate for his part in the attack on Charles Dingley's saw-mill;[67] William Hawkins, a lighterman of Old Street, was tried at the Old Bailey on 13 July, fined 1*s*. and committed to Newgate for one year, for breaking windows at the Mansion House on 9 May;[68] and Thomas Woodcock received the same sentence for rioting at the Mansion House on the 10th.[69] For the attack on Edward Russell's house in Southwark on 10 May, Thomas Greenwood, who was 'taken with a naked Bayonet concealed under his coat', was sentenced at the Surrey Assizes at Guildford on 3 August to fifteen months' imprisonment and a fine of 13*s*. 4*d*.;[70] and, at the Surrey Quarter Sessions in October 1768, John Percival, pewterer, of St. Saviour, Southwark, was ordered to be imprisoned for two years for assaulting Justice Capel on 11 May;[71] and James Truckle, nail-maker

66. P.R.O., Treasury Minutes, T. 29/39, p. 200.

67. Midd. R.O., Sessions Rolls (Middlesex), No. 3209, 5 December 1768; Process Register Book of Indictments, vol. 17 (1761–9), p. 823. Edward Castle was acquitted of the same charge at the Old Bailey on 6 July 1768 (*Proceedings* (1768), pp. 256–7).

68. Corp. Lond. R.O., Sessions Files, 17 May 1768; *Proceedings* (1768), pp. 285–7. Joseph Wild was, at the same time, acquitted of this charge (*ibid.*).

69. Corp. Lond. R.O., Sessions Files, 17 May 1768; *Proceedings* (1768), pp. 287–8. Henry Davis and John Williams were charged with the same offence (Sessions Files, 17 May 1768). There is no further record of Davis; and Williams, too, having been ordered to appear for a fresh trial in February 1769 owing to an error in the first bill of indictment, 'disappears' from the records (Guild. Lib., MS. 3724).

70. S.P. 37/6, No. 80/49, fos. 297–8; Assizes 35/208. Surrey Summer Assizes. 8th Geo. 3rd 1768.

71. Surrey R.O., Sessions Rolls, 1768 (Midsummer); Process Register Bks. of Indictments (1767–86), QS. 3/5/9, p. 24; QS. Order Bk. (1767–71), QS. 2/1/22, p. 134. William Gilbert, gentleman, of Edward Street, Marylebone, charged with obstructing Justice Capel in the execution of his office, was 'removed by certiorari' (Surrey R.O.,

of the City parish of Allhallows the Great, was sentenced to nine months in the County Gaol for obstructing Nathaniel Skinner, constable, on the same occasion.[72] In addition, some twenty persons of varying occupations were committed to the Surrey County Gaol, charged with 'unlawful' or 'riotous assembly' or 'divers misdemeanours' as the result of the affray in St. George's Fields on 10 May; these were all admitted to bail, and subsequently released.[73]

The Government was to be considerably embarrassed by the affair. A coroner's inquest into the death of William Allen found that Captain Murray and two of the grenadiers (unhappily for the Government, all three Scots!)

feloniously, wilfully and of their malice aforethought, did kill and murder, against the peace of our said Lord the King, his crown and dignity.[74]

Sessions Rolls, 1768 (Midsummer); Process Register Bks. of Indictments, p. 32).

72. Surrey R.O., Session Rolls, 1768 (Midsummer); Process Register Bks., p. 25; Order Bk., pp. 134–5.

73. These were (in order of their appearance before the magistrates): Samuel Bennett and Jacob Tarr, labourers of St. Saviour, Southwark; Richard Johnson, shoe-maker, St. James's, Westminster; Michael Harrison, labourer, St. Olave's, Southwark; Samuel Wanhagen, carver, St. Clement Dane's, Middlesex; Charles Musto, peruke-maker, St. John, Southwark; William Bailey, labourer, Christ Church, Surrey; Francis Morgan, labourer, Suffolk Street, St. Margaret's, Westminster; Benjamin Ruffey, labourer, Bell Yard, Gracechurch Street, City of London; David Venner, Blacksmith, Christ Church, Surrey; Thomas French, mariner, St. Saviour, Southwark; John Rouden, cooper, Kent Street, Newington, Surrey; Peter Jones, porter, John Street, Clerkenwell; William Tear, shoemaker, White Street, St. George, Southwark; Joseph Rivington, Oliver Lane, St. Leonard, Shoreditch; James Lovet, weaver, Green Harbour Court, Golden Lane, St. Luke, Middlesex; Michael Budd, sawyer, Ewers Street, St. Saviour, Southwark; Elizabeth Munday, wife of a dealer in clothes, Black Raven Yard, Nightingale Lane, St. John, Wapping; George Minor, labourer, Woolpack Yard, St. George, Southwark; and Ann Nicholas, widow, St. James's Street, Grosvenor Square (Surrey R.O., Sessions Rolls, 1768 (Midsummer); Sessions Bundles, 1768 (Midsummer); QS. Minute Bk., 1768–9 (QS. 2/2/10).

74. *English Liberty*, I, 173–5. In all other cases verdicts of 'chance medley' were returned (*ibid.*, I, 185–8).

Subsequently, at Guildford on 8 August, a Grand Jury, having heard nineteen witnesses (including Wilkes), returned a true bill against Donald McLane, one of the grenadiers, while discharging Alexander Murray and Donald M'Laury.[75] On the day following, in the face of conflicting evidence, the jury could do no other than return a verdict of Not Guilty against McLane.[76] Yet it was widely believed that another grenadier, Peter MacLaughlin, had done the actual shooting, and had been allowed to 'desert' by his superiors.[77] Meanwhile, a Middlesex Grand Jury, on 7 July, found a bill for 'wilful murder' against Samuel Gillam, one of the justices present in St. George's Fields, who had given the order to fire, resulting in the death of William Redburn, a weaver;[78] but he was acquitted at the Old Bailey a few days later.[79]

Further damage was done to the Government's reputation by the publication, on 12 May, of a letter sent by Lord Barrington, Secretary at War, to the 'Field officer in waiting of the Foot Guards', complimenting the military on their conduct in St. George's Fields.[80] Even more damaging was the publication by Wilkes himself in the *St. James's Chronicle*, some weeks later, of a letter sent by Lord Weymouth, Secretary of State, to magistrates in April, offering military support to police the crowds that had surrounded the King's Bench prison since 27 April.[81] This, together with the news of Wilkes's sentence on 18 June to a total of twenty-two months' imprisonment on a number of charges,[82] all served to keep the agitation

75. *G.M.* (1768), p. 394.
76. B.M., Add. MSS. 30,884, fos. 65–76: 'The King ag't McLane (for murder)'.
77. *G.M.* (1768), p. 395.
78. *Ibid.*, p. 346.
79. *Proceedings* (1768), pp. 274–83.
80. *G.M.* (1768), p. 244.
81. Maccoby, *op. cit.*, p. 102.
82. *G.M.* (1768), pp. 299–300.

going, of which an indication is afforded by the following news item of 4 July:

At the sessions of the peace at Guildhall, a woman was tried for assaulting Mr. Emmerton, a constable, at St. Bride's parish. He had taken her into custody for bawling *Wilkes and Liberty*, when for his folly, she said, she would take the liberty to break his head, which she accordingly did. The jury found her guilty, and the Court fined her one shilling.[83]

Wilkes's birthday on 28 October was the occasion for further demonstrations, and 'a great number of disorderly persons went in a body through the principal streets, breaking windows on pretence of their not being illuminated'.[84] Among the victims was one James Pearson, linen-draper, of 106 Cheapside, opposite Bow Church Yard,[85] whose house was attacked by James Jacob, servant to John Mills of Great St. Helen, London, 'with 40 other persons'. Jacob was charged with

making a noise and disturbance before the house of . . . James Pearson with a lighted candle in his hand at eleven o'clock last Friday night . . . and throwing a great quantity of dirt and stones against his house and windows and violently knocking at his door;[86]

and, on 20 February 1769, was sentenced at General Quarter Sessions to a fine of £5 and to provide surety for his good behaviour for one year.[87]

A few weeks later, George Cooke, Wilkes's fellow-Member for Middlesex, died; the vacant seat was contested by Serjeant Glynn, Wilkes's counsel, and Sir William

83. *G.M.* (1768), p. 346. I have found no record of this case in the London Sessions papers for this period.

84. *Ibid.*, p. 539.

85. James Pearson & Co. were assessed for the Sewer Rate in 1771 at a rent of £96 per annum (Guild. Lib., MS. 2137/1-4, Sewer Rate 1771 (Cheap Ward), p. 6).

86. Corp. Lond. R.O., Sessions Files, 5 December 1768.

87. Corp Lond. R.O., Sessions Minute Bks., vol. 17 (December 1768–November 1769).

Beauchamp Proctor, the Court candidate defeated at the General Election. The election took place in Brentford Butts on 8 December and was attended by violent disturbances, provoked by Sir William Proctor's supporters. The poll, which had opened at eleven o'clock, proceeded peacefully enough until 2 p.m. when a band of twenty-five to thirty persons, armed with bludgeons and bearing the device 'Liberty and Proctor' in their hats,[88] appeared from the direction of the Castle Inn and drove the startled freeholders from the hustings. Polling was suspended but, being resumed, Glynn was, a week later, declared elected with 1,542 votes against his opponent's 1,278.[89] The usual round of illuminations followed in the Strand and City to celebrate another Wilkite victory.[90]

But, soon after, George Clarke, a young Wilkite lawyer, died from blows received during the disturbance; and proceedings were opened against two Irish chairmen, Lawrence Balfe and Edward McQuirk, in the first instance for assaulting 'one William Beale' and Samuel Clay, a High Constable of the Hundred of Ossulston.[91] At their trial at the Old Bailey in January, it appeared evident that the two men had been hired and armed to 'protect' the Court candidate[92] and the jury took only twenty minutes to find

88. At the subsequent Old Bailey trial, even some of Proctor's witnesses admitted that the 'desparate sort of ruffians' who caused the disturbance wore this insignia, though it was claimed that they did so to incriminate Proctor and that they shouted 'Glynn for ever!' (*Proceedings* (1769), pp. 66–84, 87–100; see also *G.M.* (1768), p. 587). According to Walpole, 'this mob seems to have been hired by Sir William Beauchamp Proctor for defence, but, by folly or ill-management, proved the sole aggressors' (*Letters*, V, 140).

89. *G.M.* (1768), p. 587.

90. *Ibid.*

91. Mid. R.O., Process Register Bks. of Indictments, vol. 17 (1761–9), pp. 837–8; Sessions Rolls (Middlesex), No. 3211 (a), 9 January 1769.

92. Robert Jones Esq., J.P., of Fonmon Castle, Glamorganshire, told how, posing as a friend of Sir William Proctor, he had arranged to meet McQuirk and Balfe, on the evening following the Brentford riot, at the Shakespeare Tavern in Covent Garden; and that there

them guilty of the murder of Clarke.[93] They were sentenced to death but, after a number of respites, the case was allowed to drop.[94] The atmosphere of suspicion engendered by this affair may well have contributed to Wilkes's election as Alderman of the ward of Farringdon Without on 27 January, when he was returned unopposed at a Wardmote Court held in the parish church of St. Bride's.[95]

Soon after, came Wilkes's expulsion from the Commons of 3 February and the famous series of Middlesex elections, culminating in Colonel Luttrell's recognition by the House as the lawful Member. The story has often been told, and here it will only be recalled in so far as it served as a background or stimulus to the popular movement of the spring of 1769. On the night of Wilkes's expulsion, there was a riot in Drury Lane, where 'a number of persons riotously assembled' and 'pulled down' some old houses. The peace officers were overwhelmed, but the 'most active' of the rioters were arrested after the Guard had been summoned.[96] There followed, in quick succession, Wilkes's readoption

---

McQuirk had told him, 'he was hired by a person, whose name was Tetam, or Chetham, and he was to have the same wages as at Northampton election; he said he was hired to go down there; that this Tetam was agent to Lord Halifax, that the wages was two guineas a week, victuals and drink for himself; and as many men as he brought should have the same; and thought he had done the work completely for that day' (*Proceedings* (1769), p. 69).

93. *Ibid.*, p. 100.

94. *G.M.* (1769), pp. 53, 166–7, 212, 269.

95. In the first instance, Wilkes was opposed by Thomas Bromwich. The result of the poll held on 2 January was as follows: *St. Bride's*: Bromwich, 36 votes, Wilkes, 72; *St. Dunstan's*: Bromwich, 11, Wilkes, 43; *St. Sepulchre's*: Bromwich, 15, Wilkes, 85; *St. Andrew's*: Bromwich, 5, Wilkes, 42; *St. Martin's Ludgate*: Bromwich, 2, Wilkes, 6; *White Fryars*: Bromwich, 0, Wilkes, 7. There was a further poll on 27 January owing to an alleged irregularity; this time, Wilkes was returned unopposed. (Guild. Lib., St. Bride, Fleet Street, Vestry Minute Book, 1767–1810, MS. 6554/6, pp. 32–4; St. Dunstan in the West, Wardmote Inquest, 1558–1823, MS. 3018/1, pp. 253–4.)

96. *G.M.* (1769), p. 106. I have found no trace of this incident in the QS. records; but these are not complete for the period.

by the Middlesex electors on 14 February and his unopposed return on the 16th; his further disqualification by
the Commons on the 17th; his third unopposed election,
after the withdrawal of Charles Dingley, on 16 March;
its annulment by Parliament on the 17th and the reaffirma-
tion of the electors to return the candidate of their choice
on the 20th.[97]

Meanwhile, Wilkes's City friends had, at the London
Tavern, on 20 February, after numerous meetings called
in his support by Middlesex and Westminster freeholders,
formed the Society of Supporters of the Bill of Rights. Its
immediate object was to raise money to settle 'Mr Wilkes's
affairs' and, on 7 March, it was agreed 'that £300 be sent to
Mr Wilkes for his immediate use'.[98] But, doubtless, it was
the Society's potentialities as the spearhead of the Wilkite
political movement that prompted Court supporters in the
City to stage the ill-fated 'loyal' Address of merchants to
the King. The first meeting of the 'loyalists' on 8 March was
taken over by Wilkes's supporters; but, led by Charles
Dingley, smarting no doubt from his humiliating experience at Brentford on 16 March, they persisted and duly
presented their Address at St. James's Palace on the 22nd.
It was the occasion of a considerable Wilkite counter-
demonstration in the Cities of London and Westminster.
The *Annual Register* reported that the merchants' cavalcade

were interrupted by a desperate mob, on passing through the
city, who insulted, pelted and mal-treated the principal con-
ductors; so that several coaches were obliged to withdraw,
some to return back, others to proceed by bye-ways, and those
who arrived at St. James's were so daubed with dirt, and
shattered, that both masters and drivers were in the utmost peril
of their lives.

In the Strand [continued the report] a hearse with two white

97. *G.M.* (1769), pp. 108, 165.
98. *A.R.* (1769), pp. 74-5, 79. Eventually, when the Society issued
a final statement of accounts in the spring of 1770, Wilkes was left
with a net income of £350 p.a. and a lump sum of £2,000 (Almon's
Letters, III, 8B; quoted by Postgate, *op. cit.*, p. 144).

and two black horses, took the lead of the cavalcade. On one side of the hearse were strikingly represented the soldiers firing at young Allen, and on the other the murder at Brentford. An attempt was made to drive it into the court-yard at St. James's; but the riot-act being read, it drove off to Carleton-house, afterwards to Cumberland-house, and last of all to Lord Weymouth's; at all of which places, the driver made a particular compliment, and then retired.[99]

The disturbances continued within the Palace gates. Here fifteen rioters were secured by the military. Of these, five only were indicted: according to their indictments, they

unlawfully, riotously, routously and tumultuously did assemble & meet together to disturb the peace of the said Lord the King at and before the Palace or usual place of Residence of our said Lord the King, commonly called Saint James's Palace.

The indicted persons, who were discharged by a Grand Jury at the New Guildhall, Westminster, a week later, were: Joseph Rawlinson, Robert Spencer and Thomas Hughes, 'labourers' of the parish of St. James; Samuel Westguard, bottle merchant, Thames Street, City of London; and Thomas Rose, shoemaker, of St. James's Street. A recognisance also appears for Stephen Parrant, coachman to Richard Davenport Esq., St. James's.[100]

This was the last of the great Wilkite political demonstrations of the period.[101] The next Middlesex election was duly held at Brentford on 13 April, and Wilkes was returned for a fourth time—on this occasion, with 1,143 votes against the 296 votes won by his opponent, Henry Lawes Luttrell.

99. *A.R.* (1769), p. 84. This account is fully quoted by Maccoby, *op. cit.*, p. 114. Other accounts appear in *G.M.* (1769), pp. 165–6, 210; and in Walpole's *Letters*, V. 148–9, 151.

100. Midd. R.O., Sessions Rolls (Westminster), No. 3212, 28 March 1769. No recognisances—hence no occupations or addresses—survive in the case of Rawlinson, Spencer and Hughes.

101. Maccoby may be correct in estimating that 'the political rioting of March 1769, was never again equalled until the "Gordon Riots" of 1780' (*op. cit.*, p. 115); but the disturbances of 22 March cannot be compared in scope and violence with those of 28–9 March and 9–11 May 1768.

After the poll was over [it was reported], a number of horsemen, with colours flying and musick playing, attended by several thousand people went through St. James's Street, the Strand and over London Bridge to the King's Bench, to congratulate Mr Wilkes on his success.[102]

The next day, the Commons once more declared Wilkes's election null and void and declared Luttrell elected. No popular outburst followed; yet a news report of 6 May suggests that sympathy for Wilkes had not abated. The King and Queen being at Epsom races, we are told that

a fellow who stood near his Majesty had the audacity to hallow out, 'Wilkes and Liberty for ever!'

Swords were drawn, but the demonstrator escaped.[103]

Nevertheless, the creation of the Society of Supporters of the Bill of Rights—aided, no doubt, by the rapid fall in the prices of wheat and bread[104]—had ushered in a new phase of political agitation in which, for the time being at least, street demonstrations and 'Wilkes and Liberty' calls gave way to the petitions and counter-petitions of 'respectable' freeholders and burghers.[105] The next round of the popular political movement—apart from occasional City demonstrations—was not to begin until March 1771, when the King's State coach, passing down Parliament Street, was hailed with shouts of 'No Lord Mayor, no King!'[106]

Historians have drawn attention to the considerable industrial unrest of 1768–9:[107] these disputes generally ran side by side with the Wilkite political movement, though, on occasion—as in the case of the weavers and

102. *G.M.* (1769), pp. 212–13.

103. *Ibid.*, p. 268.

104. See pp. 263–5 below.

105. See Maccoby, *op. cit.*, pp. 115 *et seq.*

106. This was the occasion of the City's struggle with Parliament over the printing of parliamentary proceedings. Gregory Brown, a hosier of St. Stephen, Coleman Street, indicted for shouting the offensive slogan, was released by a Westminster Grand Jury (Midd. R.O., Sessions Rolls (Westminster), No. 3240, 2 April 1771).

107. See e.g., Maccoby, *op. cit.*, pp. 94–6, 458–60.

coal-heavers—they temporarily 'merged' with it. But most of them had no connection whatever with the 'Wilkes and Liberty' movement either as to their origin, course or outcome.[108] Let us examine them briefly.

Apart from the coal-heavers and weavers, whose activities will be considered later, the sailors appear to have been first in the field. On 5 May, the press reported that

a great body of sailors assembled at Deptford, forcibly went on board several ships, unreefed their top-sails, and vowed no ships should sail till the merchants had consented to raise their wages.

Two days later, they assembled in St. George's Fields and marched to St. James's Palace, 'with colours flying, drums beating and fifes playing', and presented a petition to the King.[109] This was followed, on the 11th, by a petition to Parliament: a 'great body of sailors'—estimates vary between 5,000 and 15,000—marched to Palace Yard where, having been addressed by two gentlemen 'mounted on the roof of a hackney coach', they 'gave three cheers and dispersed'.[110] Further incidents took place along the waterfront in August and the following March;[111] but there is no evidence of any link between the sailors' movement and Wilkite agitation—such evidence as there is points rather the other way[112]—and too much importance should not be attached to a report of 27 April that

At Newcastle the cry for Wilkes and Liberty is said to be as loud among the sailors as at London, and attended with the same violence.[113]

108. Postgate's characterization of them as 'an outbreak of political strikes' is, in fact, singularly inappropriate (*op. cit.*, p. 158).

109. *G.M.* (1768), p. 242. Meanwhile, sailors' strikes and riots had been reported from North Shields and Sunderland in early April (*A.R.* (1768), p. 92; S.P. Dom, Entry Bks., 44/142, pp. 47–51, 54, 74).

110. *G.M.* (1768), p. 243.

111. *Ibid.* (1768), p. 442; 1769, p. 162.

112. According to Walpole, the sailors petitioning Parliament on 11 May 'declared for the King and Parliament and beat and drove away Wilkes's mob' (*Letters*, V, 100).

113. *G.M.* (1768), p. 241. For the London sailors' strike, see also Entry Bks., 44/142, pp. 79–81, 94–7, 162–3, 165–6.

On 9 May the Thames watermen demonstrated outside the Mansion House. Having been advised by the Lord Mayor to appoint 'a proper person' to draw up a petition to Parliament, they gave three huzzas and went off.[114]

The same day, 'the hatters struck and refused to work till their wages had been raised'.[115] The dispute seems to have lasted some weeks. According to the 'information' of John Dyer, hat-maker of St. Olave's, Southwark, taken on oath on 21 June:

On Thursday last,[116] a Mob or Gang of Hatters to the number of thirty came to his House in the Maze in the Parish of St. Olave's, Southwark, about one o'clock at noon, in a riotous manner, and insisted on this Informant turning off the men he then had at work, which he refused; and, upon such refusal, the said Mob or Gang of Hatters threatened to pull his House down and take this Informant thereout. And this Informant saith they would have begun to execute such threats if it had not been for one Mr Philips who accidentally was at this Informant's house, and did prevail on them to omit it. And this Informant's business now stands still on account of the said Mob coming to his House, and his apprentices are now unemployed. And this Informant saith that there was one Thomas Fitzhugh present and aiding & assisting among ye sd Mob, and came & asked this Informant whe[r] he wo[d] turn off his men which he refused; and upon that the said Fitzhugh declared, if he wo[d] not, 'damn them that wo[d] not have you out (meaning this Inform't) & the House down'.[117]

On 10 May, Charles Dingley's saw-mill in Limehouse was attacked by 500 sawyers. From the evidence of Christopher

114. *G.M.* (1768), p. 242.
115. *Ibid.*
116. I.e., 16 June 1768.
117. Surrey R.O., Sessions Bundles, 1768 (Midsummer). A recognisance for Thomas Fitzhugh, hatter of Holland's Leagues, Christ Church, Surrey, appears in the Surrey Sessions Roll for 1768 (Midsummer), according to which he is charged with 'a breach of the peace and a misdemeanour', released on a bail of £50 and required to appear at Guildford Quarter Sessions on 12 July. There is no further mention of him in the Q.S. records.

Robertson, Dingley's principal clerk, it appears that the main grievance was that new machinery had been recently installed: when he asked 'the mob of sawyers and other people' what they wanted,

They told me the saw-mill was at work when thousands of them were starving for want of bread. I then represented to them that the mill had done no kind of work that had injured them, or prevented them receiving any benefit. I desired to know which was their principal man to whom I might speak. I had some conversation with him and represented to him that it had not injured the sawyers. He said it partly might be so, but it would hereafter if it had not; and they came with a resolution to pull it down, and it should come down.[118]

A week later, the glass-grinders and journeymen tailors assembled to present a petition to Parliament in support of higher wages;[119] but no more is heard of these claims. More complex and protracted was the movement of East London coal-heavers. It had its origins in a dispute over wages going back to early February 1768: the coal-heavers who unloaded coals on the Thames, having compelled their masters, after a short strike, to increase their wages to 'fifteen pence a score' (of sacks), raised their demand to 18*d*.;[120] and, on their masters' refusal,

unanimously determined to desist from their labour; whereby a total stop was put to the business of unloading coals in the port of London.

Rioting by some 800 coal-heavers followed in Wapping and Shadwell.[121] The dispute became further complicated by the 'war' between two groups of agents operating rival

118. *Proceedings* (1768), p. 256.
119. *G.M.* (1768), p. 245. For the tailors, see Entry Bks., 44/142, pp. 92–4.
120. *Proceedings* (1768), p. 244.
121. Midd. R.O., Sessions Papers (Middlesex), September 1768: 'To the Honorable the Lord High Chancellor of Great Britain. The Representation of His Majesty's Justices of the Peace for the County of Middlesex in the General Sessions assembled at Hicks Hall on Thursday the 8th of Sept'r 1768'.

schemes for registering coal-heavers. The 'official' scheme, generally recognised until this dispute, had been set up under an Act of Parliament of 1758 and was administered by William Beckford, Alderman of Billingsgate Ward, and his agents.[122] Taking advantage of the wages dispute, Ralph Hodgson, a Middlesex justice resident in Shadwell, appears to have won wide support for his own 'unofficial' scheme, whereby only those coal-heavers paying him a registration fee were recognised as fully qualified. To win further favour among them, it was alleged that Hodgson had, on St. Patrick's Day, headed a demonstration of 400 coal-heavers—the great majority of whom were Irishmen —parading with shamrocks in 'the high streets and public highways of Shadwell, Ratcliff and the parish of Stepney ... with drums beating and colours flying'.[123] Violent clashes followed: on 18 April, John Green, publican of the *Round About Tavern*, Shadwell, himself a coal 'under-taker' and an agent of Alderman Beckford's, was threatened by Hodgson's men in Billingsgate that 'they would do for (him), if (he) did not desist in (his) proceedings'; and, on the 20th, Green's public house was besieged by armed coal-heavers who, to the accompaniment of shouts of 'Wilkes and coal-heavers for ever!',[124] swore 'they would have his heart and liver, and cut him in pieces and hang him on his sign'. Green defended himself stoutly and, before escaping to a neighbouring shipyard, shot dead two of his assailants—Thomas Smith, a cobbler, and William Wake, a coal-heaver.[125] Subsequently, seven coal-heavers—John Grainger, Daniel Clark, Richard Cornwall, Patrick Lynch, Thomas Murray, Peter Flaherty and Nicholas McCabe—were sentenced to death at the Old Bailey and hanged at the Sun Tavern Fields in Stepney

122. *Proceedings* (1768), *loc. cit.*
123. Midd. R.O., Sessions Papers (Middlesex), September 1768.
124. See pp. 231–2 above.
125. *Proceedings* (1768), pp. 204–7, 207–14, 244–56. John Green was subsequently tried on two charges of murder, but acquitted, at the Old Bailey on 18–21 May 1768 (*ibid.*, pp. 204–14).

before a crowd of 50,000, attended by 300 soldiers and 'a prodigious number of peace officers'.[126]

A week after the riot, there appears to have been a temporary settlement, when the coal-heavers' foremen, after meeting Alderman Beckford and other justices, agreed to register their gangs and return to work;[127] but, on 12 May, having failed to win their masters' consent in writing for a rise in wages, the coal-heavers marched to the Mansion House; 'his Lordship', however, 'very prudently declined intermeddling with their affairs'.[128] A series of violent affrays followed between coal-heavers and sailors who continued to man colliers on the Thames. On 23 May, coal-heavers boarded the *Thomas and Mary*, lying in Shadwell dock, and threatened to murder any sailor who continued to load; on the next day, a fight followed in the course of which a young sailor, John Beattie, was stabbed to death.[129] Again, on 1 June, two captains of colliers, who had come ashore at King James's Steps, Wapping, to purchase provisions, were beaten up by fifty coal-heavers.[130] Another clash was reported on 6 June;[131] but, after the military had, a few days later, been called in to help 'the civil power', twenty of the 'desperadoes' were

126. *Proceedings* (1768), pp. 244-56; *A.R.* (1768), pp. 139-40; *G.M.* (1768), p. 348. It appears that six of the convicted men were Catholics; but 'one, being a Protestant (was) attended by a gentleman of Mr. Wesley's persuasion' (*A.R.* (1768), p. 140). In September 1769, another coal-heaver, David Creamer, was sentenced to seven years in Newgate for firing at John Green (Midd. R.O., Sessions Rolls (Middlesex), No. 3217a, 26 June 1769; Process Register Bks. of Indictments, vol. 18 (1769-75), p. 8).

127. *A.R.* (1768), pp. 101-2.

128. *G.M.* (1768), p. 243.

129. For the Old Bailey trial of nine coal-heavers charged with this murder—Thomas Carnan, James Murphy, James Dogan, John Castillo, Thomas Davis, James Hammond, Hugh Henley, Michael (Malachi) Doyle and Thomas Farmer—see *Proceedings* (1768), pp. 264-74. Murphy and Dogan were executed at Tyburn on 11 July (*G.M.* (1768), p. 347).

130. *A.R.* (1768), p. 119.

131. *Ibid.*, p. 121.

taken into custody,[132] and the movement seems to have collapsed.[133]

Even more protracted was the weavers' dispute, which forms but an episode in the stormy history of the silk-weavers of Spitalfields, Stepney and Bethnal Green with their long tradition of action—both industrial and political —to promote their trade interests.[134] This particular dispute began as one between the masters and their journeymen over wages, but quickly developed into warfare between journeymen engaged in different types of work. Early in January 1768, the masters reduced the price of work by 4*d.* a yard;[135] yet, on 12 January, we find masters and journeymen combining in a great march of Spitalfields weavers to St. James's to thank the King for shortening the period of Court mournings;[136] and, later in the month, we hear of masters expressing their readiness 'to give to that useful body of men, their journeymen, the wages they themselves had requested'.[137] Meanwhile, in Stepney, a dispute had broken out between 'single-handed' and 'engine-loom' weavers; and three 'single-handed' weavers, charged with attacking their opponents' houses and destroying their work in the loom, were handed over to the magistrates by their rivals and ordered to appear at Middlesex Quarter Sessions.[138]

132. *A.R.* (1768), p. 124. The names of ten of these appear in Midd. R.O., Process Register Bks. of Indictments, vol. 17 (1761–9), p. 799; but I have found no record of any judgment.

133. The movement left some memories. Applying on 26 July 1779 to the Duke of Northumberland, Lord Lieutenant of Middlesex, for consideration as a Volunteer 'in some of our newe leveys for our home defence', John Green of Westminster Bridge Road, Lambeth, reminds the Duke of 'a detail of my conduct in repelling the Hostile proceedings of the Coal Heavers in the year 1768' (Midd. R.O., Mil. 90/2/2). I am indebted to Miss E. D. Mercer, B.A., F.S.A., County Archivist, Middlesex County Record Office, for drawing my attention to this document.

134. See Maccoby, *op. cit.*, pp. 453–5.

135. *A.R.* (1768), p. 57.

136. *Ibid.*, pp. 59–60.

137. *Ibid.*, p. 68.

138. This appears to have been Peter Perryn, John Read and Corne-

A lull followed; and then, on 26 July, reports the *Annual Register*,

a great number of evil-disposed persons, armed with pistols, cutlasses and other offensive weapons, and in disguise, assembled themselves together about the hour of twelve in the night . . . and entered the houses and shops of several journeymen weavers in and near Spitalfields . . . and . . . cut to pieces and destroyed the silk works then manufacturing in nine different looms there, belonging to Mr. John Baptist Herbert, of Stewart-Street Spitalfields, the damage of which is very considerable.[139]

Again, on 20 August, we read that the Spitalfields weavers 'rose in a body', broke into the house of Nathaniel Farr in Pratt's Alley, cut to pieces the silk in two looms and, in the house of Elizabeth Farr, shot dead Edward Fitchett, a lad of seventeen.[140] Rewards were offered in both these cases, but no prosecutions followed. After a further lull, the disturbances began again in the spring. On 9 May 1769, William Tilley of St. Leonard's, Shoreditch, was fined 12*d*. at Middlesex Quarter Sessions for having, on 10 April, cut and destroyed a loom 'and a warp of thread therein of the value of ten shillings', belonging to Lydia Fowler.[141] Meanwhile, the 'cutters' had formed committees, which met at the *Dolphin Ale-house*, Spitalfields, and other taverns, to levy contributions for a strike fund from both masters and journeymen:[142] on 10 March 1769, we read that Spitalfields 'throwsters' had 'extorted money from the

---

lius Cavalier, tried at the Old Bailey in October 1769 on a charge of forcibly entering the house of John Clare in Stepney on 4 January 1768, with intent to destroy 4 looms. Read and Cavalier were acquitted and Perryn sentenced to death (*Proceedings* (1769), pp. 446–7). Another 'single-handed' journeyman weaver, William Evans, was examined by Sir John Fielding late in January 1768 and committed to Newgate, charged with cutting and destroying 'works out of the loom' (*A.R.* (1768), p. 68); he does not appear in the Q.S. records.

139. *A.R.* (1768), p. 139.
140. *Ibid.*, p. 157; see also *G.M.* (1768), p. 442.
141. Midd. R.O., Sessions Rolls (Middlesex), No. 3214, 9 May 1769; Process Register Bks. of Indictments, vol. 17 (1761–9), p. 874.
142. *A.R.* (1769), p. 136.

masters and committed other outrages';[143] and when John Doyle and John Valline were tried and capitally convicted at the Old Bailey for having broken into the house of Thomas Poor, weaver of Stocking-Frame Alley, Shoreditch, on 7 August, 'with intent to cut and destroy a loom', their victim testified that

'he was obliged to pay 6d a week for each loom to the cutters . . . the weavers called it the Defiance.'[144]

A number of other outrages, leading to capital convictions, followed: on 9 August, Thomas Poor's house was again broken into and raw silk destroyed in a loom;[145] on 11 September, William Eastman forcibly entered the house of Daniel Clarke at 11 Artillery Lane, Bishopsgate, and destroyed 20 yards of silk and one *monteur* value 5s.;[146] a few days later, similar 'outrages' were committed against John Dupree of St. John's Street, Bethnal Green,[147] and Robert Cromwell of Moorfields.[148] Meanwhile, fifteen

143. *A.R.* (1769), p. 164.

144. *Proceedings* (1769), pp. 438–42. The evidence suggests that Valline was a member of the committee meeting at the *Duke of Northumberland's Head*, See also the case of Michael Duff of Christ Church, Middlesex, found Not Guilty at Middlesex Quarter Sessions of having, on 4 October 1769, extorted money from John Gorman, journeyman weaver, on the pretence 'that this 6d was for the poor men in prison, meaning certain persons . . . called Cutters who were in custody for feloniously cutting and destroying divers looms, utensils and works', etc. (Midd. R.O., Sessions Rolls (Middlesex), No. 3218, 5 October 1769; Process Register Bks. of Indictments, vol. 18 (1769–75) p. 31).

145. For this offence, William Horsford, aged 22, was sentenced to death at the Old Bailey on 9 December 1769 (*Proceedings* (1770), pp. 31–46).

146. Eastman was sentenced to death at the Old Bailey on 6 December 1769 (*Ibid.*, pp. 23–8). In a recognisance of 4 November 1769, the name of Thomas Haddon appears with that of Eastman (Corp. Lond. R.O., Sessions Files, 4 December 1769).

147. See the case of John Fessy, capitally convicted at the Old Bailey in October 1769 (*Proceedings* (1769), pp. 450–53).

148. See the case of John Carmichael of Half-Moon Alley, Bishopsgate Street, sentenced to death at the Old Bailey on 6 December 1769 (*Ibid.* (1770), pp. 46–51).

weavers of Christ Church, Middlesex (many of them Irishmen), had been taken into custody and charged with parading with swords, hangers, pistols, blunderbusses and other offensive weapons, and engaging in sundry 'riots' and 'tumults', during August.[149]

To intimidate the weavers, the Government now decided to post troops in Spitalfields, and a number of clashes followed between the strikers and the military.[150] On 6 December, John Doyle and John Valline, two of the convicted 'cutters', were executed before great crowds of weavers near the Salmon and Ball, Bethnal Green;[151] and, the same day, Lewis Chauvet, a prosperous silk-manufacturer,[152] whose house had already been attacked,[153] had his windows broken by Simon Rawlings and 'others unknown'.[154] The agitation for the release of the other convicted 'cutters' received official support in both London and Middlesex;[155] and, on 18 December, we read of Alderman John Sawbridge, Wilkite Sheriff of Middlesex, advising the weavers to appoint a committee and to present a petition to the King 'in favour of their unfortunate brethren now under sentence of death'.[156] 'Parson' Horne also claimed later to have paid £20 out of his own pocket

149. Midd. R.O., Sessions Rolls (Middlesex), No. 3218, 5 October 1769; Process Register Bks. of Indictments, vol. 18 (1769–75), pp. 27, 33.

150. *A.R.* (1769), pp. 136, 138.

151. *Ibid.*, pp. 159–60.

152. In 1771, Chauvet had a house in Broad Street Ward (precinct of St. Peter le Poor) of an annual value of £90; and the firm of Lewis Chauvet & Co. at 10, St. Olave's Jewry, was valued at £165 p.a. (Guild. Lib., Sewer Rate 1771, MS. 2137/1–4 (Broad Street), p. 47; (Coleman Street), p. 59).

153. On 4 December 1769, Nathaniel Norris was sentenced at Middlesex Quarter Sessions to one year's jail for a previous 'riot' at Lewis Chauvet's house (Midd. R.O., Process Register Bks. of Indictments, vol. 18 (1769–75), p. 40. There are no Sessions Rolls (Middlesex) for 4 December 1769).

154. Midd. R.O., Sessions Rolls (Middlesex), No. 3222, 8 January 1770; Process Register Bks. of Indictments, vol. 18 (1769–75), pp. 43–4.

155. Maccoby, *op. cit.*, p. 459.

156. *A.R.* (1769), p. 161.

to procure counsel for Baker, an indicted journeyman weaver.[157] Yet Wilkes and his closest associates do not appear to have played any significant part in the agitation, and Horne wrote to Wilkes in July 1771 that he 'never did receive any subscription for the affair of the weavers of Spitalfields'.[158]

What, then, were the social ingredients of the 'Wilkes and Liberty' movement of 1768–9 and whence did it receive its stimulus and driving force? In a review of the events of the spring and summer of 1768, the *Annual Register* observed:

A general dissatisfaction unhappily prevailed among several of the lower orders of the people. This illtemper, which was partly occasioned by the high price of provisions, and partly proceeded from other causes, too frequently manifested itself in acts of tumult and riot, which were productive of the most melancholy consequences.[159]

Yet George III's reply to Parliament's Address of 11 May significantly noted that a 'spirit of outrage and violence' prevailed 'among different classes of my subjects';[160] and it would be a mistake to follow certain historians in presenting the 'Wilkes and Liberty' movement almost exclusively in terms of working-class unrest.[161]

In fact, it drew its strength from widely different social groups. First, there was Wilkes's growing support among a substantial section of the merchants and property-owners of the City of London and elsewhere—a support that, with all its vagaries and desertions, long outlived the movement that is the subject of the present paper.[162] During the

157. *Controversial Letters of John Wilkes Esq., the Rev. John Horne, and their principal adherents* (1772), p. 21.

158. *Ibid.*

159. *A.R.* (1768), pp. 83–4.

160. *G.M.* (1768), p. 243.

161. See, e.g., Postgate, *op. cit.*, p. 155: 'Wilkes's supporters were notoriously overwhelmingly of the working class.'

162. Again to quote the *Annual Register*: 'Nor were the marks of public regard which he received confined solely to the lower order of people; several merchants and other gentlemen of large property and of considerable interest openly espoused his cause' (*A.R.* (1769), p. 60).

period under review, we may recall the vote cast for him in the City—considerable under the circumstances—in the General Election of March 1768; his unopposed return as Alderman for Farringdon Without in January 1769; and, above all, the financial support and sympathy that he received among prosperous citizens in London, Westminster and Southwark after the creation of the Society of Supporters of the Bill of Rights. The founders of the Society included such prominent public figures and men of wealth as Alderman John Sawbridge, M.P.,[163] James Townsend, M.P.,[164] Richard Oliver, M.P., [165] Sir Joseph Mawbey, M.P.,[166] Sir Cecil W.Ray, Bart,[167] and Samuel

163. M.P. for Hythe (1768) and for London (1774–90). Inherited large fortune from grandfather, Jacob Sawbridge, former director of South Sea Company. Liveryman of Framework Knitters' Company; Sheriff, midsummer 1768; Alderman of Langbourne Ward, July 1769; Lord Mayor, 1775–6 (*D.N.B.*, XVII, 868–9). His house in New Burlington Street, St. James's, had a rentable value of £90 p.a. (West. Lib., St. James's, Westminster, Watch Rate, 1769, D 595, p. 27).

164. M.P. for West Looe and Westbury, Wilts. Inherited Bruce Castle, Tottenham, and property in Norfolk. Member of Mercers' Company; Alderman of Bishopsgate Ward, June 1769; Sheriff, 1770; Lord Mayor, 1772–3 (Guild. Lib., Noble Coll., C78 (Wilkes)). Family house in Austin Friars, London, was, in 1771, assessed at rent of £60 p.a. (Guild. Lib., Sewer Rate 1771, MS. 2137, 1–4 (Broad Street), p. 20).

165. M.P. for London, 1770–80. Grandson of Richard Oliver, Speaker of House of Assembly, Antigua. Freeman of Drapers' Company, June 1770; Alderman of Billingsgate, July 1770; Sheriff, 1772. Committed to Tower on 26 March 1771 during City's dispute with Commons over printing parliamentary proceedings. Returned to Antigua, 1778 (*D.N.B.*, XIV, 1043–4). His house at 107, Fenchurch Street, was assessed at rent of £65 p.a. and stables at £8 (Guild. Lib., Sewer Rate 1771, MS. 2137/1–4 (Aldgate), pp. 37, 41).

166. M.P. for Southwark, 1761–74. Malt-distiller and estate-owner. Sheriff for Surrey, 1757; Baronet, 1765; Chairman of Surrey Quarter Sessions, 1763–90 (*D.N.B.*, XIII, 109–10). His distillery at Vauxhall was assessed at rent of £26 p.a. (London County R.O., Surrey and Kent Commissioners of Sewers, Rate book No. 516, Vauxhall Creek Rate (duplicate), January 1774, p. 7).

167. M.P. for E. Retford (1768–80) and for Westminster (1782–4). Baronetcy and large house and estate at Lincoln, 1752. Opponent of Fox in Westminster, 1783–4 (*D.N.B.*, XXI, 989–90).

Vaughan, City merchant.[168] Through them he was able to win the even more influential—though less consistent—support of 'patriots' like William Beckford[169] and Brass Crosby,[170] who doubtless saw in Wilkes—with much of which they disapproved—Chatham's disciple as the stalwart champion of 'Revolution principles' and the City interest.

More important, however, for the present study was Wilkes's support among the Middlesex freeholders. These of course, by the very nature of their electoral qualification, formed an amorphous body of property owners and cannot be related to any particular social group; though it may be presumed that the 'inferior freeholders' predominated among them[171] and could, therefore, on occasion, exercise a decisive electoral influence. It was later noted of the signatories to the nation-wide Wilkite petitions of 1769–70 that they were drawn in the main from these 'inferior freeholders' and 'that the majority of gentlemen of large fortunes, of justices of the peace, and of the clergy,

168. Common Council man and merchant. His house at 1, Dunster's Court, Mincing Lane, was assessed at rent of £43 p.a. (Guild. Lib., Sewer Rate 1771, MS. 2137/1–4 (Tower), p. 9).

169. M.P. for Shaftesbury (1747–54) and for London (1754–70). Alderman of Billingsgate, 1752; Sheriff, 1755; Lord Mayor, 1762–3 and 1769–70 (*D.N.B.*, II, 80–1). Beckford was extremely popular in the City: on his death in June 1770, the various Vestries in the Billingsgate Ward joined together in pairs to mourn his loss by draping the pulpit and desks of their churches in black and displaying his coat-of-arms with the motto: 'Amicum populi munerabit Deus' (Guild. Lib., St. George, Botolph Lane, Vestry Minutes, 1685–1782, MS. 952/2, p. 312; St. Andrew Hubbard, V.M., 1753–84, MS. 1278/3; St. Mary at Hill, Vestry Bk., 1752–1804, MS. 1240/2; St. Botolph, Billingsgate, V.M., 1757–1859, M.S., 943/3, p. 66).

170. M.P. for Honiton, 1768–74. Sheriff, 1764–5; Alderman of Bread Street, February 1765; Lord Mayor, 1770–1. Committed to Tower by order of Commons, 27 March–8 May 1771 (*D.N.B.*, V, 210).

171. Thus, in Brentford, twenty-four out of forty-five properties owned by freeholders voting in one or more of the Middlesex elections of 1768–9 were assessed for the Poor Rate at an annual value of under £12 (Midd. R.O., Middlesex Poll Books 1768–9 (transcript in one volume, undated), pp. 103–7; Brentford Lib., New Brentford MSS., No. 17612, Poors Rate, August 1768).

in some of the counties, had not signed the petition';[172] and it would be instructive to use the available records— the Middlesex Poll Books and the surviving Poor Rate and Land Tax registers—to attempt to arrive at some rough social analysis of the Wilkite voters of 1768–9.[173] This would be a long task and might not yield positive results; but even a preliminary glance at the Poll Books suggests that the Esquires, Knights, Church of England clergy and more prominent lawyers and property-holders tended to vote for the anti-Wilkite candidates. In the Middlesex election of December 1768, for example, whereas Serjeant Glynn won the support of eight Esquires and 'Parson' Horne of Brentford, Sir William Proctor, the defeated Court candidate, received the votes of twenty-eight Esquires, two Knights, a Baronet and four Church of England ministers;[174] and, in Brentford alone, we find that three out of five freeholders whose properties were assessed for the Poor Rate at an annual value of over £25 voted for Luttrell against Wilkes in April 1769.[175]

Yet the most active elements in the 'Wilkes and Liberty'

172. *A.R.* (1770), p. 60; quoted by Postgate, *op. cit.*, p. 154.

173. Unfortunately, neither the Poll Books nor Poor Rate or Land Tax registers give occupations; but the latter give the annual values, or rents, of the properties occupied.

174. Guild. Lib., Middlesex Poll, December 1768. Among prominent freeholders voting for Glynn were Aldermen John Sawbridge and James Townsend of Tottenham (p. 6); among Proctor's supporters were The Hon. Charles Yorke, M.P., of Lincoln's Inn; Samuel Whitbread, brewer, of Chiswell Street, St. Luke's; David Wilmot, justice, of Bethnal Green; and Sir James Esdaile, City Alderman, of Bunhill Row, St. Luke's (pp. 1, 2, 30, 47).

175. Of the remainder, one voted for the Wilkite candidate in all three elections and the other did not vote in April 1769. (Midd. R.O., Middlesex Poll Books, 1768–9, pp. 103–7; Brentford Lib., New Brentford MSS., No. 17612, Poors Rate, August 1768.) In spite of 'Parson' Horne's efforts, the Wilkite vote in Brentford was relatively low: whereas Proctor received 3·5 per cent of his vote there in March and 2·9 per cent in December 1768 and Luttrell received 5·4 per cent of his support there in April 1769, Glynn received only 2·2 per cent of his vote in Brentford in December 1768, and Wilkes himself only 2·3 per cent of his vote there in March 1768 and 2 per

movement of 1768–9 were presumably those who demon-strated in St. George's Fields, at the Mansion House and St. James's Palace, and shouted, or chalked up, Wilkite slogans in the streets of the City, Westminster and South-wark. While it is difficult, for lack of precise evidence, to classify these elements exactly, it is fairly certain that they were not composed of City merchants or Aldermen, or even of the 'middling' sort of freeholders. We have the evidence of Horace Walpole that—on one occasion, at least—they included weavers of Spitalfields, and the more certain evidence of the Old Bailey trials that the riotous coal-heavers of Wapping and Shadwell were drawn into the movement, if only for a brief while. We know, too, from the few available 'informations' that Mathew Chris-tian, 'a gentleman of character and fortune', was drawn into the riots of March 1768 and, whether by compulsion or inclination, drank with the rioters to 'Wilkes and Liberty';[176] that Robert Chandler, a City tea-broker, was believed to have 'headed a Mob in Westminster' on the same occasion;[177] and that, in Southwark on 11 May, Justice Capel was 'insulted' by Richard Gilbert, who stood in a group with 'several well-dressed persons'.[178] Beyond this, we have to rely on the comparatively small sample afforded by those who were committed to prison or released on bail as the result of their activities, or who appeared for trial at the Old Bailey or before the justices in Quarter Sessions in London, Westminster, Middlesex and Surrey. Occupation or social status[179] is given in the case of thirty-

cent of his vote in April 1769 (Midd. R.O., Middlesex Poll Books, 1768–9, pp. 103–7).

176. S.P. 37/6, No. 80/13, fos. 225–6. See pp. 227–8 above.

177. S.P. Dom, Entry Bks. 44/142, p. 157.

178. Surrey R.O., Sessions Bundles, 1768 (Midsummer). See pp. 236–7 above.

179. By 'social status' I mean such broad classifications as 'gentle-man', 'yeoman' or 'labourer'. The latter is commonly used in indict-ments to include urban workers, small traders and craftsmen; in recognisances the precise occupation is more frequently given, and the term 'labourer' is generally reserved for wage-earners.

seven of forty-six such persons. These included two gentlemen; two merchants or dealers;[180] eleven tradesmen (who may have been small masters, journeymen or independent craftsmen);[181] five vaguely classified as 'labourers'; and seventeen who were probably wage-earners.[182] The great majority were, in fact, labourers, servants, journeymen, small craftsmen or petty traders; and we must assume that nearly all lived in lodgings, as not one of those whose addresses appear in the records—not even the two 'gentlemen'—are to be found in the lists of householders assessed for the Poor Rate, Sewer Rate or Land Tax in the various parishes or precincts in which they resided.[183] So, in spite of the occasional report of 'well-dressed persons' among the rioters, for lack of further evidence, we must conclude that these formed but a small minority, that even the 'middling' sort of householder played little part in the disturbances, and that the most active elements in Wilkite street demonstrations and riots, while not being drawn exclusively from the 'working class', were overwhelmingly composed of 'the lower orders of the people'.

This is not the place to enquire what prompted City merchants and Middlesex freeholders to support Wilkes in 1768; but we must briefly consider why so many from London's 'lower orders' gave him such enthusiastic and vocal allegiance. Much has been written of Wilkite 'mobs', as of other 'mobs' of the eighteenth century: the term is misleading, as it suggests that there was a criminal, or at

180. These were one bottle merchant and the wife of a dealer in old clothes.

181. They were: three shoemakers, a peruke-maker, a sail-maker, a carver, a sawyer, a cooper, a weaver, a blacksmith and a pewterer.

182. These were: nine labourers, two lightermen, a mariner, a 'servant', a coachman, a porter, a paper-hanger and a watch-finisher.

183. Land Tax registers (or duplicates), Poor Rate and Sewer Rate Books have been examined for this purpose in the Guildhall Library, the Middlesex and London County Record Offices, and the Westminster and Southwark Libraries.

least a pecuniary, motive behind the actions of the persons concerned. Yet there is, in this case, no evidence of the 'hiring' of bands of demonstrators;[184] and loot played no part in these disturbances. We have, then, to look for other explanations, such as Wilkes's personal appeal or the influence of social or economic factors.

Indeed, the evidence already presented suggests that such factors as prices and wages played a considerable part in stimulating unrest during the spring and summer of 1768. This is, of course, self-evident in the case of the industrial disputes running 'parallel' with the 'Wilkes and Liberty' movement itself, in which wages—in spite of their occasional diversion into political channels—were the essential issue. And, quite apart from the particular circumstances affecting each trade, we may assume that the almost simultaneous presentation of claims for higher wages by tailors, coal-heavers, sailors and other workers was prompted by the need to adjust wages to the rising cost of living. 'The high price of provisions' was stressed by the *Annual Register* as being the main cause of the 'illtemper' of the coal-heavers and sailors in the spring of 1768;[185] and prevailing public concern with the cost of food is underlined by the following news item in the same journal, dated 18 April 1768:

Yesterday a ½-penny loaf, adorned with mourning Crape, was hung up at several parts of the Royal Exchange, with an inscription thereon, containing some reflections touching the high price of bread and other provisions. It was nailed up at the northside of the building, & there left for the inspection of the public.[186]

More solid evidence is provided by the monthly tables of wheat and bread prices published in the *Gentleman's*

---

184. The question does arise, of course, in the case of Balfe and McQuirk; but they were hired by the Court party (see pp. 242–3 and note 92 above).

185. *A.R.* (1768), pp. 83–4.

186. *Ibid.*, p. 69.

Magazine.[187] From these it appears that the price of the quarter of wheat, having remained remarkably stable for the years 1763–4,[188] reached a 'peak' of 50*s.* in October 1766; after considerable fluctuation, it rose to new (though slightly lower) 'peaks' in July and October 1767,[189] fell to 44*s.* 9*d.* in December, and then rose steeply to a new 'peak' of 50*s.* 6*d.* in May 1768. After that, there was a sharp drop to 31*s.* 9*d.* in January 1769, followed by slight rises to 35*s.* 9*d.* in July–August and to 35*s.* 2*d.* in December; but, generally, the price of wheat in London remained low throughout 1769 and continued to be so in the early months of 1770.[190] The price of the wheaten peck-loaf followed a similar—though less erratic—course, and reached its highest point for the years 1763 to 1770 at 2*s.* 9*d.* in July 1767, in October–November 1767 and in February–July 1768; after which, it fell, by stages, to 2*s.* 2*d.* in October–December, and fluctuated between 2*s.*

187. *G.M.*, vols. 33–40 (1763–70), *passim*. Prices quoted are for the quarter (generally) of wheat at the London Corn Exchange and for the wheaten peck-loaf at the Assize of Bread in London. No prices of wheat appear for the period January 1765 to May 1766 and December 1766 to May 1767; and no prices of bread for October 1766 to June 1767. Monthly *minima* and *maxima* over which the price of the quarter of wheat ranges are given for the period January 1763 to November 1767; from July 1767 to October 1770, a weekly range of prices is quoted. In both cases, I have calculated a single monthly 'mean' for the sake of uniformity. In November–December 1770, a single London price is quoted in bushels: these I have converted into quarters (London used the Winchester measure: 1 quarter = 8 bushels). According to the 'observations' of London bakers to a Parliamentary Committee in 1768, the Cities of London and Westminster jointly consumed 600,000 quarters of wheat per annum (i.e. approx. 1 quarter per person p.a.), sufficient to bake 7,200,000 wheaten peck-loaves and 7,200,000 household peck-loaves (Guild. Lib., MS. 7799: 'Observations humbly submitted to the consideration of the Honourable Committee of the House of Commons appointed to enquire into the Assize of Bread').

188. It fluctuated between a monthly 'mean' of 32*s.* and 32*s.* 6*d.* per quarter.

189. In July 1767, 47/10; in October 1767, 49*s.* 6*d.* per quarter.

190. In January–June 1770, it never rose above 32*s.* per quarter; it rose to 37*s.* 11*d.* in July, to 42*s.* 8¼*d.* in August, and then fluctuated slightly below this price.

and 2*s*. 2½*d*. in 1769 and between 2*s*. and 2*s*. 3½*d*. in 1770.

These figures do, in fact, suggest a certain concordance between the movement of prices and the popular movements—for, at least, a part of the period under review. This is striking in the months January–May 1768, which marked the final phase of the high-prices cycle of August 1766 to May 1768 and witnessed both the origins of the movements of weavers and coal-heavers and the violent Wilkite riots of March and May 1768. Thus, food prices appear to have been an important factor at this stage, at least, of the 'Wilkes and Liberty' movement, in contrast with a movement like the Gordon Riots of 1780, in which they played an insignificant part.[191] Yet this is no longer true of the subsequent period: as we have seen, prices dropped very sharply after May 1768 and remained low in 1769; so we can obviously not explain the excitement over the Middlesex election of December 1768 or the new outbreak of political rioting in London in March 1769 in such terms.[192]

Due account must, of course, be taken of the power of Wilkes's personality, political principles and courageous defiance of authority to evoke a more than ephemeral response among the small property owners and propertyless classes of the capital. They had already, on more than one occasion, in the name of 'Revolution principles', championed the cause of the City magistrates and of the Earl of Chatham; and, in a sense, their 'adoption' of Wilkes

191. In January–July 1780 (the riots took place in early June), the price of wheat did not rise above 30*s*. 8*d*. per quarter, nor did the price of the wheaten peck-loaf rise above 2*s*. (*G.M.*, vol. 50 (1780), *passim*).

192. Further point is lent to this argument by extending it to the two other phases of the 'Wilkes and Liberty' movement—in 1763 and 1771–5. The year 1763 was a year of exceptionally low food prices, and the 'peak' price-periods of July 1771, April–November 1772, July–August 1773 and January–April 1775 were not particularly distinguished by Wilkite agitation or disturbances (*G.M.*, vols. 40–45, *passim*).

was but a logical sequence to the former popularity of Chatham. Besides, Wilkes knew, on occasion, how to address himself to, or solicit the support of, the 'inferior sort of people', though be it in the most general terms. During his trial at Westminster Hall in May 1763, he had declared:

The liberty of all peers and gentlemen—and (what touches me most sensibly) that of *all the middling and inferior set of people, who stand most in need of protection*—is, in my case, this day to be finally decided upon.[193]

Not that he formulated—then or later—any social programme of particular concern to the 'inferior', or working, people: he certainly remained oblivious or indifferent to the particular interests of workers in dispute with their employers. Nor was there anything original, let alone of specific concern to working people, in his formulation of political principles.[194] Yet the survival of a 'radical' tradition in the City of London, the sharpening antagonism of Court and Opposition Whigs, the electoral excitement of March 1768, Wilkes's own particular record and championship of 'Revolution principles'—not to mention his colourful personality and willingness to appeal to the political energies of the unenfranchised—all combined to make him the centre of a considerable popular, political movement. This, as we have seen, was all the more likely to develop in a period of rising prices and of general social unrest.[195]

The 'Wilkes and Liberty' movement marks an important stage in the political education of the 'middling' and common people of Britain; yet it marked but the early

193. Bleackley, *op. cit.*, pp. 105–6 (my *italics*).
194. S. Maccoby, *op. cit.*, pp. 82–8.
195. This is, of course, not an exhaustive treatment of the various elements contributing to the outbreak and protraction of the 'Wilkes and Liberty' movement of 1768–9. In such a treatment, proper account would have to be taken of additional social factors like unemployment, immigration and growth of London's population.

beginnings of a Radical movement with a stable popular base. This base was still insecure and the political lessons were as yet imperfectly learned: so much is evident from the ease with which it allowed itself, a dozen years later, to be diverted—though, professedly, in the name of the same 'Revolution principles'—into the dangerous course of the Gordon Riots. Yet it revived and bore richer fruit in the 1790s, under the impact of the French Revolution, the new factory system and the work and writings of the democrats.

The Gordon Riots: A Study of the Rioters and their Victims

The Gordon Riots made a profound impression on contemporaries. They took a place at a time of acute political crisis, at the most dangerous moment of the American war, when the country, after numerous defeats and counter-alliances, found itself virtually isolated. At their height, on the night of 7 June 1780, London appeared to onlookers to be a sea of flames. 'I remember,' wrote Horace Walpole on the 8th 'the Excise and the Gin Act and the rebels at Derby and Wilkes' interlude and the French at Plymouth, or I should have a very bad memory; but I never till last night saw London and Southwark in flames!'[1] Sébastien Mercier, in his *Tableau de Paris*, wrote nine years before the attack on the Bastille that such 'terrors and alarms' as were spread by Lord George Gordon in London would be inconceivable in a city as well-policed as Paris.[2]

It is perhaps not surprising that later writers should have felt something of the awe and fascination which the riots aroused in those who witnessed them. Dickens gave a vivid, though romanticised, account in *Barnaby Rudge*, and the origins and significance of the riots have become a favourite theme of historical speculation. Historians have, of course, not failed to point to their important political implications: to the unexpected strengthening of Lord North's administration which followed;[3] to the sharp divisions which they

From *Transactions of the Royal Historical Society*, 5th series, VI (1956), 93–114.

1. *The Letters of Horace Walpole, Earl of Orford*, ed. P. Cunningham, 9 vols. (1891), VII, 388.

2. L. S. Mercier, *Tableau de Paris*, 12 vols. (Amsterdam, 1783), VI, 22–5.

3. Ian R. Christie, 'The Marquis of Rockingham and Lord North's offer of a Coalition, June–July 1780', *Eng. Hist. Rev.*, LXIX, 388–407.

brought out between the government and the City of London on the bearing of arms; to the particular anxieties of the Roman Catholic community;[4] and, perhaps most important of all, to the permanent strengthening of the executive by the powerful arguments which they provided in favour of a professional police force. These and other aspects have been treated at length by Mr. Paul de Castro in his book on the Gordon Riots written nearly thirty years ago[5]. But neither Mr. de Castro nor any other historian has attempted to portray the rioters themselves, beyond dismissing them as a nameless 'mob', nor even to look closely at any but the more prominent of their victims.

In the present study an attempt is made to begin to bridge this gap by drawing, in the main, on new materials—on judicial and financial records relating to the riots in the Public Record Office, the Record Offices of the Corporation of London, of the London County Council and of the Counties of Middlesex and Surrey, and in the archives of the Westminster, Holborn and Guildhall Libraries;[6] on the Papist returns ordered by Parliament in 1767 and 1780;[7] and by an extensive use of the Proceedings of the Old Bailey and of the Special Commission set up to judge rioters in Southwark.[8] With their aid it is hoped not only to identify the rioters and their victims, but to throw a fresh light on the pattern of the riots and on the motives that prompted their participants.

4. See E. H. Burton, *The Life and Times of Bishop Challoner, 1691–1791*, 2 vols. (1909).

5. J. P. de Castro, *The Gordon Riots* (Oxford, 1926).

6. Use has also been made of Land Tax and Poor Rate registers in the Bethnal Green, Islington, Shoreditch and Stepney Libraries.

7. House of Lords R.O., Returns of Papists for 1767 and 1780; Catholic Record Society, Papist Return for 1780 (St. Andrew, Holborn).

8. *The whole Proceedings on the King's Commission of the Peace, Oyer and Terminer and Gaol Delivery for the City of London and . . . for the County of Middlesex*, ed. J. Gurney (1780), pp. 358–640 (hereafter cited as *Proceedings* (London)); and (bound in the same volume) *The Proceedings on the King's Special Commission of Oyer and Terminer for the County of Surrey*, ed. J. Gurney (1780), pp. 1–168 (hereafter cited as *Proceedings* (Surrey)).

The outline of events need here be only briefly given.[9] It was on Friday, 2 June 1780, that a huge concourse of some 60,000 persons gathered at the summons of the Protestant Association in St. George's Fields, Southwark, to present a monster petition to Parliament, calling for the repeal of the partial measures of Roman Catholic relief enacted in 1778.[10] After listening to a harangue by Lord George Gordon, the Association's president, the demonstrators marched in four contingents to Palace Yard, where they reassembled between half past two and three in the afternoon. It was noted by a bystander that the marchers were composed of 'the better sort of tradesmen; they were all well-dressed decent sort of people';[11] though earlier it had been reported that the journeymen weavers of Spitalfields were mustering.[12] While Lord George was presenting his petition to the Commons, violent scenes were taking place outside: to shouts of 'No Popery!' members of both Houses—but particularly of the Lords—were hustled and buffeted and several only escaped severe injury by ignominious retreat or by the intervention of the Guards. The anger of the crowds was raised to a higher pitch by the periodic appearance of Lord George Gordon at the top of the gallery stairs, announcing that consideration of the Petition was to be postponed and naming members who had expressed hostility to their cause. After hours of uproar, the Guards were able to clear a way for the imprisoned members; at eleven o'clock the Commons adjourned until the following Tuesday and parts of the crowds dispersed.

At this point, a section of the demonstrators moved off towards the private chapel of the Sardinian ambassador in

9. I have generally followed de Castro's account (*op. cit.*, pp. 28–167), except where indicated in the footnotes.

10. The main provisions of the Catholic Relief Act of 1778 were to repeal those portions of an Act of 1699–1700 which condemned Papists keeping schools to perpetual imprisonment and which disabled Papists from inheriting or purchasing land (W. E. H. Lecky, *A History of England in the Eighteenth Century*, 7 vols. (1906), IV, 307).

11. Howell's *State Trials*, XXI, 578.

12. *Ibid.*, XXI, 572.

Duke Street, Lincoln's Inn Fields; another to the chapel attached to the Bavarian Embassy in Warwick Street, St. James's. The first, known to be frequented by English Catholic gentry, was burned to the ground;[13] both were plundered and ransacked and their contents burned in the street. Fourteen persons were arrested, of whom five were later committed to Newgate.

The next evening, crowds gathered in Ropemakers' Alley, Moorfields, where there were known to be a Roman mass-house and the houses of a number of prosperous Catholics. At first, they were dissuaded or dispersed by the constables; but the next night and the day following, doubtless encouraged by the supineness of the Lord Mayor, Brackley Kennet,[14] and the reluctance of the constables to intervene,[15] they pulled down the Roman chapel, destroyed the personal property of the priest, Mr. Dillon, and of four of his lodgers, and damaged a number of neighbouring houses, not all of them occupied by Roman Catholics.[16] The same day, the houses of Messrs. Maberley and Rainforth, two justices who had played a part in the arrest of prisoners, were pulled down in Westminster; Sir George Savile, the promoter of the Catholic Relief Bill, was threat-

13. More frequently, during these riots, buildings marked for destruction were pulled down and their movable contents burned in the street. This both made it difficult for the victim to claim insurance money and avoided damage to neighbouring houses We shall see, however, that there were some notable exceptions to this rule.

14. De Castro's contention that, at this stage of the riots, the City magistrates acted with extreme reluctance—both through fear of reprisals and lack of conviction—is well supported by the State Papers.

15. The Minutes of the Court of Aldermen give more than one instance of the unwillingness of City constables to protect Roman Catholic property: one such case was that of John Bradley, marshalman, who was suspended by the Court for refusing to 'protect any such Popish rascals' (*Repertory of the Court of Aldermen*, no. 184 (1779–80), p. 209).

16. A list of 'Catholic Houses attacked during the Gordon Riots' is given in the Westminster Diocesan Archives, vol. XLI (1758–81), fo. 227. Further names of Catholic victims are indicated in one of the two registers of claimants for damages drawn up by the Board of Works (P.R.O., Works 6, no. 111).

ened. An expedition was made to Virginia Street, by Wapping, where, in spite of the efforts of the local Irish to rally in support of their priest, Dr. Copps, the mass-house was destroyed and neighbouring Catholic dwelling-houses were attacked. In adjoining Spitalfields rioters damaged the houses of a number of Catholic brokers and manufacturers.

Parliament reassembled on Tuesday, 6 June, at three o'clock; but crowds had once more gathered at its approaches wearing blue cockades and shouting slogans; it was decided to adjourn until Thursday morning. At about five o'clock, Justice Hyde attempted to overawe the demonstrators by reading the Riot Act and ordering the Horse to disperse them; whereupon James Jackson, a watch-wheel cutter, is said to have hoisted a black and red flag and shouted: 'Hyde's house a-hoy!'[17] The crowds followed him to St. Martin's Street, Leicester Fields, where Hyde's townhouse lay. By six o'clock the work of destruction had begun and the cry went up 'To Newgate!'[18] While the mass of the rioters made off, through Long Acre and Holborn, to Newgate Gaol, where the prisoners of 2 June were lodged, another party destroyed the Police Office of Sir John Fielding, who had committed them. Preceded by thirty men, armed with bludgeons, crowbars and chisels, the main column arrived at the Old Bailey shortly before eight o'clock. Having fired the house of the keeper, Mr. Akerman, they wrenched open the prison gates, released all prisoners and set fire to the buildings.[19] The same night, an assault was made on the Clerkenwell Bridewell and New Prison; here, too, prisoners were set free.

The next point of attack was Lord Mansfield's house in Bloomsbury Square. Lord Mansfield had earned the particular hostility of the rioters both as Lord Chief Justice and as a warm advocate of the Catholic Relief Act; in fact, it was

17. *Proceedings* (London), pp. 615–20.
18. *Ibid.* Hyde's country-house in Islington was destroyed the next day (S. Lewis, *History and Topography of St. Mary, Islington,* 2 vols. (1842), I, 164).
19. *Proceedings* (London), pp. 442–52, 570–83.

even claimed that, in order to direct the rioters to his house, the rumour was spread 'that he had advised the Dragoons to ride over the Protestants, that he was a Roman Catholic and that he had made the King one'.[20] An orgy of looting and destruction followed; Lord Mansfield's residence and his library of precious books and manuscripts were gutted or pulled to pieces; firemen, called to the scene, were forced to stand idly by. It was here that the military fired for the first time and, when the crowds dispersed at daybreak, they left several dead behind them.

During the day, two Catholic school-houses had been destroyed in Bloomsbury ahd Soho; that night, the house of David Miles, a constable who had been active in apprehending rioters, was ransacked in King Street, Golden Square.

The next day ('Black Wednesday', Walpole called it),[21] the riots reached their climax. Destruction was widespread: in Westminster, the City and the Middlesex 'out-parishes', houses, shops and offices occupied by Catholic merchants, businessmen, shopkeepers and justices were attacked and pulled down or damaged; public houses were destroyed in Golden Lane and Whitechapel. But, that evening, the main centre of disturbance was to lie to the west and south of the City. At about six o'clock, a band of rioters arrived at the premises of Thomas Langdale, a wealthy Roman Catholic distiller, who occupied two great blocks of buildings between Holborn and Field Lane. It was said 'that there was a Roman chapel in the house';[22] and, whether it was due to this or to the attraction of the vast quantities of gin (estimated at 120,000 gallons and valued at £38,000)[23] stored in their cellars, the two distilleries were eventually broken into and fired. The consequences were appalling: the vats ignited and the fire spread to adjoining buildings. While men, women and children sought to rescue or lap up the flam-

20. P.R.O., State Papers 37, no. 20, fo. 219.
21. *Letters*, VII, 394.
22 *Proceedings* (London), pp. 516–19.
23. Works 6, no. 110.

ing liquor,[24] twenty-one neighbouring houses caught fire[25] and it seemed to onlookers that the whole City was ablaze.[26]

More was to come. The Fleet Prison, a few hundred yards away, was attacked, the dwelling-house of the keeper fired and the prisoners were released. Marchers crossed the river to St. George's Fields and joined local rioters in setting fire to the King's Bench Prison, the New Gaol, Southwark and the Surrey House of Correction; the Marshalsea—a debtors' prison—was attacked and its inmates turned loose. In East Lane, Bermondsey, a Roman mass-house was destroyed and neighbouring Catholic houses damaged or pulled down. Blackfriars Bridge was taken by storm, the halfpence removed from its tills and the toll-houses set ablaze. As a climax, an attempt was made to capture the Bank of England; but by this time the City wards had begun to organise themselves for defence, and the London Military Association— in whose ranks Alderman Wilkes played a distinguished part—and regular troops made a stand at the Royal Exchange and repulsed the rioters with heavy casualties.

The next day, the riots continued in Southwark and Bermondsey; the public houses and dwellings of Roman Catholics and others were attacked in a dozen streets. A Catholic pastry-cook's shop was destroyed in the City; in Bishopsgate and Holborn, men were arrested for soliciting with threats. Fifty persons were arrested in the ruins of Newgate.[27] There were bloody skirmishes in Fleet Street and St. George's Fields. But the riots were all but over. The military, by now numbering more than 10,000 men,[28] were in full possession of the streets. On the 9th, Lord George

24. Referring to this incident, Walpole wrote: 'As yet there are more persons killed by drinking than by ball or bayonet' (*Letters,* VII, 392).

25. These figures, higher than those given by de Castro, are from the claim for compensation made by the Hand-in-Hand Fire Office, Works 6, no. 111.

26. Langdale received a total compensation in February 1782 of £18,974 ('Riots 1780', Corp. Lond. R.O., CR 13A).

27. 'Papers concerning the riots in 1780', Corp. Lond. R.O., Alchin Papers, Box H, no. 77.

28. De Castro, *op. cit.*, p. 163.

Gordon was escorted to the Tower from his house in Welbeck Street. Nothing remained but the judicial reckoning.

Of more than 450 persons arrested in the Gordon Riots, 160 appeared for trial at the Old Bailey, before a Special Commission in Southwark and at the Surrey Assizes at Guildford.[29] Of these, 62 were sentenced to death (25 being eventually hanged), 12 were sentenced to terms of imprisonment ranging from one month to five years and one to be 'privately whipped'; 85 were found not guilty and discharged. Gordon himself—the most notable participant, if not the prime mover, in the affair—came up for trial for high treason before the King's Bench on 5 February 1781, and was acquitted after a remarkable defence by his counsel, Thomas Erskine.[30]

The toll taken by the military was considerably greater: 210 persons were killed outright, 75 died in hospital and 173 others were treated for wounds.[31] The damage to property was unexpectedly small after a full week of riot-

29. One hundred and seven of these were tried at the Old Bailey Sessions of June–July, September and December 1780, fifty in Southwark in June–July and three at Guildford in August. These and the figures for arrested persons, substantially in excess of those cited by de Castro (*op. cit.*, p. 208), are based on a detailed examination of the Sessions Minute Books (1779–80), Sessions Files: index to persons indicted (1750–92), and Sessions Papers (June–July 1780) in the Corporation of London R.O.; of the Sessions Rolls (nos. 3389–90, June 1780), Calendar of Indictments (1770–85), and Commitment Books (1748–9 and 1771–80) in the Middlesex R.O.; of the Sessions Bundles (1780) in the Surrey R.O.; and of P.R.O., Assizes 35/220 (Indictments Surrey. Summer Assizes, 20 George III 1780). I have found no record of any commitments or indictments connected with the Gordon Riots in Kent, Essex or Hertfordshire (Assizes 35/220).

30. *State Trials*, XXI, 587–621, 647.

31. *Annual Register*, XXIII, 262. On 9 June, thirty-six wounded were brought to St. Bartholomew's, where eight died (press reports, quoted by de Castro, *op. cit.*, p. 189). On 7–9 June, seven persons 'with gun shot wounds' were admitted to the Middlesex, where three died (Middlesex Hospital, Apothecary's Book, 1777–82, p. 186). At Guy's, two died after receiving burns at the King's Bench (Guy's Hospital, Death Book, 1757–1804). No such records exist or survive for St. Thomas's, the London and Westminster Hospitals.

ing and the sensational blaze of the night of 7 June: in the City of London and the County of Middlesex, eighty-one persons were eventually paid varying sums of compensation for damage to private property, amounting in all to £63,269 6s. 1d.;[32] in Surrey, an additional twenty-nine persons filed claims amounting to a little over £7,000. But, of these numerous claimants and recipients, only forty-seven claimed or received sums of £200 or more; and only thirty-two private houses were actually destroyed or substantially damaged.[33] The damage to public buildings (including Newgate Gaol, but—mysteriously—excluding the King's Bench Prison) was assessed at a little over £30,000.[34]

It is hardly surprising that such a colourful event as the Gordon Riots should have given rise to a rich crop of rumours of plots and conspiracies, of which the major part seem quite fantastic in retrospect and need not therefore be taken too seriously. Among the more plausible, fostered by some supporters of the Opposition, was that the Government had allowed the riots to develop as a pretext for calling in the Army and imposing Martial Law[35]: this explanation found some credence in France also, if we are to trust the evidence of the Parisian bookseller and diarist, Sébastien Hardy.[36] It is true enough that only the Government gained any advantage from their outcome: the riots deepened the division with the Opposition[37] and Lord North's administration received two years' lease of life.

32. 'Riots 1780', Corp. Lond. R.O., CR. 13A; 'The Gordon Riots' (account book), Middlesex R.O.

33. Among houses 'destroyed or substantially damaged' I have included only those in respect of which £200 or more damages were claimed and, in the case of houses rented at less than £20 a year, those in respect of which claims were made for sums equal to or exceeding 10 times the annual rent. For sources for rents, see p. 287 and n. 78 below.

34. Works 6, nos. 110–11.

35. See, e.g., The Letters of Horace Walpole, VII, 408.

36. S. Hardy, Mes Loisirs, ou Journal des événements tels qu'ils parviennent à ma connoissance (Bibliothèque Nationale, MSS. français, nos. 6680–87), IV, 303.

37. Ian R. Christie, loc. cit.

Yet, were there any substance in the report, the rioters were presumably unaware of it, as they showed no inclination to distinguish between the administration and its opponents; not only were the houses of Opposition leaders like Burke, Dunning, Lord Rockingham and Sir George Savile directly threatened, but equally those of the archbishops of York and Canterbury and of Lords North, Stormont, and the Earl of Sandwich—not to mention that of Lord Mansfield.[38]

The case for the complicity of certain members of the Opposition might seem better founded: John Wilkes still had the reputation of being a dangerous Radical; Lord Shelburne demanded the repeal of the Quebec Act, which granted freedom of worship to Roman Catholics in Canada, on the day following the presentation of the Protestant Petition;[39] and the Court of Common Council of the City of London, two days before the riots, supported the Protestant Association's demand that the Catholic Relief Act be repealed,[40] and decided to present a petition to Parliament for this purpose on 7 June, at the very height of the disturbances.[41] The Government certainly did not hesitate to spread this rumour and even found some credence for it at the courts of the kings of France and Spain by means of an agent employed at the Hague.[42] Yet it had little substance: Rockingham and Portland, at least, zealously supported the administration in quelling the riots,[43] and John Wilkes, although tardily, played an active part in shooting and driving out rioters from the City.[44]

Even more colourful were the stories of French and American agents slipping across the Channel, distributing gold and instigating disturbances as a prelude to causing chaos in the City and falling upon Admiral Geary's fleet. According to one version, at least, this plot was to be carried

38. S.P. 37, no. 20, fos. 81, 97–8, 111, 113–14, 127.

39. Christie, *loc. cit.*   40. De Castro, *op. cit.*, pp. 26–7.

41. 'Proceedings of the Common Council' (7 June 1780), Corp. Lond. R.O., Box 18, no. 32.

42. F. P. Renaut, *L'Affaire Montagu Fox, 1780–1781* (Paris, 1937).

43. Christie, *loc. cit.*   44. De Castro, *op. cit.*, pp. 142, 192–3, 232.

out in London by Roman Catholics acting on behalf of the French government.[45] Fantastic as such suggestions may appear, they had their influence on the defensive measures of the administration, and the orders to guard the New River and the water works by London Bridge were given in direct response to such communications.[46]

There is more substance, of course, in the suggestion that the riots were deliberately fostered by the Protestant Association and, in particular, by its President, Lord George Gordon, either to serve the immediate purpose of securing the repeal of the Catholic Relief Act or to overthrow the administration. A detailed examination of this charge would be beyond the scope of the present paper; but it is incontrovertible that the riots sprang directly from the agitation carried on over many months by the Association and, more particularly, from the vast assembly in St. George's Fields and the march to Parliament on 2 June. The immoderate language used, on more than one occasion, by Lord Gordon suggests, to say the least, that its leaders did not scruple to stir up violent feelings against the Roman Catholic minority to achieve their ends. Theirs, too, were the banners, blue cockades and slogans that were a feature both of the procession to Palace Yard and of the riots that followed. And yet Lord George Gordon was acquitted of the charge of high treason, and the case against the Association's secretary, James Fisher, was dropped—precisely because it was not possible to prove beyond reasonable doubt that Gordon or the Association had deliberately planned or intended the disturbances that followed from their speeches, manifestos and activities. Thomas Erskine, Gordon's defence counsel, was also able to make the telling point that not a single one of the 44,000 signatories of the Petition had, in the course of the riots, been 'convicted, tried, or even apprehended on suspicion'.[47]

45. S.P. 37, no. 20, fos. 172–3, 278–9, 280–1.

46. See correspondence between Lord Amherst and Alderman Wooldridge (Corp. Lond. R.O., Alchin Papers, Box H, no. 77).

47. *State Trials*, XXI, 613, 620.

In fact, there emerges neither from Gordon's trial nor from any other source the proof of such a co-ordinated plan of action as imagined by Dickens in *Barnaby Rudge*. Witnesses at the trials of the rioters spoke of lists of houses 'that had to come down',[48] yet there is no trace of such a list among the judicial records consulted. Nor do they suggest that the rioters were, in the main, composed of itinerant bands moving from one scene of action to another under the guidance of some central authority. It is, in fact, remarkable what a large proportion of those brought to trial resided in the neighbourhood, if not in the actual parish, of the incident with which they were supposed to be concerned. This does not, of course, apply in the case of the destruction of Justice Hyde's house, to which people came direct from the demonstration in Palace Yard of 6 June, or in that of the firing of Newgate and the King's Bench Prison, to which bands of demonstrators evidently came from a greater distance, either from curiosity or as direct participants.[49] This is not, however, to suggest that the great majority of the actions were purely spontaneous and that there was no organisation even at a local level: each group of rioters appears to have had its recognised 'captain', sometimes armed 'with a drawn sword' or even riding on a horse—though he seems as often as not to have been a local man, probably emerging as a leader by temporary circumstance, rather than an outsider sent into the community from outside. Such 'captains' were Robert Smille at Langdale's—not arrested, presumably because he used his influence to

48. *Proceedings* (Surrey), pp. 105, 125.

49. Of 66 rioters brought to trial, whose addresses are reasonably clearly established, 46 lived in the locality in which the offence with which they were charged was committed, 10 lived within a mile of the incident concerned and 10 as far as 2–4 miles distant (most of the latter cases relate to the firing of Newgate and the King's Bench Prison). The point is further emphasized by the frequent recognition of prisoners by local witnesses: thus, Hull, a publican of Arundel Street, claimed to recognise 'all the mob' at Sir John Fielding's; and Bradbury, a publican of Golden Lane whose house was attacked, testified: 'I know all the prisoners.' (*Proceedings* (London), pp. 360, 621.)

dissuade his followers from attacking the house earlier in the afternoon; William Pateman, journeyman wheelwright, at Robert Charlton's house in Coleman Street; and Thomas Taplin, a coach-master, who 'captained' the rioters collecting funds 'for the poor Mob' in Great Russell Street on 7 June.[50]

But what is known of the mass of the rioters and their aims? An anonymous informer, who claimed to have 'been amongst them' but to have repented of his ways, addressed the following picture of the 'Mob' to Lord North's secretary:

200 house brakers with tools;
550 pick-pockets;
6,000 of alsorts;
50 men that . . . gives them orders what to be done; they only come att night.[51]

Walpole, after various attempts to define them, decided that they were 'chiefly apprentices, convicts and all kinds of desperadoes'.[52] Dr. George ascribes a major share in the riots to 'the inhabitants of the dangerous districts in London who were always ready for pillage'.[53] 'Desperadoes' and criminal elements no doubt played a part in an event which so obviously favoured their activities, but not so large a part as the sensational accounts spread about of the release of thousands of criminals from the prisons would suggest. The released debtors, in fact, far outnumbered the criminals: whereas only 134 were set free from Newgate and 119 from Clerkenwell Bridewell (and several of these surrendered or were retaken)[54] 853 debtors were released from the King's Bench[55] and probably as many from the Fleet.[56] Many of

50. *Ibid.*, pp. 516–19, 484–6, 409–13.
51. S.P. 37, no. 20, fo. 200.
52. *Letters*, VII, 391.
53. M. D. George, *London Life in the XVIII Century*, pp. 118–19.
54. Corp. Lond. R.O., Newgate and Clerkenwell Bridewell Calendars, June 1780.
55. Surrey R.O., Insolvent Debtors' Books (King's Bench Prison, 1780).
56. In 1728, a committee of enquiry into the state of the prisons reported that there were 'at least 1,000 prisoners' at the Fleet (*Com-*

these unfortunates, besides, found themselves in pitiable straits as the result of their unsolicited discharge and later petitioned Parliament for relief.[57] It is true that two of the prisoners released from the New Gaol in Southwark on 7 June were, on the next day, involved in an attack on a public house in Kent Street;[58] and John Burgess, 'a boy not yet 14', sentenced to death for rioting in Golden Lane on 7 June, was said to have been before the magistrates two or three times before.[59] Yet these are quite exceptional, and a remarkably high proportion of the remaining 157 prisoners up for trial received testimonials of good character from their neighbours and, very often, from their employers.[60] This contrasts strikingly with the bad record of several of those who informed against them (encouraged in a large number of instances by the bait of a £50 reward): in more than one case, the prosecution was compelled to drop its charges in view of the unsavoury reputation of the Crown witness; in another, an informer was subsequently sentenced to seven years' jail for bearing false witness; in a further case, two of the witnesses were shown to be felons, one of whom had not yet completed a sentence of seven years' transportation.[61] Bribery, in spite of lurid accounts by interested persons, can be discounted as a serious cause of the rioting;[62] and, though looting undoubtedly played a

---

mons Journals, XXI, 274 ff.); in 1830–4, there were between 700 and 884 prisoners (J. Ashton, *The Fleet* (1888), p. 313). In June 1780, there were only 27 prisoners at the New Gaol, Southwark, and about 30 in the Marshalsea (Surrey R.O., Insolvent Debtors' Books); 23 were released from the House of Correction, Surrey, and 40 from the New Gaol (Surrey R.O., Sessions Bundles, Midsummer–Michaelmas 1780).

57. *Journals of the House of Lords*, XXXVI, 155–6.

58. They were Henry Wadham and Edward Doreman, the latter a sailor on H.M.S. *Serapis* (*Proceedings* (Surrey), pp. 29–40; S.P. 37, no. 21, fos. 300–1, 356–8).

59. *Proceedings* (London), pp. 429–30.

60. *Proceedings* (London and Surrey), *passim*; see also numerous petitions and declarations in State Papers 37, no. 21, fos. 194–410.

61 *Proceedings* (London), pp. 584, 621, 579–83; Assizes 35/220 (Indictments Surrey, Summer Assizes 1780).

62. The only specific accusations on this score appearing in the

part—there were numerous complaints of theft made by householders and landlords and there was considerable looting at Lord Mansfield's and at Thomas Langdale's[63]— it is doubtful if desire for loot and plunder was a primary factor in the disturbances. The general rule seems to have been to destroy movable objects and personal effects on bonfires in the streets. Only fifteen persons among those up for trial were specifically charged with theft, and seven of these were found not guilty.[64]

It is, of course, impossible to determine with any degree of accuracy the composition of the rioters as a whole. We have next to no information in the case of the 458 persons killed or wounded by the Volunteers and the military; and very little in the case of the majority of those arrested.[65] We have, in fact, to rely almost entirely on the comparatively small sample of 160 who appeared for trial at the Old Bailey, in Southwark and at the Surrey Assizes. Even in their case, the information is often sketchy and depends on the chance word of a witness, or a phrase used in a petition or bill of indictment. Yet it is reasonably certain that the majority of these, at least, were working men. Dickens does not, in fact, appear to err greatly when he wrote of a fair proportion of the rioters as 'sober workmen';[66] nor does

---

State Papers are those made by Benjamin Bowsey, a Negro cook, while awaiting execution after conviction for taking part in the assault on Newgate (S.P. 37, no. 20, fos. 316–18, 320; no. 21, fos. 367, 376–7, 380–1).

63. A plasterer's labourer, arrested at Langdale's was reported to have said, 'he made better there than he did at work' (*Proceedings* (London), pp. 558–60).

64. *Ibid.*, pp. 514–16, 555–60, 583, 603–6, 632–4.

65. Apart from the 160 actually brought to trial, occupations are known in the case of thirteen out of fourteen arrested at the Sardinian and Bavarian chapels (*A Narrative of the Proceedings of Lord George Gordon* (1780), pp. 7–9, 20) and of twenty-four out of forty-nine arrested in the ruins of Newgate on 8 June (Corp. Lond. R.O., Alchin Papers, Box H, no. 77). These are, almost without exception, wage-earners—a large proportion of them journeymen and apprentices.

66. Charles Dickens, *Barnaby Rudge* (1894), p. 133.

Walpole when he repeatedly stresses the number of 'apprentices'.[67] Of 110 persons whose occupations are stated, one was a professional man—the apothecary Maskall, who may have been denounced through the spite of political opponents; one was the public executioner, Edward Dennis; 22 were small employers, shopkeepers, pedlars and independent craftsmen; 4 were soldiers and 6 were sailors (2 from the *Serapis*, lately captured by Paul Jones); while the remaining 76—nearly 70 per cent of the whole—appear to have been wage-earners. Of these, 36 were journeymen and apprentices, 13 were waiters and domestic servants, and 11 labourers of various kinds. There were 20 women among them. Few appear to have been unemployed. Thus, while the majority of those whose addresses are given in any detail lived in lodgings, they do not appear, in the main, to have belonged to the very poorest sections of the working population.

What, then, prompted these 'sober workmen' and others to resort to such destructive violence?[68] Having witnessed the fires in Holborn and the attacks on the prisons and the Bank, Walpole discounted the idea that the prime motive of the rioters was religious zeal and wrote: 'The Pope need not be alarmed: the rioters thought more of plundering those of their own communion than His Holiness's flock.'[69] Bishop Newton, too, claimed that the excesses of the Gordon Riots were committed 'under the cloake of religion'.[70] Following this lead, some historians have suggested that the riots, while originally prompted by religious fanaticism, underwent a change of character around 6 June, and that, from this time on, religious enthusiasm gave way to more material considerations.[71] At first sight, there is much that is attractive in this argument. There was the attack on

67. *Letters*, VII, 387, 388, 390, 391, 400.
68. It should be noted, however, that there were no fatal casualties among the victims of the rioters.
69. *Letters*, p. 400.
70. Guildhall Lib., MS. 3638.
71. See, e.g., E. H. Burton, *The Life and Times of Bishop Challoner*, II, 250.

Newgate and on Lord Mansfield's on the night of the 6th and, the following night, there were the drunken orgies performed outside Thomas Langdale's distilleries, the firing of the King's Bench, the Fleet and New Gaol, the looting of the toll-money on Blackfriars Bridge and the assault on the Bank of England, none of which might seem to have anything in common with the pious professions of the zealots who marched to Parliament from St. George's Fields. Furthermore, considerably less than half of all the victims of the riots—large and small—were Roman Catholics; and, in the parish of St. Andrew, Holborn, which suffered more damage than any other parish in the metropolis, only five out of twenty-six houses damaged or destroyed were occupied by Roman Catholics.[72]

Yet this argument will not stand the test of closer examination. The release of the prisoners and the attacks on the houses of certain non-Catholic magistrates and justices —including that of the Lord Chief Justice, Lord Mansfield himself—mark no departure from the original character of the riots. Rather, they were the logical consequences of the failure to secure the repeal of the Relief Act either by peaceful demonstration or the burning of Catholic mass-houses, the refusal of Parliament to consider the Protestant Petition and the part played by certain magistrates and constables in apprehending rioters. Even the scenes enacted outside Langdale's distilleries do not prove that the riots had changed their pattern: Langdale was a wealthy and well-known manufacturer and—though here, as elsewhere, drunkenness gave a special twist to events—it may well be that it was the belief that he had a Roman mass-house on his extensive premises that prompted the initial attack rather than the reputed strength of the liquor in his vaults. It is probable that the attacks on Blackfriars Bridge and on the Bank had implications beyond the immediate aims of the riots—to these we shall return later—but the riots that broke out the same night in Southwark and Bermondsey followed exactly the same pattern as those previously witnessed in

72. Works 6, nos. 110–11; West. Dioc. Arch., vol. XLI, fo. 227.

Westminster, Moorfields and Wapping and were accompanied by the same chanting of anti-Papist slogans. Of seventeen private houses (including chapels and public houses) damaged or destroyed in these two Boroughs on 7 and 8 June, thirteen were occupied by Roman Catholics; and it is a striking fact that, for the whole period of the riots, of forty-seven recipients or claimants of substantial sums of compensation, all but four were either Papists, or magistrates, justices, prison-keepers, constables and 'thief-takers' involved in quelling the riots, or the owners or occupiers of buildings damaged as the direct result of assaults made on Catholic property. Even in St Andrew, Holborn, where we noted so large a proportion of non-Catholic property among the damaged houses, the riots did not depart from their general pattern: no less than twenty-one of the twenty-two non-Catholic houses mentioned were damaged by the conflagration spreading from Langdale's distilleries and, as such, appear on the list of claims submitted by the Hand-in-Hand Fire Office to the Board of Works.[73]

Yet the riots were not directed against the Roman Catholic community as a whole. Had they been, they would have been most violent and widespread in those parishes and districts in which the largest numbers of Roman Catholics lived, particularly in those in which the great mass of the Catholic working population was concentrated. This, however, was not the case. The following are the six parishes in the metropolis in which the largest number of houses were damaged or destroyed, presented in descending order of magnitude (with Roman Catholic population in brackets):

St. Andrew, Holborn,	26	(443);
St. Luke, Old Street,	8	(188);
St. Giles in the Fields,	7	(1,223);
St. George, Southwark,	6	(39);
St. Mary Magdalene, Bermondsey,	6	(199);
St. Giles, Cripplegate,	5	(138).

73. Works 6, no. 111; *Minutes of the Hand-in-Hand Fire Office*, XXVII (May 1780 to July 1783), 131–2 (Guild. Lib., MS. 8666/24).

Now follow, also in descending order of magnitude, the six with the largest number of Catholic residents (this time with the number of destroyed and damaged houses in brackets):

St. George in the East,	1,581	(2);
St. John, Wapping,	1,364	(nil);
St. Giles in the Fields,	1,223	(7);
St. James, Piccadilly (adults),	987	(2);
St. George, Hanover Square,	860	(1);
St. Leonard, Shoreditch,	536	(3).[74]

It will be seen that there is little concordance between the two sets of figures. In fact, there does not appear at any time to have been the intention of making a general and indiscriminate attack on the houses of the 14,000 Roman Catholics in the metropolitan area[75]—let alone on the mythical figure of '35,000 Roman Catholic houses' imagined by Lord Bute three weeks after the event.[76] At most, there were sixty Catholic houses destroyed or damaged (very few of these beyond repair) in the course of a full week's comparatively unrestricted rioting—and hardly one of these lay in the crowded courts and alleys in which lived the Catholic lodgers and labourers of Saffron Hill and St. Sepulchre, Holborn; the weavers and worsted twiners of St. Botolph, Aldgate; the labourers of St. Giles, Cripplegate and St. Luke, Old Street; and, above all, the lodgers, labourers, riverside workers and weavers of Whitechapel, Wapping and St. George in the East.

There was, in fact, a distinct class bias in the direction of the attack made by the rioters on the Roman Catholic community. A glance at the composition of the victims of the riots will confirm this point: once the priest and the school-

74. Works 6, nos. 110–11; H. of Lords R.O., Return of Papists for 1780 (return for 1767 in the case of St. Mary Magdalene, Bermondsey).

75. Included in this total are all Catholics (13,379) appearing in the return made by the Bishop of London and those made for Southwark and Bermondsey by the Bishop of Winchester (390). In using the term 'metropolis' or 'metropolitan area' I have generally followed the boundaries suggested by Dr. George (*op. cit.*, p. 329).

76. Quoted by de Castro, *op. cit.*, p. 218.

master had been dealt with (these were undoubtedly the primary targets, as the whole pattern of the riots suggests), it was the gentleman, the manufacturer, the merchant, or the publican, rather than the independent craftsman or the wage-earner, who was the main object of the rioters' attention. Of 136 claimants for damages whose occupation or status is given, there were one peer; two ambassadors; two doctors; two priests; three magistrates, five school-teachers; thirty gentleman; twenty-nine publicans, distillers, brewers and brandy-merchants; nine other merchants and dealers; ten manufacturers; twenty-four shopkeepers; fifteen independent craftsmen (or persons appearing to be such); and four wage-earners.[77] That the victims of the riots were, on the whole, persons of substance is further confirmed by a study of the Rate Books and Land Tax registers for the period: of more than a hundred victims appearing in the ledgers of thirty parishes affected by the riots, all but eight live in houses of an annual rent of £10 or more; two in every three occupy premises whose rent ranges from £20 to £230 a year.[78]

77. Works 6, nos. 110–11.

78. Guild. Lib., Sewer Rate (1779), MS. 2137/13–16; Riot Rate (Feb. 1782) for St. Andrew Holborn and St. Bride Fleet Street, MSS. 9073, 3427/1–10; Poor Rate (1779–80) for Allhallows London Wall, St. Botolph Aldgate, St. Botolph Bishopsgate, St. Giles Cripplegate, St. Sepulchre London, St. Stephen Coleman Street, MSS. 5347/3, 2534/367–77, 5419/317, 6104/160–4, 3120/24, 2433/8–9. Midd. R.O., Land Tax duplicates (1780–2) for St. Catherine's, Christchurch Spitalfields, St. George Middlesex, St. Luke Old Street, St. Mary Whitechapel, nos. 5205, 5258, 5314–5, 2134–5, 2196, 2248, 6137. London County Council R.O., Surrey and Kent Commissioners of Sewers (1779–85), nos. 102, 113, 127–8, 137, 158, 176, 412, 454. West. City Arch., Poor Rate (1774–80) for St. Anne, St. George Hanover Square, St. James Piccadilly, St. Martin in the Fields, St. Paul Covent Garden (A 276, C 355, D 101, F 574, H 105); Riot Rate (Feb. 1782) for St. Clement Danes (B 934). Holborn Lib., Poor Rate (1780) for St. George Bloomsbury, St. George the Martyr, St. Giles in the Fields; Church Rate (1780) for Liberty of Saffron Hill. Bethnal Green Lib., Land Tax assessments (1779–81) for St. Matthew B. Green. Islington Lib., Poor Rate (1780–4) and Church, Lamp and Watch Rate (1770–6) for St. Mary Islington. Shoreditch Lib., Land Tax assessments (1778–

It has been suggested by G. M. Trevelyan and others that the violence meted out to the Roman Catholics during the Gordon Riots sprang, in large measure, from the English workman's hostility to the immigrant Irish.[79] In Bermondsey, the trials of rioters gave evidence of local anti-Irish feeling. The Crown chose a number of Irishmen to give evidence against some tanners' journeymen who were charged with attacking Laurence Welch's ale-house in Long Lane; some lively exchanges resulted between defence counsel and witnesses; and William Inbest, one of the accused, declared in a statement read to the Court: 'All the men that have given evidence against me are Irishmen of the lowest class, and people of abandoned character.'[80] Irishmen and Catholics were, naturally enough, closely identified in the popular mind: in Golden Lane, one Susannah Clark was supposed to have said that Cornelius Murphy's house must come down, 'for Mr. Murphy's was a Roman Catholic's house' and 'if they were not Roman Catholics, why did they keep Irish wakes there?'[81] In both Golden Lane and Southwark, there was a tendency to attack Irish public houses; but in these riots there is no sign of that fury which was expressed against the Irish immigrants in the savage brawls that broke out in Spitalfields in 1736 and in Covent Garden in 1763.[82] The main centres of the Irish population were then, as somewhat later, in St. Giles in the Fields; Whitechapel; St. George in the East; St. Andrew, Holborn; and Bermondsey-Southwark.[83] In none of these was there any attack made on the alleys and tenements where

---

81) for St. Leonard Shoreditch. I hope to elaborate this point elsewhere.

79. G. M. Trevelyan, *History of England*, p. 608; see also M. D. George, *op. cit.*, pp. 117–19

80. *Proceedings* (Surrey), pp. 67–70.

81. *Proceedings* (London), pp. 459–60.

82. M. D. George, *loc. cit.*

83. H. of Lords R.O., Return of Papists for 1767 (that of 1780 gives no details of households); *Report from the Select Committee on the Education of the Lower Orders in the Metropolis*, p. 261, H.C. (1816), IV, 1.

the Irish population lived closely packed together; the only Irish Catholic labourer appearing on the lists of victims was Doyle Kone of St. Catharine's Lane, Tower Hill, who put in a claim for £3 4s. 1d. as compensation for damage to his personal effects.[84]

Our analysis suggests, in fact, that behind the slogan of 'No Popery' and the other outward forms of religious fanaticism there lay a deeper social purpose: a groping desire to settle accounts with the rich, if only for a day, and to achieve some rough kind of social justice. This element of social protest is expressed in the reported remark of a barge-builder in East Lane, Bermondsey, who, told that a threatened housholder (a prosperous iron manufacturer) was no Papist, countered: 'Protestant or not, no gentleman need be possessed of more than £1,000 a year; that is enough for any gentleman to live upon.'[85] It may, again, be implicit in the answer of Thomas Haycock, a waiter at the St. Alban's Tavern, St. James's, who, when questioned by a neighbour on the part he had claimed to take in the assault on Newgate, said: 'Damn my eyes, I have no religion, but I have to keep it up for the good of the cause.'[86] It explains perhaps why Negroes, as well as Protestant Englishmen, took part in the release of prisoners at Newgate;[87] and why Samuel Solomons, a Jew, should risk his neck during the riots to settle accounts with a Roman Catholic publican, because he thought him to be a 'thief-taker' who had lived 'by the price of blood'.[88] It may also explain—unless we are to read a more sinister implication into the event—the seizure of the toll-houses on Blackfriars Bridge and the blind, desperate, costly assault on the Bank.

This does not mean that religion—to repeat Bishop Newton's phrase—was merely the 'cloak' for some form of deeper social protest in which men other than Protestant

84. *Works* 6, no. 111.
85. *Proceedings* (Surrey), p. 11.
86. *Proceedings* (London), pp. 446–52.
87. *Ibid.*, pp. 479–83.
88. S.P. 37, no. 21. fo. 225.

fanatics might share. The two went side by side. It is doubtful if the mass of the participants in the riots considered
themselves as direct supporters, or even shared the religious
convictions, of the Protestant Association; and yet they
gaily destroyed Roman chapels and mass-houses, echoed the
Association's slogans and wore its insignia, the blue cockade; and even collected funds 'for the Protestant religion'
or—perhaps more significantly—'for the poor Mob'.[89] The
contradiction is more apparent than real. Popery still remained, two hundred years after Philip of Spain and the
Armada, associated in the popular mind with 'wooden
shoes' and foreign enslavement. There had been the dread
of a massacre of Protestant Englishmen by Irish Catholics
on the eve of the Civil War; again, there was the panic
aroused by James II's reputed Catholic army of 1688, following hard on the heels of the scares fomented by Titus
Oates at the time of the Popish Plot. Anti-Catholicism
remained part of the political tradition of the people, continually nourished by Republican, Whig or nationalist
agitation, and closely linked with abiding memories of 'the
Good Old Cause'. For all the distaste of cultured Englishmen like Horace Walpole for 'enthusiasm', such a tradition
might, in moments of national emergency, be turned to
direct advantage by bodies of religious fanatics like the
Protestant Association. Only half a dozen years before, the
passage of the Quebec Act had been greeted by angry
crowds with shouts of 'No Popery!' and its terms denounced by a chorus of Whig politicians, the Earl of Chatham and the City of London,[90] Besides, it was widely
believed that the Catholic minority was far larger and more
influential than in fact it was;[91] also that the Catholic
Relief Act entirely removed all those disabilities which had
hitherto kept it within bounds.[92] Moreover, in 1780,

89. *Proceedings* (London), pp. 471–2, 409.
90. Lecky, *op. cit.*, IV, 299–300.
91. See B. Magee, *The English Recusants* (1938), pp. 195–6.
92. The Government found it necessary, in the course of the riots,
to reassure 'many well-disposed Protestants' that Catholics were still

England found herself at war, not only with American colonists—for whom there was much sympathy—but with the Catholic Powers of France and Spain, the traditional enemy, who had joined the coalition against her at a moment of acute national peril.[93] This may directly account for the prevalence of sailors among the rioters and the reluctance of soldiers to shoot at the crowds so long as their activities appeared to be directed solely against Catholic property.[94] It may also explain why the panic fear of the Roman Catholic minority spread so rapidly to Bath and Bristol without any direct encouragement from Lord George Gordon or the Protestant Association;[95] and why the anxiety was expressed (probably with reason) that the movement would find support, if the occasion arose, among the labouring population of the countryside.[96] At the same time, once launched by the Protestant Association, being a movement of the poor, it began to assume, however confusedly, a social complexion which its original promoters had not intended and with which they had little sympathy.

---

liable to severe penalties for keeping schools, saying mass, etc. (S.P. 37, no. 21, fos. 28, 141).

93. The riots revealed considerable hostility to foreigners: Hardy wrote (on hearsay, it is true) that no Frenchman dared show his face in the streets (*Journal*, IV, 303); and the Italian, Thomas Lebarty, was threatened with the words: 'I will have your house down, you outlandish bouger' (*Proceedings* (London), p. 509).

94. *Vide* a letter to Lord Stormont of 13 June: 'The doctrine said to be got among the soldiers that, having taken an oath that they were Protestants, it would be a breach of their oaths to assist the Catholics, and that therefore they would not fire on any persons destroying Roman chapels . . .' (S.P. 37, no. 21, fo. 64).

95. A letter of 15 June from the mayor of Bath to Lord Hillsborough discounted the suggestion that anyone had come from London to provoke the riots that took place in Bath on 9–10 June (S.P. 37, no. 21, fos. 155–6).

96. A letter of 10 June from Alton, Surrey, to Lord Hillsborough runs: 'I am sorry to say when the unhappy commotions in London reached the country, the lower class of the people seemed inclineable to join them . . .' (S.P. 37, no. 21, fo. 77).

Many questions, of course, still remain unanswered. What links existed between the Protestant Association and the journeymen, servants and labourers who formed the bulk of the rioters? By what channels were the Association's ideas and slogans communicated to them? How far did economic factors, such as wages and food-prices,[97] play a part in stimulating unrest? How do the motive forces underlying the riots of June 1780 compare with those underlying other 'panic' movements of the seventeenth, eighteenth and early nineteenth centuries? On some of these the documents are silent and, for lack of certain evidence, they will doubtless continue to provoke surmise and speculation. Others lie outside the scope of the present study and, for their answer, must await the results of enquiries conducted over a wider field of research.

97. The prices of cereals and of bread, in London and Middlesex at least, appear to have been comparatively low for the time of year and had not risen since March (*Gentleman's Magazine*, XLVII–LI (1777–81), *passim*).

The London 'Mob' of the Eighteenth Century

IN their use of the term 'mob', historians of the eighteenth century have generally neglected to define and to analyse it and have often shown a tendency to confuse the uses to which it might reasonably be applied. These may perhaps be summarised as follows:

First, its use as an omnibus term for the 'lower orders', common people, 'inferior set of people' (Wilkes's phrase), 'fourth estate', or what the French later called 'sans-culottes' —in brief, the lower strata of society in the pre-industrial age. Henry Fielding, in 1752, writes of 'that very large and powerful body which form the fourth estate in this community and have long been dignified by the name of the Mob'.[1] A more uncommon use of the term is from 1736—a year of considerable popular disturbance—when one of Sir Robert Walpole's informers speaks of the discontents and murmurings prevalent 'through all this Mobbish part of the Town'.[2] The people so described are, of course, sharply distinguishable from 'the people' in the sense used by William Beckford in Parliament in November 1761: 'I don't mean the mob; neither the top nor the bottom, the scum is perhaps as mean as the dregs. I mean the middling people of England, the manufacturer, the yeoman, the merchant, the country gentleman, they who bear all the heat of the day.'[3]

Secondly, the use of 'mob' when referring to a hired gang acting in the interest of a particular political group or

From *The Historical Journal*, II, no. 1 (1959), 1–18

1. Cit. J. P. de Castro, *The Gordon Riots* (Oxford, 1926), p. 249.
2. Cambridge University Library, Cholmondeley (Houghton) MSS., Group P/70, file 2/14.
3. See Lucy S. Sutherland, 'The City in Eighteenth-Century Politics', in *Essays presented to Sir Lewis Namier* (1957), p. 66.

faction. In this sense, we might apply it to the gang, or 'mob', of Irish chairmen hired by the Court candidate, Sir William Beauchamp Proctor, to protect him and beat up his rival's supporters in the Middlesex election of December 1768.[4]

Thirdly—and perhaps most commonly—we find the term 'mob' used by contemporaries, and repeated by historians, to apply indiscriminately to crowds engaged in riots, strikes or political demonstrations. The most common confusion arises perhaps between these two last uses, as crowds so engaged are frequently assumed, without further investigation, to be the passive instruments of outside parties and to have no particular motives of their own other than loot, lucre, free drinks or the satisfaction of some lurking criminal instinct.

It is in this third sense of 'crowd' rather than of a stratum of society or hired strong-arm gang that the term is generally used in this paper. The main sources on which I have drawn are the Old Bailey printed *Proceedings*, the Sessions papers in the London, Middlesex and Surrey Record Offices; and the Rate Books and Land Tax assessments of the metropolitan parishes.[5] In addition to these, there are, for the year 1736, two files among the private papers of Sir Robert Walpole deposited with the Cambridge University Library, which are both of considerable general interest and of particular importance to my subject.[6] With the aid of these materials a study has been made of three episodes in the history of eighteenth-century London which, between them, form the substance of the present paper: the London riots of 1736; the 'Wilkes and Liberty' movement of 1768–9; and the Gordon Riots of 1780.[7] While these episodes can,

---

4. See p. 243 above.

5. For fuller details of sources, see the articles listed in n. 7 below.

6. Cholmondeley (Houghton) MSS., Group P/70. I am indebted to the Most Hon. the Marquess of Cholmondeley, G.C.V.O., for his kind permission to use these papers.

7. For a fuller treatment of these episodes, see the three preceding papers: ' "Mother Gin" and the London Riots of 1736', ' "Wilkes and Liberty", 1768–69', and 'The Gordon Riots: a Study of the Rioters and their Victims'.

of course, not claim to be fully representative of all the varied London movements and popular disturbances of the century, they may help to indicate certain lines of approach to the subject as a whole, point to some general conclusions and suggest further steps in research. With the aid of these samples, then, it is here proposed to discuss how London 'mobs' behaved, how they were composed, what motives or ideas impelled or prompted them, and what further light such movements help to throw on the origins of a mass Radical movement in Britain.

The typical form of activity to which eighteenth-century urban demonstrators and rioters resorted was not the strikes, petitions and public mass meetings with which we have grown familiar. There are, indeed, important exceptions: strikes were already frequent and sometimes took forms that were not substantially different from those we know today;[8] and the great rallies of Wilkes's supporters in May 1768 and of Lord George Gordon's Protestant petitioners in June 1780, both in St. George's Fields, were, in many respects, similar to more recent gatherings in Trafalgar Square or Hyde Park in the nineteenth and twentieth centuries. Yet more typical of the times were the parades of itinerant bands, marching (or running) through Shoreditch, the City of London, Westminster or Southwark, gathering fresh forces on the way, that were a feature of all three of these episodes. Frequently they were 'captained' by men whose personality, speech, dress or momentary assumption of authority marked them out as leaders: such 'captains', sometimes described by eyewitnesses as 'carrying a drawn sword' or 'riding on a horse', were Tom the Barber, who led a contingent of demonstrators in Goodman's Fields during the riots of July 1736; William Pateman, a journeyman wheelwright, who directed the attack made on Robert Charlton's house in Coleman Street during the Gordon Riots; and Thomas Taplin, a coach-master, who 'captained' the rioters collecting money 'for the poor Mob'[9] in Great

8. For the numerous London trade disputes of 1768-9, see p. 247-57.
9. See pp. 210, 279-280.

Russell Street on the same occasion. They may, too, have passed on to their followers the slogans of the day, whose chanting in unison both terrified 'respectable' onlookers and served so effectively to rally supporters—such slogans as 'Down with the Irish!' (1736), 'Wilkes and Liberty!' (1768) and 'No Popery!' (1780). It is also frequently alleged by eyewitnesses that these 'captains' carried 'lists' of houses that had to 'come down', or whose windows were due to be smashed—as they often were, anyway, if their owners did not respond promptly enough to the summons to put out candles or 'light up', when bidden to do so by the crowds.[10] But, whether such 'lists' ever existed in fact or were entirely apocryphal, the purposes that they were supposed to serve were genuine enough: in all three disturbances a common feature was the picking out of the houses of selected victims, whose property might be partly destroyed—or 'pulled down'—in the traditional manner;[11] or who, if the occasion appeared to demand less drastic reprisals, might escape with a few broken panes.

In either event, the damage was often considerable and led to substantial claims for compensation by the rioters' victims. Among the more modest of such claims was that put in by John Walden, publican of *The Bull and Butcher* in Cable Street, whose eighteen lodgers were all in bed when the rioters of July 1736 advanced on his house, shouting, 'Down with the Irish!' He later reported the loss of a joint of meat and the smashing of six shutters and seventy-odd panes of glass to a gross value of £3 13s.[12] Far more ex-

10. I have found no trace of any such lists in the sessions records consulted; but, as arrests were frequently made as the result of information received some days after the event, it is not suggested that this is clear proof of their never having existed.

11. 'Pulling down' rarely meant total destruction: most frequently it involved the pulling out of windows and smashing of shutters, banisters, doors, movable furniture and other accessible woodwork. Even in the Gordon Riots, when some 100 houses were 'pulled down', only about one-third of these were damaged substantially or beyond repair. Though personal effects were frequently burned in the streets, houses themselves were seldom fired.

12. See p. 209.

tensive was the damage done to the Mansion House by crowds celebrating Wilkes's first election victory in Middlesex on the night of 28 March 1768. Nearly every lamp and window in the building was broken. One of the six glaziers commissioned to restore the damage later sent in an account for £20 5s. 'to 136 Sash sqrs of the Best Crown Glass cont. 270 Ft . . . at 1s. 6d. per foot'; while the total cost incurred by the Mansion House Committee was no less than £174 in respect of glass and a further £30 4s. 'to the supply of Lighting Lamps'.[13] Yet even this was small compared to the sums claimed as compensation by the victims of the Gordon Riots. Once the cumbrous machinery for levying the Riot Tax had been set in motion, eighty-one residents of the City of London and of the County of Middlesex were eventually paid a total of £63,269 6s. to meet these claims; while, in Surrey, a further twenty-nine persons filed claims amounting to a little over £7000.[14] These amounts would, however, have been immeasurably greater if, during a week of almost undisturbed rioting, the demonstrators had not confined their attention to selected targets: it was, for example, only the conflagration spreading from Thomas Langdale's distilleries in Holborn and Field Lane that destroyed several non-Catholic houses—a result that had in no way been intended by the rioters.[15] Such discrimination was not peculiar to the Gordon Riots and appears in other social disturbances of the period.

There are certain features, too, common to the active participants in these events. In the first place, they rarely operated at any great distance from their local street or parish: in any given incident it was always the local people, and not the outsiders that predominated. There were, of course, occasions when curiosity or partisan commitment drew large numbers from widely scattered parishes to some

13. Cf. the Treasury award of £69 4s. 7d. as compensation to Richard Capel and of £491 5s. 6d. to Edward Russell, both Southwark magistrates, whose houses had been 'pulled down' after the 'massacre' of St George's Fields on 10 May 1768 (*ibid.*, 11).

14. See pp. 275–6.

15. See p. 285.

central meeting place or scene of operations. Thus, the crowds that gathered in St. George's Fields on 10 May 1768, many of them in the expectation of seeing John Wilkes escorted from the King's Bench prison to Westminster, were drawn from a wide variety of parishes in London, Westminster, Middlesex and Surrey; and we find that several of those taking part in the assault on Newgate and King's Bench prisons during the Gordon Riots lived as far as from two to four miles distant from the scene of their present activities. In the anti-Irish disturbances of July 1736, too, it appears that a part of the Spitalfields rioters, having completed their work locally, moved down into Whitechapel and joined or instigated those who, later that evening, attacked Irish dwellings and ale-houses in Goodman's Fields and Rosemary Lane. Yet, even on this latter occasion, the majority of those arrested were local men; and it is remarkable how frequently persons brought to trial for presumed complicity in some incident were recognised by publicans and other local witnesses. All this, of course, suggests both that the sphere of operations of the itinerant bands was generally limited and that the element of spontaneity in these affairs was greater than contemporary comment would often allow; to this point we shall return later.

A more important consideration is the social and occupational composition of these crowds. Historians have been inclined to shrug them off with such ready-made labels as 'mobs', 'slum-dwellers', or 'criminal elements'. Contemporaries had more excuse for resorting to these generalised definitions; yet, on occasion, they were more precise, though not necessarily more exact, in their assessment. Thus, an anonymous informer of 1780 gave the following description of the Gordon rioters:

200 house brakers with tools;
550 pick-pockets;
6000 of alsorts;
50 men that . . . gives them orders what to be done; they only come att night.[16]

16. See p. 280, n. 51.

With the aid of the judicial records of the period—imperfect and inadequate as they are—we may hope to present a more accurate picture. In the first place, they suggest that what Wilkes termed 'the inferior set' predominated among the participants in these riots—that is, not only wage-earners (journeymen, apprentices, labourers and 'servants'), but also craftsmen, shopkeepers and tradesmen; while 'gentlemen' and other middle-class elements were only occasionally to be found among them. But while this pattern is generally valid, there are significant differences in detail as between one riot and another. In the anti-Irish riots of 1736, as we might expect from their nature and origins, it was wage-earners that formed the dominant element. On this occasion, the initial impetus came from the English building workers engaged on the site of the new Church of St. Leonard's, Shoreditch, many of whom had been dismissed by the contractor, William Goswell, and replaced by Irish labour from Shoreditch and Spitalfields at one-half or two-thirds of the Englishmen's wages; they were joined by local unemployed weavers who shared their grievance, as several master weavers had chosen to employ Irishmen at lower rates of pay. In the case of those arrested a few days later in Goodman's Fields, the emphasis was again on wage-earners: among seven of nine arrested persons whose occupations appear in the records, there were two craftsmen, two journeymen, two labourers and a brewer's servant. Among the 'Wilkes and Liberty' demonstrators of 1768–9, elements other than wage-earners seem to have played a slightly larger part. Yet here, too, Horace Walpole picks out for special mention the Spitalfields weavers, who, he claimed, mustered in full strength in Piccadilly on the morning of the first Middlesex election, distributing blue cockades and papers inscribed, 'No. 45, Wilkes and Liberty'.[17] The East London coal-heavers also espoused Wilkes's cause and, on the night of his surrender to his outlawry at the Court of King's Bench, a large number of

17. *The Letters of Horace Walpole, Fourth Earl of Orford*, ed. P. Cunningham, 9 vols. (1906), V, 91–2.

them, already engaged in a mortal dispute with an unpopular coal-'undertaker', paraded the Ratcliffe Highway and New Gravel Lane, Shadwell, shouting, 'Wilkes and Liberty, and coal-heavers for ever!' and 'Damn you, light up your candles for Wilkes!' Yet these were only passing phases in the weavers' and coal-heavers' wages movements of that time, and no coal-heaver, and only one weaver, appears among those arrested in the course of Wilkite riots. Wage-earners, however, are again much in evidence: of thirty-seven persons arrested in such incidents and whose occupations are given, a score or more appear to have been journeymen, labourers or 'servants'; while the remainder included a dozen independent craftsmen, shopkeepers and small manufacturers, two small merchants or dealers, and two gentlemen.[18] Our documentation is considerably richer in the case of the Gordon Riots. Here again, according to bystanders' reports, certain occupations were in particular evidence among the demonstrators: mention is, once more, made of the Spitalfields weavers (said to have mingled with the 'respectable' middle-class folk of the Protestant Association in their march from St. George's Fields to Westminster), also of tanners, brewers' draymen and sailors: the latter's presence is hardly surprising at a time when Britain was at war with, or faced with the armed neutrality of, every other major maritime Power. More precise, of course, is the evidence of the judicial records. They give us the occupations of 110 of the 160 who were brought to trial at the Old Bailey, in Southwark and at the Surrey Assizes. Of these, over two in every three were wage-earners —journeymen, apprentices, waiters, domestic servants and labourers; some twenty were small employers, petty tradesmen or craftsmen; and two were professional men, if we may include in this category Edward Dennis, the public executioner, who was sentenced to death though (Dickens's account notwithstanding) never hanged.[19]

Yet, whether wage-earners, independent craftsmen or

18. See pp. 261–2.
19. See pp. 282–3.

petty employers or traders, these rioters of 'the inferior set' had an important social feature in common, which separates them from the 'middling sort' of people standing directly above them in the social scale. It is that their names appear but rarely among the householders listed in the parish Rate Books. In some two hundred cases of persons arrested, committed to prison or brought to trial in the course of these disturbances I have found the name of only one in the numerous Rate Books or Land Tax registers of the period: he was John Bates, a brewer's servant arrested at Goodman's Fields in July 1763. This is certainly no coincidence, nor is it due to any serious gaps in the records. Such there are, of course; but, if we turn to the victims of the riots—those who had their windows broken or their houses 'pulled down'—we find a very different picture: while only two of seven victims of the anti-Irish riots of 1736 appear in such registers, every one of the known victims of the Wilkite disturbances of 1768–9 (admittedly few in number) is listed, and the names of no less than 111 out of 136 claimants for damages resulting from the Gordon Riots appear in the Poor Rate, Riot Tax and Land Tax registers of thirty parishes within the metropolitan area. This merely serves to underline the sharp social differences that generally separated the London 'mob' from its selected victims—a factor of some significance, as we shall see later. Meanwhile, however, it would be wrong to conclude from the above that rioters on such occasions tended to be drawn from the poorest of the poor, from vagrants or homeless persons, or even from those shadowy 'criminal elements' that have such a fascination for certain writers. It is not proposed to re-examine the evidence here; suffice it to say that, in the Gordon Riots at least, comparatively few persons brought to trial were unemployed, all were of settled abode, few were given a bad character by witnesses, fewer still had previous convictions, and that of the many hundreds released from prison by the rioters the great majority were debtors rather than criminals.[20] Dickens, in fact for all his

20. See p. 280–1.

romantic exaggeration of certain aspects of the riots, was not far from the truth when, in *Barnaby Rudge*, he wrote of a fair proportion of the participants as 'sober workmen';[21] nor, for that matter, was Horace Walpole when he repeatedly stressed the number of 'apprentices' involved.[22]

But why did the 'inferior set of people' engage in such activities? Contemporaries, who were singularly ill-informed on the origins of similar movements, tended to oversimplify the problem. While conceding that 'mobs' might be prompted by hunger, they were even more ready to believe that the desire for loot or drink acted as the major factor in such disturbances; any sort of social idealism or the dawning of political awareness, however rudimentary, was not seriously considered. The 'mobbish sort' being notoriously venal, bribery by interested parties was deemed a sufficient stimulant to touch off riot or rebellion. Sir Robert Walpole, however, tended to take a more cautious view. Of the riots in 1736 he wrote: 'It is said that money was dispersed'; 'but', he added, 'that does not as yett appear to be certain.'[23] In the Gordon Riots, there was plenty of talk of bribery and looting and the quest for cheap liquor—with some justification, it is true; but here, too, it was grossly exaggerated. Having witnessed the drunken orgies performed around Langdale's distilleries and the attacks on the prisons and the Bank of England, Horace Walpole concluded that the prime motive of the rioters was something other than religious zeal and wrote: 'The Pope need not be alarmed: the rioters thought more of plundering those of their own communion than His Holiness's flock.'[24] The charge is plausible enough: there was considerable looting at Lord Mansfield's house in Bloomsbury Square,

21. Charles Dickens, *Barnaby Rudge* (1894), 133.

22. *Letters*, VII, 387, 388, 390–1, 400.

23. W. Coxe, *Memoirs of the Life and Administration of Sir Robert Walpole*, 3 vols. (1798), III, 349–50.

24. *Letters*, VII, 400. More pointedly, he wrote to another correspondent: 'Anti-Catholicism seems not only to have had little, but even only a momentary, hand in the riots' (*ibid.*, p. 407).

at Langdale's and at various public houses (by no means all run by Irishmen), and it seems probable that a fair proportion of the funds collected for the 'Protestant cause' or even for 'the poor Mob'—found its way into the wrong pockets. Yet the Assizes records show that only fifteen out of 160 persons brought to trial were specifically charged with looting; and of these only half were found guilty.[25] In the 'Wilkes and Liberty' movement of 1768–9, at least, the boot appears to have been on the other foot: the only sign of bribery that emerges is that of the two Irish chairmen, McQuirk and Balfe, whose group of rowdies seem to have been paid two guineas a head per week, allegedly by an agent of Lord Halifax, to 'protect' the Court candidate, Sir William Beauchamp Proctor, against the supporters of Serjeant Glynn.[26]

Companion to the charge of bribery in such cases was that of 'conspiracy': it was almost axiomatic that a 'hidden hand' should be sought behind all outbursts of popular violence. Lord Carteret's comments on the riots of 1736 in the Lords' debate on 10 February 1737 are of interest as being the very opposite of typical of the period in which they were voiced. 'The people', declared his Lordship, 'seldom or never assemble in any riotous or tumultuous Manner, unless when they are oppressed, or at least imagine they are oppressed.'[27] But Lord Carteret was speaking as a leader of the Opposition, anxious to press home an advantage. The Government could hardly be expected to be so sanguine; and Sir Robert Walpole, though he was prepared to acknowledge the presence of more immediate motives (such as 'the complaint of the Irish'), attributed all the varied disturbances of that year to the common origin of Jacobite agitation. Others, his own agents among them, spoke

25. For this point and a more detailed examination of the whole problem, see pp. 280–2.

26. See the evidence of Robert Jones, Esq., J.P., of Fonmon Castle, Glam., at McQuirk's and Balfe's subsequent trial for murder at the Old Bailey in January 1769 (Old Bailey *Proceedings* (1769), 69).

27. *Gent[leman's] Mag[azine]* (1737), p. 374.

darkly of 'high church' and 'popish priests'. In 1768 no such explanations were put forward: 'that Devil Wilkes' was considered by King and Parliament alike as a sufficiently potent power for evil to stir the passions of 'the mobbish sort' without the aid of any outside agency. A similar compliment, however, was not paid to Lord George Gordon in June 1780. Though he and his Protestant Association were generally believed to have deliberately fostered the 'No Popery' disturbances for political ends, far more fantastic explanations of their origins were in circulation. It was said, for example, that the Government had allowed the riots to develop as a pretext for calling in the Army and imposing Martial Law;[28] and lurid tales were current of French and American agents slipping across the Channel, distributing gold and instigating disturbance under cover of which an assault was to be made on Admiral Geary's fleet. But, though several of these tales were treated with all solemnity at the time, they were soon forgotten as serious explanations of the riots; and even Lord George Gordon was acquitted, when tried for treason at Westminster Hall, because it was not possible to convince a jury that he had deliberately planned the disturbances that followed from his speeches and activities.

The ostensible causes of these movements are, of course, not in dispute: here, at least, we can see eye to eye with contemporary observers and commentators. Yet the motives underlying them were far from being so simple; and it is only by looking at these a little more closely that we shall get some picture of the deeper urges and impulses of the 'mob' of the eighteenth century. In July 1736, 'the first motive' (to quote Walpole) 'was the complaint of the Irish'; but, even after Mr. Goswell, the offending contractor, had dismissed his Irish workmen and the master weavers had promised to do the same, the riots went on. Judging from the continued shouting of the slogan 'Down with the Irish!' when the movement spread to Whitechapel this could only be because the grievance was long-standing and deep-felt.

28. See, e.g., Horace Walpole's *Letters*, VII, 408.

Yet it seems likely that the recent passing of the Gin Act, which threatened to tax the small gin-shops out of existence,[29] had something to do with it. Certainly, some of Walpole's informers held this view: one of them was told on the second day of the riots in Shoreditch 'that their meeting was to prevent the putting Down Ginn'. In early September, too, some weeks before the main campaign aganst the Act came to a head, threats were being voiced 'in the Tippling Ale houses and little Gin Shops' in Shoreditch against the lives of both Sir Robert himself and of the Master of the Rolls, Sir Joseph Jekyll, M.P., who had sponsored the Bill in Parliament. Similarly, the campaign against the Gin Act itself, which followed in the wake of the anti-Irish disturbances in East London, appears to have drawn strength from the long-standing opposition of farmers, distillers and City merchants to Sir Robert Walpole's earlier proposals for a general Excise; fears were naturally expressed that the newly enacted duty on 'spirituous liquors' was but a further step in this direction.[30] This interplay of motive was, on occasion, well appreciated by contemporary observers, as witness the following letter addressed to Walpole in early September:

It is evident that there are great discontents and murmurings through all this Mobbish part of the Town. The Gin Act and the Smuggling act sticks hard in the Stomachs of the meaner sort of People, and the Bridge act greatly Exasperates the Watermen insomuch that they make no scruple of declaring publiquely that they will join in any Mischief that can be set on foot.[31]

Finally, we must not leave out of account the possible effects on this 'Mobbish part' of a recent rise in the price of wheat

29. The Act levied a duty of 20*s.* per gallon on all 'spirituous liquors' sold by retailers and obliged innkeepers, brandy-shopkeepers and others dealing in spirits to hold a £50 licence (*Commons Journals*, XII, 585–7).

30. A circular letter addressed to a Mr. Moor, distiller of Long Ditch, Westminster, claimed that the Gin Act 'struck at the very roots of Property' and was 'a prelude to general Excise next Session' (see p. 215 and n. 54 above).

31. See p. 220.

and bread: the quarter of wheat in London rose sharply from 20–25s. in June to 26–36s. in July, falling again slightly to 24–33s. in August–November.[32] We can, of course, only speculate how far events were influenced by this factor.

A similar medley of motives appears to lie behind the Wilkes movement. It is, of course, important to note that Wilkes performed the remarkable feat of making a particular and distinctive appeal to three separate social groups—to the merchants and householders of the City (men like Aldermen John Sawbridge, James Townsend and Richard Oliver were, for a considerable time, among his most fervent supporters); to the 'middling folk' among the Middlesex freeholders; and (what concerns us more directly here) to the 'inferior set of people' in London, Westminster and Southwark. Unless, in order to explain this phenomenon, we are to fall back on a conspiracy-cum-bribery theory—for which there is no supporting evidence—we must assume that Wilkes's personality, political principles (however lacking in originality), and courageous defiance of authority had the power to evoke a more than ephemeral response among not only large and small property-owners in City and County, but among the small shopkeepers, craftsmen and wage-earners as well. They had already, on more than one previous occasion, in the name of 'Revolution principles', championed the cause of the City magistrates and of the Earl of Chatham; and, in a sense, their 'adoption' of Wilkes was but a logical sequel to the former popularity of Chatham. Yet, by this time, political passions had become more deeply and widely aroused, the divisions between Court and Opposition had grown apace, and Wilkes's own willingness to tap the political energies of those normally untouched by parliamentary or municipal contests must have contributed not a little to make this response more widespread, more urgent and more sustained.

32. *Gent. Mag.* (1736), pp. 357, 425, 489, 554, 612, 676. Unfortunately the price of the wheaten peck-loaf (17 lb. 6 oz.), quoted daily at the Assize of Bread in London, is not given for this period.

In this case, the part played by social and economic factors emerges more clearly; yet it is important to place them in their proper perspective. A feature of the year 1768 was the almost simultaneous presentation of wages claims by a wide variety of London trades. Historians have naturally been inclined to relate these disputes to the political movement of the period, and one of Wilkes's biographers has even gone so far as to characterise them as an 'outbreak of political strikes'.[33] Yet, with the exception of the coal-heavers and weavers, who appear for a short while to have been caught up in the Wilkite movement, these workers do not seem to have been particularly affected by the current political agitation,[34] and the two movements should be seen as parallel rather than as closely related manifestations. The high cost of living during the earlier months of 1768 certainly gave an impetus to both. The price of wheat had risen steadily since the end of 1767: having fallen temporarily from a peak of 50*s.* per quarter in July and October of that year to 44*s.* 9*d.* in December, it rose by stages to a new and higher peak of 50*s.* 6*d.* in May; the price of bread followed a similar, though less erratic, course.[35] Not surprisingly, we find the discontent that this aroused reflected in the agitation of the period. In mid-April, for instance, the *Annual Register* reported: '. . . a ½-penny loaf, adorned with mourning crape, was hung up at several parts of the Royal Exchange, with an inscription thereon, containing some reflections touching the high price of bread and other provisions';[36] and—even more significantly—demonstrators at the House of Lords on 10 May accompanied their chanting of the slogan 'Wilkes and Liberty!' with shouts of: 'We might as well be hanged as starved!'[37]

33. R. W. Postgate, *That Devil Wilkes*, 2nd edn. (1956), p. 158.

34. Horace Walpole even wrote that sailors petitioning Parliament for higher wages on 11 May 'declared for the King and Parliament and beat down and drove away Wilkes's mob' (*Letters*, V, 100).

35. See pp. 263–64.

36. *Annual Register* (1768), p. 96.

37. Cit. John Brooke, *The Chatham Administration 1766–1768* (1957), pp. 357–8.

But, after that, there was a sharp drop in wheat prices to
31*s.* 9*d.* in January 1769, followed by slight rises in July–
August and December; yet, generally, the price of wheat
and bread in London remained low throughout 1769
and continued to be so in the early months of 1770. In
fact, for some time after the early summer of 1768, rising
food prices cease to be a factor for consideration; and the
later phases of the 'Wilkes and Liberty' movement—
including the excitement over the Middlesex election of
December 1768 and the new outbreak of political rioting
in London in March 1769—cannot be explained in such
terms.

In the case of the Gordon Riots , while the famine
motive may have lurked in the background, there is no
obvious evidence of dissatisfaction with low wages or high
prices. For the first seven months of 1780, the price of the
quarter of wheat did not rise above 30*s.* 8*d.*; and the price
of the wheaten peck-loaf remained correspondingly low.[38]
Here then, we must look to other factors for an explanation. In the first place, an examination of the documents
confirms the first casual impression—that the riots were
essentially an outburst of anti-Catholicism, expressing the
deep, traditional hatred of Popery (with all its associations)
and the panic-fear that, under cover of war with the
Catholic Powers of France and Spain, both 'Protestant
religion' and 'Revolution principles' would be swept aside.
This conclusion emerges not only from the repeated chanting of the 'No Popery' slogan at every stage of the riots and
the obvious priority accorded by the rioters to Catholic
chapels and schools; but, even more strikingly, from a
closer study of the victims of the attacks. While these were
far from all being Roman Catholics, it appears none the less
that nearly every one of the claimants of substantial sums
for compensation were either Papists, persons actively

38. The price of the wheaten peck-loaf, 2*s.* 9*d.* in October–November 1767 and February–July 1768, was 1*s.* 11*d.* in January–June 1780
and only rose to 2*s.* in July.

engaged in quelling the disturbances, or the owners or occupiers of buildings damaged in the course of assaults made on Catholic property. The primary motive, then, was political-religious; but the way in which the blow was directed against the Roman Catholic community and its defenders suggests that it had a distinct social bias as well.

There was no indiscriminate attack made on the Roman Catholic population as a whole; had this been so, the main assault would have been against the humble Catholic communities of St. Giles in the Fields and St. Sepulchre, Holborn; of St. Giles, Cripplegate, and St. Luke, Old Street; and, above all, against the lodgers, labourers, riverside workers and weavers of Whitechapel, Wapping and St. George in the East. The lists of claimants for damages show us that once the priest and the schoolmaster had been dealt with, it was the gentleman, the manufacturer, the merchant or the publican, rather than the craftsman or wage-earner, who was the main object of the rioters' attention. This impression is confirmed by the Rate Books and Land Tax registers of the parishes concerned. Of 111 claimants whose rents are listed, only nine paid or were assessed for rents of less than £10 a year, and nearly two in every three paid rents of £20 or more; the average rent paid was a little over £34.[39] In fact, they were householders of some substance and hardly typical of London's 14,000 Catholics as a whole. This element of social protest, while by no means peculiar to the Gordon Riots, is one of their more remarkable features.

We may now attempt to draw some general conclusions. First, as to the composition and behaviour of these 'mobs'. We have seen that they shared certain common traditions of behaviour, with their ready resort to such activities as house-'breaking', window-smashing, burning their victims in effigy, parading under recognised 'captains', hallooing, huzzaing, slogan-shouting and so forth. Yet they appear as

39. See p. 286–7 and n. 78.

socially identifiable crowds of men and women and do not correspond to the static-abstract picture of the 'mob' presented by hostile contemporary witnesses or later historians. Above all, they were not simply passive instruments of outside agents or conspirators, whether Government, Opposition, Jacobite, Wilkite or Franco-American. Of course, they borrowed the ideas of their heroes of the hour —men such as Chatham and Wilkes, or even Lord George Gordon—but to present this aspect alone is to give a one-sided picture and to ignore the particular grievances and social impulses of the 'inferior set of people', which were by no means the same as those of the 'middling sort', such as voted for Wilkes in Middlesex or that rallied to St. George's Fields at the summons of Lord George Gordon; still less were they those of the City merchants or members of the Opposition in Parliament. We must now look at this factor a little more closely.

First of all, there were the social and economic grievances. Wages, as we have seen, played an important part in the anti-Irish riots of July 1736 and influenced one phase, at least, of the Wilkes movement of 1768-9. It would, of of course, require a far more detailed study of wages movements during the period as a whole than has here been attempted to determine how far this was a general underlying grievance. High food prices were a more likely common source of dissatisfaction, as they affected all small consumers; but they were certainly not a continuous cause of complaint, as we can see from our study of the disturbances under review and from a brief glance at the fluctuations in the price of bread and wheat in the course of the century. In London, wheat prices were high—or appreciably above average—in 1736, 1740, 1756-8, 1766-8, 1772-3, 1775, 1777 and in 1793-5.[40] Yet, taking the period as a whole, there was not in London—as there was in English rural districts and, for that matter, in Paris both before and during the

40. For prices of bread and wheat, see the *Gent. Mag.* for the appropriate years.

Revolution—a close general concordance between high food prices and popular disturbance.[41]

A more generalised social grievance must have lain behind the more or less spontaneous protest of poor against rich which we have noted as a feature of certain of these outbreaks. A similar desire to achieve some rough kind of social justice is evident in the Wilkes riots of March 1768, when the windows of lords and ladies of opulence and fashion were smashed with gay abandon: the names of the victims read almost like a page from Debrett. And it is no doubt significant that in the course of such outbreaks we do not find any clear distinction made by the rioters between Government and Opposition members.

Equally significant is the emergence of a nucleus of ideas and impulses not limited to the satisfaction of immediate material needs. One of the most frequently recurring themes in the popular ideology of this time was that of the Englishman's 'liberty'. The belief that Englishmen were 'free' and not 'slaves', and did not starve or wear 'wooden shoes'— such as foreigners in general and Papists in particular— was strongly entrenched, and had been so since the religious and social conflicts of the previous century. The view finds an echo in the riots of 1736, though, in this case, it appears to have been voiced by the 'middling' rather than by the 'mobbish' sort. The 'Liberty and Property' slogan was heard in the Shoreditch riots in July; and, in September, while the campaign against the Gin Act was at its height, a circular letter addressed to London distillers declared: 'If we are Englishmen let us show that we have English spirits and not tamely submit to the yoak just ready to be fastened about our necks . . . Let them [Sir Robert Walpole and Sir Joseph Jekyll, M.P.] see that *wooden shoes* are not so easy to be worn as they imagine.'[42] This concept of 'liberty', of

41. For English rural and provincial riots of the period, see R. W. Wearmouth, *Methodism and the Common People of the Eighteenth Century* (1945), chaps. 1–3; for Paris, see my *The Crowd in the French Revolution* (Oxford, 1959).

42. Coxe, *op. cit.*, III, 349.

course, runs through the Wilkes movement as a whole and here it is essentially a popular slogan. It is significant, no doubt, that Sir William Proctor should have found it expedient to adopt it at Brentford in December 1768, where it was reported that arm-bands issued by the Court candidate bore the inscription 'Liberty and Proctor!' In the Gordon Riots, we find another form of this assertion of an Englishman's liberties—this time, by the property-owners and householders of the City of London. They demanded the right to set up voluntary associations commanded by their own officers in order to protect their rights and properties both against the depredations of the rioters and the encroachment of government—a sort of citizens' militia, or *milice bourgeoise*, nine years before the siege of the Bastille![43] A similar spirit of sturdy independence and hostility to the executive was shown in the flat refusal of a majority of the City companies to contribute financially to the upkeep of troops quartered in the City during the disturbances.[44]

Closely related to the theme of 'liberty' and similarly linked with 'wooden shoes' was the theme of 'No Popery'. In popular ideology, at least, this had as strong a political as a religious bias and probably derived equally from memories of seventeenth-century conflicts and of 'the Good Old Cause'. It appears in all three of these movements. In 1736, the rioters' slogan in Goodman's Fields, 'King George for

43. The St. Marylebone Associates, headed as they were by seven noblemen and fifty-seven gentlemen and esquires, were more in the nature of a *milice aristocratique*.

44. See the Court Minutes for July–October 1780 of the Apothecaries, Barber-Surgeons, Blacksmiths, Butchers, Carpenters, Cordwainers, Dyers and Fishmongers (Guild. Lib., MSS. 8201/13, 5258/8, 6443/9, 4329/20, 7353/7, 4329/20, 8154/4, 5571/4). Among twenty-two Companies whose Court Minutes and/or Account Books I have examined for this period and for this purpose, the Upholders at first voted £20 towards the cost of the upkeep of troops and later rescinded it (MS. 7141/2), and the Grocers alone seem to have been fully cooperative (MSS. 7302/10, 7305/1).

ever and down with the Irish!' was countered by a shout of 'King George and no Popery!' from Walpole's agent, John Ibutt, and his friends. In 1774, both Wilkes and Serjeant Glynn, as M.P.s for Middlesex, felt obliged to give a pledge to their constituents to work for the repeal of the Quebec Act, 'establishing Popery' and French Laws in Canada; the demand was backed by the City's Common Council and the Earl of Chatham, and supported by popular demonstrations at the House of Commons.[45] The riots of 1780 provided, or course, a more striking example; yet it is sometimes wrongly supposed that, in this case, active support for the repeal of the Catholic Relief Act and for the 'No Popery' demand was confined to the 'lunatic fringe' around Lord George Gordon and the Protestant Association, to the irresponsible London 'mob' and the associates of John Wesley. This was, in fact, far from being the case. The Protestant Association's campaign had stirred a response among those professing the most traditional and secular of 'Revolution principles' in the City of London. Four days before the riots the Lime Street Ward, by unanimous vote, instructed its Alderman, Sir Watkin Lewes, and its Common Council men to press for repeal; and two days later, the Common Council followed suit and even urged their demand on Parliament, supported by a deputation on 7 June —when the riots were at their height. Little wonder that magistrates were chary of risking their necks or reputations in order to protect Catholic property or that troops were unwilling to fire on citizens engaged in destroying Catholic chapels and schools! In this sense, of course—though not in every other—the Gordon Riots fall within the main Whig-Radical tradition and are not just a crazy, isolated phenomenon. The same theme of anti-Popery persists as

45. *Gent. Mag.* (1774), pp. 283, 444; (1775), p. 348; W. E. H. Lecky, *A History of England in the Eighteenth Century*, 7 vols. (1906), IV, 299–300. The Earl of Shelburne was repeating this demand as late as June 1780 (I. R. Christie, *The End of North's Ministry 1780–1782* (1958), p. 25).

a live political issue as late as the General Election of 1830.[46]

Another related theme is chauvinism, or hostility to foreigners—particularly, though by no means exclusively, from Catholic countries. Anti-Irish agitation was sustained by religious differences, historical memories and the importation of cheap labour from Ireland. The latter consideration was, no doubt, predominant in the East London disturbances of 1736 and in the Covent Garden riots of 1763;[47] the former in 1780. In this case, several Irish public houses were wrecked in Golden Lane and Southwark, and the choice of Irish witnesses for the Crown in one of the trials that followed at St. Margaret's Hall led to a lively exchange between defence counsel and prosecution. Yet, as we have noted, there was clearly no attempt to make a wholesale and indiscriminate attack on the Irish Catholic population. In 1768, the position was more confused: on the one hand, Wilkes received considerable support among Irish coal-heavers and weavers; on the other, it was Irish chairmen who threw in their lot—at a price, it is true!—with Sir William Proctor at Brentford.

Anti-Scottish feeling was shorter-lived. Whatever its exact origins, it was strong in the 1760s and was ably exploited by Wilkes in the *North Briton* and after the 'massacre' of St. George's Fields. It was certainly not confined to London: Sir Lewis Namier gives an interesting example from the Canterbury election of 1761, when Bute's 'Whig' candidate is opposed by local Tories with the slogan, 'No Scotch—no foreigner!'[48] But it was clearly a diminishing asset after Bute's retirement from the scene. In the Gordon Riots, for example, it was the Scots that gave the lead to

46. Norman Gash, 'English Reform and the French Revolution in the General Election of 1830', in *Essays presented to Sir Lewis Namier*, pp. 258–88.

47. M. D. George, *London Life in the XVIII Century* (1925), pp. 117–19.

48. Sir Lewis Namier, *The Structure of Politics at the Accession of George III* (1957), pp. 101–2.

London in destroying Papist chapels, and Lord George Gordon himself was a Scot. It is not doubt significant of a change in popular mood (as well as of Wilkes's conversion to more sober habits) that neither Wilkes not any other determined opponent of the riots sought to exploit this fact.

The deepest hostility was, with little doubt, reserved for the French and Spaniards, who were not only Papists but traditional national enemies. In the course of the St. George's Fields affray of May 1768—when Britain was at peace—a soldier was heard to say that he would never shoot at Englishmen, though he was ready to fire on Frenchmen and Spaniards at any time. The same hostility came to the surface again in the protests against the Quebec Act of 1774.[49] It was more violently expressed in the Gordon Riots, though this is hardly surprising as, by this time, Britain was at war with both France and Spain. Frenchmen, wrote a French diarist, did not dare show their faces in the streets of London; and the Portuguese Lebarty was told: 'I'll have your house down, you outlandish bouger!' Hostility to France was once more evident in the campaign against the Eden–Vergennes Treaty of 1786 and may have played some part in the Birmingham and Manchester 'Church and King' riots of 1791–2. By contrast, there is little evidence, during the Gordon Riots, though they took place at the height of the American War of Independence, of any anti-American feeling among the 'mobbish sort'. Pro-Americanism, too, seems to have been confined to higher social circles and does not appear as an expression of popular opinion.

Yet it was from elements such as these, tenuous and even irrelevant as they may appear, that there gradually developed a mass basis for the Radical movement of the later eighteenth century. There has been a tendency to trace the origins of such a movement almost exclusively to the political awakening of the 'middling sort' of people—Middlesex

---

49. Lecky, *loc. cit.*; *Gent. Mag.* (1774), pp. 283, 444.

freeholders, City liverymen and the like—while the 'mob' in London as elsewhere is left out of the picture, except in so far as it is represented as indulging in dangerous diversionary activities like the Gordon Riots or in blind outbursts motivated by hunger or the quest for loot. Yet this is a profound mistake. Hardy's Corresponding Society of 1792 (composed of similar elements to those who shouted 'Wilkes and Liberty!' and 'pulled down' Catholic chapels) could hardly have appeared without a sustained political tradition behind it. The crucial years are perhaps 1768–9: the period of the General Election of March 1768,[50] of the various contests in Middlesex, of the founding of the Society of Supporters of the Bill of Rights and—most crucial for the 'inferior set of people' in London—the years of the fullest flowering of the 'Wilkes and Liberty' agitation. It is, of course, only too easy to exaggerate its maturity: at this stage, it is by no means a fully-fledged political movement in which devotion to a set of political principles is in greater evidence than attachment to the person of a popular leader or hero. It was only later that such concepts as 'liberty' became clothed in the more tangible form of demands for Annual Parliaments, the rights of electors, or the extension of the franchise—demands as yet only voiced by the higher social strata of freeholders, City merchants and tradesmen. The American War may have hastened the process in the long run, though appeals by Wilkes and others to the common people fell off steeply after October 1774, when Wilkes was elected Lord Mayor at his third attempt. After that, there was the refusal of Lord Mayor Sawbridge in 1776 to allow the Navy to impress men in the City;[51] but, generally speaking, no attempt was made to enlist the sympathies of the 'mobbish sort' for the views of the pro-American elements in the City. And, as is well known, the Gordon Riots—though by no means marking

---

50. See S. Maccoby, *English Radicalism 1762–1785* (1955), pp. 79–88.

51. *Gent. Mag.* (1776), p. 528. With.in a month, however, under Sawbridge's successor, Sir Thomas Halifax, the press gangs were once more freely operating in the City (*ibid.*, p. 530).

a complete break with a Radical tradition—discouraged any further appeals of this kind for a decade to come: Dr. Sutherland quotes a City worthy, Joseph Brasbridge, as saying—'From that moment . . . I shut my ears against the voice of popular clamour';[52] and Wilkes himself had by this time, quite apart from the riots, become a thoroughly respectable citizen with a safe seat in the Commons and a lucrative City sinecure and was not likely to bother himself any more with appeals to the 'inferior set'. So the political development of the London 'mob' had to proceed by other means. How far the Westminster election of 1784 contributed to the process it would be hard to say, as it would be to estimate how far London craftsmen and working men were influenced by the opening stages of the French Revolution or the factory system, just then beginning in the North; but it is evident that the more thoughtful of them were touched by the writings of Tom Paine. In fact, with the founding of Hardy's Corresponding Society in 1792, a stable base seems at last to have been found for the Radical movement among the petty craftsmen and wage-earners of the metropolis.

This takes us, of course, a long way beyond the groping, tentative and immature displays of 1736, and even of 1768. Much work needs to be done to fill in the gaps in our knowledge of the subject—including the role of the 'mob' in the outcry over Excise, during the Jacobite agitation of the 1740s, at the time of Chatham's ascendancy, or in 1784. Again, we need to pay more attention to factors like Irish immigration and the growth of London's population; and, perhaps even more important, to the influence exerted on the 'mobbish sort' by the 'middling sort' of people—such as those who supported Wilkes in Middlesex and the City of London; who escorted Crosby and Oliver to Parliament and the Tower in the course of the City–Commons dispute over the publication of parliamentary debates; who gave such solid backing to Beckford and other City 'Patriots'; and who formed the rank and file of Lord George Gordon's

52. Cit. Dr. L. S. Sutherland, *op. cit.*, p. 73.

Protestant Association. This would enable us to draw more confident conclusions; but, even within the limitations of our present knowledge, we may tentatively suggest that the first beginnings of this mass Radical movement should be sought in these immature, groping, and often violent, efforts of the common people of London to express themselves in social and political terms.

Collusion and Convergence in Eighteenth-Century English Political Action

It is now more than thirty-five years since Sir Lewis Namier gave his famous shot in the arm to the study of the parliamentary politics of the eighteenth century. Under his impact, the great Tory and Whig monoliths have been effectively dethroned and their places taken by 'connections' and 'groups', by 'ins' and 'outs'—and among the 'outs' the 'loyal', or sometimes 'factious', opposition. But Namier's preoccupations, and the enthusiasm they inspired, far from stimulating research into the whole field of political action, have rather had the effect of confining its operation to Parliament alone. Hence, the unofficial opposition—that of the 'political nation' *without-doors*—has tended to be neglected. Yet, in this more spontaneous, unofficial opposition from 'without doors', it is instructive to see the way in which different actions, starting in different quarters of the community converge for more or less brief periods and exert a common pressure. Anomic and associational movements, social protest and political demands, well-organised and clear-sighted interest groups and 'direct-action' crowds, leaders and follows come together in a chorus of united opposition, in which, however, the individual parts can still be distinguished and identified.

It is with this opposition in the Greater London context of the eighteenth century, with its components, its issues, its forms of action, its scope and its influence, that this essay is concerned.

City politics

In eighteenth-century London, this opposition characteristically took the form of a loose and temporary alliance

From *Government and Opposition*, I, no. 4 (July–Sept. 1966), 511–28.

between the 'middling' elements and the streets—between
the freemen, liverymen, merchants, householders and
tradesmen of the City—with occasional support from
Westminster, Middlesex and Surrey—on the one hand and
the craftsmen, shopkeepers, labourers and servants—those
whom Wilkes once termed 'the inferior set of people'—on
the other. But, naturally, so loose and unwieldy a medley of
disparate social groups had to find a common focal point,
a common mouth-piece to give them unity and express
their grievances in political terms. This function was
generally fulfilled by the City's Court of Common Council
—elected by the Common Hall, the freemen and liverymen
of the City companies: sometimes by initiating or directing
action, at other times by merely setting an example. In
addition to this extra-parliamentary combination, there was
nearly always—particularly when City interests were
involved—a group of opposition M.P.s and peers who
could be counted on to act as spokesmen and supporters
within-doors.

   This was of course no eighteenth-century innovation. In
the early 1640s, on the eve of the great Civil War, the City
of London, having gone through an internal 'revolution'
of its own, emerged as a champion of the popular and
Puritan cause against the 'tyranny' of Charles I and Laud.[1]
A generation later, at the time of the Exclusion Crisis, the
Earl of Shaftesbury's 'country party', City politicians and
London's *mobile vulgus*, with the Green Ribbon Club as
their organising centre, formed a powerful extra-parliamentary pressure group.[2] But in the reaction that followed
Shaftesbury's fall and exile and Monmouth's abortive
insurrection, the City's influence declined and it ceased to
play, for several years, an independent role.

   With the new century, however, the City began to reassert
its independence and to draw support once more from the

   1. See Valerie Pearl, *The City of London and the Outbreak of the
Puritan Revolution* (1961), pp. 107–59.
   2. See Iris Morley, *A Thousand Lives. An Account of The English
Revolutionary Movement, 1660–1685* (London, 1954).

streets for its anti-government agitation. It proclaimed its loyalty to George I on his accession to the throne; but, soon after, as Walpole rose to power, the alliance between Court and City broke down and, for nearly sixty-five years, the City was more often than not in opposition to Whitehall and St. James's.[3] As a bulwark of 'country' *versus* Court, the City was, until the 1750s, more Tory than Whig and its policies, even when its 'party' affiliations were ill-defined, were more often tainted with Toryism than with Whiggery. At this time, too, the London 'crowd', though by no means always reflecting City views, had generally a similar complexion; and it was 'Church and King' rather than radical-political causes that prompted its frequent appearance on the streets. This was evidently the case in the Sacheverell Riots of 1709, which were provoked and exploited by the Tories to 'dish' their Whig opponents. Again in 1715 and 1716, though the City had officially rallied to George I, there were certainly Jacobite undertones in the activities of the 'High Church' crowds that paraded the streets of the City, Holborn and Whitechapel to shouts of 'High Church and Ormonde', smashed the windows of government supporters, and attacked a Presbyterian Meeting House in Highgate.[4] Even thirty years later, at the time of the 'Forty-Five', the Jacobite cause had a powerful group of supporters within the City's Common Council; and had Prince Charles marched south from Derby there is more than a strong possibility that he would have received a tumultuous welcome in London's streets.[5]

Meanwhile, the City had become a major thorn in the

3. Lucy S. Sutherland, 'The City of London in Eighteenth-Century Politics,' in *Essays presented to Sir Lewis Namier*, eds. R. Pares and A. J. P. Taylor (1956), pp. 53–5. For an explanation of this opposition, see *ibid.*, pp. 55–8.

4. D. G. D. Isaac, 'A Study of Popular Disturbances in Britain, 1714–1754', Ph.D. thesis, University of Edinburgh (1953), pp. 143–85 (consulted by permission of the Librarian of the University of Edinburgh).

5. A. A. Mitchell, 'London and the Forty-Five,' *History Today* (October 1965), pp. 719–26.

flesh of Sir Robert Walpole in the 1730s. Led by Sir John Barnard, a 'Tory' in sympathy if not in name, it allied itself with the 'Patriots'—a combination of Tories and 'considerable grumbling Whiggs'—inside the House of Commons to oppose Walpole over Excise in 1733, the Septennial Act in 1734 and the Gin Act in 1736. On the first and third of these occasions it relied on the streets as well. The Excise Bill was withdrawn after Sir Robert had been besieged at the doors of Parliament by London crowds chanting 'No slavery—no excise—no wooden shoes!'[6] The Gin Act encountered comparatively little opposition within the House; but when it became law, 'Mother Geneva's lying-in-state' was attended by a campaign of letters urging gin-shops to distribute free gin in order to provoke disturbance. This time, however, there were no riots as the Government took firm measures to avert them: its determination was all the greater as, two months before, Irish dwellings and pubs had been attacked, or 'pulled down', in Shoreditch, Spitalfields and Whitechapel by crowds angered by the employment of cheap Irish labour. (In this case, too, it was strongly suspected that hostility to the Gin Act had played a part.)[7]

The last occasion when the City joined with the old Tory interest in an anti-government campaign was when it raised a hue and cry against the Jewish Nationalisation Act of 1753. This measure was promoted by the Pelham Ministry with the limited aim of making it easier for alien Jews to become British subjects, and seemed at first a matter of relatively little importance. Yet, as the Bill went through its various stages of legislative enactment, it stirred up a gathering storm of abuse and denunciation. At first, its opponents— a combination of London merchants engaged in the Spanish and Portuguese trade and a group of Tory Members—had objected on mainly economic grounds; but a new and more

6. Sutherland, *op. cit.*, pp. 62–3; R. R. Sharpe, *London and the Kingdom*, 3 vols. (1895), III, 4–9, 36–8.
7. See '"Mother Gin," and the London Riots of 1736,' p. 201 *et seq.* above.

threatening note was struck when the City's Lord Mayor, aldermen and Common Council blasted the Bill in a denunciatory petition as one that would 'tend greatly to the dishonour of the Christian religion, [and] endanger our excellent Constitution'. As the Bill became law, the campaign—stoked up by further petitions, Press and public meetings—gathered momentum; and, in the end, the government, alarmed for its chances of survival, took the initiative in repealing its own act.[8]

It was through its long connection with William Pitt that the City began gradually to change its political orientation, disengage itself from the 'old' Tory connection and strike out on a new 'radical' line of its own; and the London crowd, while continuing on occasion to act as an independent agent, soon followed suit. As an ally of Pitt, the City had helped to bring Britain into war with Spain over Jenkins' Ear and to drive Walpole from office—an event that it celebrated by urging Parliament to promote a Place Bill and a Pensions Bill and to repeal the Septennial Act. It also helped, with some support 'from below', to bring Pitt into office during the Seven Years War; and, after his resignation in October 1761, Pitt was rapturously acclaimed by the citizens of London, while Bute, the royal favourite, was booed and pelted with mud.[9]

Meanwhile, George III had come to the throne; and it was against the background of the ensuing 'palace revolution', the dismissal or resignation of the 'Patriot' Ministers, the disappointments attending the peace negotiations with France and Spain, and the elections of 1761 that City 'radicalism' was born. In March that year, William Beckford, twice Lord Mayor of London and Pitt's chief lieutenant in the City, fired the opening shot in the campaign for a radical reform of Parliament by calling for an end of the 'little, pitiful boroughs' as a step towards the 'more equal

---

8. Thomas W. Perry, *Public Opinion, Propaganda, and Politics in Eighteenth-Century England. A Study of the Jewish Naturalization Act of 1753* (Cambridge, Mass., 1962).

9. See Sharpe, *op. cit.*, III, 38, 48, 58–65.

representation of the people'.[10] This campaign, as it gained momentum, would embrace a variety of issues: shorter parliaments (triennial or annual); the rights of electors to be represented by the member of their choice; an end of placemen and 'rotten' and 'pocket' boroughs; and, above all, a 'more equal representation': at first, by giving more seats to the counties and later (from 1776 on) by giving the vote (in Wilkes's words) to 'the meanest mechanic, the poorest peasant and day labourer'—in short, to the whole male adult population.

Of course, this 'radicalism', like the assertion of the City's independence, was not entirely new. A similar programme of manhood or 'freemen's' suffrage as part of 'the common rights of man' had been variously voiced by Levellers, Diggers, Fifth Monarchy and Commonwealth Men in Cromwell's day; and Colonel Rainborough had, in the Putney debates of 1647, demanded full citizen rights for 'the poorest he that is in England'. This earlier radicalism had also made a deliberate point of enlisting its support without-doors by appealing 'from the degenerate representative body, the Commons of England, to the body represented, the free people'.[11] The City radicals of the 1760s followed the example and revived both a programme and a means of agitation that had lain dormant since Monmouth's west-country rising of 1685, and whose embers had first been stirred by the opposition to Walpole over the Septennial Act in 1734.

The new radicalism

It was inevitable that political radicalism, once reborn, should arouse a response among the unenfranchised 'lower

---

10. Lucy S. Sutherland, *The City of London and the Opposition to Government, 1768–1774* (1959), pp. 10–11. Strictly speaking, the term 'radicalism' applied to a political movement is an anachronism, as it was only invented by the Benthamites in the 1830s. But I use it here, as no doubt, Dr. Sutherland does too, for the sake of convenience.

11. C. Hill, *The Century of Revolution, 1603–1714* (1961).

orders'. There were the precedents of the Good Old Cause and of the 'levelling' movement and Shaftesbury's Green Ribbon Club, of which the memory, though long submerged, had survived in popular tradition. Besides, there was the deep-felt belief in the Englishman's 'birthright' and 'liberties' and the hatred of 'Popery and wooden shoes', which, though they might find an outlet in xenophobia and religious intolerance, might equally well be harnessed to a radical cause.[12] In addition, there were other demographic and social factors, such as the rapid rise of London's population and its development into a unified capital city. The ground was thus well prepared. But, equally, there had to be an issue around which a movement could take shape.

The issue was the 'Wilkes affair', and the slogan 'Wilkes and Liberty' became for nearly a dozen years the rallying cry of City merchants, London's labourers and craftsmen, and the freeholders and householders of Westminster, Middlesex and Surrey. It began in May 1763, when Wilkes was released from the Tower to which he had been committed by order of the Secretaries of State for publishing an attack on George III in his paper *The North Briton*. The City and the London 'mob' sprang to his defence and this basic partnership not only survived, but found valuable additional allies through the eleven years of Wilkes's exile and outlawry, his return as Member for Middlesex, his imprisonment, expulsion and exclusion from Parliament and repeated re-election, his City career as alderman and sheriff, his election as the City's Lord Mayor, and his return to Parliament in 1774.

This 'Wilkite' movement had quite remarkable results. Not only did it win a startling series of victories at the government's expense (of which more later); but it greatly extended the social, geographical, and political boundaries of the new radical movement. Thus, in addition to the London merchants and their partners in the streets, it came to embrace the freeholders of Middlesex and Surrey

12. See 'The London "Mob" of the Eighteenth Century', pp. 311–16.

and (for a short while at least) a substantial body of city freemen and county gentry in the provinces. Simultaneously, under Wilkite influence, radicalism spread out from its home base in London, Westminster, and Middlesex to envelop whole counties in the west and cities as far afield as Dover, Newcastle, Liverpool and Bristol.[13] Moreover, the whole arena of public political debate was enlarged. New issues were flung into the contest with the executive and Parliament: the rights of electors and of the American colonists, the privileges of the City of London, freedom of the press, and freedom from general warrants and from the operations of the press-gang.

Yet, despite these promising beginnings, the City's popular radicalism had as yet a fragile and unstable base, and there would be numerous setbacks before it attained its fulfilment as a part of the national reform movement of the early nineteenth century. For one thing, the purely temporary alliance of City radicalism with the aristocratic opposition in Parliament, as represented by Rockingham and Burke and later by Fox, broke down soon after the reformers' activities revived (following the Wilkes affair) in 1779. When it came to the point, the Whig opposition in the Lords were quite unwilling to support demands for shorter parliaments, to abolish 'rotten' or 'pocket' boroughs, or substantially to enlarge the electorate. The consequence was that the London and Yorkshire radicals not only fell out with Fox over reform, but when Fox went into partnership with his (and their) old enemy Lord North, they joined the younger Pitt to defeat him and soon found themselves no longer among the supporters of radical reform, but of a new Tory party pledged to the service of the King.[14]

13. For the above, see my *Wilkes and Liberty. A Social Study of 1763 to 1774* (Oxford, 1962). For the geographical limits of the Wilkite and radical movement in 1774, see I. R. Christie, 'The Wilkites and the General Election of 1774', *The Guildhall Miscellany*, II, no. 4, (1962), pp. 155–64; and Sutherland, *op. cit.*, pp. 15–19.

14. For the reform movement of 1779–82, see I. R. Christie, *Wilkes, Wyvill and Reform*, (1962), and for the radical-Tory line-up against the

The Gordon Riots

But, even before this, a wedge had been driven into the alliance of city radicals with London's 'inferior set of people' by the extraordinary episode of the Gordon Riots of June 1780. Two years earlier, Parliament had enacted a limited measure of relief for Roman Catholics. Before the new law was introduced in Scotland, riots directed against Catholic chapels and schools took place in Edinburgh and Glasgow; and following the Scots' example, a Protestant Association was formed in London, with Lord George Gordon as its president, to work for its repeal. The agitation found supporters in the City and, on 31 May, the Common Council moved for a repeal of the Act. Two days later, Lord George Gordon addressed a great rally of 60,000 Protestants, said to be composed of 'the better sort of tradesmen', and marched them to Westminster to present a monster petition to Parliament. As the crowd, by now reinforced by others of 'the meaner sort', waited in Parliament Square to hear the Commons' decision, the demonstration changed its character and was transformed into a violent attack on Catholic properties and chapels and the houses of Catholic supporters; and, in the course of a week's rioting, 100 buildings were damaged or destroyed to a value of some £100,000, while 285 rioters were killed and 173 were wounded. As the riots reached their climax on 7 June, the Common Council decided to petition for the repeal of the Act. So, up to this point, there had been a certain collusion between the City, the Protestants and the rioters. But when, a day later, crowds marched on the Bank of England, the City changed its tune and called in the army, while several City 'fathers' (Wilkes among them) shouldered muskets and shot down rioters at the Royal Exchange.[15] After this, the links between the City and its

---

Fox–North coalition in Yorkshire, see N. C. Phillips, *Yorkshire and English National Politics, 1783–1784* (Christchurch, N.Z., 1961).

15. See 'The Gordon Riots. A Study of the Rioters and their Victims', p. 274 above.

followers in the streets were severed for a decade or more; and, recalling the event, a City worthy later observed: 'From that moment, I shut my ears against the voices of popular clamour.'[16]

Yet though these were their political results, the Gordon Riots were by no means a return to the 'Church and King' movements of the early eighteenth century. In this instance, the King himself was under fire: it was said that he had broken his coronation oath by consenting to give relief to Roman Catholics; and it was even rumoured that he had become Catholic himself through the evil machinations of the Earl of Mansfield! Moreover, the 'No Popery' slogan of Lord George's Protestant Association lay in the radical tradition and evoked memories of the Popish Plot and James's 'tyranny'; and, only six years before, the passage of the Quebec Act had been greeted by angry crowds with shouts of 'No Popery!', and its terms had been denounced by a chorus of Whig and radical politicians, the Earl of Chatham, the Middlesex freeholders and the City of London.[17] Besides, there was another respect in which the riots marked continuity rather than a breach in popular tradition. For it was not the religious fanaticism or xenophobia of the riots that shocked the City 'fathers', but their threat to property and their animosity towards the rich. This became the more evident when they began to besiege the Bank; but, all along, they had shown a nice discrimination in the selection of their targets: whether

16. Sutherland, 'The City of London in Eighteenth-Century Politics', p. 73. It should be noted that the City's own radicalism, though wrenched from its popular moorings, did not die a sudden death. In the aftermath of the riots, it fought a protracted duel with the government over its claim to form voluntary associations with their own appointed officers—ostensibly to protect City properties against 'the rabble', but also as an assertion of its traditional privileges against ministerial encroachment. (See my article, 'Some Financial and Military Aspects of the Gordon Riots', *The Guildhall Miscellany*, no. 6 (February 1956), pp. 31–42.)

17. W. E. H. Lecky, *A History of England in the Eighteenth Century*, 7 vols. (1906), IV, 299–300.

Catholic or not, they were generally among the more substantial citizens and very rarely among the poor. One rioter in Bermondsey, when told that a threatened householder was no Papist, was actually heard to say: 'Protestant or not, no gentleman needs to be possessed of more than £1,000 a year; that is enough for any gentleman to live upon.'[18]

In fact, this element of social protest is an important feature of the Gordon Riots; but not of them alone. The Wilkite disturbances of a dozen years before also reflect a certain desire among the poor to settle accounts, if only briefly, with the rich. This is suggested, at least, by the gay abandon with which Wilkes's supporters in the streets greeted his victory at the polls by smashing the windows of lords and ladies, regardless of their party affiliations, in the more opulent parishes of Westminster and London. This same element of class hostility appears in some of the earlier London riots, as it does in the Priestley Riots in Birmingham in 1791.[19] Nor need this surprise us, unless we assume that the 'mob' could only be roused by its 'middling' partners by bribery or the prospect of loot or gin.

The causes of social protest

But social protest might take other forms and be prompted by more immediate considerations, such as low wages or rising prices. Such issues lay naturally to the fore in industrial disputes and food riots, which in the countryside and market towns far outweighed (particularly the latter) all other types of popular disturbance. In London, the case was somewhat different, as political questions were liable to intervene and energetic measures were taken to avert food riots by keeping a close watch on prices and stocking the markets with adequate supplies of wheat and bread.

18. See 'The Gordon Riots. A Study of the Rioters and their Victims', p. 289 above.

19. R. B. Rose, 'The Priestley Riots of 1791', *Past and Present* (November 1960), pp. 68–88.

Strikes were common enough and might even (though the case was rare) obtrude on a political movement: as in March and April 1768, when Spitalfields weavers, in the course of a trade dispute, cheered Wilkes on his way to the hustings and striking coal-heavers in East London raised the cry of 'Wilkes and coal-heavers for ever!'[20] Concern over wages certainly played a part in the anti-Irish rioting of 1736, and it may have been reflected in the hostility shown to the Irish during the Gordon Riots. But, more often, it was concern for cheaper bread rather than for higher wages that was liable to serve as an accompaniment to London's popular disturbances. Sometimes this concern found vocal expression, as in the spring of 1768, when the Royal Exchange was festooned with $\frac{1}{2}d.$ loaves bearing a protesting caption 'adorned with mourning crepe', and Wilkite demonstrators at the House of Lords were heard to say 'that bread and beer were too dear & that it was as well to be hanged as starved'.

In other cases, we may infer that high food prices were a factor making for popular participation in disturbance (other than actual food riots), though we may find no direct evidence to prove it. This appears to have been the case in some of London's popular outbreaks, but not in others. During the anti-Irish rioting and commotion over the Gin Act in 1736, for example, the price of the quarter of wheat in London rose from 20*s.*–25*s.* in June to 26–36*s.* in July (the month the riots started), falling again slightly to 24–33*s.* in August–November. The Wilkite riots of 1768, though not those of 1763 and 1769, came at the tail-end of a two-year cycle when the price of bread and wheat had been abnormally high; and the riots over the 'printers' case' of 1771 were preceded by another sharp upward movement in the price of bread. Yet, in the Gordon Riots, the most violent popular outbreak of

20. Yet there is little justification for calling the whole crop of London industrial disputes of 1768–9 'an outbreak of political strikes' (see Raymond Postgate, *That Devil Wilkes* (1956), p. 181; and *Wilkes and Liberty*, pp. 90–104).

the century, it seems unlikely that food prices played any
part at all, as the price of bread during June of that year
was almost abnormally low and had been so for the past
six months. This is just another indication that in London,
unlike the provinces, there was no close concordance
between years of high prices and years of popular disturbance. Yet, as we have seen in the case of the Gordon Riots,
social protest might take other forms and be stirred by
other, more long-standing, causes. Or again, it might be
aroused by a variety of grievances. In 1736, for example,
one of Sir Robert Walpole's informants wrote to him at
the time of the agitation against the Gin Act:

It is evident that there are great discontents and murmurings
throughout the Mobbish part of the Town. The Gin Act and
the Smuggling act Sticks hard in the Stomachs of the meaner
sort of People and the Bridge Act greatly Exasperates the
Watermen insomuch that they make no scruple of declaring
publiquely that they will join in any Mischief that can be set on
foot.[21]

Such cases, of course, simply underline the fact that in all
protest movements, whether concerted with other social
groups or not, the 'mobbish', like the 'middling sort' of
people, had interests of their own. These might constitute a
divisive factor, tending (as in the later stages of the Gordon
Riots) to alienate them from their middle-class allies;
but, equally, if suitably canalised, exploited and directed,
they might prove an asset to those anxious to harness
popular energies to a political cause.

The mechanics of extra-parliamentary agitation

This brings us to such problems as the organisation of
political action, the channels of communication between
leaders and followers, and the actual mechanics of the
extra-parliamentary agitation of the day. All campaigns

21. Cambridge University Library, Cholmondeley (Houghton) MSS.
P/70, file 2/14 (consulted by permission of the Most Hon. the Marquess
of Cholmondeley).

were by no means conducted on identical lines; but there was a certain common pattern of petitions or 'remonstrances', parliamentary lobbying, speech-making both inside and outside Parliament, and a synchronised chorus of press, pamphlet and satirical broadsheet directed towards the wider reading public, and, when the popular element was actively involved (whether by intrusion or by invitation), demonstrations, marches and attacks or threats to properties and persons. And in these operations there was always a fairly clear-cut division of labour that followed a broadly social pattern. It was the leaders at the top (often the City's Common Council, but sometimes such associated bodies as the Supporters of the Bill of Rights in Wilkes's day) who took decisions, issued petitions, instructed M.P.s, supplied the arguments, made speeches, and gave the orders. At the next level, there were the followers of the 'middling sort', who signed petitions, voted in elections, lobbied Parliament, and occasionally took part in peaceful demonstrations. Such were the Middlesex freeholders, Wilkes's devoted electors and supporters, who, besides voting for their hero in one election after another, supported his cause by marches and processions—as when 'a great body' of them, 'preceded by a band of music, with colours flying, marched along Pall Mall, and stopped fronting the Palace, gave three loud huzzas, and the music began to play'.[22] Also of the 'middling sort' were Lord George Gordon's Protestants of June 1780, who gave a fine display of organized strength when he lined them up in disciplined columns on St. George's Fields and, having harangued them, marched them in four great contingents to Palace Yard to present their petition to the House of Commons.

The third partner was of course the 'mob', whose job lay in the streets and whose function it was to cheer and acclaim the leaders, fill the hustings at election times, chant and chalk up slogans, and to riot. And even at this

22. *Middlesex Journal*, 13–15 April 1769.

level, spontaneous as many of such manifestations might appear, there was always a degree of organisation, with some elementary channels of communication and command. Generally, its nucleus was formed by the itinerant band, based on a single parish or neighbourhood, which ran, marched or paraded through the streets, gathering forces on its way, sometimes engaging in a peaceful display of numbers, at other times breaking the windows of its victims, burning them in effigy, or 'pulling down' their houses. Such bands might gather quite spontaneously, but they generally acquired a degree of cohesion through the emergence from their ranks of a leader or 'riot captain'— such men as Tom the Barber, who led anti-Irish rioters in Goodman's Fields in July 1736, or Thomas Taplin, a coach-master, who 'captained' the rioters collecting money 'for the poor Mob' in Great Russell Street in the course of the Gordon Riots. Such leaders were more often thrown up by the occasion than previously appointed; but they played an important part in directing local operations, rallying supporters by leading the chant of slogans such as 'No excise!' or 'Wilkes and Liberty!'; and ordering which windows were to be broken and which houses were to 'come down', whether orally or by reading from pre-prepared 'lists' (as was frequently charged yet never proved).

The co-ordination of effort

Such, broadly, were the respective functions of the partners. But how were these functions directed or related, and what were the channels of communication between them? These would, naturally vary with the occasion. In the first place, there were those movements in which the 'lower orders' were not directly involved or played an altogether minor role. We have quoted two such cases: the later stages of the campaign against the Gin Act and the Jewish Naturali-sation Act of 1753. In the first, the campaign was limited to a flow of letters; and as the Government had already had riots on its hands a few weeks before, it yielded to the threat rather than to the reality of popular disturbance. In the second case, the agitation was on a far greater scale. An important part was played, as we saw, by the petition presented by the Common Council. The City's action was vigorously supported by the *London Evening Post*; and, in the provinces, the City's arguments and those of their High Church and Tory allies were taken up and embellished upon by *Jackson's Oxford Journal*. Thus there appears to have been a certain degree of co-ordination between the partners at the top; but here again the streets (and certainly in London) played little part.[23]

There was a far closer degree of co-ordination—and at all three levels—in the Gordon Riots and in the various Wilkite episodes of the 1760s and 1770s. In the first case, we saw that the City ended by shooting down its one-time partners in the streets. But if we look at the affair more closely, we shall see how deeply the City authorities were originally involved. The first step in the London campaign to repeal the Catholic Relief Act was taken not by the City but by Lord George Gordon, who launched his Protestant Association in the early months of 1780. It was the Association, too, that decided to draft and circulate a petition to be signed in St. George's Fields on 2 June. But, by this time, the City, which had close associations with Lord George Gordon through one of its aldermen, Frederick Bull, was already deeply engaged. On 30 May, the Lime Street Ward had unanimously carried the following resolution:

That it is the opinion of this Wardmote that Sir Watkin Lewes, Knight and Alderman, Mr. Deputy Samuel Brown, Mr. James Sharp, Mr. John William Benson and Mr. John Hardy, their Representatives in Common Council, be desired to concur and assist in promoting any Resolutions of that Court to procure a Repeal of the late Act of Parliament in favour of Roman Catholicks so far as respects the establishment of Seminaries for the

23. Perry, *op. cit.*, pp. 72–122.

Education of Youth & the purchasing of Lands within this Realm of England.[24]

A similar motion was passed by the Common Council the next day; and a week later, after the Protestants had presented their petition and when the riots were at their height, the Council, far from being deterred by the spectacle of popular disturbance, persisted in pursuing its course and resolved unanimously 'to petition the Hon. House of Commons against the Act of Parliament passed in favour of the Roman Catholics'. It followed this up the next day by appointing a drafting committee of fifteen members, which included Gordon's friend, Alderman Frederick Bull; and so the petition went forward.[25]

After this, the partnership broke up. The Common Council continued to support its anti-Catholic petition; but it ordered in the military against the rioters whose activities, until 7 June, it had virtually condoned; and when Lord George Gordon, the Protestants' leader, was committed to the Tower to await his trial for high treason the incident raised no protest. Yet, up to a day or two before, it is evident that the cooperation between the City and the Protestants had, through the medium of Frederick Bull, been cordial and close. While the magistrates did little, at least before 6 June, to stop the spread of the riots, we cannot, however, say that they had any direct connection with the 'No Popery' rioters in the streets. But was there such a connection between the rioters and the Protestant Association? Did these, in fact, serve as a link between the leaders at the top and their followers in the streets? Up to a point, it may be so; for the rioters certainly took their cue from the Association, borrowed its slogan, carried its banner and wore its blue cockade; and there is little doubt that they were incited to behave as they did by the violence

24. Lime Street Wardmote Minute Book, 1780–1866, Guildhall Library, MS. 1169/2, p. 2.

25. 'Proceedings of the Common Council' (7 June 1780), Corp. London R.O., Box 18, no. 32.

of Lord George Gordon's attacks on the Roman Catholics. Yet their methods were entirely different; and Gordon's defence counsel was able to show at his trial that not one of the 44,000 signatories of the Protestant Petition had, in the course of the riots, been 'convicted, tried, or even apprehended on suspicion'.[26] In brief, we have here the case of a campaign carried on concurrently at three levels, each one running parallel to the other, inspired by a common aim though using different methods, with certain lines of communication between City and Protestants and between Protestants and rioters, but with no direct chain of command except that between Gordon and his Protestant supporters.

The Wilkite movement was a far more varied and complex affair and, in some of its manifestations, was far more highly organised than any other concerted movement of the period; yet, even here, we shall find little evidence of a chain of command linking the leaders at the top with their followers in the streets. If we consider the movement as a whole, spread over nearly a dozen years (though mainly concentrated in the seven years, 1763 and 1768–74), we encounter a bewildering kaleidoscope of changing leadership, alliances and issues. The only constants are Wilkes himself, the slogan 'Wilkes and Liberty', and the continuous and vociferous support that he elicited from London's 'lower orders' from start to finish and from the Middlesex electors after 1768. The other pieces of the jigsaw were in a continuous state of flux, constantly changing, regrouping, expanding or contracting. The issues—if we except the Wilkes affair as a whole—changed from freedom of the press and the persons of M.P.s and general warrants in 1763 to Wilkes's electoral victory in Middlesex, his right to take his seat in Parliament, and the 'tyranny' of the executive (over the 'massacre' of St. George's Fields) in 1768. In 1769, the Middlesex election case raised the wider issue of the rights of electors to the member of their

26. *State Trials*, XXI, 620.

choice. The 'printers' case' of 1771 was fought over the newspapers' right to print parliamentary debates and Parliament's encroachment on the City's privileges and prerogatives; while the issue in 1772–4 was Wilkes's claim to the mayoralty of London. As the issues changed, so the pattern of alliances changed with them. The *North Briton* affair of 1763 won Wilkes, in addition to the support of the City and the streets, that of a considerable body of opposition Members in both Houses of Parliament; but this latter force dwindled over the scandal that followed his printing of the *Essay on Woman*. On his return from exile in 1768, Wilkes extended his support in the City, in the streets of Westminster and Surrey, and among the freeholders of Middlesex; and he built up a fair, though unstable, measure of support in Parliament. This following was enlarged, the next year, when the Commons' decision to seat Luttrell in the place of Wilkes roused a storm of protest which extended to county freeholders and gentry and city freemen who had been left untouched by the earlier agitation. After his release from prison in 1770, Wilkes built up a large organised following in the City and was elected sheriff; but, a year later, the 'Patriot' forces split, and he had to depend on a new combination of supporters (first in the Common Council, later in the Court of Aldermen) to assure his election as Lord Mayor in 1774.

Similarly, there was a changing pattern of command. In the *North Briton* affair, Wilkes himself initiated action and played the leading role. Five years later, when he returned from France, his election campaign was astutely conducted by his counsel, Serjeant Glynn, and the ever-resourceful 'Parson' Horne. While Wilkes was in prison, the Wilkite leadership was divided between himself—he wrote some of his most effective letters and addresses from the King's Bench prison—and the City's radical (or 'Patriot') leaders, Beckford, Oliver, Townsend and Sawbridge. Early in 1769, these men and others among Wilkes's influential supporters in Surrey and the City formed the Society of Supporters of the Bill of Rights, ostensibly to pay his debts; but it gradually assumed the direction of the whole Wilkite movement; in particular, it played the leading role in promoting the nationwide campaign of petitions, protesting against Wilkes's exclusion from Parliament, in the spring, summer and autumn of 1769. In 1771, the City's radical and conservative groups temporarily combined over the 'printers' case', which, though handled directly by the Lord Mayor himself, owed its inspiration largely to Wilkes.[27] Soon after, the split in the 'Patriot' forces (Wilkes broke with Oliver, Townsend and Sawbridge) weakened Wilkes's position and gave a temporary majority to the 'court party' in the City. But the Wilkites regained the leadership and the majority in the Common Council two years later and conducted the campaign that led to Wilkes's election to the mayoralty.

So here it is quite impossible to establish a common pattern of political action and direction; and to present the *mechanics* of the Wilkite agitation in anything but a generalised form we should have to consider its successive manifestations each in turn. Here we will merely add, by way of a summary, that the movement was more protracted and diverse, and more highly organised, than any other of its time; it created new forms of organisation (such as the Bill of Rights Society); it devised new methods of propaganda (such as its uniform slogan, its election handbills and 'stickers', its 'instructions' to M.P.s). Moreover, it embraced a wider range of issues than any other movement of its kind, and it drew support from a wider range of social classes: above all, it brought into political action great numbers of unenfranchised citizens who had never been similarly involved before. Within it, as with other concerted opposition movements, there was a clear division of function between leaders and followers, whether of the 'middling' or 'meaner' sort. Through its changing pattern we can easily trace, as with the Gordon Riots, the links

27. Peter D. G. Thomas, 'John Wilkes and the Freedom of the Press (1771)', *Bulletin of the Institute of Historical Research*, XXXIII (May 1960), 86–98.

between the leaders and their 'middling' followers among the more respectable City tradesmen and shopkeepers and county freeholders. But who acted as intermediaries between the leaders or the 'middling' strata and the rioters in the streets? Who organised them? Who passed on the slogans, or brought them, so constantly and continuously, into the streets? We may assume that there were such links, but we have no certain evidence to prove it. Occasionally, we read of the presence in riots of 'well-dressed persons' or 'tradesmen of the better sort'; and, in March 1768, there were reports that a City tea-broker had 'headed a Mob' in Westminster and that a 'gentleman of character and fortune' had ordered beer and drunk with the rioters to 'Wilkes and Liberty'. But even if such cases are authentic, they tell us very little.

The effectiveness of extra-parliamentary opposition

Finally, to return from Wilkes to the eighteenth-century protest movements as a whole. What did they achieve? By and large, their successes were remarkable and form an impressive list. The Excise Bill was withdrawn. The Gin Act was allowed to die a natural death. The Jewish Naturalisation Act was repealed by the government itself. William Pitt became War Minister in spite of the personal hostility of George II. Above all, the 'Wilkes affair' led to the abandonment of general warrants, the free publication of parliamentary debates, Wilkes's return to Parliament in 1774, the temporary removal of press-gangs from the City; and—most remarkable of all—the Commons' vote declaring his 'incapacity' to sit in the House was expunged from its Journals, on his own proposal, in 1782. On the other hand, the anti-Irish rioters of 1736 failed to gain full satisfaction for their demand that Irishmen should not be employed at lower wages; and the 'No Popery' rioters of 1780 failed to gain anything at all. What conclusions may be drawn from this balance-sheet of failure and success? First, where the 'mob' was on its own, as in the anti-Irish disturbances and the closing stages of the Gordon Riots, its chances of success were very slim. Secondly, there were occasions when the City, or the 'middling' element, might achieve its objects even without the active intervention of the streets. This might happen where the issue was of relatively small importance or the government's supporters themselves were divided or half-hearted. This was notably the case with the Jewish Naturalisation Act, which was of little interest even to its promoters; so once the commotion had started, it was a matter of choosing the right moment for backing down without too much loss of face. Again, in the case of the Gin Act, Walpole, though nominally one of its sponsors, showed such little regard for it that he wrote to his brother Horace, even before the Bill became law, that he doubted if it would fulfil the purposes for which it was intended.[28]

And, thirdly, the record suggests that the more spectacular victories could only be won by a broader alliance of which the streets formed an integral part. Walpole's concern for his Excise Bill was certainly greater than it was for his Gin Act; yet when faced with a powerful combination of City and farming interests and opposition M.P.s, and the hostile attentions of the London 'mob', he was compelled to withdraw it. Even this remarkable victory, however, was eclipsed by the succession of trophies carried off by the Wilkite movement in its numerous encounters with Parliament, George III and his Ministers. The experience then gained had important lessons for the future. And it was not until the days of the Reform Bill and the agitation against the Corn Laws in the early nineteenth century that an extra-parliamentary opposition, organised on broadly similar lines and conducting its campaigns by broadly similar means, would achieve successes on an even greater scale.

28. Archdeacon William Coxe, *Memoirs of the Life and Administration of Sir Robert Walpole*, 3 vols. (1798), III, 357.

Index

Index